Mastering Reinforcement Learning with Python

Build next-generation, self-learning models using reinforcement learning techniques and best practices

Enes Bilgin

BIRMINGHAM—MUMBAI

Mastering Reinforcement Learning with Python

Commissioning Editor: Sunith Shetty

Acquisition Editor: Siddharth Mandal

Senior Editor: David Sugarman

Content Development Editor: Joseph Sunil

Technical Editor: Sonam Pandey

Copy Editor: Safis Editing

Project Coordinator: Aishwarya Mohan

Proofreader: Safis Editing

Indexer: Manju Arasan

Production Designer: Shankar Kalbhor

First published: December 2020

Production reference: 2250121

Published by Packt Publishing Ltd.

Livery Place

35 Livery Street

Birmingham

B3 2PB, UK.

ISBN 978-1-83864-414-7

www.packt.com

`Packt.com`

Subscribe to our online digital library for full access to over 7,000 books and videos, as well as industry leading tools to help you plan your personal development and advance your career. For more information, please visit our website.

Why subscribe?

- Spend less time learning and more time coding with practical eBooks and Videos from over 4,000 industry professionals

- Improve your learning with Skill Plans built especially for you

- Get a free eBook or video every month

- Fully searchable for easy access to vital information

- Copy and paste, print, and bookmark content

Did you know that Packt offers eBook versions of every book published, with PDF and ePub files available? You can upgrade to the eBook version at `packt.com` and as a print book customer, you are entitled to a discount on the eBook copy. Get in touch with us at `customercare@packtpub.com` for more details.

At `www.packt.com`, you can also read a collection of free technical articles, sign up for a range of free newsletters, and receive exclusive discounts and offers on Packt books and eBooks.

Contributors

About the author

Enes Bilgin works as a senior AI engineer and a tech lead in Microsoft's Autonomous Systems division. He is a machine learning and operations research practitioner and researcher with experience in building production systems and models for top tech companies using Python, TensorFlow, and Ray/RLlib. He holds an M.S. and a Ph.D. in systems engineering from Boston University and a B.S. in industrial engineering from Bilkent University. In the past, he has worked as a research scientist at Amazon and as an operations research scientist at AMD. He also held adjunct faculty positions at the McCombs School of Business at the University of Texas at Austin and at the Ingram School of Engineering at Texas State University.

About the reviewers

Juan Tomás Oliva Ramos is an environmental engineer from University of Guanajuato, Mexico, with a master's degree in administrative engineering and quality. He is an expert in technologies used to improve processes and project management. He also works in statistical studies and develop processes around it. He has been part of the design of surveillance and technology alert models as support for education, and the development of new products and processes. His specialities include the design of professional, engineering, and postgraduate updating programs in face-to-face and virtual environments.

I want to thank God for giving me the wisdom and humility to review this book. I want to thank my family for staying with me all this time (Brenda, Regina, Renata and Tadeo), I love you.

Satwik Kansal is a freelance software developer by profession. He has been working on data science and Python projects since 2014. Satwik has a keen interest in content creation and runs DevWriters, a tech content creation agency. A couple of his authored works are the *What the f*ck Python* project and the *Hands-on Reinforcement Learning with TensorFlow* course by Packt.

Packt is searching for authors like you

If you're interested in becoming an author for Packt, please visit `authors.packtpub.com` and apply today. We have worked with thousands of developers and tech professionals, just like you, to help them share their insight with the global tech community. You can make a general application, apply for a specific hot topic that we are recruiting an author for, or submit your own idea.

Table of Contents

3

Contextual Bandits

4

Makings of a Markov Decision Process

5

Solving the Reinforcement Learning Problem

Section 2:
Deep Reinforcement Learning

6
Deep Q-Learning at Scale

7
Policy-Based Methods

Section 3:
Advanced Topics in RL

10
Introducing Machine Teaching

11
Achieving Generalization and Overcoming Partial Observability

12

Meta-Reinforcement Learning

13

Exploring Advanced Topics

Section 4: Applications of RL

14
Solving Robot Learning

15
Supply Chain Management

16

Personalization, Marketing, and Finance

17

Smart City and Cybersecurity

18
Challenges and Future Directions in Reinforcement Learning

Other Books You May Enjoy

Index

Preface

Reinforcement Learning (RL) is a field of artificial intelligence used for creating self-learning autonomous agents. On a strong theoretical foundation, this book takes a pragmatic approach and uses examples inspired by real-world industry problems to teach you about state-of-the-art RL.

Starting with bandit problems, Markov decision processes, and dynamic programming, the book provides an in-depth review of the classical RL techniques, such Monte Carlo methods and temporal-difference learning. After that, you will learn about deep Q-learning, policy gradient algorithms, actor-critic methods, model-based methods, and multi-agent reinforcement learning. Then, the book will introduce you to some of the key approaches behind the most successful RL implementations, such as domain randomization and curiosity-driven learning.

As you advance, you'll delve into many novel algorithms with advanced implementations using modern Python libraries such as TensorFlow and Ray/RLlib. You'll also find out how to implement RL in areas such as robotics, supply chain management, marketing, finance, smart cities, and cybersecurity while assessing the tradeoffs between different approaches and avoiding common pitfalls.

By the end of this reinforcement learning book, you'll have mastered how to train and deploy your own RL agents for solving RL problems.

Who this book is for

This book is for expert machine learning practitioners and deep learning researchers looking to implement advanced RL concepts in real-world projects. This book will also appeal to RL experts who want to tackle complex sequential decision-making problems through self-learning agents. Working knowledge of Python programming and machine learning along with prior experience with reinforcement learning is required.

What this book covers

Chapter 1, Introduction to Reinforcement Learning, provides an introduction to RL, presents motivating examples and success stories, and looks at RL applications in industry. It then gives some fundamental definitions to refresh your mind on RL concepts and concludes with a section on software and hardware setup.

Chapter 2, Multi-Armed Bandits, covers a rather simple RL setting, bandit problems without context, which, on the other hand, has tremendous applications in industry as an alternative to the traditional A/B testing. The chapter also describes a very fundamental RL trade-off: exploration versus exploitation. It then presents three approaches to tackle this trade-off and compares them against A/B testing.

Chapter 3, Contextual Bandits, takes the discussion on multi-armed bandits to an advanced level by adding context to the decision-making process and involving deep neural networks in decision making. We adapt a real dataset from the U.S. Census to an online advertising problem. We conclude the chapter with a section on the applications of bandit problems in industry and business.

Chapter 4, Makings of a Markov Decision Process, builds the mathematical theory behind sequential decision processes that are solved using RL. We start with Markov chains, where we describe types of states, ergodicity, transitionary, and steady-state behavior. Then we go into Markov reward and decision processes. Along the way, we introduce return, discount, policy, value functions, and Bellman optimality, which are key concepts in RL theory that will be frequently referred to in later chapters. We conclude the chapter with a discussion on partially observed Markov decision processes. Throughout the chapter, we use a grid world example to illustrate the concepts.

Chapter 5, Solving the Reinforcement Learning Problem, presents and compares dynamic programming, Monte Carlo, and temporal-difference methods, which are fundamental to understanding how to solve a Markov decision process. Key approaches such as policy evaluation, policy iteration, and value iteration are introduced and illustrated. Throughout the chapter, we solve an example inventory replenishment problem. Along the way, we motivate the reader for deep RL methods. We conclude the chapter with a discussion on the importance of simulation in reinforcement learning.

Chapter 6, Deep Q-Learning at Scale, starts with a discussion on why it is challenging to use deep neural networks in reinforcement learning and how modern deep Q-learning addresses those challenges. After a thorough coverage of scalable deep Q-learning methods, we introduce Ray, a distributed computing framework, with which we implement a parallelized deep Q-learning variant. We finish the chapter by introducing RLlib, Ray's own scalable RL library.

Chapter 7, Policy-Based Methods, introduces another important class of RL approaches: policy-based methods. You will first learn how they are different than Q-learning and why they are needed. As we build the theory for contemporary policy-based methods, we also show how you can use RLlib for their application to a sample problem.

Chapter 8, Model-Based Methods, presents how learning a model of the environment can help an RL agent to plan its actions efficiently. In the chapter, we implement and use variants of cross-entropy methods and present Dyna, an RL framework that combines model-free and model-based approaches.

Chapter 9, Multi-Agent Reinforcement Learning, increases gears, goes into multi-agent settings and present the challenges that come with it. In the chapter, we train tic-tac-toe agents through self-play, which you also can play against for fun.

Chapter 10, Introducing Machine Teaching, introduces an emerging concept in RL that focuses on leveraging the subject matter expertise of a human "teacher" to make learning easy for RL agents. We present how reward function engineering, curriculum learning, demonstration learning, and action masking can help with training autonomous agents effectively.

Chapter 11, Achieving Generalization and Overcoming Partial Observability discusses why it is important to be concerned about generalization capabilities of trained RL policies for successful real-world implementations. To this end, the chapter focuses on simulation-to-real gap, connects generalization and partial observability, and introduces domain randomization and memory mechanisms. We also present the CoinRun environment and results on how traditional regularization methods can also help with generalization in RL.

Chapter 12, Meta-Reinforcement Learning, introduces approaches that allow an RL agent to adapt to a new environment once it is deployed for its task. This is one of the most important research directions towards achieving resilient autonomy through RL.

Chapter 13, Exploring Advanced Topics, brings you up to speed with some of the most recent developments in RL, including state-of-the-art distributed RL, SEED RL, approaches that cracked all the Atari benchmarks, Agent57, and RL without simulation, offline RL.

Chapter 14, Solving Robot Learning, goes into implementations of the methods covered in the earlier chapters by training a robot hand to grasp objects using manual and automated curriculum learning in PyBullet, a famous physics simulation in Python.

Chapter 15, Supply Chain Management, gives you hands-on experience in modeling and solving an inventory replenishment problem. Along the way, we perform hyperparameter tuning for our RL agent. The chapter concludes with a discussion on how RL can be applied to vehicle routing problems.

Chapter 16, Personalization, Marketing, and Finance goes beyond bandit models for personalization and discusses a news recommendation problem while introducing dueling bandit gradient descent and action embeddings along the way. The chapter also discusses marketing and finance applications of RL and introduces the TensorTrade library for the latter.

Chapter 17, Smart City and Cybersecurity starts with solving a traffic light contsrol scenario as a multi-agent RL problem using the Flow framework. It then describes how RL can be applied to two other problems: providing ancillary service to a power grid and discovering cyberattacks in it.

Chapter 18, Challenges and Future Directions in Reinforcement Learning wraps up the book by recapping the challenges in RL and connects them to the recent developments and research in the field. Finally, we present practical suggestions for the reader who want to further deepen their RL expertise.

To get the most out of this book

If you are using the digital version of this book, we advise you to type the code yourself or access the code via the GitHub repository (link available in the next section). Doing so will help you avoid any potential errors related to the copying and pasting of code.

Download the example code files

You can download the example code files for this book from your account at www.packt.com. If you purchased this book elsewhere, you can visit www.packtpub.com/support and register to have the files emailed directly to you.

You can download the code files by following these steps:

1. Log in or register at www.packt.com.
2. Select the **Support** tab.
3. Click on **Code Downloads**.
4. Enter the name of the book in the **Search** box and follow the onscreen instructions.

Once the file is downloaded, please make sure that you unzip or extract the folder using the latest version of:

- WinRAR/7-Zip for Windows
- Zipeg/iZip/UnRarX for Mac
- 7-Zip/PeaZip for Linux

The code bundle for the book is also hosted on GitHub at `https://github.com/PacktPublishing/Mastering-Reinforcement-Learning-with-Python`. In case there's an update to the code, it will be updated on the existing GitHub repository.

We also have other code bundles from our rich catalog of books and videos available at `https://github.com/PacktPublishing/`. Check them out!

Download the color images

We also provide a PDF file that has color images of the screenshots/diagrams used in this book. You can download it here: `https://static.packt-cdn.com/downloads/9781838644147_ColorImages.pdf`.

Conventions used

There are a number of text conventions used throughout this book.

`Code in text`: Indicates code words in text, database table names, folder names, filenames, file extensions, pathnames, dummy URLs, user input, and Twitter handles. Here is an example: "Install NVIDIA Modprobe, for example, for Ubuntu, using `sudo apt-get install nvidia-modprobe`."

A block of code is set as follows:

```
ug = UserGenerator()
visualize_bandits(ug)
```

When we wish to draw your attention to a particular part of a code block, the relevant lines or items are set in bold:

```
./run_local.sh [Game] [Agent] [Num. actors]
./run_local.sh atari r2d2 4
```

> **Tips or important notes**
> Appear like this.

Get in touch

Feedback from our readers is always welcome.

General feedback: If you have questions about any aspect of this book, mention the book title in the subject of your message and email us at customercare@packtpub.com.

Errata: Although we have taken every care to ensure the accuracy of our content, mistakes do happen. If you have found a mistake in this book, we would be grateful if you would report this to us. Please visit www.packtpub.com/support/errata, selecting your book, clicking on the Errata Submission Form link, and entering the details.

Piracy: If you come across any illegal copies of our works in any form on the Internet, we would be grateful if you would provide us with the location address or website name. Please contact us at copyright@packt.com with a link to the material.

If you are interested in becoming an author: If there is a topic that you have expertise in and you are interested in either writing or contributing to a book, please visit authors.packtpub.com.

Reviews

Please leave a review. Once you have read and used this book, why not leave a review on the site that you purchased it from? Potential readers can then see and use your unbiased opinion to make purchase decisions, we at Packt can understand what you think about our products, and our authors can see your feedback on their book. Thank you!

For more information about Packt, please visit packt.com.

Section 1: Reinforcement Learning Foundations

This part covers the necessary background of **Reinforcement Learning (RL)** to prepare you for the advanced material in later chapters. This includes definitions, mathematical foundations, and an overview of RL solution methodology.

This section contains the following chapters:

- *Chapter 1, Introduction to Reinforcement Learning*
- *Chapter 2, Multi-Armed Bandits*
- *Chapter 3, Contextual Bandits*
- *Chapter 4, Makings of a Markov Decision Process*
- *Chapter 5, Solving the Reinforcement Learning Problem*

1
Introduction to Reinforcement Learning

Reinforcement Learning (**RL**) aims to create **Artificial Intelligence** (**AI**) agents that can make decisions in complex and uncertain environments, with the goal of maximizing their long-term benefit. These agents learn how to do it through interacting with their environments, which mimics the way we as humans learn from experience. As such, RL has an incredibly broad and adaptable set of applications, with the potential to disrupt and revolutionize global industries.

This book will give you an advanced level understanding of this field. We will go deeper into the theory behind the algorithms you may already know, and cover state-of-the art RL. Moreover, this is a practical book. You will see examples inspired by real-world industry problems and learn expert tips along the way. By its conclusion, you will be able to model and solve your own sequential decision-making problems using Python.

So, let's start our journey with refreshing your mind on RL concepts and get you set up for the advanced material upcoming in the following chapters. Specifically, this chapter covers:

- Why reinforcement learning?
- The three paradigms of ML
- RL application areas and success stories
- Elements of a RL problem
- Setting up your RL environment

Why reinforcement learning?

Creating intelligent machines that make decisions at or superior to human level is a dream of many scientist and engineers, and one which is gradually becoming closer to reality. In the seven decades since the **Turing test**, AI research and development has been on a roller coaster. The expectations were very high initially: In the 1960s, for example, Herbert Simon (who later received the Nobel Prize in Economics) predicted that machines would be capable of doing any work humans can do within twenty years. It was this excitement that attracted big government and corporate funding flowing into AI research, only to be followed by big disappointments and a period called the "AI winter." Decades later, thanks to the incredible developments in computing, data, and algorithms, humankind is again very excited, more than ever before, in its pursuit of the AI dream.

> **Note**
> If you're not familiar with Alan Turing's instrumental work on the foundations of AI in 1950, it's worth learning more about the Turing Test here: `https://youtu.be/3wLqsRLvV-c`

The AI dream is certainly one of grandiosity. After all, the potential in intelligent autonomous systems is enormous. Think about how we are limited in terms of specialist medical doctors in the world. It takes years and significant intellectual and financial resources to educate them, which many countries don't have at sufficient levels. In addition, even after years of education, it is nearly impossible for a specialist to stay up-to-date with all of the scientific developments in her field, learn from the outcomes of the tens of thousands of treatments around the world, and effectively incorporate all this knowledge into practice.

Conversely, an AI model could process and learn from all this data and combine it with a rich set of information about a patient (medical history, lab results, presenting symptoms, health profile) to make diagnosis and suggest treatments. Such a model could serve even in the most rural parts of the world (as far as an internet connection and computer are available) and direct the local health personnel about the treatment. No doubt that it would revolutionize international healthcare and improve the lives of millions of people.

> **Note**
>
> AI is already transforming the healthcare industry. In a recent article, Google published results from an AI system surpassing human experts in breast cancer prediction using mammography readings (McKinney et al. 2020). Microsoft is collaborating with one of India's largest healthcare providers to detect cardiac illnesses using AI (Agrawal, 2018). IBM Watson for Clinical Trial Matching uses natural language processing to recommend potential treatments for patients from medical databases (`https://youtu.be/grDWR7hMQQQ`).

On our quest to develop AI systems that are at or superior to human level, which is -sometimes controversially- called **Artificial General Intelligence (AGI)**, it makes sense to develop a model that can learn from its own experience - without necessarily needing a supervisor. RL is the computational framework that enables us to create such intelligent agents. To better understand the value of RL, it is important to compare it with the other ML paradigms, which we'll look into next.

The three paradigms of ML

RL is a separate paradigm in **Machine Learning (ML)** along **supervised learning (SL)** and **unsupervised learning (UL)**. It goes beyond what the other two paradigms involve – perception, classification, regression and clustering – and makes decisions. Importantly however, RL utilizes the supervised and unsupervised ML methods in doing so. Therefore, RL is a distinct yet a closely related field to supervised and UL, and it's important to have
a grasp of them.

Supervised learning

SL is about learning a mathematical function that maps a set of inputs to the corresponding outputs/labels as accurately as possible. The idea is that we don't know the dynamics of the process that generates the output, but we try to figure it out using the data coming out of it. Consider the following examples:

- An image recognition model that classifies the objects on the camera of a self-driving car as pedestrian, stop sign, truck

- A forecasting model that predicts the customer demand of a product for a particular holiday season using past sales data.

It is extremely difficult to come up with the precise rules to visually differentiate objects, or what factors lead to customers demanding a product. Therefore, SL models infer them from labeled data. Here are some key points about how it works:

- During training, models learn from ground truth labels/output provided by a supervisor (which could be a human expert or a process),

- During inference, models make predictions about what the output might be given the input,

- Models use function approximators to represent the dynamics of the processes that generate the outputs.

Unsupervised learning

UL algorithms identify patterns in data that were previously unknown. While using such models, we might have an idea of what to expect as a result, but we don't supply the models with labels. For example:

- Identifying homogenous segments on an image provided by the camera of a self-driving car. The model is likely to separate the sky, road and buildings based on the textures on the image.

- Clustering weekly sales data into 3 groups based on sales volume. The output is likely to be weeks with low, medium, and high sales volume.

As you can tell, this is quite different than how SL works, namely:

- UL models don't know what the ground truth is, and there is no label to map the input to. They just identify the different patterns in the data. Even after doing so, for example, the model would not be aware that it separated sky from road, or a holiday week from a regular week.

- During inference, the model would cluster the input into one of the groups it had identified, again, without knowing what that group represents.

- Function approximators, such as neural networks, are used in some UL algorithms, but not always.

With supervised and UL reintroduced, we'll now compare them with RL.

Reinforcement learning

RL is a framework to learn how to make decisions under uncertainty to maximize a long-term benefit through trial and error. These decisions are made sequentially, and earlier decisions affect the situations and benefits that will be encountered later. This separates RL from both supervised and UL, which don't involve any decision-making. Let's revisit the examples we provided earlier to see how a RL model would differ from supervised and UL models in terms of what it tries to find out.

- For a self-driving car, given the types and positions of all the objects on the camera, and the edges of the lanes on the road, the model might learn how to steer the wheel and what the speed of the car should be to pass the car ahead safely and as quickly as possible.

- Given the historical sales numbers for a product and the time it takes to bring the inventory from the supplier to the store, the model might learn when and how many units to order from the supplier, so that seasonal customer demand is satisfied with high likelihood while the inventory and transportation costs are minimized.

As you will have noticed, the tasks that RL is trying to accomplish are of different nature and more complex than those simply addressed by SL and UL alone. Let's elaborate on how RL is different:

- The output of an RL model is a decision given the situation, not a prediction or clustering.

- There are no ground truth decisions provided by a supervisor that tell what the ideal decisions are in different situations. Instead, the model learns the best decisions from the feedback from its own experience and the decisions it made in the past. For example, through trial and error, an RL model would learn that speeding too much while passing a car may lead to accidents; and ordering too much inventory before holidays will cause excess inventory later.

- RL models often use outputs of SL models as inputs to make decisions. For example, the output of an image recognition model in a self-driving car could be used to make driving decisions. Similarly, the output of a forecasting model is often an input to an RL model that makes inventory replenishment decisions.

- Even in the absence of such an input from an auxiliary model, RL models, either implicitly or explicitly, predict what situations its decisions will lead to in the future.

- RL utilizes many methods developed for supervised and UL, such as various types of neural networks as function approximators.

So, what differentiates RL from other ML methods is that it is a decision-making framework. What makes it exciting and powerful, though, is its similarities to how we learn as humans to make decisions from experience. Imagine a toddler learning how to build a tower from toy blocks. Usually, the taller the tower, the happier the toddler is. Every increment in height is a success. Every collapse is a failure. She quickly discovers that the closer the next block is to the center of the one beneath, the more stable the tower is. This is reinforced when a block placed too close to the edge more readily topples. With practice, she manages to stack several blocks on top of each other. She realizes how she stacks the earlier blocks creates a foundation which determines how tall of a tower she can build. Thus, she learns.

Of course, the toddler did not learn these architectural principles from a blueprint. She learnt from the commonalities in her failure and success. The increasing height of the tower or its collapse provided a feedback signal upon which she refined her strategy accordingly. Learning from experience, rather than a blueprint is at the center of RL. Just as the toddler discovers which block positions lead to taller towers, an RL agent identifies the actions with the highest long-term rewards through trial and error. This is what makes RL such a profound form of AI; it's unmistakably human.

Over the past several years, there have been many amazing success stories proving the potential in RL. Moreover, there are many industries it is about to transform. So, before diving into the technical aspects of RL, let's further motivate ourselves by looking into what RL can do in practice.

RL application areas and success stories

RL is not a new field. Many of the fundamental ideas in RL were introduced in the context of dynamic programming and optimal control throughout the past seven decades. However, successful RL implementations have taken off recently thanks to the breakthroughs in deep learning and more powerful computational resources. In this section, we talk about some of the application areas of RL together with some famous success stories. We will go deeper into the algorithms behind these implementations in the following chapters.

Games

Board and video games have been a research lab for RL, leading to many famous success stories in this area. The reasons of why games make good RL problems are as follows:

- Games are naturally about sequential decision-making with uncertainty involved.

- They are available as computer software, making it possible for RL models to flexibly interact with them and generate billions of data points for training. Also, trained RL models are then also tested in the same computer environment. This is as opposed to many physical processes for which it is too complex to create accurate and fast simulators.

- The natural benchmark in games are the best human players, making it an appealing battlefield for AI vs. human comparisons.

After this introduction, let's go into some of the most exciting RL work that made to the headlines.

TD-Gammon

The first famous RL implementation is TD-Gammon, a model that learned how to play super-human level backgammon - a two-player board game with 10^{20} possible configurations. The model was developed by Gerald Tesauro at the IBM Research in 1992. TD-Gammon was so successful that it created a great excitement in the backgammon community back then with the novel strategies it taught humans. Many methods used in that model (temporal-difference, self-play, use of neural networks) are still at the center of the modern RL implementations.

Super-human performance in Atari games

One of the most impressive and seminal works in RL was that of Volodymry Mnih and his colleagues at Google DeepMind that came out in 2015. The researchers trained RL agents that learned how to play Atari games better than humans by only using screen input and game scores, without any hand-crafted or game-specific features through deep neural networks. They named their algorithm **deep Q-network** (**DQN**), which is one of the most popular RL algorithms today.

Beating the world champions in Go, chess and Shogi

The RL implementation that perhaps brought the most fame to RL was Google DeepMind's AlphaGo. It was the first computer program to beat a professional player in the ancient board game of Go in 2015, and later the world champion Lee Sedol in 2016. This story was later turned into a documentary film with the same name. The AlphaGo model was trained using data from human expert moves as well as with RL through self-play. The later version, AlphaGo Zero reached a performance of defeating the original AlphaGo 100-0, which was trained via just self-play and without any human knowledge inserted to the model. Finally, the company released AlphaZero in 2018 that was able to learn the games of chess, shogi (Japanese chess) and Go to become the strongest player in history for each, without any prior information about the games except the game rules. AlphaZero reached this performance after only several hours of training on **tensor processing units** (**TPUs**). AlphaZero's unconventional strategies were praised by world-famous players such as Garry Kasparov (chess) and Yoshiharu Habu (shogi).

Victories in complex strategy games

RL's success later went beyond just Atari and board games, into Mario, Quake III Arena, Capture the Flag, Dota 2 and StarCraft II. Some of these games are exceptionally challenging for AI programs with the need for strategic planning, involvement of game theory between multiple decision makers, imperfect information and large number of possible actions and game states. Due to this complexity, it took enormous amount of resources to train those models. For example, OpenAI trained the Dota 2 model using 256 GPUs and 128,000 CPU cores for months, giving 900 years of game experience to the model per day. Google DeepMind's AlphaStar, which defeated top professional players in StarCraft II in 2019, required training hundreds of copies of a sophisticated model with 200 years of real-time game experience for each, although those models were initially trained on real game data of human players.

Robotics and autonomous systems

Robotics and physical autonomous systems are challenging fields for RL. This is because RL agents are trained in simulation to gather enough data; but a simulation environment cannot reflect all the complexities of the real-world. Therefore, those agents often fail in the actual task, which is especially problematic if the task is safety critical. In addition, these applications often involve continuous actions, which require different types of algorithms than DQN. Despite these challenges, on the other hand, there are numerous RL success stories in these fields. In addition, there is a lot of research on using RL in exciting applications such autonomous ground and air vehicles.

Elevator optimization

An early success story that proved RL can create value for real-world applications was about elevator optimization in 1996 by Robert Crites and Andrew Barto. The researchers developed an RL model to optimize elevator dispatching in a 10-story building with 4 elevator cars. This was a much more challenging problem than the earlier TD-gammon due to the possible number of situations the model can encounter, partial observability (the number of people waiting at different floors was not observable to the RL model), and the possible number of decisions to choose from. The RL model substantially improved the best elevator control heuristics of the time across various metrics such as average passenger wait-time and travel-time.

Humanoid robots and dexterous manipulation

In 2017, Nicolas Heess et al. of Google DeepMind were able to teach different types of bodies (humanoid) various locomotion behaviors such as how to run, jump in a computer simulation. In 2018, Marcin Andrychowicz et al. of OpenAI trained a five-fingered humanoid hand that is able to manipulate a block from an initial configuration to a goal configuration. And in 2019, again researchers from OpenAI, Ilge Akkaya et al. were able to train a robot hand that can solve a Rubik's cube.

(a) Simulation   (b) Physical robot

Figure 1.1 – OpenAI's RL model that solved Rubik's cube is trained in simulation (a) and deployed on a physical robot (b). (Image source: OpenAI Blog, 2019)

Both of the latter two models were trained in simulation and successfully transferred to physical implementation using domain randomization techniques (*Figure 1.1*).

Emergency response robots

In the aftermath of a disaster, using robots could be extremely helpful especially when operating in dangerous conditions. For example, robots could locate survivors in damaged structures, turn off gas valves Creating intelligent robots that operate autonomously would allow to scale emergency response operations and provide the necessary support to many more people than it is possible with manual operations.

Self-driving vehicles

Although a full self-driving car is too complex to solve with an RL model alone, some of the tasks could be handled by RL. For example, we can train RL agents for self-parking, and making decisions for when and how to pass a car on a highway. Similarly, we can use RL agents to execute certain tasks in an autonomous drone, such as how to take off, land, avoid collusions

> Info
>
> In a phenomenal success story that came in late 2020, Loon and Google AI deployed a superpressure balloon in the stratosphere that is controlled by a RL agent. You can read about this story at `https://bit.ly/33RqQCh`.

As in many areas, we see RL appearing as a competitive alternative to traditional controllers for vehicles.

Supply chain

Many decisions in supply chain are of sequential nature and involve uncertainty, for which RL is a natural approach. Some of these problems are as follows:

- **Inventory planning** is about deciding when to place a purchase order to replenish the inventory of an item and at what quantity. Ordering less than necessary causes shortages and ordering more than necessary causes excess inventory costs, product spoilage and inventory removal at reduced prices. RL models are used to make inventory planning decisions to decrease the cost of these operations.

- **Bin packing** is a common problem in manufacturing and supply chain where items arriving at a station are placed into containers to minimize the number of containers used, and to ensure smooth operations in the facility. This is a difficult problem that can be solved using RL.

Manufacturing

An area where RL will have a great impact is manufacturing, where a lot of manual tasks can potentially be carried out by autonomous agents at reduced costs and increased quality. As a result, many companies are looking into bringing RL to their manufacturing environment. Here are some example RL applications in manufacturing.

- **Machine calibration** is a task that is often handled by human experts in manufacturing environments, which is inefficient and error prone. RL models are often capable of achieving these tasks at reduced costs and increased quality.

- **Chemical plant operations** often involve sequential decision making, which are often handled by human experts or heuristics. RL agents are shown to be effectively controlling these processes with better final product quality and less equipment wear and tear.

- **Equipment maintenance** requires planning down-times to avoid costly breakdowns. RL models can effectively balance the cost of downtime and cost of a potential breakdown.

- In addition to the examples above, many successful RL applications in **robotics** can be transferred to manufacturing solutions.

Personalization and recommender systems

Personalization is arguably the area where RL has created the most business value so far. Big tech companies provide personalization as a service with RL algorithms running under the hood. Here are some examples.

- In **advertising**, the order and content of promotional materials delivered to (potential) customers is a sequential decision-making problem that can be solved using RL, leading to increased customer satisfaction and conversion.

- **News recommendation** is an area where Microsoft News has famously applied RL and increased visitor engagement by improving the article selection and the order of recommendation.

- **Personalization of the artwork** that you see for the titles on Netflix is handled by RL algorithms. With that, the viewers better identify the titles relevant to their interests.

- **Personalized healthcare** is becoming increasingly important as it provides more effective treatments at reduced costs. There are many successful applications of RL picking the right treatment for patients.

Smart cities

There are many areas RL can help improve how cities operate. Below are couple examples.

- In a traffic network with multiple intersections, the **traffic lights** should work in harmony to ensure the smooth flow of the traffic. It turns out that this problem can be modeled as a multi-agent RL problem and improve the existing systems for traffic light control.

- **Balancing the generation and demand in electricity grids** in real-time is an important problem to ensure the grid safety. One way of achieving this is to control the demand, such as charging electric vehicles and turning on air conditioning systems when there is enough generation, without sacrificing the service quality, to which RL methods have successfully been applied.

This list can go on for pages, but it should be enough to demonstrate the huge potential in RL. What Andrew Ng, a pioneer in the field, says about AI is very much true for RL as well.

Just as electricity transformed almost everything 100 years ago, today I actually have a hard time thinking of an industry that I don't think AI will transform in the next several years. ("Andrew Ng: Why AI is the new electricity;" Stanford News; March 15, 2017)

RL today is only at the beginning of its prime time; and you are making a great investment by putting effort to understand what RL is and what it has to offer. Now, it is time to get more technical and formally define the elements in a RL problem.

Elements of a RL problem

So far, we have covered the types of problems that can be modeled using RL. In the next chapters, we will dive into state-of-the-art algorithms that will solve those problems. However, in between, we need to formally define the elements in an RL problem. This will lay the ground for the more technical material by establishing our vocabulary. After providing these definitions, we then look into what these concepts correspond to in a tic-tac-toe example.

RL concepts

Let's start with defining the most fundamental components in an RL problem.

- At the center of a RL problem, there is the learner, which is called the **agent** in RL terminology. Most of the problem classes we deal with has a single agent. On the other hand, if there are more than one agent, that problem class is called a **multi-agent RL**, or **MARL** for short. In MARL, the relationship between the agents could be cooperative, competitive or the mix of the two.

- The essence of an RL problem is the agent learning what to do, that is which **action** to take, in different situations in the world it lives in. We call this world the **environment** and it refers to everything outside of the agent.

- The set of all the information that precisely and sufficiently describes the situation in the environment is called the **state**. So, if the environment is in the same state at different points in time, it means everything about the environment is exactly the same - like a copy-paste.

- In some problems, the knowledge of the state is fully available to the agent. In a lot of other problems, and especially in more realistic ones, the agent does not fully observe the state, but only part of it (or a derivation of a part of the state). In such cases, the agent uses its **observation** to take actions. When this is the case, we say that the problem is **partially observable**. Unless we say otherwise, we assume that the agent is able to fully observe the state that the environment is in and is basing its actions on the state.

> **Info**
>
> The term *state* and its notation s is more commonly used during abstract discussions, especially when the environment is assumed to be fully observable, although *observation* is a more general term: What the agent receives is always an observation, which is sometimes just the state itself, and sometimes a part of or a derivation from the state, depending on the environment. Don't get confused if you see them used interchangeably in some contexts.

So far, we have not really defined what makes an action good or bad. In RL, every time the agent takes an action, it receives a **reward** from the environment (albeit it is sometimes zero). Reward could mean many things in general, but in RL terminology, its meaning is very specific: it is a scalar number. The greater the number is, the higher also is the reward. In an iteration of an RL problem, the agent observes the state the environment is in (fully or partially) and takes an action based on its observation. As a result, the agent receives a reward and the environment transitions into a new state. This process is described in Figure 2 below, which is probably familiar to you.

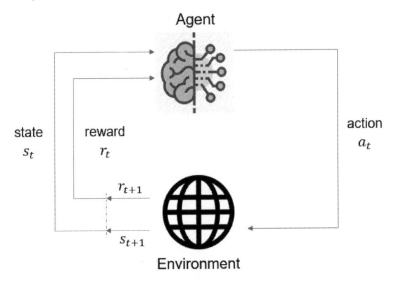

Figure 1.2 – RL process diagram

Remember that in RL, the agent is interested in actions that will be beneficial over the long term. This means the agent must consider the long-term consequences of its actions. Some actions might lead the agent to immediate high rewards only to be followed by very low rewards. The opposite might also be true. So, the agent's goal is to maximize the cumulative reward it receives. The natural follow up question is over what time horizon? The answer depends on whether the problem of interest is defined over a finite or an infinite horizon.

- If it is the former, the problem is described as an **episodic task** where an **episode** is defined as the sequence of interactions from an initial state to a **terminal state**. In episodic tasks, the agent's goal is to maximize the expected total cumulative reward collected over an episode.

- If problem is defined over an infinite horizon, it is called a **continuing task**. In that case, the agent will try to maximize the average reward since the total reward would go up to infinity.

- So, how does an agent achieve this objective? The agent identifies the best action(s) to take given its observation of the environment. In other words, the RL problem is all about finding a **policy**, which maps a given observation to one (or more) of the actions, that maximizes the expected cumulative reward.

All these concepts have concrete mathematical definitions, which we will cover in detail in later chapters. But for now, let's try to understand what these concepts would correspond to in a concrete example.

Casting Tic-Tac-Toe as a RL problem

Tic-tac-toe is a simple game, in which two players take turns to mark the empty spaces in a 3 × 3 grid. We now cast this as a RL problem to map the definitions provided above to the concepts in the game. The goal for a player is to place three of their marks in a vertical, horizontal or diagonal row to become the winner. If none of the players are able to achieve this before running out of the empty spaces on the grid, the game ends in a draw. Mid-game, a tic-tac-toe board might look like this:

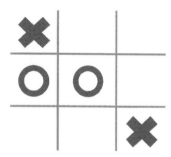

Figure 1.3 – An example board configuration in tic-tac-toe

Now, imagine that we have an RL agent playing against a human player.

- The action the agent takes is to place its mark (say a cross) in one of the empty spaces on the board when it is the agent's turn.

- Here, the board is the entire environment; and the position of the marks on the board is the state, which is fully observable to the agent.

- In a 3x3 tic-tac-toe game, there are 765 states (unique board positions, excluding rotations and reflections) and the agent's goal is to learn a policy that will suggest an action for each of these states so as to maximize the chance of winning.

- The game can be defined as an episodic RL task. Why? Because the game will last for a maximum 9 turns and the environment will reach a terminal state. A terminal state is one where either three Xs or Os make a row; or one where no single mark makes a row and there is no space left on the board (a draw).

- Note that no reward is given as the players make their moves during the game, except at the very end if a player wins. So, the agent receives +1 reward if it wins, -1 if it loses and 0 if the game is a draw. In all the iterations until the end, the agent receives 0 reward.

- We can turn this into a multi-agent RL problem by replacing the human player with another RL agent to compete with the first one.

Hopefully, this refreshes your mind on what agent, state, action, observation, policy and reward mean. This was just a toy example and rest assured that it will get much more advanced later. With this introductory context out of the way, what we need to do is to setup our computer environment to be able to run the RL algorithms we will cover in the following chapters.

Setting up your RL environment

RL algorithms utilize state-of-the-art ML libraries that require some sophisticated hardware. To follow along the examples we will solve throughout the book, you will need to set up your computer environment. Let's go over the hardware and software you will need in your setup.

Hardware requirements

As mentioned previously, state-of-the-art RL models are usually trained on hundreds of GPUs and thousands of CPUs. We certainly don't expect you to have access to those resources. However, having multiple CPU cores will help you simultaneously simulate many agents and environments to collect data more quickly. Having a GPU will speed up training deep neural networks that are used in modern RL algorithms. In addition, to be able to efficiently process all that data, having enough RAM resources is important. But don't worry, work with what you have, and you will still get a lot out of this book. For your reference, here are some specifications of the desktop we used to run the experiments:

- AMD Ryzen Threadripper 2990WX CPU with 32 cores

- NVIDIA GeForce RTX 2080 Ti GPU

- 128 GB RAM

As an alternative to building a desktop with expensive hardware, you can use **Virtual Machines (VM)** with similar capabilities provided by various companies. The most famous ones are:

- Amazon AWS

- Microsoft Azure

- Google Cloud

These cloud providers also provide data science images for your virtual machines during the setup and it saves the user from installing the necessary software for deep learning (CUDA, TensorFlow). They also provide detailed guidelines on how to setup your VMs, to which we defer the details of the setup.

A final option that would allow small-scale deep learning experiments with TensorFlow is Google's Colab, which provides VM instances readily accessible from your browser with the necessary software installed. You can start experimenting on a Jupyter Notebook-like environment right away, which is a very convenient option for quick experimentation.

Operating system

When you develop data science models for educational purposes, there is often not a lot of difference between Windows, Linux or MacOS. However, we plan to do a bit more than that in this book with advanced RL libraries running on a GPU. This setting is best supported on Linux, of which we use Ubuntu 18.04.3 LTS distribution. Another option is macOS, but that often does not come with a GPU on the machine. Finally, although the setup could be a bit convoluted, Windows Subsystem for Linux (WSL) 2 is an option you could explore.

Software toolbox

One of the first things people do while setting up the software environment for data science projects is to install **Anaconda**, which gives you a Python platform along with many useful libraries.

> Tip
> The CLI tool called **virtualenv** is a lighter weight tool compared to Anaconda to create virtual environments for Python, and preferable in most production environments. We, too, will use it in certain chapters. You can find the installation instructions for virtualenv at `https://virtualenv.pypa.io/en/latest/installation.html`.

We will particularly need the following packages:

- **Python 3.7**: Python is the lingua franca of data science today. We will use version 3.7.

- **NumPy**: It is one of the most fundamental libraries used in scientific computing in Python.

- **Pandas**: Pandas is a widely used library that provides powerful data structures and analysis tools.

- **Jupyter Notebook**: This is a very convenient tool to run Python code especially for small-scale tasks. It usually comes with your Anaconda installation by default.

- **TensorFlow 2.x**: This will be our choice as the deep learning framework. We use version 2.3.0 in the book. Occasionally, we will refer to repos that use TF 1.x as well.

- **Ray & RLlib**: Ray is a framework for building and running distributed applications and it is getting increasingly popular. RLlib is a library running on Ray that includes many popular RL algorithms. At the time of writing this book, Ray supports only Linux and macOS for production, and Windows support is in alpha phase. We will use version 1.0.1, unless noted otherwise.

- **Gym**: This is an RL framework created by OpenAI that you have probably interacted with before if you ever touched RL. It allows us to define RL environments in a standard way and let them communicate with algorithms in packages like RLlib.

- **OpenCV Python Bindings**: We need this for some image processing tasks.

- **Plotly**: This is a very convenient library for data visualization. We will use Plotly together with the **Cufflinks** package to bind it to pandas.

You can use one of the following commands on your terminal to install a specific package. With Anaconda:

```
conda install pandas==0.20.3
```

With virtualenv (Also works with Anaconda in most cases)

```
pip install pandas==0.20.3
```

Sometimes, you are flexible with the version of the package, in which case you can omit the equal sign and what comes after.

> **Tip**
>
> It is always a good idea to create a virtual environment specific to your experiments for this book and install all these packages in that environment. This way, you will not break dependencies for your other Python projects. There is a comprehensive online documentation on how to manage your environments provided by Anaconda available at `https://bit.ly/2QwbpJt`.

That's it! With that, you are ready to start coding RL!

Summary

This was our refresher on RL fundamentals! We began this chapter by discussing what RL is, and why it is such a hot topic and the next frontier in AI. We talked about some of the many possible applications of RL and the success stories that made it to the news headlines over the past several years. We defined the fundamental concepts we will use throughout the book. Finally, we covered the hardware and software you need to run the algorithms we will introduce in the next sections. Everything so far was to refresh your mind about RL, motivate and set you up for what is upcoming next: Implementing advanced RL algorithms to solve challenging real-world problems. In the next chapter, we will dive right into it with multi-armed bandit problems, an important class of RL algorithms that has many applications in personalization and advertising.

References

1. Sutton, R. S., Barto, A. G. (2018). *RL: An Introduction*. The MIT Press.

2. Tesauro, G. (1992). *Practical issues in temporal difference learning*. ML 8, 257–277.

3. Tesauro, G. (1995). *Temporal difference learning and TD-Gammon*. Commun. ACM 38, 3, 58-68.

4. Silver, D. (2018). *Success Stories of Deep RL*. Retrieved from `https://youtu.be/N8_gVrIPLQM`.

5. Crites, R. H., Barto, A.G. (1995). *Improving elevator performance using RL*. In Proceedings of the 8th International Conference on Neural Information Processing Systems (NIPS'95).

6. Mnih, V. et al. (2015). *Human-level control through deep RL*. Nature, 518(7540), 529–533.

7. Silver, D. et al. (2018). *A general RL algorithm that masters chess, shogi, and Go through self-play.* Science, 362(6419), 1140–1144.

8. Vinyals, O. et al. (2019). *Grandmaster level in StarCraft II using multi-agent RL.*

9. OpenAI. (2018). *OpenAI Five.* Retrieved from `https://blog.openai.com/openai-five/`.

10. Heess, N. et al. (2017). *Emergence of Locomotion Behaviours in Rich Environments.* ArXiv, abs/1707.02286.

11. OpenAI et al. (2018). *Learning Dexterous In-Hand Manipulation.* ArXiv, abs/1808.00177.

12. OpenAI et al. (2019). *Solving Rubik's Cube with a Robot Hand.* ArXiv, abs/1910.07113.

13. OpenAI Blog (2019). *Solving Rubik's Cube with a Robot Hand.* URL: `https://openai.com/blog/solving-rubiks-cube/`

14. Zheng, G. et al. (2018). *DRN: A Deep RL Framework for News Recommendation.* In Proceedings of the 2018 World Wide Web Conference (WWW '18). International World Wide Web Conferences Steering Committee, Republic and Canton of Geneva, CHE, 167–176. DOI: `https://doi.org/10.1145/3178876.3185994`

15. Chandrashekar, A. et al. (2017). *Artwork Personalization at Netflix.* The Netflix Tech Blog. URL: `https://medium.com/netflix-techblog/artwork-personalization-c589f074ad76`

16. McKinney, S. M. et al. (2020). *International evaluation of an AI system for breast cancer screening.* Nature, 89-94.

17. Agrawal, R. (2018, March 8). *Microsoft News Center India.* Retrieved from `https://news.microsoft.com/en-in/features/microsoft-ai-network-healthcare-apollo-hospitals-cardiac-disease-prediction/`

2

Multi-Armed Bandits

When you log on to your favorite social media app, chances are you see one of the many versions of the app that are tested at that time. When you visit a website, the ads displayed to you are tailored to your profile. In many online shopping platforms, the prices are determined dynamically. Do you know what all these have in common? They are often modeled as **multi-armed bandit (MAB)** problems to identify optimal decisions. A MAB problem is a form of **reinforcement learning (RL)**, where the agent makes decisions in a problem horizon that consists of a single step. Therefore, the goal is to maximize only the immediate reward, and there are no consequences considered for any subsequent steps. While this is a simplification over multi-step RL, the agent must still deal with a fundamental trade-off of RL: Exploration of new actions that could possibly lead to higher rewards, versus exploitation of the actions that are known to be decent. A wide range of business problems, like the ones above, involve optimizing this exploration-exploitation trade-off. Throughout the following two chapters, you will understand the implications of this trade-off -which will be a recurring theme in almost all RL methods- and learn how to effectively address them.

In this chapter, we lay the ground by solving MAB problems that don't take into account the "context" in which the actions are taken, such as the profile of the user visiting the website/app of interest, time of the day etc. To that end, we cover four fundamental exploration strategies. In the next chapter, we are going the extend these strategies to solve **contextual MABs.** In both chapters, we use online advertising, an important application of bandit problems, as our running case study.

So, let's get started! Here is what we specifically cover in this chapter:

- Exploration-exploitation trade-off
- What is a MAB?
- Case study: online advertising
- A/B/n testing as an exploration strategy
- ε-greedy actions for exploration
- Action selection using upper confidence bounds
- Thompson (posterior) sampling

Exploration-Exploitation Trade-Off

As we mentioned earlier, RL is all about learning from experience without a supervisor labeling correct actions for the agent. The agent observes the consequences of its actions, identifies what actions are leading to the highest rewards in each situation and learns from this experience. Now, think about something you learned from your own experience. For example, how to study for a test. Chances are you explored different methods until you discovered what works the best for you. Maybe you studied regularly for your tests first, but then you tried whether studying the last night before the test could work well enough - and maybe it does for certain types of tests. The point is that you had to **explore** to find the method(s) that maximizes your "reward," which is a function of your test score, time spent for leisure activities, your anxiety levels before and during the test etc. In fact, exploration is essential for any learning that is based on experience. Otherwise we may never discover better ways of doing things, or a way that works at all! On the other hand, we cannot always be trying new ways. That would be silly to not exploit what we have already learned! So, there is a *trade-off between exploration and exploitation*; and this trade-off is at the very center in reinforcement learning. And it is crucial to balance this trade-off for an efficient learning.

If the exploration-exploitation trade-off is a challenge in all across all RL problems, why do we specifically bring it up in the context of MAB? For two main reasons:

1. MAB is one-step RL. Therefore, it allows us to study various exploration strategies in isolation from the complexities of multi-step RL, and potentially prove how good they are theoretically.

2. While in multi-step RL we often train the agent offline (and in simulation) and use its policy online, in MAB problems, the agent is often trained and used (almost) online. Therefore, inefficient exploration costs more than just computer time: It actually burns real money through bad actions. Therefore, it becomes absolutely crucial to balance exploration and exploitation effectively in MAB problems.

With this in mind, now it is time to define what a MAB problem is and then see an example.

What is a MAB?

A MAB problem is all about identifying the best action among a set of actions available to an agent through trial and error, such as figuring out the best look for a website among some alternatives, or the best ad banner to run for a product. We will focus on the more common variant of MABs where there are k discrete actions available to the agent, also known as k-**armed bandit problem**.

Let's define the problem in more detail through the example it got its name from.

Problem definition

The MAB problem is named after the case of a gambler who needs to choose a slot machine (bandit) to play in a row of machines:

- When the lever of a machine is pulled, it gives a random reward coming from a probability distribution specific to that machine.
- Although the machines look identical, their reward probability distributions are different.

The gambler is trying to maximize his total reward. So, in each turn, he needs to decide whether to play the machine that has given the highest average reward so far, or to try another machine. Initially, the gambler has no knowledge of the machines' reward distributions.

Clearly, the gambler needs to balance between exploiting the one that has been the best thus far and exploring the alternatives. Why is that needed? Well, because the rewards are stochastic. A machine that won't give the highest average reward in the long-term may have looked like the best just by chance!

Figure 2.1 – MAB problems involve identifying the best lever to pull among multiple options.

So, to summarize what a MAB problem looks like:

- The agent takes sequential actions. After each action, a reward is received.

- An action affects only the immediate reward, not the subsequent rewards.

- There is no "state" in the system that changes with the actions that the agent takes.

- There is no input that the agent uses to base his decisions on. That will come later in the next chapter when we discuss contextual bandits.

So far so good! Let's better understand this by actually coding an example.

Experimenting with a simple MAB problem

In this section, you will experience through an example how tricky it could be to solve even a simple MAB problem. We will create some virtual slot machines and try to maximize the total reward by identifying the luckiest machine. This code is available at **Chapter02/Multi-armed bandits.ipynb** on the GitHub repo.

Setting up the virtual environment

Before we start, we suggest you create a virtual environment for the exercise using `virtualenv` or using Conda commands. In a folder that you would like to place the virtual environment files in, execute the following commands in your terminal:

```
virtualenv rlenv
source rlenv/bin/activate
```

```
pip install pandas==0.25.3
pip install plotly==4.10.0
pip install cufflinks==0.17.3
pip install jupyter
ipython kernel install --name "rlenv" -user
jupyter notebook
```

This will open a browser tab with Jupyter notebook. Find the .ipynb file you get from the repo, open it, and set your kernel to be the "rlenv" environment we just created.

The bandit exercise

Let's get started with the exercise:

1. First, let's create a class for a single slot machine that gives a reward from a normal (Gaussian) distribution with respect to a given mean and standard deviation:

```python
import numpy as np

# Class for a single slot machine. Rewards are Gaussian.
class GaussianBandit(object):
    def __init__(self, mean=0, stdev=1):
        self.mean = mean
        self.stdev = stdev

    def pull_lever(self):
        reward = np.random.normal(self.mean, self.stdev)
        return np.round(reward, 1)
```

2. Next, we create a class that will simulate the game:

```python
class GaussianBanditGame(object):
    def __init__(self, bandits):
        self.bandits = bandits
        np.random.shuffle(self.bandits)
        self.reset_game()

    def play(self, choice):
        reward = self.bandits[choice - 1].pull_lever()
        self.rewards.append(reward)
        self.total_reward += reward
```

```
            self.n_played += 1
            return reward

    def user_play(self):
        self.reset_game()
        print("Game started. " +
            "Enter 0 as input to end the game.")
        while True:
            print(f"\n -- Round {self.n_played}")
            choice = int(input(f"Choose a machine " +
                f"from 1 to {len(self.bandits)}: "))
            if choice in range(1, len(self.bandits) + 1):
                reward = self.play(choice)
                print(f"Machine {choice} gave " +
                    f"a reward of {reward}.")
                avg_rew = self.total_reward/self.n_played
                print(f"Your average reward " +
                    f"so far is {avg_rew}.")
            else:
                break
        print("Game has ended.")
        if self.n_played > 0:
            print(f"Total reward is {self.total_reward}"
 +
                f" after {self.n_played} round(s).")
            avg_rew = self.total_reward/self.n_played
            print(f"Average reward is {avg_rew}.")

    def reset_game(self):
        self.rewards = []
        self.total_reward = 0
        self.n_played = 0
```

A game instance receives a list of slot machines as inputs. It then shuffles the order of the slot machines so that you won't recognize which machine gives the highest average reward. In each step, you will choose a machine and aim to get the highest reward.

3. Then, we create some slot machines and a game instance:

```
slotA = GaussianBandit(5, 3)
slotB = GaussianBandit(6, 2)
slotC = GaussianBandit(1, 5)
game = GaussianBanditGame([slotA, slotB, slotC])
```

4. Now, start playing the game by calling the user_play() method of the game object:

```
game.user_play()
```

5. The output will look like the following:

```
Game started. Enter 0 as input to end the game.
-- Round 0
Choose a machine from 1 to 3:
```

6. As you enter your choice, you will observe the reward you got in that round. We don't know anything about the machines, so let's start with 1:

```
Choose a machine from 1 to 3: 1
Machine 1 gave a reward of 8.4.
Your average reward so far is 8.4.
```

It looks like we started pretty good! One might think that this reward is closest to what we could expect from the "slotB" machine, so there is no reason to try something else and lose money!

7. Let's play the same machine couple more rounds:

```
-- Round 1
Choose a machine from 1 to 3: 1
Machine 1 gave a reward of 4.9.
Your average reward so far is 6.65.


-- Round 2
Choose a machine from 1 to 3: 1
Machine 1 gave a reward of -2.8.
Your average reward so far is 3.5.
```

Snap! This in fact looks like the worst machine! It is very unlikely for "slotA" or "slotB" machines to give a reward of -2.8.

8. Let's check what we have as the first machine in the game (remember that the first machine would correspond to index 0 in the bandits list) by looking at its mean value parameter. Executing game.bandits[0].mean gives us 1 as the output!

Indeed, we thought we had chosen the best machine although it was the worst! Why did that happen though? Well, again, the rewards are stochastic. Depending on the variance of the reward distribution, a particular reward could be wildly different from the average reward we could expect from that machine. For this reason, it is not quite possible to know which lever to pull before we experience enough rounds of the game. In fact, with only a few samples, our observations could be quite misleading as it has just happened. In addition, if you play the game yourself, you will realize that it will be quite difficult to differentiate between "slotA" and "slotB," because their reward distributions are similar. And you might be thinking "is it a big deal?" Well, it kind of is, if the difference corresponds to significant money and resources, as it is the case in many real-world applications.

Next, we introduce such an application, online advertising, which is going to be our running example throughout this chapter and the next.

Case study: Online advertising

Consider a company that wants to advertise a product on various websites through digital banners, aiming to attract visitors to the product landing page. Among multiple alternatives, the advertiser company wants to find out which banner is the most effective and has the maximum **click-through rate (CTR)**, which is defined as the total number of clicks an ad receives divided by the total number of impressions (number of times it is shown).

Every time a banner is about to be shown on a website, it is the advertiser's algorithm that chooses the banner (for example, through an API provided by the advertiser to the website) and observes whether the impression has resulted in a click or not. This is a great use case for a MAB model, which could boost the clicks and product sales. What we want the MAB model to do is to identify the ad that performs the best as early as possible, display it more, and write off the ad(s) that is(are) a clear loser(s) as early as possible.

> **Tip**
> The probability of observing a click or no click after an impression, a binary outcome, can be modelled using the Bernoulli distribution. It has a single parameter, p, which is the probability of receiving a click, or more generally observing a "1" as opposed to a "0." Note that this is a discrete probability distribution, whereas normal distribution we used earlier is a continuous one.

In the prior example, we had rewards coming from a normal distribution. In the online ad case, we have a binary outcome. For each ad version, there is a different probability of click (CTR), which the advertiser does not know but is trying to discover. So, the rewards will come from different Bernoulli distributions for each ad. Let's code these to use with our algorithms later.

1. We start by creating a class to model the ad behavior:

```
class BernoulliBandit(object):
    def __init__(self, p):
        self.p = p
    def display_ad(self):
        reward = np.random.binomial(n=1, p=self.p)
        return reward
```

2. Now, let's create five different ads (banners) with the corresponding CTRs we arbitrarily pick.

```
adA = BernoulliBandit(0.004)
adB = BernoulliBandit(0.016)
adC = BernoulliBandit(0.02)
adD = BernoulliBandit(0.028)
adE = BernoulliBandit(0.031)
ads = [adA, adB, adC, adD, adE]
```

So far so good. Now it is time to implement some exploration strategies to maximize the CTR of the ad campaign!

A/B/n testing

One of the most common exploration strategies is what is called **A/B testing**, which is a method to determine which one of the two alternatives (of online products, pages, ads etc.) performs better. In this type of testing, the users are randomly split into two groups to try different alternatives. At the end of the testing period, the results are compared to choose the best alternative, which is then used in production for the rest of the problem horizon. In our case, we have more than two ad versions. So, we will implement what is called **A/B/n testing**.

We will use A/B/n testing as our baseline strategy for the comparison with the more advanced methods that we will introduce afterwards. Before going into the implementation, we need to define some notation that we will use throughout the chapter.

Notation

Throughout the implementations of various algorithms, we will need to keep track of some quantities related to a particular action (ad chosen for display) a. Now, we define some notation for those quantities. Initially we drop a from our notation for brevity, but at the end of this section we will put it back:

- First, we denote the reward (i.e. 1 for click, 0 for no click) received after selecting the action a for the ith time by R_i.

- The average reward observed prior to the nth selection of this same action is defined as

$$Q_n \triangleq \frac{R_1 + R_2 + \cdots + R_{n-1}}{n - 1}$$

which estimates the expected value of the reward that this action yields, R, after $n - 1$ observations.

- This is also called the **action value** of a. Here, Q_n estimates of the action value after selecting this action $n - 1$ times.

- Now, we need a bit of a simple algebra and we will have a very convenient formula to update the action values.

$$Q_{n+1} = \frac{R_1 + R_2 + \cdots + R_n}{n}$$

$$= \frac{R_1 + R_2 + \cdots + R_{n-1}}{n} + \frac{R_n}{n}$$

$$= \frac{n-1}{n-1} \cdot \frac{R_1 + R_2 + \cdots + R_{n-1}}{n} + \frac{R_n}{n}$$

$$= \frac{n-1}{n} \cdot \frac{R_1 + R_2 + \cdots + R_{n-1}}{n-1} + \frac{R_n}{n}$$

$$= \frac{n-1}{n} \cdot Q_n + \frac{R_n}{n}$$

$$= Q_n + \frac{1}{n} \cdot (R_n - Q_n)$$

- Remember that Q_n is our estimate for the action value of a before we take it for the nth time. When we observe the reward R_n, it gives us another signal for the action value. We don't want to discard our previous observations, but we also want to update our estimate to reflect the new signal.

- So, we adjust our current estimate, Q_n, in the direction of the **error** that we calculate based on the latest observed reward, $R_n - Q_n$, with a **step size** $1/n$ and obtain a new estimate Q_{n+1}. This means, for example, if the latest observed reward is greater than our current estimate, we revise the action value estimate upward.

- For convenience, we define $Q_0 \triangleq 0$.

- Notice that the rate at which we adjust our estimate will get smaller as we make more observations due to the $1/n$ term. So, we put less weight on the most recent observations and our estimate for the action value for a particular action will settle down over time.

- However, this might be a disadvantage if the environment is not stationary but changing over time. In those cases, we would want to use a step size that does not diminish over time, such as a fixed step size of $\alpha \in (0,1)$.

- Note that this step size must be smaller than 1 for the estimate to converge (and larger than 0 for a proper update).

- Using a fixed α will make the weights of the older observations to decrease exponentially as we take action α more and more.

Let's bring α back to the notation, so we can obtain our formula to update action values.

$$Q_{n+1}(a) = Q_n(a) + \alpha(R_n(a) - Q_n(a))$$

Where α is a number between 0 and 1. For stationary problems, we usually set $\alpha = 1/N(a)$, where $N(a)$ is the number of times the action a has been taken that far (which was denoted by n initially). In stationary problems, this will help action values converge quicker, due to the diminishing $1/N(a)$ term, rather than chasing after noisy observations.

That's all we need. Without further ado, let's implement an A/B/n test.

Application to the online advertising scenario

In our example, we have five different ad versions, which we randomly show to the users with equal probabilities. Let's implement this in Python.

1. We start with creating the variables to keep track of the rewards in the experiment.

```
n_test = 10000
n_prod = 90000
n_ads = len(ads)
Q = np.zeros(n_ads)   # Q, action values
N = np.zeros(n_ads)   # N, total impressions
total_reward = 0
avg_rewards = []   # Save average rewards over time
```

2. Now, let's run the A/B/n test.

```
for i in range(n_test):
    ad_chosen = np.random.randint(n_ads)
    R = ads[ad_chosen].display_ad() # Observe reward
    N[ad_chosen] += 1
    Q[ad_chosen] += (1 / N[ad_chosen]) * (R - Q[ad_
chosen])
    total_reward += R
    avg_reward_so_far = total_reward / (i + 1)
    avg_rewards.append(avg_reward_so_far)
```

Remember that we randomly select an ad to display during the test and observe whether it gets a click. We update the counter, the action value estimate and the average reward observed that far.

3. At the end of the test period, we choose the winner as the ad that has achieved the highest action value.

```
best_ad_index = np.argmax(Q)
```

4. And we display the winner using a print statement:

```
print("The best performing ad is {}".format(chr(ord('A')
+ best_ad_index)))
```

5. The outcome is the following:

> **The best performing ad is D.**

In this case, the A/B/n test has identified D as the best performing, which is not exactly correct. Apparently, the test period was not long enough.

6. Let's run the best ad identified in the A/B/n test in production.

```
ad_chosen = best_ad_index
for i in range(n_prod):
    R = ads[ad_chosen].display_ad()
    total_reward += R
    avg_reward_so_far = total_reward / (n_test + i + 1)
    avg_rewards.append(avg_reward_so_far)
```

In this stage, we don't explore other actions anymore. So, the incorrect selection of the ad D will have its impact throughout the production period. We continue to record the average reward observed that far to later visualize the ad campaign performance.

Now, time to visualize the results.

1. Let's create a Pandas DataFrame to record the results from the A/B/n test.

```
import pandas as pd
df_reward_comparison = pd.DataFrame(avg_rewards,
columns=['A/B/n'])
```

2. To display the progress of the average rewards, we use Plotly with Cufflinks.

```
import cufflinks as cf
import plotly.offline
cf.go_offline()
cf.set_config_file(world_readable=True, theme="white")

df_reward_comparison['A/B/n'].iplot(title="A/B/n Test
Avg. Reward: {:.4f}"
                                    .format(avg_reward_so_
far),
                                    xTitle='Impressions',
                                    yTitle='Avg. Reward')
```

This results in the following output:

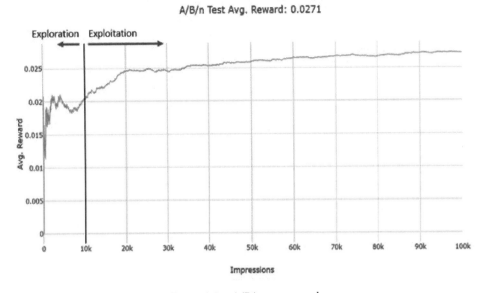

Figure 2.2 – A/B/n test rewards

You can see from Figure 2.2 that after the exploration ends, the average reward is approaching the 2.8%, which is the expected CTR for the ad D. On the other hand, due to the exploration during the first 10k impressions, in which we tried several bad alternatives, the CTR after 100k impressions ended up being 2.71%. We could have achieved a higher CTR if the A/B/n test had identified ad E as the best alternative.

That's it! We have just implemented an A/B/n test. Overall, the test was able to identify one of the best ads for us, although not the best. Next, we discuss the pros and cons of A/B/n testing.

Advantages and Disadvantages of A/B/n Testing

Now, let's qualitatively evaluate this method and discuss its shortcomings.

- **A/B/n testing is inefficient as it does not modify the experiment dynamically by learning from the observations.** Instead, it explores in a fixed time budget with pre-determined probabilities of trying the alternatives. It fails to benefit from the early observations in the test by writing off/promoting an alternative even though it is obviously underperforming/outperforming the others.

- **It is unable to correct a decision once it's made.** If, for some reason, the test period identifies an alternative as the best incorrectly (mostly because of a not-sufficiently-long test duration), this selection remains fixed during the production period. So, there is no way to correct the decision for the rest of the deployment horizon.

- **It is unable to adapt to the changes in a dynamic environment.** Related to the previous note, this approach is especially problematic for environments that are not stationary. So, if the underlying reward distributions change over time, plain A/B/n testing has no way of detecting such changes after the selection is fixed.

- **The length of the test period is a hyperparameter to tune, affecting the efficiency of the test.** If this period is chosen to be shorter than needed, an incorrect alternative could be declared the best because of the noise in the observations. If the test period is chosen to be too long, too much money gets wasted in exploration.

- **A/B/n testing is simple.** Despite all these shortcomings, it is intuitive and easy to implement, therefore widely used in practice.

So, the vanilla A/B/n testing is a rather naive approach to MAB. Next, let's look into some other and more advanced approaches that will overcome some of the shortcomings of A/B/n testing, starting with ε-greedy.

ε-greedy actions

An easy to implement, effective and widely used approach to exploration-exploitation problem is what is called **ε-greedy** actions. This approach suggests, most of the time, greedily taking the action that is the best according to the rewards observed that far in the experiment (i.e. with 1-ε probability); but once in a while (i.e. with ε probability) take a random action regardless of the action performances. Here ε is a number between 0 and 1, usually closer to zero (e.g. 0.1) to "exploit" in most decisions. This way, the method allows continuous exploration of the alternative actions throughout the experiment.

Application to the online advertising scenario

Now, let's implement the ε-greedy actions to the online advertising scenario that we have.

1. We start with initializing the necessary variables for the experiment, which will keep track of the action value estimates, number of times each ad has been displayed and the moving average for the reward.

```
eps = 0.1
n_prod = 100000
```

```
n_ads = len(ads)
Q = np.zeros(n_ads)
N = np.zeros(n_ads)
total_reward = 0
avg_rewards = []
```

Note that we choose ε as 0.1, but this is somewhat an arbitrary choice. Different ε values will lead to different performances, so this should be treated as a hyperparameter to be tuned. A more sophisticated approach would be to start with a high ε value and gradually reduce it. We'll talk about this a bit more later.

2. Next, we run the experiment. Pay attention to how we select a random action with ε probability, and the best action otherwise. We update our action value estimates according to the rule we previously described.

```
ad_chosen = np.random.randint(n_ads)
for i in range(n_prod):
    R = ads[ad_chosen].display_ad()
    N[ad_chosen] += 1
    Q[ad_chosen] += (1 / N[ad_chosen]) * (R - Q[ad_
chosen])
    total_reward += R
    avg_reward_so_far = total_reward / (i + 1)
    avg_rewards.append(avg_reward_so_far)
    # Select the next ad to display
    if np.random.uniform() <= eps:
        ad_chosen = np.random.randint(n_ads)
    else:
        ad_chosen = np.argmax(Q)
df_reward_comparison['e-greedy: {}'.format(eps)] = avg_
rewards
```

3. Run the steps (1) and (2) above for different ε values, namely 0.01, 0.05, 0.1 and 0.2. Then compare how the ε selection affects the performance as below.

```
greedy_list = ['e-greedy: 0.01', 'e-greedy: 0.05',
'e-greedy: 0.1', 'e-greedy: 0.2']
df_reward_comparison[greedy_list].iplot(title="ε-Greedy
Actions",
  dash=['solid', 'dash', 'dashdot', 'dot'],
```

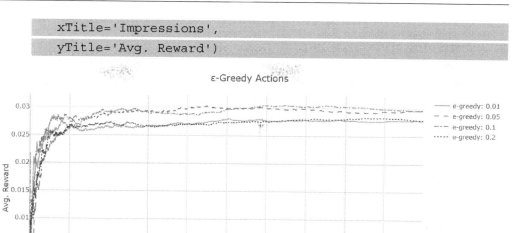

```
xTitle='Impressions',
yTitle='Avg. Reward')
```

Figure 2.3 – Exploration using ε-greedy actions

The best rewards are given by ε=0.05 and ε=0.1 as 2.97%. It turns out the exploration with the other two ε were either too low or high. In addition, all of the ε-greedy policies gave better results than the A/B/n test, particularly because the A/B/n test happened to make an incorrect choice in that specific case.

Advantages and disadvantages of ε-greedy actions

Let's talk about the pros and cons of using ε-greedy actions.

- **ε-greedy actions and A/B/n tests are similarly inefficient and static in allocating the exploration budget.** The ε-greedy approach, too, fails to write off actions that are clearly bad and continues to allocate the same exploration budget to each alternative. For example, halfway through the experiment, it is pretty clear that ad "A" is performing pretty poorly. It would have been more efficient to use the exploration budget to try to differentiate between the rest of the alternatives to identify the best. On a related note, if a particular action is under-explored/ over-explored at any point, the exploration budget is not adjusted accordingly.

- **With ε-greedy actions, exploration is continuous, unlike in A/B/n testing.** This means if the environment is not stationary, the ε-greedy approach has the potential to pick up the changes and modify its selection of the best alternative. In stationary environments though, we can expect the A/B/n testing and the ε-greedy approach to perform similarly, since they are very similar in nature except when they do the exploration.

- **The ε-greedy actions approach could be made more efficient by dynamically changing the ε.** For example, one could start with a high ε to explore more at the beginning and gradually decrease it to exploit more later. This way, there is still continuous exploration, but not as much as at the beginning when there was no knowledge of the environment.

- **The ε-greedy actions approach could be made more dynamic by increasing the importance of the more recent observations.** In the standard version, the Q values above are calculated as simple averages. Remember that, in dynamic environments, we could instead use the formula below.

$$Q_{n+1}(a) = Q_n(a) + \alpha(R_n(a) - Q_n(a))$$

This would exponentially diminish the weights of the older observations and enable the approach to detect the changes in the environment more easily.

- **Modifying the ε-greedy actions approach introduces new hyperparameters, which need to be tuned.** Both suggestions above, i.e. gradually diminishing ε and using exponential smoothing for Q, come with additional hyperparameters, and it may not be obvious what values to set these to. Moreover, incorrect selection of these hyperparameters may lead to worse results than what the standard version would yield.

So far so good! We have used ε-greedy actions to optimize our online advertising campaign and obtained better results than A/B/n testing. We have also discussed how we can modify this approach to use in a broader set of environments. However, ε-greedy selection of the actions is still too static, and we can do better. Now, let's look into another approach, Upper Confidence Bounds, which dynamically adjusts the exploration of the actions.

Action selection using upper confidence bounds

Upper confidence bounds (UCB) is a simple yet effective solution to exploration-exploitation trade-off. The idea is that at each time step, we select the action that has the highest potential for reward. The potential of the action is calculated as the sum of the action value estimate and a measure of the uncertainty of this estimate. This sum is what we call the upper confidence bound. So, an action is selected either because our estimate for the action value is high, or the action has not been explored enough (i.e. as many times as the other ones) and there is high uncertainty about its value, or both.

More formally, we select the action to take at time t using:

$$A_t \triangleq \arg\max_a \left[Q_t(a) + c\sqrt{\frac{\ln t}{N_t(a)}} \right]$$

Let's unpack this a little bit:

- Now we have used a notation that is slightly different from what we introduced earlier. $Q_t(a)$ and $N_t(a)$ have essentially the same meanings as before. This formula looks at the variable values, which may have been updated a while ago, at the time of decision making t, whereas the earlier formula described how to update them.

- In this equation, the square root term is a measure of the uncertainty for the estimate of the action value of a.

- The more we select a, the less we are uncertain about its value, and so is the $N_t(a)$ term in the denominator.

- As the time passes, however, the uncertainty grows due to the $\ln t$ term (which makes sense especially if the environment is not stationary), and more exploration is encouraged.

- On the other hand, the emphasis on uncertainty during decision making is controlled by a hyperparameter, c. This obviously requires tuning and a bad selection could diminish the value in the method.

Now, it is time to see UCB in action.

Application to the online advertising scenario

Follow along to implement the UCB method to optimize the ad display:

1. As usual, let's initialize the necessary variables first.

```
c = 0.1
n_prod = 100000
n_ads = len(ads)
ad_indices = np.array(range(n_ads))
Q = np.zeros(n_ads)
N = np.zeros(n_ads)
total_reward = 0
avg_rewards = []
```

2. Now, implement the main loop to use UCB for action selection.

```
for t in range(1, n_prod + 1):
    if any(N==0):
        ad_chosen = np.random.choice(ad_indices[N==0])
    else:
        uncertainty = np.sqrt(np.log(t) / N)
        ad_chosen = np.argmax(Q + c * uncertainty)
    R = ads[ad_chosen].display_ad()
    N[ad_chosen] += 1
    Q[ad_chosen] += (1 / N[ad_chosen]) * (R - Q[ad_
chosen])
    total_reward += R
    avg_reward_so_far = total_reward / t
    avg_rewards.append(avg_reward_so_far)
df_reward_comparison['UCB, c={}'.format(c)] = avg_rewards
```

Note that we select the action in each time step with the highest UCB. If an action has not been selected yet, it has the highest UCB. We break the ties randomly if there are multiple such actions.

3. As mentioned before, different c selections will lead to different levels of performance. Run the steps (1) and (2) with different selections of the c hyperparameter. Then compare the results as below.

```
ucb_list = ['UCB, c=0.1', 'UCB, c=1', 'UCB, c=10']
best_reward = df_reward_comparison.loc[t-1,ucb_list].
max()
df_reward_comparison[ucb_list].iplot(title="Action
Selection using UCB. Best avg. reward: {:.4f}"
                                      .format(best_reward),
                             dash = ['solid',
'dash', 'dashdot'],
                                      xTitle='Impressions',
                                      yTitle='Avg. Reward')
```

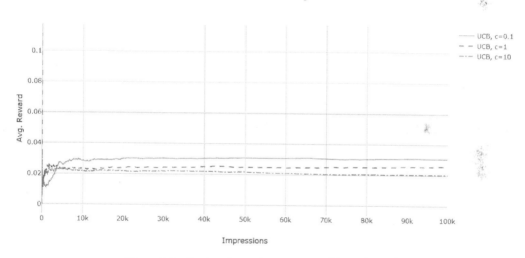

Figure 2.4 – Exploration using upper confidence bounds

In this case, using UCB for exploration, after some hyperparameter tuning, gave a better result (3.07% CTR) than ε-greedy exploration and A/B/n testing! Of course, the elephant in the room is how to do this hyperparameter tuning. Interestingly, this is itself a MAB problem! First, one has to form a set of plausible c values and choose the best one using one of the methods we described so far.

> **Tip**
> Try hyperparameters in a logarithmic scale, such as [0.01, 0.1, 1, 10] rather than a linear scale, such as [0.08, 0.1, 0.12, 0.14]. The former allows exploring different orders of magnitude, where we could see significant jumps in performance. A search in linear scale could be used after identifying the right order of magnitude.

To make things less complicated, you can use an A/B/n test to choose c. This might look like an infinite loop, you form a MAB to solve a MAB, which itself may have a hyperparameter to tune and so on. Fortunately, once you identify a good c that works for your problem type (e.g. online advertising), you can usually use the same value over and over again in later experiments as far as the reward scale remains similar (e.g. around 1-3% CTR for online ads).

Advantages and disadvantages of using UCBs

Finally, let's discuss some of the pros and cons of the UCB approach.

- **UCB is a set-and-forget approach.** It systematically and dynamically allocates the budget to alternatives that need exploration. If there are changes in the environment, for example, if the reward structure changes because one of the ads gets more popular for some reason, the method will adapt its selection of the actions accordingly.

- **UCB can be further optimized for dynamic environments, potentially at the expense of introducing additional hyperparameters.** The formula we provided for UCB is a common one, but it can be improved, for example, by using exponential smoothing to calculate the Q values. There are also more effective estimations of the uncertainty component in literature. These modifications, though, could potentially make the method more complicated.

- **UCB could be hard to tune.** It is somewhat easier make the call and say "I want to explore 10% of the time, and exploit for the rest" for the ε-greedy approach than saying "I want my c to be 0.729" for the UCB approach, especially if you are trying these methods on a brand new problem. When not tuned, an UCB implementation could give unexpectedly bad results.

There you go! You now have implemented multiple approaches to the online advertising problem, and using the UCB approach has particularly equipped you to manage the exploration effectively in potentially non-stationary environments. Next, we cover another very powerful approach, Thompson sampling, which will be a great addition to your arsenal.

Thompson (Posterior) sampling

The goal in MAB problems is to estimate the parameter(s) of the reward distribution for each arm (that is ad to display in the above example). In addition, measuring our uncertainty about our estimate is a good way to guide the exploration strategy. This problem very much fits into the Bayesian inference framework, which is what Thompson sampling leverages. Bayesian inference starts with a prior probability distribution, an initial idea, for the parameter θ, and updates this prior as data becomes available. Here, θ refers to the mean and variance for a normal distribution, and to the probability of observing a "1" for Bernoulli distribution. So, the Bayesian approach treats the parameter as a random variable given the data.

The formula for this is given by:

$$p(\theta|X) = \frac{p(X|\theta)p(\theta)}{p(X)}$$

In this formula, $p(\theta)$ is the **prior distribution** of θ, which represents the current hypothesis on its distribution. X represents the data, with which we obtain a **posterior distribution**, $p(\theta|X)$. This is our updated hypothesis on the distribution of the parameter given the data we observe. $p(X|\theta)$ is called the **likelihood** (of observing the data X given the parameter) and $p(X)$ is called the **evidence**.

Next, let's look into how we can implement Thompson Sampling for cases with 0-1 type of outcome, like what we have in the online advertising scenario.

Application to the online advertising scenario

In our example, for a given ad k, observing a click is a Bernoulli random variable with parameter θ_k, which we are trying to estimate. Since θ_k is essentially the probability that the ad k is clicked when displayed, equivalently the CTR, it is between 0 and 1. Note that many problems other than online advertising have such a binary outcome. Therefore, our discussion and the formulas here can be extended to such other cases.

Details of Thompson sampling

For now, let's see how we can use a Bayesian approach to our problem.

- Initially, we don't have any reason to believe that the parameter is high or low for a given ad. Therefore, it makes sense to assume that θ_k has a uniform distribution over $[0, 1]$.

- Assume that we display the ad k and it results in a click. We take this as a signal to update the probability distribution for θ_k so that the expected value shifts a little bit towards 1.

- As we collect more and more data, we should also see the variance estimate for the parameter shrink. Well, this is exactly how we want to balance exploration and exploitation. We did something similar when we used UCB: We used our estimate of a parameter together with the associated uncertainty around the estimate to guide the exploration. Thompson sampling does exactly the same, using Bayesian inference.

- This method tells us to take a sample from the posterior distribution of the parameter, $p(\theta_k|X)$. If the expected value of θ_k is high, we are likely to get samples closer to 1. If the variance is high because ad k has not been selected many times that far, our samples will also have high variance, which will lead to exploration. At a given time step, we take one sample for each ad and select the greatest sample to determine the ad to display.

In our example, the likelihood (chance of an impression resulting in a click) is Bernoulli distribution, to which we will apply the logic we described above. Here is what is really going on in less technical terms:

- We want to understand what CTR is for each ad. We have estimates, but we are unsure about them, so we associate a probability distribution with each CTR.

- We update the probability distributions for CTRs as new data come in.

- When it is time to select an add, we make a guess about the CTR for each ad, that is, sample θ_ks. We then pick the ad for which we happened to guess the highest CTR.

- If the probability distribution for the CTR of an ad has a high variance, it means we are very uncertain about it. This will cause us to make wild guesses about that particular ad and select it more often, until the variance reduces, i.e., we become more certain about it.

Now, let's talk about the update rules for the Bernoulli distribution. It is okay if you don't fully grasp the terms here. The explanations above should tell you about what is going on.

- A common choice to use for the prior is beta distribution. If you think for a moment, parameter θ takes values within $[0, 1]$. So, we need to use a probability distribution with the same support to model θ, which beta distribution has.

- In addition, if we use beta distribution for the prior and plug it in the Bayes formula with a Bernoulli likelihood, the posterior also becomes a beta distribution. This way, we can use the posterior as the prior for the next update when we observe new data.

- Having the posterior in the same distribution family with the prior is such a convenience that it even has a special name: They are called **conjugate distributions**, and the prior is called a **conjugate prior** for the likelihood function. Beta distribution is a conjugate prior for the Bernoulli distribution. Depending on your choice of modeling the likelihood, it is possible to find a conjugate prior to implement Thompson sampling.

Without further ado, let's implement Thompson sampling for our online advertising example.

Implementation

The beta distribution for the prior of the ad k is given by

$$p(\theta_k) = \frac{\Gamma(\alpha_k + \beta_k)}{\Gamma(\alpha_k)\Gamma(\beta_k)} \theta_k^{\alpha_k - 1}(1 - \theta_k)^{\beta_k - 1}$$

Where α_k and β_k are the parameters characterizing the beta distribution, and $\Gamma(\cdot)$ is the gamma function. Don't let this formula scare you! It is actually pretty easy to implement it. To initialize the prior, we use $\alpha_k = \beta_k = 1$, which makes θ_k uniformly distributed over $[0, 1]$. Once we observe a reward R_t after selecting the ad k, we obtain the posterior distribution as follows:

$$\alpha_k \leftarrow \alpha_k + R_t$$

$$\beta_k \leftarrow \beta_k + 1 - R_t$$

Now, let's do this in Python.

1. First, initialize the variables we will need.

```
n_prod = 100000
n_ads = len(ads)
alphas = np.ones(n_ads)
betas = np.ones(n_ads)
total_reward = 0
avg_rewards = []
```

2. Now the main loop with Bayesian updates.

```
for i in range(n_prod):
    theta_samples = [np.random.beta(alphas[k], betas[k])
    for k in range(n_ads)]
```

```
ad_chosen = np.argmax(theta_samples)
R = ads[ad_chosen].display_ad()
alphas[ad_chosen] += R
betas[ad_chosen] += 1 - R
total_reward += R
avg_reward_so_far = total_reward / (i + 1)
avg_rewards.append(avg_reward_so_far)
df_reward_comparison['Thompson Sampling'] = avg_rewards
```

We sample θ_k for each k from their corresponding posteriors and display the ad that corresponds to the greatest sampled parameter. Once we observe the reward, we make the posterior the prior and update it according to the rule above to obtain the new posterior.

3. And to display the results:

```
df_reward_comparison['Thompson Sampling'].
iplot(title="Thompson Sampling Avg. Reward: {:.4f}"
                              .format(avg_reward_so_
far),
                              xTitle='Impressions',
                              yTitle='Avg. Reward')
```

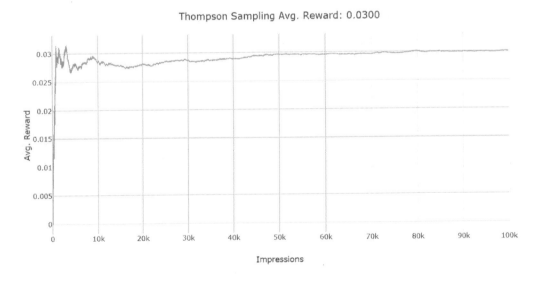

Figure 2.5 – Exploration using Thompson sampling

Thompson sampling has given a performance that is similar to ε-greedy and UCB approaches, right at 3% CTR.

Advantages and disadvantages of Thompson sampling

Thompson sampling is a very competitive approach with one major advantage over the ε-greedy and UCB approaches: *Thompson sampling did not require us to do any hyperparameter tuning.* This, in practice,

- **Saves significant time** that would have been spent on hyperparameter tuning,
- **Saves significant money** that would have been burned by ineffective exploration and incorrect selection of hyperparameters in other approaches.

In addition, Thompson sampling is shown to be a very competitive choice in many benchmarks in literature, and it has gotten increasingly popular over the last years.

Awesome job! Now that Thompson sampling is in your toolkit along with the other methods, you are set to go out and solve real-world MAB problems!

Summary

In this chapter, we've covered MAB problems, which is one-step reinforcement learning with many practical business applications. Despite its apparent simplicity, it is tricky to balance the exploration and exploitation in MAB problems, and any improvements in managing this trade-off comes with savings in costs and increases in revenue. We have introduced four approaches to this end: A/B/n testing, ε-greedy actions, action selection using upper confidence bounds and Thompson sampling. We implemented these approaches in an online advertising scenario and discussed their advantages and disadvantages.

So far, while making decisions, we have not considered any information about the situation in the environment. For example, we have not used any information about the users (e.g. location, age, previous behavior etc.) in the online advertising scenario that could be available to our decision-making algorithm. In the next chapter, you will learn about a more advanced form of MABs, namely Contextual Bandits, which can use such information to come up with better decisions.

References

1. Chapelle, O., & Li, L. (2011). An Empirical Evaluation of Thompson Sampling. *Advances in Neural Information Processing Systems* 24, (pp. 2249-2257).

2. Marmerola, G. D. (2017, November 28). *Thompson Sampling for Contextual bandits*. Retrieved from Guilherme's Blog: `https://gdmarmerola.github.io/ts-for-contextual-bandits/`

3. Russo, D., Van Roy, B., Kazerouni, A., Osband, I., & Wen, Z. (2018). *A Tutorial on Thompson Sampling. Foundations and Trends in Machine Learning*, 1-96.

3
Contextual Bandits

A more advanced version of the multi-armed bandit is the **contextual bandit (CB)** problem, where decisions are tailored to the **context** they are made in. In the previous chapter, we identified the best performing ad in an online advertising scenario. In doing so, we did not use any information about, for instance, the user persona, age, gender, location, previous visits etc., which would have increased the likelihood of a click. Contextual bandits allow us to leverage such information, which makes them play a central role in commercial personalization and recommendation applications.

Context is similar to a state in a multi-step **reinforcement learning (RL)** problem, with one key difference. In a multi-step RL problem, the action an agent takes affects the states it is likely to visit in the subsequent steps. For example, while playing tic-tac-toe, an agent's action in the current state changes the board configuration (state) in a particular way, which then affects what actions the opponent can take, and so on. In CB problems, however, the agent simply observes the context, makes a decision, and observes the reward. The next context the agent will observe does not depend on the current context/action. This setup, although simpler than multi-step RL, occurs in a very broad set of applications. So, you will add a key tool to your arsenal with what we cover in this chapter.

We continue to solve different versions of the online advertising problem, using more advanced tools, such as neural networks, together with contextual bandit models. Specifically, in this chapter, you will learn about:

- Why we need function approximations
- Using function approximation for context
- Using function approximation for action
- Other applications of multi-armed and contextual bandits

Why we need function approximations

While solving (contextual) multi-armed bandit problems, our goal is to learn action values for each arm (action) from our observations, which we have denoted by $Q(a)$. In the online advertising example, it represented our estimate for the probability of a user clicking the ad if we displayed a. Now, assume that we have two pieces of information about the user seeing the ad, namely:

- Device type (e.g. mobile vs. desktop), and
- Location (e.g. domestic / U.S. vs. international / non-U.S.)

It is quite likely that ad performances will differ with device type and location, which make up the context in this example. A CB model will therefore leverage this information, estimate the action values for each context, and choose the actions accordingly.

This would look like filling a table for each ad similar to the below:

$Q(a = D)$	Domestic	International
Mobile	0.031	0.02
Desktop	0.036	0.022

Table 1 – Sample action values for ad D

This means solving four MAB problems, one for each context:

- Mobile – Domestic
- Mobile – International
- Desktop – Domestic
- Desktop – International

While this could work fine in this simple example, think about what happens when you add additional information to the context, for example, age. This introduces a number of challenges:

- First, we may not have enough observations to (accurately) learn action values for each context, e.g., (Mobile, International, 57). However, we want to be able to cross-learn, and estimate the action values (or improve the estimate) for a 57-year-old user if we have data on users from closer ages.

- Second, the number of possible contexts increases by a factor 100. We could of course mitigate this problem by defining age groups. But then we would have to spend time and data to calibrate the groups, which is not a trivial undertaking. In addition, the growth of the context space would be more limited (i.e. growth by a factor of 10 instead of 100), but still exponential. As we add more and more dimensions to the context, which is very likely in any realistic implementation, the problem could easily become intractable.

Next, we address this problem using function approximations. This will allow us to work with very complex and high-dimensional contexts. Later, we will also use function approximations for actions, which will enable us to work with changing and / or high-dimensional action spaces.

Using function approximation for context

Function approximations allow us to model the dynamics of a process from which we have observed data, such as contexts and ad clicks. As in the previous chapter, consider an online advertising scenario with five different ads (i.e. A, B, C, D, and E), with the context comprised of user device, location and age. In this section, our agent will learn five different Q functions, one per ad, each receiving a context $x = [device, location, age]$, and return the action value estimate. This is illustrated in Figure 1.

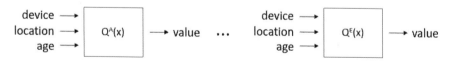

Figure 3.1 – We learn a function for each action that receives the context and returns the action value.

At this point, we have a supervised machine learning problem to solve for each action. We can use different models to obtain the Q functions, such as logistic regression or a neural network (which actually allows us to use a single network that estimates values for all actions). Once we choose the type of function approximation, we can use the exploration strategies that we covered in the previous chapter to determine the ad to display given the context. But first, let's create a synthetic process to generate click data mimicking user behavior for our example.

Case study: Contextual online advertising with synthetic user data

Assume that the true user click behavior follows a logistic function:

$$p_a(x) = \frac{1}{1 + e^{-f_a(x)}}$$

$$f_a(x = [device, location, age]) = \beta_0^a + \beta_1^a \cdot device + \beta_2^a \cdot location + \beta_3^a \cdot age$$

where $p_a(x)$ is the probability of a user click when the context is x and ad a is shown. Also, let's assume that *device* is 1 for mobile and 0 otherwise; and *location* is 1 for U.S. and 0 otherwise. There are two things important to note here:

- This behavior, particularly the β parameters, are unknown to the advertiser, which they will try to uncover,

- Note the superscript a in β_i^a, which denotes that the impact of these factors on user behavior is potentially different for each ad.

Let's now implement this in Python.

Chapter03/Contextual Bandits.ipynb

1. First, let's import the Python packages we will need.

```
import numpy as np
import pandas as pd
from scipy.optimize import minimize
from scipy import stats
import plotly.offline
from plotly.subplots import make_subplots
import plotly.graph_objects as go
import cufflinks as cf
```

```
cf.go_offline()
cf.set_config_file(world_readable=True, theme='white')
```

These include libraries for scientific computation, such as NumPy and SciPy, and Plotly, a powerful visualization tool.

2. Now, we create a class, `UserGenerator` to simulate the user dynamics. Set some true β parameters here, which the advertiser (the agent) will try to learn.

```
class UserGenerator(object):
    def __init__(self):
        self.beta = {}
        self.beta['A'] = np.array([-4, -0.1, -3, 0.1])
        self.beta['B'] = np.array([-6, -0.1, 1, 0.1])
        self.beta['C'] = np.array([2, 0.1, 1, -0.1])
        self.beta['D'] = np.array([4, 0.1, -3, -0.2])
        self.beta['E'] = np.array([-0.1, 0, 0.5, -0.01])
        self.context = None
```

3. Let's define the methods to generate a click or no clicks given the user context.

```
    def logistic(self, beta, context):
        f = np.dot(beta, context)
        p = 1 / (1 + np.exp(-f))
        return p
    def display_ad(self, ad):
        if ad in ['A', 'B', 'C', 'D', 'E']:
            p = self.logistic(self.beta[ad], self.
    context)
            reward = np.random.binomial(n=1, p=p)
            return reward
        else:
            raise Exception('Unknown ad!')
```

Note that each ad has a different set of β values. When an ad is displayed to a user, the `logistic` method calculates the probability of a click and the `display_ad` method generates a click with that probability.

4. We define a method that will generate users with different contexts randomly.

```python
def generate_user_with_context(self):
    # 0: International, 1: U.S.
    location = np.random.binomial(n=1, p=0.6)
    # 0: Desktop, 1: Mobile
    device = np.random.binomial(n=1, p=0.8)
    # User age changes between 10 and 70,
    # with mean age 34
    age = 10 + int(np.random.beta(2, 3) * 60)
    # Add 1 to the concept for the intercept
    self.context = [1, device, location, age]
    return self.context
```

As you can see, the `generate_user_with_context` method generate a U.S user with 60% chance. Also, with 80% chance, the ad is displayed on a mobile device. Finally, the user ages vary between 10 and 70 with the mean age of 34. These are some number we set somewhat arbitrarily for the sake of the example. For simplicity, we don't assume any correlations between these user attributes. You can modify these parameters and introduce correlations to create more realistic scenarios.

5. We can create some functions (outside of the class) to visualize, for our own intuition, the relationship between the context and the probability of a click associated with it. To this end, we need a function to create a scatter plot for a given ad type and data.

```python
def get_scatter(x, y, name, showlegend):
    dashmap = {'A': 'solid',
               'B': 'dot',
               'C': 'dash',
               'D': 'dashdot',
               'E': 'longdash'}
    s = go.Scatter(x=x,
                   y=y,
                   legendgroup=name,
                   showlegend=showlegend,
                   name=name,
                   line=dict(color='blue',
```

```
                                    dash=dashmap[name]))
        return s
```

6. Now, we define a function to plot how the click probabilities change with age, shown in different subplots for each device type and location pair.

```
def visualize_bandits(ug):
    ad_list = 'ABCDE'
    ages = np.linspace(10, 70)
    fig = make_subplots(rows=2, cols=2,
            subplot_titles=("Desktop, International",
                            "Desktop, U.S.",
                            "Mobile, International",
                            "Mobile, U.S."))
    for device in [0, 1]:
        for loc in [0, 1]:
            showlegend = (device == 0) & (loc == 0)
            for ad in ad_list:
                probs = [ug.logistic(ug.beta[ad],
                            [1, device, loc, age])
                                for age in ages]
                fig.add_trace(get_scatter(ages,
                                        probs,
                                        ad,
                                        showlegend),
                            row=device+1,
                            col=loc+1)
    fig.update_layout(template="presentation")
    fig.show()
```

7. Now, let's create an object instance to generate users and visualize the user behavior.

```
ug = UserGenerator()
visualize_bandits(ug)
```

The output is shown in Figure 2.

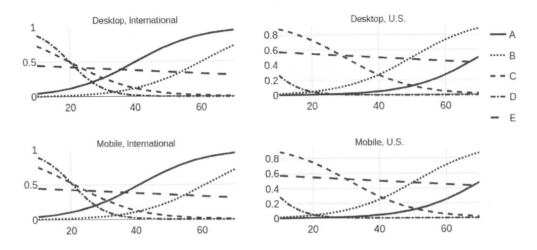

Figure 3.2 – Comparison of the true ad click probabilities given the
context (x axis – age, y axis – probability)

Looking at the plots in Figure 2, we should expect our algorithms to figure out, for
example, to display ad E for users at age around 40, who connect from the U.S. on
a mobile device. Also note that these probabilities are unrealistically high. More realistic
CTRs (click-through rates) would be less than 5%. This can be obtained by multiplying
the p calculation in the logistic class to 0.05. We will keep this as is for now to make
the problem easier.

Now we have implemented a process to generate user clicks. Here is what the scenario will
flow like:

1. We will generate a user and get the associated context using the generate_user_
    with_context method in the ug object,

2. A CB model will use the context to display one of the five ads, A, B, C, D, or E,

3. The chosen ad will be passed to the display_ad method in the ug object, giving
    a reward of 1 (click) or 0 (no click),

4. The CB model will be trained based on the reward, and this cycle will go on.

Before actually implementing this flow, let's dive into the CB approaches we will use.

Function approximation with regularized logistic regression

We want our CB algorithms to observe the user responses to the ads, update the models that estimate the action values (function approximations), and determine which ad to display given the context, the action value estimates and the exploration strategy. Note that in most realistic settings where the user traffic is high, the models would be updated not after every observation but after a batch of observations. With that, let's start with discussing what kind of a function approximator to use. There are numerous options, including many custom and sophisticated algorithms designed for contextual bandits. Many of these models are based on:

- Logistic regression,

- Decision trees / random forest,

- Neural networks.

In terms of the exploration strategy, we continue to focus on the following three fundamental approaches:

- ε-greedy

- Upper confidence bounds

- Thompson / Bayesian sampling

Now, let's assume that, as subject matter experts, we know that the CTR can be modeled using logistic regression. We also mentioned that it is not practical to update the model after every single observation, so we prefer batch updates to our models. Finally, we would like to have Thompson sampling in our exploration toolbox, therefore we need posterior distributions on the parameters of the logistic regression models. To this end, we use a regularized logistic regression algorithm with batch updates provided by (Chapelle et al, 2011). The algorithm:

- Approximates the posterior distribution on the model weights by a Gaussian distribution. This allows us to use the posterior distribution as the prior in the next batch, and also use a Gaussian for the likelihood function, since the Gaussian family is conjugate to itself.

- Uses a diagonal covariance matrix for the weights, meaning that we assume the weights are not correlated.

- Uses Laplace approximation to obtain the mean and the variance estimates of the weight distributions, one of the common methods in statistics to estimate the posterior parameters from observed data if the posterior is assumed to be Gaussian.

> **Info**
> You can learn more about Laplace approximation for computing the posterior mean at `https://bookdown.org/rdpeng/advstatcomp/laplace-approximation.html`.

Let's see this algorithm in action next.

Implementing the regularized logistic regression

We will follow the steps below to implement the regularized logistic regression, which we will use later.

1. First, we create a class and initialize the parameters we will keep track of.

```
class RegularizedLR(object):
    def __init__(self, name, alpha, rlambda, n_dim):
        self.name = name
        self.alpha = alpha
        self.rlambda = rlambda
        self.n_dim = n_dim
        self.m = np.zeros(n_dim)
        self.q = np.ones(n_dim) * rlambda
        self.w = self.get_sampled_weights()
```

Let's better understand what these parameters are.

- name is to identify which ad an object instance is estimating the action value of. Again, we have a separate model for each of the ads and they are updated separately based on their own click data.

- The hyperparameter is alpha controls the exploration and exploitation trade-off. Smaller values reduce the variance (e.g. 0.25) therefore encourages exploitation.

- This is a regularized regression, meaning that we have a regularization term λ. This is a hyperparameter to be tuned. We also use it to initialize the q array.

- n_dim is to indicate the dimension of the β parameter vector, one for each element of the context input and a bias term.

- The weights of the logistic function are denoted by the array of `w`, such that `w[i]` corresponds to β_i in our bandit dynamics model.

- The mean estimate of `w[i]` is given by `m[i]`, and the variance estimate is the inverse of `q[i]`.

2. Then, we define a method to sample the parameters of the logistic regression function.

```
def get_sampled_weights(self):
    w = np.random.normal(self.m, self.alpha *
self.q**(-1/2))
    return w
```

Note that we need this to use Thompson sampling, which requires sampling the w array parameters from the posterior, rather than using the mean values. Again, the posterior is a normal distribution here.

3. Define the loss function and a fit function, which will carry out the training.

```
def loss(self, w, *args):
    X, y = args
    n = len(y)
    regularizer = 0.5 * np.dot(self.q, (w -
self.m)**2)
    pred_loss = sum([np.log(1 + np.exp(np.dot(w,
X[j])))
                    - y[j] * np.dot(w,
X[j]) for j in range(n)])
    return regularizer + pred_loss
def fit(self, X, y):
    if y:
        X = np.array(X)
        y = np.array(y)
        minimization = minimize(self.loss,
                                self.w,
                                args=(X, y),
                                method="L-BFGS-B",
                                bounds=[(-10,10)]*3 +
[(-1, 1)],
                                options={'maxiter':
```

```
50})
                self.w = minimization.x
                self.m = self.w
                p = (1 + np.exp(-np.matmul(self.w, X.T)))**(-
1)
                self.q = self.q + np.matmul(p * (1 - p),
X**2)
```

Let's elaborate on how the fitting part works.

- We update the model using the `fit` method and the `loss` function with a given set of contexts and associated click data (1 for click, 0 for no click).

- We use SciPy's minimize function for the model training. To prevent numerical overflows in the exponential terms, we impose bounds on w. These bounds need to be adjusted depending on the range of the input values. For the binary features of device type, location [-10, +10], and for the age input, [-1, +1] are reasonable ranges for our use case.

- In each model update with a new batch of data, the previous w values serve as the prior.

4. Implement the upper confidence bounds on predictions, which is one of the exploration methods we will experiment with.

```
        def calc_sigmoid(self, w, context):
            return 1 / (1 + np.exp(-np.dot(w, context)))
        def get_ucb(self, context):
            pred = self.calc_sigmoid(self.m, context)
            confidence = self.alpha * np.sqrt(np.sum(np.
divide(np.array(context)**2, self.q)))
            ucb = pred + confidence
            return ucb
```

5. Implement two types of prediction methods, one using the mean values parameter estimates and the other using the sampled parameters to be used with Thompson sampling.

```
        def get_prediction(self, context):
            return self.calc_sigmoid(self.m, context)
        def sample_prediction(self, context):
```

```
        w = self.get_sampled_weights()
        return self.calc_sigmoid(w, context)
```

Now, before actually diving into solving the problem, we will define a metric to compare the alternative exploration strategies.

Objective: Regret minimization

A common metric that is used to compare MAB and CB algorithms is called **regret**. We define the total regret by the time we have observed the Kth user as follows:

$$\sum_{k=1}^{K} p_{a^*}(x_k) - p_a(x_k)$$

where x_k is the context for the kth user, a^* is the best action (ad) to take that gives the highest expected CTR, and a is the expected CTR for the selected action (ad). Note that we are able to calculate the regret because we have access to the true action values (expected CTRs), which would not be the case in reality (although regret can still be estimated). Not that the minimum possible regret at any step is zero.

> **Tip**
> With a good exploration strategy, we should see a decelerating cumulative regret over time as the algorithm discovers the best actions.

We will use the following code to calculate the regret given the context and the selected ad:

```
def calculate_regret(ug, context, ad_options, ad):
    action_values = {a: ug.logistic(ug.beta[a], context) for
a in ad_options}
    best_action = max(action_values, key=action_values.get)
    regret = action_values[best_action] - action_values[ad]
    return regret, best_action
```

Finally, let's write the code to actually solve the problem using different exploration strategies.

Solving the online advertising problem

As we have already defined all the auxiliary methods to use the three exploration strategies we mentioned earlier, selecting the actions accordingly will be trivial. Now, let's implement the functions for these strategies.

1. We start with writing a function to implement the ε-greedy actions, which selects the best action that far most of the time and explores a random action otherwise.

```
def select_ad_eps_greedy(ad_models, context, eps):
    if np.random.uniform() < eps:
        return np.random.choice(list(ad_models.keys()))
    else:
        predictions = {ad: ad_models[ad].get_
prediction(context)
                       for ad in ad_models}
        max_value = max(predictions.values());
        max_keys = [key for key, value in predictions.
items() if value == max_value]
        return np.random.choice(max_keys)
```

2. Next, we write a function to implement action selection using upper confidence bounds.

```
def select_ad_ucb(ad_models, context):
    ucbs = {ad: ad_models[ad].get_ucb(context)
                  for ad in ad_models}
    max_value = max(ucbs.values());
    max_keys = [key for key, value in ucbs.items() if
value == max_value]
    return np.random.choice(max_keys)
```

3. Then, we define a function to implement action selection using via Thompson sampling.

```
def select_ad_thompson(ad_models, context):
    samples = {ad: ad_models[ad].sample_
prediction(context)
                    for ad in ad_models}
    max_value = max(samples.values());
    max_keys = [key for key, value in samples.items() if
```

```
value == max_value]
    return np.random.choice(max_keys)
```

4. And finally, we perform the actual experiment, which will run and compare each strategy sequentially. We start with initializing the ad names, the experiment names, and the necessary data structures.

```
ad_options = ['A', 'B', 'C', 'D', 'E']
exploration_data = {}
data_columns = ['context',
                'ad',
                'click',
                'best_action',
                'regret',
                'total_regret']
exploration_strategies = ['eps-greedy',
                          'ucb',
                          'Thompson']
```

5. We need to implement an outer *for* loop to kick off a clean experiment with each of the exploration strategies. We initialize all the algorithm parameters and data structures.

```
for strategy in exploration_strategies:
    print("--- Now using", strategy)
    np.random.seed(0)
    # Create the LR models for each ad
    alpha, rlambda, n_dim = 0.5, 0.5, 4
    ad_models = {ad: RegularizedLR(ad,
                                   alpha,
                                   rlambda,
                                   n_dim)
                 for ad in 'ABCDE'}
    # Initialize data structures
    X = {ad: [] for ad in ad_options}
    y = {ad: [] for ad in ad_options}
    results = []
    total_regret = 0
```

6. Now, we implement an inner loop to run the active strategy for 10K user impressions.

```
for i in range(10**4):
    context = ug.generate_user_with_context()
    if strategy == 'eps-greedy':
        eps = 0.1
        ad = select_ad_eps_greedy(ad_models,
                                  context,
                                  eps)
    elif strategy == 'ucb':
        ad = select_ad_ucb(ad_models, context)
    elif strategy == 'Thompson':
        ad = select_ad_thompson(ad_models, context)
    # Display the selected ad
    click = ug.display_ad(ad)
    # Store the outcome
    X[ad].append(context)
    y[ad].append(click)
    regret, best_action = calculate_regret(ug,
                                           context,
                                           ad_
options,
                                           ad)
    total_regret += regret
    results.append((context,
            ad,
            click,
            best_action,
            regret,
            total_regret))
    # Update the models with the latest batch of data
    if (i + 1) % 500 == 0:
        print("Updating the models at i:", i + 1)
        for ad in ad_options:
            ad_models[ad].fit(X[ad], y[ad])
        X = {ad: [] for ad in ad_options}
```

```
        y = {ad: [] for ad in ad_options}

    exploration_data[strategy] = {'models': ad_models,
                                   'results':
    pd.DataFrame(results,

    columns=data_columns)}
```

Let's unpack this:

- We generate a user and use the context to decide which ad to display given the exploration strategy in each iteration.

- We observe and record the outcome. We also calculate the regret after each impression to be able to compare the strategies.

- We update the logistic regression models in batches, namely after every 500 ad impressions.

7. After executing this code block, we can visualize the results using the following code.

```
    df_regret_comparisons = pd.DataFrame({s: exploration_
    data[s]['results'].total_regret

                                        for s in
    exploration_strategies})
    df_regret_comparisons.iplot(dash=['solid', 'dash','dot'],
                               xTitle='Impressions',
                               yTitle='Total Regret',
                               color='black')
```

This gives the plot in Figure 3.

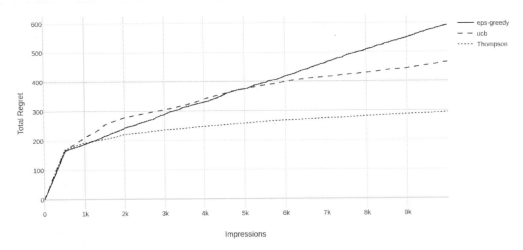

Figure 3.3 – Comparison of exploration strategies in the online advertising example

We clearly see that Thompson sampling is outperforming the ε-greedy and UCB strategies as the total regret decelerates over time faster than the other two. It writes off the inefficient ads for given contexts pretty early on, while ε-greedy and UCB continue to explore those alternatives. Also note that we have not tuned the exploration rate for ε-greedy and `alpha` for UCB, which could have led to better performances. But this is exactly the point: Thompson sampling provides a very effective exploration strategy pretty much out-of-the-box. This is what (Chapelle et al, 2011) empirically showed and helped the method gain popularity nearly a century after it was introduced.

> **Tip**
>
> In a real production system, it makes more sense to use well-maintained libraries for the supervised learning portion in contextual bandits rather than a custom implementation like we did here. One such library for probabilistic programming is PyMC3 (`https://docs.pymc.io/`). Using PyMC3, you can fit supervised learning models to your data and then sample the model parameters. As an exercise, consider implementing Thompson sampling using logistic regression model in PyMC3.

8. Let's close this section by visualizing the parameter estimates of the models. For example, when we used ε-greedy strategy, the β coefficients for ad A were estimated as follows:

```
lrmodel = exploration_data['eps-greedy']['models']['A']
df_beta_dist = pd.DataFrame([], index=np.arange(-
```

```
4,1,0.01))
mean = lrmodel.m
std_dev = lrmodel.q ** (-1/2)


for i in range(lrmodel.n_dim):
    df_beta_dist['beta_'+str(i)] = stats.
norm(loc=mean[i],
                                        scale=std_
dev[i]).pdf(df_beta_dist.index)


df_beta_dist.iplot(dash=['dashdot','dot', 'dash',
'solid'],
                   yTitle='p.d.f.',
                   color='black')
```

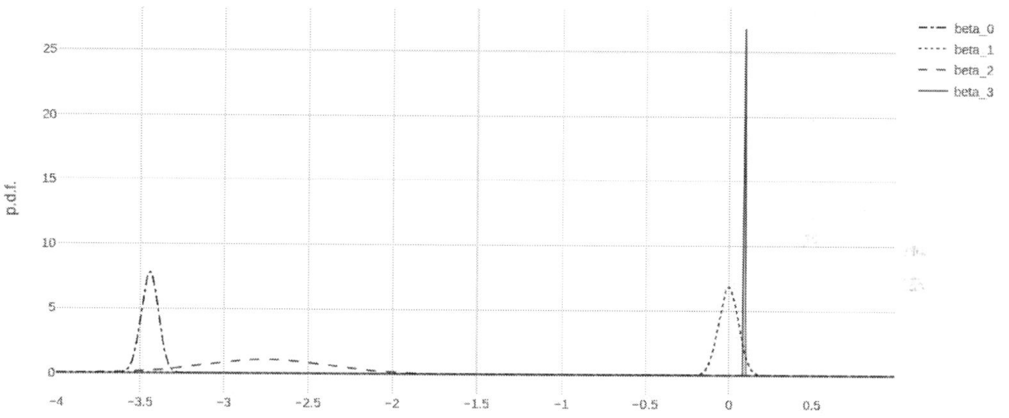

Figure 3.4 – Visualization of posterior distribution of β for ad A at the end of the experiment with ε-greedy exploration

The logistic regression model estimates the coefficients as $[-3.4, 0, -2.8, 0.09]$ whereas the actual coefficients are $[-4, -0.1, -0.3, 0.1]$. The model is especially certain about its estimate for β_3, which is indicated by a very narrow distribution in the plot.

Terrific job! This was a rather long exercise, but one that will set you up for success in your real-life implementations. Take a deep breath, and a break, and next we will look into an even more realistic version of online advertising where the ad inventory changes over time.

Using function approximation for action

In our online advertising examples so far, we have assumed to have a fixed set of ads (actions/arms) to choose from. However, in many applications of contextual bandits, the set of available actions change over time. Take the example of a modern advertising network that uses an ad server to match ads to websites/apps. This is a very dynamic operation which involves, leaving the pricing aside, three major components:

- Website/app content,
- Viewer/user profile,
- Ad inventory.

Previously, we considered only the user profile for the context. An ad server needs to take the website/app content into account additionally, but this does not really change the structure of problem we solved before. However, now, we cannot use a separate model for each ad since the ad inventory is dynamic. We handle this by using a single model to which we feed ad features. This is illustrated in Figure 5.

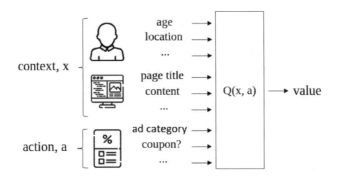

Figure 3.5 – Function approximation of action values with context and
action inputs in ad network example

While making a decision, we take the context as given. So, the decision is about which ad to display from the ad inventory that is available at the time. So, to make this decision, we generate action values for all available ads using this single model.

Now it is time to talk about what kind of model to use in this situation.

- Remember what the model does: It learns how a given user would react to a given ad that he sees on a given website/app and estimates the probability of a click.
- When you think about all possible user and website/app contexts, and all possible ads, this is a very complicated relationship to figure out.

- Such a model needs to be trained on a lot of data and it should be sophisticated enough to be able to come up with a good approximation of the true dynamics of a click.

- When we have this much of a complexity, and hopefully enough data, there is one obvious choice: Deep neural networks (DNNs).

In the previous section, we compared different exploration strategies and showed that Thompson sampling is a very competitive choice. However, Thompson sampling requires us to be able to sample from the posterior of the model parameters; and this is often intractable for complex models such as neural networks. To overcome this challenge, we rely on approximate Bayesian methods available in the literature.

> **Info**
>
> There are many approximation methods and their comparison is beyond the scope here. (Riquelme et al., 2018) provides a great comparison along with the code in TensorFlow repository.

One of these approximations involves using a dropout regularization in the DNN and keeping it active during inference time. As a reminder, dropout regularization deactivates each neuron in the DNN with respect to a given probability and increases generalization. Typically, dropout is only used during training. When it is kept active during inference, since neurons are disabled probabilistically, the output varies accordingly. (Gal et al., 2015) has shown that this works as an approximate Bayesian inference, which we need for Thompson sampling.

Case study: Contextual online advertising with user data from U.S. Census

Now, let's talk about the example we will use in this section. Previously, we crafted our own examples. This time, we use a dataset that was modified from the 1994 U.S. Census and adapt it to an online advertising setting. The dataset is known as "Census Income Dataset" and available at `https://archive.ics.uci.edu/ml/datasets/Census+Income`.

In this dataset we use the following information on the individuals participated in the census: Age, work class, education, marital status, occupation, relationship, race, gender, work hours per week, native country, and income level.

With that, let's discuss how to turn this data into an online advertising scenario.

The scenario

Consider an ad server that knows all of the information above about a user, except the education level. On the other hand, the ad network is managing ads that address a specific education level. For example, at any given time, the ad server has one ad that is targeting users with college education, one ad that is targeting users with elementary school education etc. If the target audience of the ad that is shown to a user matches the user's education level, there is a high probability of a click. If not, the probability of a click decreases gradually as the discrepancy between the target education level and the user's education level. In other words, the ad server is implicitly trying to predict users' education levels as close as possible.

Next, let's prepare the data set for our scenario.

Data preparation

Follow the steps below to clean and prepare the data.

1. We start with importing the necessary packages to use later.

```
from collections import namedtuple
from numpy.random import uniform as U
import pandas as pd
import numpy as np
import io
import requests
from tensorflow import keras
from tensorflow.keras.layers import Dense, Dropout
import cufflinks as cf
cf.go_offline()
cf.set_config_file(world_readable=True, theme='white')
```

2. Next, we need to download the data and select the columns of interest.

```
url="https://archive.ics.uci.edu/ml/machine-learning-
databases/adult/adult.data"
s=requests.get(url).content
names = ['age',
              'workclass',
              'fnlwgt',
              'education',
```

```
                        'education_num',
                        'marital_status',
                        'occupation',
                        'relationship',
                        'race',
                        'gender',
                        'capital_gain',
                        'capital_loss',
                        'hours_per_week',
                        'native_country',
                        'income']
    usecols = ['age',
                        'workclass',
                        'education',
                        'marital_status',
                        'occupation',
                        'relationship',
                        'race',
                        'gender',
                        'hours_per_week',
                        'native_country',
                        'income']
    df_census = pd.read_csv(io.StringIO(s.decode('utf-8')),
                              sep=',',
                              skipinitialspace=True,
                              names=names,
                              header=None,
                              usecols=usecols)
```

3. Let's drop the rows with missing data, marked by "?" entries.

```
    df_census = df_census.replace('?', np.nan).dropna()
```

Normally, a missing entry could be itself a valuable indicator that the model could use. In addition, it is a bit wasteful to drop a whole record just because of a single missing entry. However, data imputation is beyond our scope here, so let's keep focusing on the CB problem.

4. Let's also collapse different education levels to five categories: Elementary, middle, HS-grad, undergraduate and graduate.

```
edu_map = {'Preschool': 'Elementary',
           '1st-4th': 'Elementary',
           '5th-6th': 'Elementary',
           '7th-8th': 'Elementary',
           '9th': 'Middle',
           '10th': 'Middle',
           '11th': 'Middle',
           '12th': 'Middle',
           'Some-college': 'Undergraduate',
           'Bachelors': 'Undergraduate',
           'Assoc-acdm': 'Undergraduate',
           'Assoc-voc': 'Undergraduate',
           'Prof-school': 'Graduate',
           'Masters': 'Graduate',
           'Doctorate': 'Graduate'}
for from_level, to_level in edu_map.items():
    df_census.education.replace(from_level, to_level,
inplace=True)
```

5. Next, we convert categorical data to one-hot vectors to be able to feed into a DNN. We preserve the education column as is, since that is not part of the context.

```
context_cols = [c for c in usecols if c != 'education']
df_data = pd.concat([pd.get_dummies(df_census[context_
cols]),
           df_census['education']], axis=1)
```

By doing this conversion at the beginning, we assume that we know all possible work class categories, native countries etc.

That's it! We have the data ready. Next, we implement a logic to simulate an ad click based on the actual education level of the user and the education level the ad displayed targets.

Simulating ad clicks

In this example, the availability of ads is also random in addition to the ad clicks being stochastic. We need to come up with some logic to simulate this behavior.

1. Let's start with determining the ad availability probabilities for each education category and implement the sampling of ads.

```python
def get_ad_inventory():
    ad_inv_prob = {'Elementary': 0.9,
                   'Middle': 0.7,
                   'HS-grad': 0.7,
                   'Undergraduate': 0.9,
                   'Graduate': 0.8}
    ad_inventory = []
    for level, prob in ad_inv_prob.items():
        if U() < prob:
            ad_inventory.append(level)
    # Make sure there are at least one ad
    if not ad_inventory:
        ad_inventory = get_ad_inventory()
    return ad_inventory
```

As mentioned above, the ad server will have at most one ad for each target group. We also ensure that there is at least one ad in the inventory.

2. Then, we define a function to generate a click probabilistically, where the likelihood of a click increases to the degree that the user's education level and the ad's target match.

```python
def get_ad_click_probs():
    base_prob = 0.8
    delta = 0.3
    ed_levels = {'Elementary': 1,
                 'Middle': 2,
                 'HS-grad': 3,
                 'Undergraduate': 4,
                 'Graduate': 5}
    ad_click_probs = {l1: {l2: max(0, base_prob - delta *
abs(ed_levels[l1]- ed_levels[l2])) for l2 in ed_levels}
```

```
                                          for ll in ed_levels}
        return ad_click_probs
def display_ad(ad_click_probs, user, ad):
        prob = ad_click_probs[ad][user['education']]
        click = 1 if U() < prob else 0
        return click
```

So, when an ad is shown to a user, if the ad's target matches the user's education level, there will be 0.8 chance of a click. This probability decreases by 0.3 for each level of mismatch. For example, a person with a high school diploma has a $0.8 - 2 \cdot 0.3 = 0.2$ chance to click on an ad that targets a user group of elementary school graduates (or college graduates). Note that this information is not known to the CB algorithm. It will be used only to simulate the clicks.

We have the problem set up. Next, we turn to implementing a CB model.

Function approximation using a neural network

As mentioned above, we use a (not so) deep neural network (DNN) that will estimate the action value, given the context and the action. The DNN we use has 2 layers with 256 hidden units in each layer. This model is pretty easy to create using Keras, TensorFlow's high-level API.

> **Tip**
>
> Note that in our model, we use dropout that we leave active for the inference time as a Bayesian approximation that we need for Thompson sampling. This is configured by setting `training=True` in the dropout layer.

The network outputs a scalar, which is an estimate for the action value given the context and the action feature (target user group). Using a binary cross-entropy suits such an output the best, which we use in our model. Finally, we use the popular Adam optimizer.

> **Info**
>
> Visit `https://www.tensorflow.org/guide/keras` if you need to get started with Keras or refresh your mind. It is very simple to build the standard DNN models with it.

Now, let's create the functions for model creation and updates.

1. We create a function that returns a compiled DNN model with given input
    dimensions and a dropout rate.

```python
def get_model(n_input, dropout):
    inputs = keras.Input(shape=(n_input,))
    x = Dense(256, activation='relu')(inputs)
    if dropout > 0:
        x = Dropout(dropout)(x, training=True)
    x = Dense(256, activation='relu')(x)
    if dropout > 0:
        x = Dropout(dropout)(x, training=True)
    phat = Dense(1, activation='sigmoid')(x)
    model = keras.Model(inputs, phat)
    model.compile(loss=keras.losses.BinaryCrossentropy(),
                  optimizer=keras.optimizers.Adam(),
                  metrics=[keras.metrics.binary_
accuracy])
    return model
```

2. We will update this model in batches as data becomes available. Next, write
    a function to train the model for 10 epochs with each batch.

```python
def update_model(model, X, y):
    X = np.array(X)
    X = X.reshape((X.shape[0], X.shape[2]))
    y = np.array(y).reshape(-1)
    model.fit(X, y, epochs=10)
    return model
```

3. We then define a function that returns a one-hot representation for a specified
    ad based on the education level it targets.

```python
def ad_to_one_hot(ad):
    ed_levels = ['Elementary',
                 'Middle',
                 'HS-grad',
                 'Undergraduate',
```

```
                    'Graduate']
        ad_input = [0] * len(ed_levels)
        if ad in ed_levels:
            ad_input[ed_levels.index(ad)] = 1
        return ad_input
```

4.   We implement the Thompson sampling to select an ad given the context and the ad inventory at hand.

```
def select_ad(model, context, ad_inventory):
    selected_ad = None
    selected_x = None
    max_action_val = 0
    for ad in ad_inventory:
        ad_x = ad_to_one_hot(ad)
        x = np.array(context + ad_x).reshape((1, -1))
        action_val_pred = model.predict(x)[0][0]
        if action_val_pred >= max_action_val:
            selected_ad = ad
            selected_x = x
            max_action_val = action_val_pred
    return selected_ad, selected_x
```

The ad to be displayed is chosen based on the largest action value estimate that we obtain from the DNN. We obtain this by trying all available ads in the inventory and remember, we have at most one ad per target user group with the context of the user. Note that the target user group is equivalent to action, which we feed to the DNN in the format of one-hot vector.

5.   Finally, we write a function to generate users through a random selection from the dataset. The function will returns the user data as well as the derived context.

```
def generate_user(df_data):
    user = df_data.sample(1)
    context = user.iloc[:, :-1].values.tolist()[0]
    return user.to_dict(orient='records')[0], context
```

This concludes what we need to decide on the ad to display using Thompson sampling.

Calculating the regret

We continue to use regret for comparing various versions of the CB algorithm. We calculate it as below:

```
def calc_regret(user, ad_inventory, ad_click_probs, ad_
selected):
    this_p = 0
    max_p = 0
    for ad in ad_inventory:
        p = ad_click_probs[ad][user['education']]
        if ad == ad_selected:
            this_p = p
        if p > max_p:
            max_p = p
    regret = max_p - this_p
    return regret
```

With the regret calculation is also in place, let's now actually solve the problem.

Solving the online advertising problem

Now we are ready to put all these components together. We try this algorithm with different dropout probabilities over 5000 impressions. We update the DNN parameters after every 500 iterations. Here is the implementation in Python for various dropout rates.

```
ad_click_probs = get_ad_click_probs()
df_cbandits = pd.DataFrame()
dropout_levels = [0, 0.01, 0.05, 0.1, 0.2, 0.4]
for d in dropout_levels:
    print("Trying with dropout:", d)
    np.random.seed(0)
    context_n = df_data.shape[1] - 1
    ad_input_n = df_data.education.nunique()
    model = get_model(context_n + ad_input_n, 0.01)
    X = []
    y = []
    regret_vec = []
    total_regret = 0
```

```
    for i in range(5000):
        if i % 20 == 0:
            print("# of impressions:", i)
        user, context = generate_user(df_data)
        ad_inventory = get_ad_inventory()
        ad, x = select_ad(model, context, ad_inventory)
        click = display_ad(ad_click_probs, user, ad)
        regret = calc_regret(user, ad_inventory, ad_click_
probs, ad)
        total_regret += regret
        regret_vec.append(total_regret)
        X.append(x)
        y.append(click)
        if (i + 1) % 500 == 0:
            print('Updating the model at', i+1)
            model = update_model(model, X, y)
            X = []
            y = []

    df_cbandits['dropout: '+str(d)] = regret_vec
```

The cumulative regrets over time are stored in df_cbandits Pandas dataframe. Let
visualize how they compare.

```
df_cbandits.iplot(dash = ['dash', 'solid', 'dashdot',
                          'dot', 'longdash', 'longdashdot'],
                  xTitle='Impressions',
                  yTitle='Cumulative Regret')
```

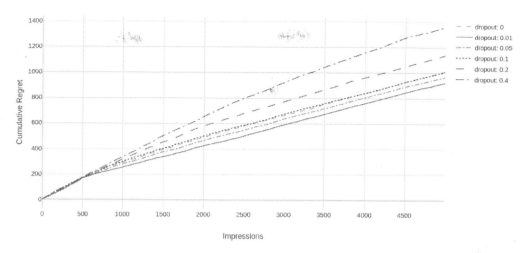

Figure 3.6 – Comparison of cumulative regret with various dropout rates

The results on Figure 6 show that our bandit models learn after some observations how to select the ads given the user characteristics. As various dropout rates have led to different algorithm performances, an important question again becomes how to select the dropout rate. One obvious answer is to try different rates over time identify what works the best in similar online advertising problems. This approach usually works if the business has to solve similar problems again and again over a long time period. A better approach though is to learn the optimal dropout rate.

> **Tip**
>
> **Concrete dropout** is a variant that tunes the dropout probabilities automatically. (Collier & Llorens, 2018) has successfully used this method on CB problems and reported superior performance over fixed dropout selections. For a TensorFlow implementation of concrete dropout, see `https://github.com/Skydes/Concrete-Dropout`.

With this, we conclude our discussion on contextual bandits. Note that we focused on two components while formulating the CB problem: 1) Function approximation and 2) exploration strategy. You can often mix and match different function approximations with various exploration techniques. While Thompson sampling with Deep Neural Networks is probably the most common choice, we encourage you to take a look at the literature for other approaches.

Other applications of multi-armed and contextual bandits

So far, we have focused on online advertising example as our running example. If you are wondering how commonly bandit algorithms are used in practice for such problems, it is actually quite common. For example, Microsoft has a service, called Personalizer, based on bandit algorithms (disclaimer: the author is a Microsoft employee at the time of writing this book). The example here itself is inspired by the work at Hubspot – a marketing solutions company (Collier & Llorens, 2018). Moreover, bandit problems have a vast array of practical applications other than advertising. In this section we briefly go over some of those applications.

Recommender systems

The bandit problems we formulated and solved in this chapter are a type of recommender system: they recommend which ad to display, potentially leveraging the information available about the users. There are many other recommender systems that use bandits in a similar way, such as:

- Artwork selection for movie titles, as Netflix famously implements (Chandrashekar, Amat, Basilico, & Jebara, 2017),

- Article recommendation on a news portal,

- Post recommendation on a social media platform,

- Product/service recommendation on an online retailer,

- Tailoring search results to the user on a search engine.

Webpage / app feature design

Most famous websites and apps that we visit every day decide which design to use for different features after extensive tests. For example, they create different designs of the "buy" button on the shopping cart and observe which design generates the most sales. Such experiments conducted nonstop for hundreds of features. An efficient way of conducting these experiments is to use multi-armed bandits. This way, bad feature designs could be identified early on and eliminated to minimize the user disturbance throughout these experiments (Lomas et al., 2016).

Healthcare

Bandit problems have important applications in healthcare. Especially with the increasing availability of patient data, through well-maintained patient databases and data collection via mobile devices, many treatments can now be personalized to individuals. Contextual bandits are therefore an important tool to use while deciding which treatment to apply to a patient in randomized controlled trials. Another application in which contextual bandits have successfully been used is for deciding the treatment dose of drugs, such as Warfarin that regulates blood coagulation (Bastani and Bayati, 2015). One more application is related to the optimal allocation of data sampling to various animal models to assess the effectiveness of a treatment. Contextual bandits have proven to increase the efficiency of this process by identifying promising treatments better than conventional methods (Durand et al., 2018).

Dynamic pricing

An important challenge for online retailers is to dynamically adjust their prices on millions of products. This can be modeled as a contextual bandit problem where the context could include product demand forecasts, inventory levels, product cost, location etc.

Finance

Contextual bandits are used in literature for optimal portfolio construction through mixing passive and active investments to achieve a balance between the risk and expected return.

Control systems tuning

Many mechanical systems use variants of **proportional-integral-derivative (PID)** controllers to control the system. PID controllers require tuning, which is often done by subject matter experts for each system separately. This is because optimal gains for the controller depend on the specifics of the equipment, such as the material, temperature, wear and tear etc. This manual process can be automated using a contextual bandit model that assesses system characteristics and tunes the controller accordingly.

Summary

In this chapter, we've concluded our discussion on bandit problems with contextual bandits. As we mentioned, bandit problems have many practical applications. So, it would not be a surprise if you already had a problem in your business or research that can be modeled as a bandit problem. Now that you know how to formulate and solve one, go out and apply what you have learned! Bandit problems are also important to develop intuition on how to solve exploration-exploitation dilemma, which will exist in almost every RL setting.

Now that you have a solid understanding of how to solve one-step RL, it is time to move on to full-blown multi-step RL. In the next chapter, we will go into the theory behind multi-step RL with Markov Decision Processes, and build the foundation for modern deep RL methods that we will cover in the subsequent chapters.

References

1. Bouneffouf, D., & Rish, I. (2019). *A Survey on Practical Applications of Multi-Armed and Contextual Bandits.* Retrieved from arXiv: `https://arxiv.org/abs/1904.10040`

2. Chandrashekar, A., Amat, F., Basilico, J., & Jebara, T. (2017, December 7). *Netflix Technology Blog.* Retrieved from Artwork Personalization at Netflix: `https://netflixtechblog.com/artwork-personalization-c589f074ad76`

3. Chapelle, O., & Li, L. (2011). An Empirical Evaluation of Thompson Sampling. *Advances in Neural Information Processing Systems 24*, (pp. 2249-2257).

4. Collier, M., & Llorens, H. U. (2018). *Deep Contextual Multi-Armed Bandits.* Retrieved from arXiv: `https://arxiv.org/abs/1807.09809`

5. Gal, Y., Hron, J., & Kendall, A. (2017). Concrete Dropout. *Advances in Neural Information Processing Systems 30*, (pp. 3581-3590).

6. Marmerola, G. D. (2017, November 28). *Thompson Sampling for Contextual bandits.* Retrieved from Guilherme's Blog: `https://gdmarmerola.github.io/ts-for-contextual-bandits/`

7. Riquelme, C., Tucker, G., & Snoek, J. (2018). Deep Bayesian Bandits Showdown: An Empirical Comparison of Bayesian Deep Networks for Thompson Sampling. *International Conference on Learning Representations, ICLR.*

8. Russo, D., Van Roy, B., Kazerouni, A., Osband, I., & Wen, Z. (2018). A Tutorial on Thompson Sampling. *Foundations and Trends in Machine Learning*, 1-96.

9. Lomas, D., Forlizzi, J., Poonawala, N., Patel, N., Shodhan, S., Patel, K., Koedinger, K., Brunskill, E. (2016). Interface Design Optimization as a Multi-Armed Bandit Problem. 4142-4153. 10.1145/2858036.2858425.

10. Durand, A., Achilleos, C., Iacovides, D., Strati, K., Mitsis, G.D. & Pineau, J. (2018). Contextual Bandits for Adapting Treatment in a Mouse Model of de Novo Carcinogenesis. Proceedings of the 3rd Machine Learning for Healthcare Conference, in PMLR 85:67-82

11. Bastani, H., Bayati, M. (2015). Online decision-making with high-dimensional covariates. Available at SSRN 2661896.

4

Makings of a Markov Decision Process

In the first chapter, we talked about many applications of **Reinforcement Learning (RL)**, from robotics to finance. Before implementing any RL algorithms for such applications, we need to first model them mathematically. **Markov Decision Process (MDP)** is the framework we use to model such sequential decision-making problems. MDPs have some special characteristics that make it easier for us to theoretically analyze them. Building on that theory, **Dynamic Programming (DP)** is the field that proposes solution methods for MDPs. RL, in some sense, is a collection of approximate DP approaches, which enable us to obtain good (but not necessarily optimal) solutions to very complex problems that are intractable to solve with exact DP methods.

In this chapter we step-by-step build the MDP, explain its characteristics, and lay down the mathematical foundation for the RL algorithms upcoming in the later chapters.

In an MDP, the actions an agent takes have long-term consequences, which is what differentiates it from the **Multi-armed Bandit** (**MAB**) problems we covered earlier. This chapter focuses on some key concepts that quantify this long-term impact. It involves a bit more theory than other chapters, but don't worry, we will quickly dive into Python exercises to get a better grasp of the concepts. Specifically, we cover the following topics in this chapter:

- Markov chains

- Markov reward processes

- Markov decision process

- Partially observable Markov decision process

Starting with Markov chains

We start this chapter with Markov chains, which do not involve any decision-making. They only model a special type of stochastic processes that are governed by some internal transition dynamics. Therefore, we don't talk about an agent yet. Understanding how Markov chains work will allow us to lay the foundation for MDPs that we will cover later.

Stochastic processes with Markov property

We already defined the **state** as the set information that completely describes the situation an environment is in. If the next state that the environment will transition into only depends on the current state, not the past, we say that the process has the **Markov property**. This is named after the Russian mathematician Andrey Markov.

Imagine a broken robot that randomly moves in a grid world. At any given step, the robot goes up, down, left and right with 0.2, 0.3, 0.25 and 0.25 probability, respectively. This is depicted in Figure 4.1, as follows:

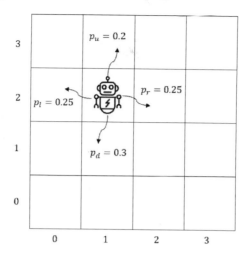

Figure 4.1 – Broken robot in grid world, currently at (1,2)

The robot is currently in state (1,2). It does not matter where it has come from; and it will be in state (1,3) with a probability of 0.2, in (0,2) with a probability of 0.25 and so on. Since, for all of the states in this example, the probability of where it will transition next depends only on the state it is currently in, but not where it was before, the process has the Markov property.

Let's define this more formally. We denote the state at time t by s_t. A process has the Markov property if the following holds for all states and times:

$$p(s_{t+1} | s_t, s_{t-1}, s_{t-2}, \dots, s_0) = p(s_{t+1} | s_t)$$

Such a stochastic process is called a **Markov chain**. Note that if the robot hits a wall, we assume that it bounces back and remains in the same state. So, while in state (0,0), for example, the robot will be still there in the next step with a probability of 0.55.

A Markov chain is usually represented using a directed graph. The directed graph for the broken robot example in a 2x2 grid world would be as in *Figure :*

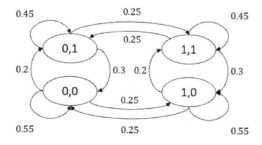

Figure 4.2 – Markov chain diagram for the robot example in a 2x2 grid world

> **Tip**
>
> Many systems/environments can be made Markovian by including historical information in the state. Consider a modified robot example where the robot is more likely to continue in the direction it moved in the previous time step. Although such a system seemingly does not satisfy the Markov property, we can simply redefine the state to include the visited cells over the last two time steps, such as $x_t = (s_t, s_{t-1}) = ((0,1), (0,0))$. The transition probabilities would be independent of the past under this new state definition and the Markov property would be satisfied.

Now that we have defined what a Markov chain is, let's go deeper. Next, we look into how to classify states in a Markov chain as they might differ in terms of their transition behavior.

Classification of states in a Markov chain

An environment that can go from any state to any other state after some number of transitions, like we have in our robot example, is a special kind of Markov chain. As you can imagine, a more realistic system would involve states with a richer set of characteristics, which we introduce next.

Reachable and communicating states

If the environment can transition from state i to state j after some number of steps with a positive probability, we say j is **reachable** from i. If i is also reachable from j, those states are said to **communicate**. If all the states in a Markov chain communicate with each other, we say that the Markov chain is **irreducible**, which is what we had in our robot example.

Absorbing state

A state s is an **absorbing state** if the only possible transition is to itself, which is $P(s_{t+1} = s | s_t = s) = 1$. Imagine that the robot cannot move again if it crashes into wall in the preceding example. This would be an example of an absorbing state since the robot can never leave it. The $2x2$ version of our grid world with an absorbing state could be represented in a Markov chain diagram as in Figure 4.3:

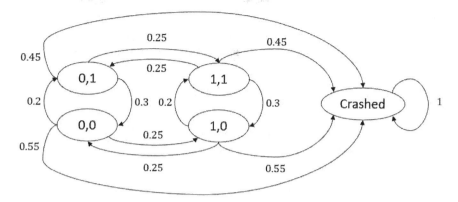

Figure 4.3 – Markov chain diagram with an absorbing state

An absorbing state is equivalent to a terminal state that marks the end of an episode in the context of RL, which we defined in Chapter 1. In addition to terminal states, an episode can also terminate after a time limit T is reached.

Transient and recurrent states

A state s is called a **transient state** if there is another state s' that is reachable from s, but s is not reachable from s'. Provided enough time, an environment will eventually move away from transient states to never come back. Consider a modified grid world with two sections; and let's call them the light side and the dark side for fun. The possible transitions in this world are illustrated in Figure 4.4. Can you identify the transient state(s)?

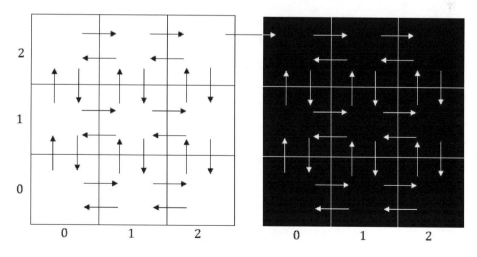

Figure 4.4 – Grid world with a light and dark side

If your answer is $(2, 2)$ of the light side, think again. For each of the states in the light side, there is a way out to the dark side without a way back. So, wherever the robot is in the light side, it will eventually transition into the dark side and won't be able to come back. Therefore, all the states in the light side are transient. Such a dystopian world... Similarly, in the modified grid world with a *crashed* state, all the states are transient, except the *crashed* state.

Finally, a state that is not transient is called a **recurrent state**. The states in the dark side are recurrent in this example.

Periodic and aperiodic states

We call a state s **periodic** if all of the paths leaving s come back after some multiple of $k > 1$ steps. Consider the example in Figure 4.5, where all the states have a period of $k = 4$:

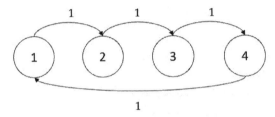

Figure 4.5 – A Markov chain with periodic states, k=4

A recurrent state is called **aperiodic** if $k = 1$.

Ergodicity

We can finally define an important class of Markov chains. A Markov chain is called **ergodic** if all states exhibit the following properties:

- Communicate with each other (irreducible)
- Are recurrent
- Are aperiodic

For ergodic Markov chains, we can calculate a single probability distribution that tells which state the system would be in, after a sufficiently long time from its initialization, with what probability. This is called the **steady state probability distribution**.

So far so good, but it has also been a bit dense set of definitions. Before we go into practical examples, though, let's also define the math of how a Markov chain transitions between states.

Transitionary and steady state behavior

We can mathematically calculate how a Markov chain behaves over time. To this end, we first need to know the **initial probability distribution** of the system. When we initialize a grid world, for example, in which state does the robot appear at the beginning? This is given by the initial probability distribution. Then, we define the **transition probability matrix**, whose entries give, well, the transition probabilities between all state pairs in from one time step to the next. More formally, the entry at the ith row and j^{th} column of this matrix gives $P_{ij} = P(s_{t+1} = j | s_t = i)$, where i and j are the state indices (starting with 1 in our convention).

Now, to calculate the probability of the system being in state i after n steps, we use the following formula:

$$p_n = qP^n$$

where q is the initial probability distribution, and P^n is the transition probability matrix raised to the power n. Note that P_{ij}^n gives the probability of being in state j after n steps when started in state i.

> **Info**
>
> A Markov chain is completely characterized by a tuple $\langle S, P \rangle$, where S is the set of all states and P is the transition probability matrix.

Yes, it has been a lot of definitions and theory so far. Now, it is a good time to finally look at a practical example.

Example: n-step behavior in the grid world

In many RL algorithms, the core idea is to arrive at a consistency between our understanding of the environment in its current state and after n steps of transitions, and to iterate until this consistency is ensured. Therefore, it is important to get a solid intuition of how an environment modeled as a Markov chain evolves over time. To this end, we look into n-step behavior in the grid world example. Follow along!

Chapter04/MDP.ipynb

1. Let's start with creating a $3x3$ grid world with our robot in it, similar to the one in Figure 4.1. For now, let's always initialize the world with the robot being at the center. Moreover, we index the states/cells so that $(0,0):1, (0,1):2, ..., (2,2):9$. So, the initial probability distribution, q, is given by the following code:

```python
import numpy as np
m = 3
m2 = m ** 2
q = np.zeros(m2)
q[m2 // 2] = 1
```

Here, q is the initial probability distribution.

2. We define a function that gives the $n \times n$ transition probability matrix:

```python
def get_P(m, p_up, p_down, p_left, p_right):
    m2 = m ** 2
    P = np.zeros((m2, m2))
    ix_map = {i + 1: (i // m, i % m) for i in range(m2)}
    for i in range(m2):
        for j in range(m2):
            r1, c1 = ix_map[i + 1]
            r2, c2 = ix_map[j + 1]
            rdiff = r1 - r2
            cdiff = c1 - c2
            if rdiff == 0:
                if cdiff == 1:
                    P[i, j] = p_left
                elif cdiff == -1:
                    P[i, j] = p_right
                elif cdiff == 0:
```

```
                    if r1 == 0:
                        P[i, j] += p_down
                    elif r1 == m - 1:
                        P[i, j] += p_up
                    if c1 == 0:
                        P[i, j] += p_left
                    elif c1 == m - 1:
                        P[i, j] += p_right
            elif rdiff == 1:
                if cdiff == 0:
                    P[i, j] = p_down
            elif rdiff == -1:
                if cdiff == 0:
                    P[i, j] = p_up
    return P
```

The code may seem a bit long but what it does is pretty simple: It just fills an $n \times n$ transition probability matrix according to the specified probabilities of going up, down, left and right.

3. Let's get the transition probability matrix for the 3×3 grid world of ours:

```
P = get_P(3, 0.2, 0.3, 0.25, 0.25)
```

4. Then, we calculate the n-step transition probabilities. For example, for $n = 1$:

```
n = 1
Pn = np.linalg.matrix_power(P, n)
np.matmul(q, Pn)
```

5. The result will look like the following:

```
array([0., 0.3, 0., 0.25, 0., 0.25, 0., 0.2, 0.])
```

Nothing surprising, right? The output just tells that the robot that starts at the center will be a cell above with a probability of 0.2, a cell down with a probability of 0.3 and so on. Let's do this for 3, 10 and 100 steps. The results are shown in *Figure 4.6*.

$n = 1$			$n = 3$			$n = 10$			$n = 100$		
0	0.2	0	0.068	0.107	0.068	0.072	0.072	0.072	0.07	0.07	0.07
0.25	0	0.25	0.137	0.061	0.137	0.105	0.106	0.105	0.105	0.105	0.105
0	0.3	0	0.124	0.176	0.124	0.156	0.156	0.156	0.158	0.158	0.158

Figure 4.6 – $\boldsymbol{n}$-step transition probabilities

You might notice the probability distribution after 10 steps and 100 steps are very similar. This is because the system has almost reached the steady state after a few steps. So, the chance that we will find the robot in a specific state is almost the same after 10, 100, or 1000 steps. Also, you should have noticed that we are more likely to find the robot at the bottom cells, simply because we have $p_{down} > p_{up}$.

Before we wrap up our discussion about the transitionary and steady state behavior, let's go back to ergodicity and look into a special property of ergodic Markov chains.

Example: Sample path in an ergodic Markov chain

If a Markov chain is ergodic, we can simply simulate it for a long time once and estimate the steady state distribution of the states through the frequency of visits. This is especially useful if we don't have access to the transition probabilities of the system, but we can simulate it.

Let's see this in an example:

1. First, let's import the SciPy library to count the number the visits. Set the number of steps to 1M in the sample path, initialize a vector to keep track of the visits, and initialize the first state to 4, which is $(1, 1)$:

```
from scipy.stats import itemfreq
s = 4
n = 10 ** 6
visited = [s]
```

2. Then, we simulate the environment for 1M steps:

```
for t in range(n):
    s = np.random.choice(m2, p=P[s, :])
    visited.append(s)
```

3. Finally, we count the number of visits to each state.

```
itemfreq(visited)
```

4. You will see numbers similar to the following:

```
array([[0, 158613],
       [1, 157628],
       [2, 158070],
       [3, 105264],
       [4, 104853],
       [5, 104764],
       [6,  70585],
       [7,  70255],
       [8,  69969]], dtype=int64)
```

The results are indeed very much in line with the steady state probability distribution we calculated.

Great job so far, as we've covered Markov chains in a fair amount of detail, worked on some examples and gained a solid intuition! Before we close this section, let's briefly look into a more realistic type of Markov process.

Semi-Markov processes and continuous-time Markov chains

All of the examples and formulas we have provided so far are related to discrete-time Markov chains, where transitions occur at discrete time steps, such as every minute or every 10 seconds. But in many real-world scenarios, when the next transition will happen is also random, which makes them a **semi-Markov process**. In those cases, we are usually interested in predicting the state after T amount of time (rather than after n steps).

One example to such scenarios is queuing systems. For instance, the number of customers waiting on a customer service line. A customer could join the queue anytime and a representative could complete the service with a customer at any time – not just at discrete time steps. Another example is a work-in-process inventory waiting in front of an assembly station to be processed in a factory. In all these cases, analyzing the behavior of the system over time is very important to be able to improve it.

In some semi-Markov processes, we may need to know the current state of the system, and also, for how long the system has been in it. This means the system depends on the past from the time perspective, but not from the perspective of the type of the transition it will make – and hence the name semi-Markov.

Let's look into several possible versions of how this be of interest to us:

- If we are only interested in the transitions themselves, not when they happen, we can simply ignore everything related to time and work with the **embedded Markov chain of the semi-Markov process**, which is essentially the same with working with a discrete-time Markov chain.

- In some processes, although the time between transitions are random, it is memoryless, which means, exponentially distributed. Then we have the Markov property fully satisfied, and the system is a **continuous-time Markov chain**. Queuing systems, for example, are often modeled in this category.

- If it is both that we are interested in the time component and the transition times are not memoryless, then we have a general semi-Markov process.

When it comes to working with these types of environments and solving them using RL, although not ideal, it is common to treat everything as discrete and use the same RL algorithms developed for discrete-time systems with some workarounds. For now, it is good for you to know and acknowledge the differences, but we will not go deeper into semi-Markov processes. Instead, you will see what these workarounds are when we solve continuous-time examples in the later chapters.

We have made a great progress towards building a solid understanding for Markov decision processes with Markov chains. The next step in this journey is to introduce a "reward" to the environment.

Introducing the reward: Markov reward process

In our robot example so far, we have not really identified any situation/state that is "good" or "bad." In any system though, there are desired states to be in and there are other states that we want to avoid. In this section, we attach rewards to states/transitions, which gives us a **Markov Reward Process** (**MRP**). We then assess the "value" of each state.

Attaching rewards to the grid world example

Remember the version of the robot example where it could not bounce back to the cell it was in when it hits a wall, but crashes in a way that it is not recoverable. From now on, we will work on that version, and attach rewards to the process. Now, let's build this example:

1. We modify the transition probability matrix to assign self-transition probabilities to the "crashed" state that we add to the matrix:

```
P = np.zeros((m2 + 1, m2 + 1))
P[:m2, :m2] = get_P(3, 0.2, 0.3, 0.25, 0.25)
for i in range(m2):
    P[i, m2] = P[i, i]
    P[i, i] = 0
P[m2, m2] = 1
```

2. Then, we assign rewards to transitions:

```
n = 10 ** 5
avg_rewards = np.zeros(m2)
for s in range(9):
    for i in range(n):
        crashed = False
        s_next = s
        episode_reward = 0
        while not crashed:
            s_next = np.random.choice(m2 + 1, \
                              p=P[s_next, :])
            if s_next < m2:
                episode_reward += 1
            else:
                crashed = True
```

```
avg_rewards[s] += episode_reward
avg_rewards /= n
```

For every transition the robot stays alive, it collects +1 reward. It collects 0 reward from the moment the robot crashes. Since "crashed" is a terminal/absorbing state, we terminate the episode there. Simulate this model for different initializations, 100K times for each initialization, and see how much total reward is collected on average until a crash for each starting state. The results will look like in *Figure 4.7* (and yours will be a bit different due to the randomness):

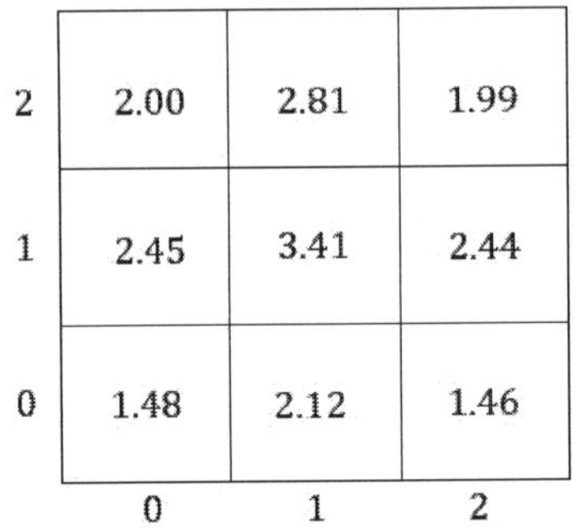

2	2.00	2.81	1.99
1	2.45	3.41	2.44
0	1.48	2.12	1.46
	0	1	2

Figure 4.7 – Average returns with respect to the initial state

In this example, if the initial state is $(1, 1)$, the average return is the highest. This makes it a "valuable" state to be in. Contrast this with the state $(2, 0)$ with an average return of 1.46. Not surprisingly, it is not a great state to be in. This is because it is more likely for the robot to hit the wall earlier when it starts in the corner. Another thing that is not surprising is that the returns are vertically symmetrical (almost), since $p_{left} = p_{right}$.

Now that we have calculated the average reward with respect to each initialization, let's go deeper and see how they are related to each other.

Relations between average rewards with different initializations

The average returns that we have observed have pretty structured relationships in between. Think about it: Assume the robot started in $(1, 1)$ and made a transition into $(1, 2)$. Since it is still alive, we collected a reward of +1. If we knew the "value" of the state $(1, 2)$, would we need to continue the simulation to figure out what return to expect? Not really! The value already gives us the expected return from that point on. And remember that this is a Markov process and what happens next does not depend on the past!

We can extend this relationship to derive the value of a state from the other state values. But remember that the robot could have also transitioned into some other state. Taking into account the other possibilities and denoting the value of a state by $v(s)$, we obtain the following relationship:

$$v(1,1) = p_{up} \cdot \big(1 + v(1,2)\big) + p_{down} \cdot \big(1 + v(1,0)\big)$$
$$+ p_{left} \cdot \big(1 + v(0,1)\big) + p_{right} \cdot \big(1 + v(2,1)\big)$$
$$= 0.2 \cdot (1 + 2.81) + 0.3 \cdot (1 + 2.12)$$
$$+ 0.25 \cdot (1 + 2.45) + 0.25 \cdot (1 + 2.44)$$
$$= 3.42 \approx 3.41$$

As you can see, some small inaccuracies in the estimations of the state values are aside, the state values are consistent with each other!

> **Tip**
>
> This recursive relationship between state values is central to many RL algorithms and it will come up again and again. We will formalize this idea using the Bellman equation in this section.

Next, let's formalize all these concepts and discussions.

Return, discount and state values

We define the **return** in a Markov process after time step t as follows:

$$G_t \triangleq R_{t+1} + R_{t+2} + \cdots + R_T$$

where R_t is the reward at time t, and T is the terminal time step. This definition, however, could be potentially problematic. In a Markov reward process that has no terminal state, the return could go up to infinity. To avoid this, we introduce a **discount rate**, $0 \le \gamma \le 1$ in this calculation and define a **discounted return** as follows:

$$G_t \triangleq R_{t+1} + \gamma R_{t+2} + \gamma^2 R_{t+3} + \gamma^3 R_{t+4} + \cdots$$

$$= \sum_{k=0}^{\infty} \gamma^k R_{t+k+1}$$

For $\gamma < 1$, this sum is guaranteed to be finite as far as the reward sequence is bounded. Here is how varying γ affects the sum:

- γ values closer to 1 place almost equal emphasis on distant rewards as immediate rewards.
- When $\gamma = 1$ all the rewards, distant or immediate, are weighed equally.
- For γ values closer to 0, the sum is more myopic.
- At $\gamma = 0$, the return is equal to the immediate reward.

Throughout the rest of the book, our goal will be to maximize the *expected discounted return*. So, it is important to understand the other benefits of using a discount in the return calculation.

- Discount diminishes the weight placed on the rewards that will be obtained in distant future. This is reasonable as our estimations about the distant future may not be very accurate when we bootstrap value estimations using other estimations (more on this later).
- Human (and animal) behavior prefers immediate rewards over future rewards.
- For financial rewards, immediate rewards are more valuable due to the time value of money.

Now that we have defined the discounted return, the **value** of a state s is defined as the expected discounted return when starting in s:

$$v(s) = E[G_t|S_t = s]$$
$$= E[\textstyle\sum_{k=0}^{\infty} \gamma^k R_{t+k+1} |S_t = s]$$

Note that this definition allows us to use the recursive relations that we already figured out in the previous section:

$$v(s) = \sum_{s',r} p(s',r|s)[r + \gamma v(s')]$$

This equation is called the **Bellman equation for MRP**. Again, this is what we utilized in the preceding grid world example when we calculated the value of a state from the other state values. Bellman equation is at the heart of many RL algorithms and is of crucial importance. We will give its full version after we introduce the Markov Decision Process.

Let's close this section with a more formal definition of a Markov reward process, which is as follows:

> **Info**
>
> An MRP is fully characterized by a tuple $\langle S, P, R, \gamma \rangle$, where S is a set of states, P is a transition probability matrix, R is a reward function and $\gamma \in [0,1]$ is a discount factor.

Next, we look into how to calculate the state values analytically.

Analytically Calculating the State Values

Bellman equation gives us the relationships between the state values, rewards and the transition probabilities. When the transition probabilities and the reward dynamics are known, we can use the Bellman equation to precisely calculate the state values. Of course, this is only feasible when the total number of states is small enough to make the calculations. Let's now see how we can do this.

When we write the Bellman Equation in matrix form, it looks as follows:

$$v = PR + \gamma Pv$$

where:

- v is a column vector, each entry of which is the value of the corresponding state (e.g., state 1, 2, and so on),

- R is another column vector, each entry of which corresponds to the reward obtained when transitioned into that state.

Accordingly, we get this expanded representation of the previous formula:

$$\begin{bmatrix} v(1) \\ \vdots \\ v(n) \end{bmatrix} = \begin{bmatrix} P_{1,1} & \cdots & P_{1,n} \\ \vdots & \ddots & \vdots \\ P_{n,1} & \cdots & P_{n,n} \end{bmatrix} \begin{bmatrix} R_1 \\ \vdots \\ R_n \end{bmatrix} + \gamma \begin{bmatrix} P_{1,1} & \cdots & P_{1,n} \\ \vdots & \ddots & \vdots \\ P_{n,1} & \cdots & P_{n,n} \end{bmatrix} \begin{bmatrix} v(1) \\ \vdots \\ v(n) \end{bmatrix}$$

> **Tip**
>
> If this representation looks complicated to you, to better understand how it works, just consider the version for a single state, for example what we illustrated for state 5 (which is $(2,2)$):
>
> $$v(5) = [P_{5,1}, \dots, P_{5,n}] \begin{bmatrix} R_1 \\ \vdots \\ R_n \end{bmatrix} + \gamma [P_{5,1}, \dots, P_{5,n}] \begin{bmatrix} v(1) \\ \vdots \\ v(n) \end{bmatrix}$$
>
> and fill in the entries on the right-hand side. You should get ≈ 3.41 with $\gamma = 1$.

We can solve this system of linear equations as follows:

$$(I - \gamma P)v = PR$$

$$v = (I - \gamma P)^{-1} PR$$

Now it is time to implement this for our grid world example. Note that, in the 3×3 example, we have 10 states, where the 10th state represents the robot's crash. Transitioning into any state results in +1 reward, except into the "crashed" state. Let's get started:

1. First, we construct the R vector.

```
R = np.ones(m2 + 1)
R[-1] = 0
```

2. We set $\gamma = 0.9999$ (something very close to 1, which is what we have in the example) and calculate the state values. We need this so that the formula works (to avoid singularity).

```
inv = np.linalg.inv(np.eye(m2 + 1) - 0.9999 * P)
v = np.matmul(inv, np.matmul(P, R))
print(np.round(v, 2))
```

3. The output will look like this:

```
[1.47 2.12 1.47 2.44 3.42 2.44 1.99 2.82 1.99 0.]
```

Remember that these are the true (theoretical, rather than estimated) state values (for the given discount rate), and they are aligned with what we estimated through simulation before in Figure 4.7!

If you are wondering why we did not simply set γ to 1: Remember that we now have introduced a discount factor, which is necessary for things to converge mathematically. If you think about it, there is a chance that the robot will randomly move but stay alive infinitely long, collecting infinite reward. Yes, this is extremely unlikely, and you will never see this in practice. So, you may think that we can set $\gamma = 1$ here. However, this would lead to a singular matrix that we cannot take the inverse of. So instead, we will choose $\gamma = 0.9999$. For practical purposes, this discount factor almost equally weighs the immediate and the future rewards.

We can estimate the state values in other ways than simulation or matrix inversion. Let's look into an iterative approach next.

Estimating the state values iteratively

One of the central ideas in RL is to use the value function definition to estimate the value functions iteratively. To achieve that, we arbitrarily initialize the state values and use its definition as an update rule. Since we estimate states based on other estimations, this is a **bootstrapping** method. We stop when the maximum update to the state value over all states is below a threshold.

Here is the code to estimate the state values in our robot example.

```python
def estimate_state_values(P, m2, threshold):
    v = np.zeros(m2 + 1)
    max_change = threshold
    terminal_state = m2
    while max_change >= threshold:
        max_change = 0
        for s in range(m2 + 1):
            v_new = 0
            for s_next in range(m2 + 1):
                r = 1 * (s_next != terminal_state)
                v_new += P[s, s_next] * (r + v[s_next])
            max_change = max(max_change, np.abs(v[s] - v_new))
            v[s] = v_new
    return np.round(v, 2)
```

The result will closely resemble the estimations in Figure 4.7. Just run the following code:

```
estimate_state_values(P, m2, 0.01)
```

And you should get something similar to the following:

```
array([1.46, 2.11, 1.47, 2.44, 3.41, 2.44, 1.98, 2.82, 1.99,
0.])
```

This looks great! Again, remember the following:

- We had to iterate over all possible states. This is intractable when the state space is large,
- We used the transition probabilities explicitly. In a realistic system, we don't know that these probabilities are.

Modern RL algorithms tackle these drawbacks by using function approximation to represent the states and sample the transitions from (a simulation of) the environment. We will visit those approaches in the later chapters.

So far so good! Now we incorporate the last major piece into this picture: actions.

Bringing the action in: Markov decision process

A Markov reward process allowed us to model and study a Markov chain with rewards. Of course, our ultimate goal is to control such a system to achieve the maximum rewards. Now, we incorporate decisions into the MRP.

Definition

A **Markov decision process (MDP)** is simply a Markov reward process with decisions affecting transition probabilities and potentially the rewards.

> **Info**
> An MDP is characterized by a tuple $\langle S, A, P, R, \gamma \rangle$, where we have a finite set of actions, A, on top of MRP.

MDP is the mathematical framework behind RL. So, this is time to remember the RL diagram that we introduced in *Chapter 1, Introduction to Reinforcement Learning*:

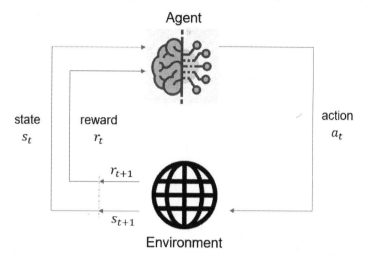

Figure 4.8 – Markov decision process diagram

Our goal in MDP is to find a **policy** that maximizes expected cumulative reward. A policy simply tells which action(s) to take for a given state. In other words, it is a mapping from states to actions. More formally, a policy is a distribution over actions given states and denoted by π.

$$\pi(a|s) = P[A_t = a|S_t = s]$$

The policy of an agent potentially affects the transition probabilities as well as the rewards and it fully defines the agent's behavior. It is also stationary and does not change over time. Therefore, the dynamics of the MDP are defined by the following transition probabilities:

$$p(s',r|s,a) \triangleq P(S_{t+1} = s', R_t = r|S_t = s, A_t = a)$$

for all states and actions.

Next, let's see how an MDP might look like in the grid world example.

Grid world as a Markov decision process

Imagine that we can control the robot in our grid world, but only to some extent. In each step, we can take one of the following actions: up, down, left and right. Then the robot goes in the direction of the action with 70% chance, and one of the other directions with 10% chance each. Given these dynamics, part a sample policy could be as follows:

- Right, when in state $(0, 0)$

- Up, when in state $(1, 0)$

- ...

The policy also determines the transition probability matrix and the reward distribution. For example, we can write the transition probabilities for state $(0, 0)$, and given our policy, as follows:

$$P(S_{t+1} = (1, 0), \ R_t = 1 | S_t = (0, 0), \ A_t = right) = 0.7$$
$$P(S_{t+1} = (0, 1), \ R_t = 1 | S_t = (0, 0), \ A_t = right) = 0.1$$
$$P(S_{t+1} = crashed, \ R_t = 0 | S_t = (0, 0), \ A_t = right) = 0.2$$

> **Tip**
>
> Once a policy is defined in an MDP, the state and reward sequence become a Markov reward process.

So far so good. Now, let's become a bit more rigorous about how we express the policy. Remember that a policy is actually a probability distribution over actions given the state. Therefore, saying that "the policy is to take the action 'right' in state $(0, 0)$" actually means "we take the action 'right' with probability 1 when in state $(0, 0)$." This can be expressed more formally as follows:

$$\pi\big(right | (0, 0)\big) = 1$$

A perfectly legitimate policy is a probabilistic one. For example, we can choose to take the action left or up when in state $(1, 0)$ with equal probability, which is

$$\pi(up | (1, 0)) = 0.5$$
$$\pi(left | (1, 0)) = 0.5.$$

Again, our goal in RL is to figure out an optimal policy for the environment and the problem at hand that maximizes the expected discounted return. Starting from the next chapter, we will go into the details of how to do that and solve detailed examples. For now, this example is enough to illustrate what an MDP looks like in a toy example.

Next, we define the value functions and the related equations for MDPs as we did for MRPs.

State-value function

We have already talked about the value of a state in the context of MRP. The value of a state, now we formally call **state-value function**, is defined as the expected discounted return when starting in state s. However, there is a crucial point here: **The state-value function in an MDP is defined for a policy**. After all, the transition probability matrix is determined by the policy. So, changing the policy is likely to lead to a different state-value function. This is formally defined as follows:

$$v_\pi(s) \triangleq E_\pi[G_t | S_t = s] = E_\pi[\textstyle\sum_{k=0}^{\infty} \gamma^k R_{t+k+1} | S_t = s]$$

Note the π subscript in the state-value function as well as the expectation operator. Other than that, the idea is the same with what we defined with MRP.

And now we can finally define the **Bellman equation for v_π**:

$$v_\pi(s) \triangleq \sum_a \pi(a|s) \sum_{s',r} p(s',r|s,a)[r + \gamma v_\pi(s')]$$

You already know the true values of the states must be consistent with each other from our discussion on MRPs. The only difference here is that now the transition probabilities depend on the actions and the corresponding probabilities of taking them in a given state as per the policy. Imagine "no action" is one of the possible actions in our grid world. The state values in Figure 4.7 would correspond to the policy of taking no actions in any state.

Action-value function

An interesting quantity we use a lot in RL is the action-value function. Now, assume that you have a policy π (not necessarily an optimal one). Consider the following:

- The policy already tells you which actions to take for each state with the associated probabilities, and you follow that policy.

- However, for the current time step, you ask "*what would be the expected cumulative return if I take action a initially while in the current state, and follow π thereafter for all states?*"

- The answer to this question is the **action-value function**.

Formally, this is how we define it in various but equivalent ways:

$$q_\pi(s, a) \triangleq E_\pi[G_t \mid S_t = s, A_t = a]$$

$$= E_\pi\left[\sum_{k=0}^{\infty} \gamma^k R_{t+k+1} \;\middle|\; S_t = s, A_t = a\right]$$

$$= E[R_{t+1} + \gamma v_\pi(s') \mid S_t = s, A_t = a]$$

$$= \sum_{s',r} p(s', r \mid s, a)[r + \gamma v_\pi(s')]$$

Now, you may ask what the point in defining this quantity is if we will follow the policy π thereafter anyway. Well, it can be shown that we can improve our policy by choosing the action that gives the highest action value for state s, represented by $\arg\max_a q_\pi(s, a)$.

We will come back to how to improve and find the optimal policies later in the next chapter.

Optimal state-value and action-value functions

An optimal policy is one that gives the optimal state-value function:

$$v_*(s) \triangleq \max_\pi v_\pi(s), \quad \text{for all } s \in S$$

An optimal policy is denoted by π_*. Note that more than one policy could be optimal. However, there is a single optimal state-value function. We can also define optimal action-value functions as follows:

$$q_*(s, a) \triangleq \max_\pi q_\pi(s, a)$$

And the relationship between the optimal state-value and action-value functions is the following:

$$q_*(s, a) = E[R_{t+1} + \gamma v_*(S_{t+1}) \mid S_t = s, A_t = a]$$

Next, we turn to an important concept, **the Bellman optimality**.

Bellman optimality

When we defined the Bellman equation earlier for $v_\pi(s)$, we needed to use $\pi(a|s)$ in the equation. This is because the state-value function is defined for a policy and we needed to calculate the expected reward and the value of the following state with respect to the action(s) suggested by the policy while in state s (together with the corresponding probabilities if multiple actions are suggested to be taken with positive probability). This equation was the following:

$$v_\pi(s) \triangleq \sum_a \pi(a|s) \sum_{s',r} p(s',r|s,a)[r + \gamma v_\pi(s')]$$

Now, let's discuss what this equation might look like for an optimal policy:

- While dealing with the optimal state-value function, v_*, we don't really need to retrieve $\pi(a|s)$ from somewhere to plug in the equation.

- Why? Because the optimal policy should be suggesting an action that maximizes the consequent expression.

- After all, the state-value function represents the cumulative expected discounted reward. If the optimal policy were not suggesting the action that maximized the expectation term, it would not be an optimal policy.

- Therefore, for the optimal policy and the state-value function, we can write a special form of the Bellman equation.

This is called the **Bellman optimality equation** and is defined as follows:

$$v_*(s) = \max_a q_*(s,a)$$
$$= \max_a E[R_{t+1} + \gamma v_*(s') \mid S_t = s, A_t = a]$$
$$= \max_a \sum_{s',r} p(s',r|s,a)[r + \gamma v_*(s')]$$

We can write the Bellman optimality equation for the action value function similarly.

$$q_*(s,a) = E[R_{t+1} + \gamma v_*(s') \mid S_t = s, A_t = a]$$
$$= E\left[R_{t+1} + \gamma \max_{a'} q_*(S_{t+1}, a') \mid S_t = s, A_t = a\right]$$
$$= \sum_{s',r} p(s',r|s,a)\left[r + \gamma \max_{a'} q_*(s',a')\right]$$

Bellman optimality equation is one of the most central ideas in RL, which will form the basis of many algorithms we will introduce in the next chapter.

With that, we have now covered a great deal of the theory behind the RL algorithms. Before we actually go into using them to solve some RL problems, we will discuss an extension to MDPs next, called partially observable MDPs, which frequently occurs in many real-world settings.

Partially observable Markov decision process

The definition of policy we have used in this chapter so far is that it is a mapping from the states of an environment to actions. Now, the question we should ask is whether the state is really known to the agent in all types of environments.

Remember the definition of the state: it describes everything in an environment related to the agent's decision-making (in the grid world example, if the color of the walls is not important, for instance, so it will not be part of the state).

If you think about it: This is a very strong definition. Consider the situation when someone is driving a car. Does the driver know everything about the world around them while making their driving decisions? Of course not! To begin with, the cars would be blocking each other in their sight more often than not. Not knowing the precise state of the world does not stop anyone from driving, though. In such cases, we base our decision on our **observations**, for example, what we see, and hear during driving, rather than the state. In those cases, we say the environment is **partially observable**. If it is a Markov decision process, we call it **partially observable MDP**, or **POMDP**.

In a POMDP, the probability of seeing a particular observation for an agent depends on the latest action and the current state. The function that describes this probability distribution is called the **observation function**.

> **Info**
> A POMDP is characterized by a tuple $\langle S, A, O, P, R, Z, \gamma \rangle$, where O is the set of possible observations and Z is an observation function such that
> $$Z(o, s', a) = P(O_{t+1} = o | S_{t+1} = s', A_t = a).$$

In practice, having a partially observable environment usually requires keeping a memory of observations to base the actions off of. In other words, a policy is formed not just based on the latest observation, but on the observations from the last k steps.

To better understand why this works, think of how much information a self-driving car can get from a single, frozen scene obtained from its camera. This picture alone does not reveal some important information about the environment, such as the speed and the exact directions of the cars. To infer that, we need a sequence of scenes and see how the cars have moved between the scenes.

> **Tip**
>
> In partially observable environments, keeping a memory of observations makes it possible to uncover more information about the state of the environment. That is why many famous RL settings utilize **LSTM (Long Short-Term Memory)** networks to process the observations. We will look into this in more detail in the later chapters.

With that, we conclude our discussion on Markov decision processes. You are now set to dive into how to solve RL problems!

Summary

In this chapter, we have covered the mathematical framework in which we model the sequential decision-making problems we face in real-life: Markov decision processes. To this end, we started with Markov chains, which do not involve any concept of reward or decision making. Markov chains simply describe stochastic processes where the system transitions based on the current state and independent of the previously visited states. We then added the notion of a reward and started discussing things like which states are more advantageous to be in in terms of the expected future rewards. This created a concept of a "value" for a state. Then, we finally brought in the concept of "decision/action" and defined the Markov decision process. Subsequently, we finalized the definitions of state-value functions and action-value functions. Lastly, we discussed what a partially observable environment is and how it affects the decision-making of an agent.

The Bellman equation variations we've introduced in this chapter are central to many of the RL algorithms today, which are called "value-based methods." Now that, you are equipped with a solid understanding of what they are, starting from next chapter, we will use these ideas to come up with optimal policies. In particular, we will first look into the exact solution algorithms to MDPs, which are dynamic programming methods. We will then go into methods such as Monte Carlo and temporal-difference learning, which provide approximate solutions but don't require knowing the precise dynamics of the environment, unlike dynamic programming methods.

Stay tuned and see you in the next chapter!

Exercises

1. Calculate n-step transition probabilities for the robot using the Markov chain model we introduced with the state initialized at $(2, 2)$. You will notice that it will take a bit more time for the system to reach the steady state.

2. Modify the Markov chain to include the absorbing state for the robot crashing into the wall. What does your P^n look like for a large n?

3. Using the state values in Figure 4.7, calculate the value of a corner state using the estimates for the neighboring state values.

4. Iteratively estimate the state values in the grid world MRP using matrix forms and operations instead of using a for loop.

5. Calculate the action value $q_\pi((1,0), up)$, where the policy π corresponds to taking no actions in any state using the values in *Figure 4.7*. Based on how $q_\pi((1,0), up)$ compares to $v_\pi((1,0))$, would you consider changing your policy to take the action 'up' instead of no actions in state $(1,0)$?

References

1. Silver, D. (2015). *Lecture 2: Markov Decision Processes.* Retrieved from UCL Course on RL: https://www.davidsilver.uk/wp-content/uploads/2020/03/MDP.pdf

2. Sutton, R. S., & Barto, A. G. (2018). *Reinforcement Learning: An Introduction.* A Bradford Book.

3. Ross, S. M. (1996). *Stochastic Processes.* 2nd ed, Wiley.

5
Solving the Reinforcement Learning Problem

In the previous chapter we provided the mathematical foundations for modeling a reinforcement learning problem. In this chapter, we lay the foundation for solving it. Many of the following chapters will focus on some specific solution approaches that will rise on this foundation. To this end, we first cover the **dynamic programming** (DP) approach, with which we introduce some key ideas and concepts. DP methods provide optimal solutions to **Markov decision processes (MDPs)**, yet they require the complete knowledge and a compact representation of the state transition and reward dynamics of the environment. This could be severely limiting and impractical in a realistic scenario, where the agent is either directly trained in the environment itself or in a simulation of it. **Monte Carlo** and **temporal difference (TD)** approaches that we cover later, unlike DP, use sampled transitions from the environment and relax the aforementioned limitations. Finally, we also talk about what makes a simulation model suitable for RL.

In particular, here are the topics we cover in this chapter:

- Exploring dynamic programming
- Training your agent with Monte Carlo methods
- Temporal-difference learning
- Understanding the importance of simulation in reinforcement learning

Exploring dynamic programming

Dynamic programming is a branch of mathematical optimization that proposes optimal solution methods to MDPs. Although most real-world problems are too complex to optimally solve via DP methods, the ideas behind these algorithms are central to many RL approaches. So, it is important to have a solid understanding of them. Throughout this chapter, we go from these exact methods to more practical approaches by systematically introducing approximations.

We start this section by describing an example that will serve as a use case for the algorithms that we will introduce throughout the chapter. Then, we will cover how to do prediction and control using DP. Let's get started!

Example use case: Inventory replenishment of a food truck

Our use case involves a food truck business that needs to decide how many burger patties to buy every weekday to replenish its inventory. Inventory planning is an important class of problems in retail and manufacturing that a lot of companies need to deal with all the time. Of course, for pedagogical reasons, our example is much simpler than what you would see in practice. However, it should still give you an idea about this problem class.

Now, let's dive into the example:

- Our food truck operates in a downtown during the weekdays.
- Every weekday morning, the owner needs to decide how many burger patties to buy with the following options: $A = \{0, 100, 200, 300, 400\}$. The cost of a single patty is $c = \$4$.

- The food truck can store the patties up to a capacity of $C = 400$ during the weekdays. However, since the truck does not operate over the weekend, any inventory unsold by Friday evening spoils. If, during a weekday, the number of patties purchased and the existing inventory exceeds the capacity, the excess inventory also spoils.

- Burger demand for any weekday is a random variable D with the following probability mass function:

$$\Pr\{D = d\} = \begin{cases} 0.3, & d = 100, \\ 0.4, & d = 200, \\ 0.2, & d = 300, \\ 0.1, & d = 400, \\ 0, & otherwise. \end{cases}$$

- Net revenue per burger (after the cost of the ingredients other than the patty is deducted) is $b = \$7$.

- Sales in a day is the minimum of the demand and the available inventory, since the truck cannot sell more burgers than the number of patties available or the demand.

So, what we have is a multi-step inventory planning problem and our goal is to maximize the total expected profit $(b - c)$ in a week.

Info

One-step inventory planning problem is often called "the newsvendor problem." It is about balancing the cost of overage and underage given a demand distribution. For many common demand distributions, this problem can be solved analytically. Of course, many real-world inventory problems are multi-step, similar to what we will solve in this chapter. You can read more about the newsvendor problem at https://en.wikipedia.org/wiki/Newsvendor_model. We will solve a more sophisticated version of this problem in *Chapter 15, Supply Chain Management*.

So far so good. Next, let's create this environment in Python.

Implementing the food truck environment in Python

What we are about to create is a simulation environment for the food truck example as per the dynamics we described above. In doing so, we will use the popular framework designed exactly for the same purpose, which is OpenAI's Gym library. Chances are you have probably come across it before. But if not, that is perfectly fine since it is not playing a critical role in this example. We will cover what you need to know as we go through it.

> **Info**
>
> OpenAI's Gym is the standard library for defining reinforcement learning environments and developing and comparing solution methods. It is also compatible with various RL solution libraries, such as RLlib. If you are not already familiar with the Gym environment, take a look at its concise documentation here: `https://gym.openai.com/docs/`

Chapter05/Solving RL.ipynb

Now, let's go into the implementation:

1. We start with importing the libraries we will need:

    ```python
    import numpy as np
    import gym
    ```

2. Next, we create a Python class, which is initialized with the environment parameters we described in the previous section.

    ```python
    class FoodTruck(gym.Env):
        def __init__(self):
            self.v_demand = [100, 200, 300, 400]
            self.p_demand = [0.3, 0.4, 0.2, 0.1]
            self.capacity = self.v_demand[-1]
            self.days = ['Mon', 'Tue', 'Wed',
                         'Thu', 'Fri', "Weekend"]
            self.unit_cost = 4
            self.net_revenue = 7
            self.action_space = [0, 100, 200, 300, 400]
            self.state_space = [("Mon", 0)] \
                                + [(d, i) for d in self.days[1:]
                                   for i in [0, 100, 200, 300]]
    ```

The state is a tuple of the day of the week (or the weekend) and the starting inventory level for the day. Again, the action is the number of patties to purchase at the beginning of the day. This purchased inventory becomes available immediately. Note that this is a fully observable environment, so the state space and the observation space are the same. Possible inventory levels are 0, 100, 200, and 300 at the beginning of a given day (because of how we defined the action set, possible demand scenarios, and the capacity); except we start Monday with no inventory.

3. Next, let's define a method that calculates the next state and the reward along with the relevant quantities, given the current state, the action, and the demand. Note that this method does not change anything in the object.

```python
def get_next_state_reward(self, state,
                          action, demand):
    day, inventory = state
    result = {}
    result['next_day'] = \
            self.days[self.days.index(day) + 1]
    result['starting_inventory'] = min(self.capacity,
                                       inventory
                                       + action)
    result['cost'] = self.unit_cost * action
    result['sales'] = \
        min(result['starting_inventory'], demand)
    result['revenue'] = \
        self.net_revenue * result['sales']
    result['next_inventory'] \
        = result['starting_inventory'] - \
        result['sales']
    result['reward'] = result['revenue'] - \
                       result['cost']
    return result
```

4. Now, we define a method that returns all possible transitions and rewards for a given state and action pair using the `get_next_state_reward` method, together with the corresponding probabilities. Notice that different demand scenarios will lead to the same next state and reward if the demand exceeds the inventory.

```python
def get_transition_prob(self, state, action):
    next_s_r_prob = {}
    for ix, demand in enumerate(self.v_demand):
        result = self.get_next_state_reward(state,
                                            action,
                                            demand)
        next_s = (result['next_day'],
```

```
                       result['next_inventory'])
          reward = result['reward']
          prob = self.p_demand[ix]
          if (next_s, reward) not in next_s_r_prob:
              next_s_r_prob[next_s, reward] = prob
          else:
              next_s_r_prob[next_s, reward] += prob
      return next_s_r_prob
```

That's all we need for now. Later, we will add other methods to this class to be able to simulate the environment. Now, we dive into DP with the policy evaluation methods.

Policy evaluation

In MDPs (and RL), our goal is to obtain (near) optimal policies. But how do we even evaluate a given policy? After all, if we cannot evaluate it, we cannot compare it against another policy and decide which one is better. So, we start discussing the DP approaches with **policy evaluation** (also called the **prediction problem**). There are multiple ways to evaluate a given policy. In fact, in *Chapter 4, Makings of a Markov Decision Process*, when we defined the state-value function, we discussed how to calculate it analytically and iteratively. Well, that is policy evaluation! In this section, we will go with the iterative version, which we turn to next.

Iterative policy evaluation

Let's first discuss the iterative policy evaluation algorithm and refresh your mind on what we covered in the previous chapter. Then, we will evaluate a policy that the owner of the food truck already has (base policy).

Iterative policy iteration algorithm

Recall that the value of a state is defined as follows for a given policy π:

$$v_\pi(s) \triangleq E_\pi[G_t|S_t = s] = E_\pi[\sum_{k=0}^{\infty} \gamma^k R_{t+k+1} | S_t = s]$$

$v_\pi(s)$ is the expected discounted cumulative reward starting in state s and following policy π. In our food truck example, the value of the state $(Monday, 0)$ is the expected reward (profit) of a week that starts with zero inventory on Monday. The policy that maximizes $v(Monday, 0)$ would be the optimal policy!

Now, the Bellman equation tells us the state values must be consistent with each other. It means that the expected one-step reward together with the discounted value of the next state should be equal to the value of the current state. More formally:

$$v_\pi(s) \triangleq E_\pi[\sum_{k=0}^{\infty} \gamma^k R_{t+k+1} | S_t = s]$$

$$= E_\pi[R_{t+1} + \gamma G_{t+1} | S_t = s]$$

$$= E_\pi[R_{t+1} + \gamma v_\pi(S_{t+1}) | S_t = s]$$

Since we know all the transition probabilities for this simple problem, we can analytically calculate this expectation:

$$v_\pi(s) \triangleq \sum_a \pi(a|s) \sum_{s',r} p(s',r|s,a)[r + \gamma v_\pi(s')]$$

The $\sum_a \pi(a|s)$ term at the beginning is because the policy may suggest taking actions probabilistically given the state. Since the transition probabilities depend on the action, we need to account for each possible action the policy may give us.

Now, all we need to do to obtain an iterative algorithm is to convert the Bellman equation into an update rule as below.

$$v_\pi^{k+1}(s) := \sum_a \pi(a|s) \sum_{s',r} p(s',r|s,a)[r + \gamma v_\pi^k(s')]$$

A single round of updates, k, *involves updating all the state values.* The algorithm stops until the changes in state values are sufficiently small in successive iterations. We won't go into the proof, but this update rule can be shown to converge to v_π as $k \to \infty$. This algorithm is called **iterative policy evaluation** with **expected update** since we take into account all possible one-step transitions.

One last note before we implement this method is that rather than carrying two copies of the state values for k and $k + 1$, and replacing v_π^k with v_π^{k+1} after a full round of updates, we'll just make in-place updates. This tends to converge faster since we make the latest estimate for the value of a state immediately available to be used for other state-value updates.

Next, let's evaluate a base policy for the inventory replenishment problem.

Iterative evaluation of a base inventory replenishment policy

Imagine that the owner of the food truck has the following policy: At the beginning of a weekday, the owner replenishes the inventory up to 200 or 300 patties, with equal probability. For example, if the inventory at the beginning of the day is 100, she is equally likely to purchase 100 or 200 patties. Let's evaluate this policy and see how much profit we should expect in the course of a week.

1. We first define a function that returns a `policy` dictionary, in which the keys correspond to the states. The value that corresponds to a state is another dictionary that has actions as the keys and the probability of selecting that action in that state as the values.

```python
def base_policy(states):
    policy = {}
    for s in states:
        day, inventory = s
        prob_a = {}
        if inventory >= 300:
            prob_a[0] = 1
        else:
            prob_a[200 - inventory] = 0.5
            prob_a[300 - inventory] = 0.5
        policy[s] = prob_a
    return policy
```

2. Now the policy evaluation. We define a function that will calculate the expected update for a given state and the corresponding policy for that state.

```python
def expected_update(env, v, s, prob_a, gamma):
    expected_value = 0
    for a in prob_a:
        prob_next_s_r = env.get_transition_prob(s, a)
        for next_s, r in prob_next_s_r:
            expected_value += prob_a[a] \
                            * prob_next_s_r[next_s, r] \
                            * (r + gamma * v[next_s])
    return expected_value
```

In other words, this function calculates $\sum_a \pi(a|s) \sum_{s',r} p(s',r|s,a)[r + \gamma v_\pi^k(s')]$ for a given s.

3. The policy evaluation function executes the expected updates for all states until the state values converge (or it reaches a maximum number of iterations).

```python
def policy_evaluation(env, policy, max_iter=100,
                      v = None, eps=0.1, gamma=1):
    if not v:
        v = {s: 0 for s in env.state_space}
    k = 0
    while True:
        max_delta = 0
        for s in v:
            if not env.is_terminal(s):
                v_old = v[s]
                prob_a = policy[s]
                v[s] = expected_update(env, v,
                                       s, prob_a,
                                       gamma)
                max_delta = max(max_delta,
                                abs(v[s] - v_old))
        k += 1
        if max_delta < eps:
            print("Converged in", k, "iterations.")
            break
        elif k == max_iter:
            print("Terminating after", k, "iterations.")
            break
    return v
```

Let's elaborate on how this function works:

a) The `policy_evaluation` function receives an environment object, which will be an instance of the `FoodTruck` class in our example.

b) The function evaluates the specified policy, which is in the form of a dictionary that maps states to action probabilities.

c) All the state values are initialized to 0 unless an initialization is passed into the function. The state values for the terminal states (states corresponding to weekend in this example) are not updated since we don't expect any reward from that point on.

d) We define an epsilon value to use as a threshold for convergence. If the maximum change between updates among all the state values is less than this threshold in a given round, the evaluation is terminated.

e) Since this is an episodic task with finite number of steps, we set the discount factor gamma to 1 by default.

f) The function returns the state values, which we will need later.

4. Now, we evaluate the base policy using this function. First, we create a `foodtruck` object from the class we defined above.

```
foodtruck = FoodTruck()
```

5. Then, we get the base policy for the environment.

```
policy = base_policy(foodtruck.state_space)
```

6. Finally, we evaluate the base policy and get the corresponding state values – specifically for the initial state.

```
v = policy_evaluation(foodtruck, policy)
print("Expected weekly profit:", v["Mon", 0])
```

7. The results will look like the following.

```
Converged in 6 iterations.
Expected weekly profit: 2515.0
```

The state-value of (`"Mon"`, `0`), which is the initial state, is 2515 under this policy. Not a bad profit for a week!

Great job so far! Now you are able to evaluate a given policy and calculate the state values corresponding to that policy. Before going into improving the policy, though, let's do one more thing. Let's verify that simulating the environment under this policy leads to a similar reward.

Comparing the policy evaluation against simulation

In order to be able to simulate the environment, we need to add a few more methods to the FoodTruck class.

1. Create a reset method, which simply initializes/resets the object to Monday morning with zero inventory. We will call this method every time before we start an episode.

```
def reset(self):
    self.day = "Mon"
    self.inventory = 0
    state = (self.day, self.inventory)
    return state
```

2. Next, define a method to check if a given state is terminal or not. Remember that episodes terminate at the end of the week in this example.

```
def is_terminal(self, state):
    day, inventory = state
    if day == "Weekend":
        return True
    else:
        return False
```

3. Finally, define the step method that simulates the environment for one-time step given the current state and the action.

```
def step(self, action):
    demand = np.random.choice(self.v_demand,
                              p=self.p_demand)
    result = self.get_next_state_reward((self.day,
                                         self.inventory),
                                        action,
                                        demand)
    self.day = result['next_day']
    self.inventory = result['next_inventory']
    state = (self.day, self.inventory)
    reward = result['reward']
    done = self.is_terminal(state)
```

```
            info = {'demand': demand,
                    'sales': result['sales']}
        return state, reward, done, info
```

The method returns the new state, one-step reward, whether the episode is complete and any additional information we would like to return. This is the standard Gym convention. It also updates the state stored within the class.

4. Now that our FoodTruck class is ready for simulation. Next, let's create a function that chooses an action from a -possibly probabilistic- policy given a state.

```
def choose_action(state, policy):
    prob_a = policy[state]
    action = np.random.choice(a=list(prob_a.keys()),
                              p=list(prob_a.values()))
    return action
```

5. Let's create a function (outside of the class) to simulate a given policy.

```
def simulate_policy(policy, n_episodes):
    np.random.seed(0)
    foodtruck = FoodTruck()
    rewards = []
    for i_episode in range(n_episodes):
        state = foodtruck.reset()
        done = False
        ep_reward = 0
        while not done:
            action = choose_action(state, policy)
            state, reward, done, info = \
                            foodtruck.step(action)
            ep_reward += reward
        rewards.append(ep_reward)
    print("Expected weekly profit:", np.mean(rewards))
```

The simulate_policy function simply performs the following actions:

a) Receives a policy dictionary that returns the actions and the corresponding probabilities the policy suggests for a given state,

b) It simulates the policy for a specified number of episodes,

    c) Within an episode, it starts at the initial state and probabilistically selects the actions suggested by the policy at each step,

    d) The selected action is passed to the environment which transitions into a next state as per the dynamics of the environment.

6.   Now, let's simulate the environment with the base policy!

```
simulate_policy(policy, 1000)
```

7.   The result should look like the following.

```
Expected weekly profit: 2518.1
```

Great! This closely matches what we calculated analytically! Now it is time to use this iterative policy evaluation method for something more useful: Finding optimal policies!

Policy iteration

Now that we have a way of evaluating a given policy, we can use it to compare two policies and iteratively improve them. In this section, we first discuss how policies are compared. Then, we introduce the policy improvement theorem and finally put everything together in the policy improvement algorithm.

Policy comparison and improvement

Suppose that we have two policies, π' and π', we would like to compare. We say π is as good as π if

$$v_{\pi'}(s) \geq v_{\pi}(s) \quad \forall s \in S$$

In other words, if the state values under a policy π' is greater than or equal to the state values under another policy π for all possible states, then it means π' is as good as π. If this relation is a strict inequality for any state s, then π' is a better policy than π. This should be intuitive since a state-value represents the expected cumulative reward from that point on.

Now, the question is how we go from π to a better policy π'. For that, we need to recall the action-value function we defined in *Chapter 4, Makings of a Markov Decision Process*.

$$q_{\pi}(s, a) \triangleq E[R_{t+1} + \gamma v_{\pi}(s') \mid S_t = s, A_t = a]$$

Remember that the definition of the action-value function is a bit nuanced. It is the expected cumulative future reward when:

- Action a is taken at the current state s, and then,

- The policy π is followed.

The nuance is that policy π may normally suggest another action when in state s. The q-value represent a one-time deviation from policy π that happens in the current step.

How does this help with improving the policy though? The **policy improvement theorem** suggests that *if it is better to select* a *initially when in state* s *and then follow* π *rather than following* π *all along; selecting* a *every time when in state* s *is a better policy than* π. In other words, if $q_\pi(s, a) > v_\pi(s)$, then we can improve π by taking action a when in state s and following π for the rest of the states. We don't include it here but the proof of this theorem is actually quite intuitive, and it is available in (Sutton & Barto, 2018).

Let's generalize this argument say some policy π is at least as good as another policy π if, for all $s \in S$, the following holds.

$$q_\pi(s, \pi'(s)) \geq v_\pi(s)$$

Then, all we need to do to improve a policy is to choose actions that maximize the respective q-values for each state. Namely,

$$\pi'(s) \triangleq \arg\max_a q_\pi(s, a)$$

One last note before we close this discussion: Although we described the policy improvement method for deterministic policies, which suggest only a single action for a given state s, the method holds for stochastic policies as well.

So far so good! Now, let's turn this policy improvement into an algorithm that will allow us to find optimal policies!

Policy iteration algorithm

Policy Iteration algorithm simply includes a starting with an arbitrary policy, followed by a policy evaluation step and then with a policy improvement step. This procedure, when repeated, eventually leads to an optimal policy. This process is depicted in the figure below.

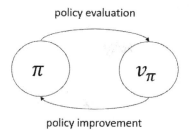

policy evaluation

$$\pi \qquad v_\pi$$

policy improvement

Figure 5.1 – Generalized policy iteration

Actually, iterating between some forms of policy evaluation and policy improvement steps is a general recipe for solving RL problems. That is why this idea is named as **generalized policy iteration (GPI)** (Sutton & Barto, 2018). It is just that the policy iteration method we describe in this section involves specific forms of these steps.

Let's implement a policy iteration for the food truck environment.

Implementing a policy iteration for the inventory replenishment problem

We have already coded the policy evaluation and expected update steps. What we need additionally for the policy iteration algorithm is the policy improvement step, and then we can obtain an optimal policy! This is exciting, so, let's dive right in.

1. Let's start with implement the policy improvement as we described above.

```python
def policy_improvement(env, v, s, actions, gamma):
    prob_a = {}
    if not env.is_terminal(s):
        max_q = np.NINF
        best_a = None
        for a in actions:
            q_sa = expected_update(env, v, s,
                                   {a: 1}, gamma)
            if q_sa >= max_q:
                max_q = q_sa
                best_a = a
        prob_a[best_a] = 1
    else:
        max_q = 0
    return prob_a, max_q
```

This function searches for the action that gives the maximum q-value for a given state using the value functions obtained under the current policy. For the terminal states, the q-value is always equal to 0.

2. Now, we put everything together in a policy iteration algorithm.

```python
def policy_iteration(env,  eps=0.1, gamma=1):
    np.random.seed(1)
    states = env.state_space
    actions = env.action_space
    policy = {s: {np.random.choice(actions): 1}
            for s in states}
    v = {s: 0 for s in states}
    while True:
        v = policy_evaluation(env, policy, v=v,
                            eps=eps, gamma=gamma)
        old_policy = policy
        policy = {}
        for s in states:
            policy[s], _ = policy_improvement(env, v, s,
                                actions, gamma)
        if old_policy == policy:
            break
    print("Optimal policy found!")
    return policy, v
```

This algorithm starts with a random policy, and in each iteration, implements the policy evaluation and improvement steps. It stops when the policy becomes stable.

3. And the big moment! Let's find out the optimal policy for our food truck and see what the expected weekly profit is!

```python
policy, v = policy_iteration(foodtruck)
print("Expected weekly profit:", v["Mon", 0])
```

4. The result should look like the following.

```
Converged in 6 iterations.
Converged in 6 iterations.
Converged in 5 iterations.
```

```
Optimal policy found!
Expected weekly profit: 2880.0
```

We have just figured out a policy that gives an expected weekly profit of $2,880. This is a significant improvement over the base policy! Well, thanks for supporting your local business!

You can see from the output that there were two policy improvement steps over the random policy. The third policy improvement step did not lead to any changes in the policy and the algorithm terminated.

Let's see what the optimal policy looks like:

Starting Inventory / Day	Monday	Tuesday	Wednesday	Thursday	Friday
0	400	400	400	300	200
100		300	300	200	100
200		200	200	100	0
300		100	100	0	0

Figure 5.2 – Optimal policy for the food truck example

What the policy iteration algorithm comes up with is quite intuitive. Let's analyze this policy for a moment:

- On Monday and Tuesday, it is guaranteed that 400 burgers will be sold in the remainder of the week. Since the patties can be safely stored during the weekdays, it makes sense to fill the inventory up to the capacity.

- At the beginning of Wednesday, there is a chance that the total number sales will be 300 till the end of the week and 100 patties will be spoiled. However, this is a rather small likelihood and the expected profit is still positive.

- For Thursday and Friday, it makes more sense to be more conservative de-risk a costly spoilage in case the demand is less than the inventory.

Congratulations! You have successfully solved an MDP using policy iteration!

> **Tip**
> The optimal policy we have found heavily depends on the cost of patties, the net revenue per unit as well as the demand distribution. You can gain more intuition about the structure of the optimal policy and how it changes by modifying the problem parameters and solving it again.

You have come a long way! We built an exact solution method starting with the fundamentals of MDP and DP. Next, we will look into another algorithm that is often more efficient than policy iteration.

Value iteration

Policy iteration requires us to fully evaluate the policies, until the state values converge, before we perform an improvement step. In more sophisticated problems, it could be quite costly to wait for a complete evaluation. Even in our example, a single policy evaluation step took 5-6 sweeps over all states until it converged. It turns out that we can get away with terminating policy evaluation before it converges without losing the convergence guarantee of the policy iteration. In fact, we can even combine policy iteration and policy improvement into a single step by turning the Bellman optimality equation we introduced in the previous chapter into an update rule:

$$v_{k+1}(s) := \max_a q_k(s, a)$$

$$= \max_a E[R_{t+1} + \gamma v_k(S_{t+1}) \mid S_t = s, A_t = a]$$

$$= \max_a \sum_{s',r} p(s', r \mid s, a)[r + \gamma v_k(s')]$$

We simply perform the update for all states again and again until the state values converge. This algorithm is called **value iteration**.

Tip

Notice the difference between a policy evaluation update and a value iteration update. The former selects the actions from a given policy, hence the $\sum_a \pi(a \mid s)$ term in front of the expected update. The latter, on the other hand, does not follow a policy but actively searches for the best actions through the $\max_a$ ... operator.

This is all we need to implement the value iteration algorithm. So, let's dive right into the implementation.

Implementing the value iteration for the inventory replenishment problem

To implement value iteration, we will use the `policy_improvement` function we defined earlier. However, after improving the policy for each state, we also update the state-value estimate of the state.

Now, let's go ahead with the following steps for the implementation:

1. We first define the value iteration function with in-place replacement of the state values.

```python
def value_iteration(env, max_iter=100, eps=0.1, gamma=1):
    states = env.state_space
    actions = env.action_space
    v = {s: 0 for s in states}
    policy = {}
    k = 0
    while True:
        max_delta = 0
        for s in states:
            old_v = v[s]
            policy[s], v[s] = policy_improvement(env,
                                                 v,
                                                 s,
                                                 actions,
                                                 gamma)
            max_delta = max(max_delta, abs(v[s] - old_v))
        k += 1
        if max_delta < eps:
            print("Converged in", k, "iterations.")
            break
        elif k == max_iter:
            print("Terminating after", k, "iterations.")
            break
    return policy, v
```

2. Then, we execute the value iteration and observe the value of the initial state.

```
policy, v = value_iteration(foodtruck)
print("Expected weekly profit:", v["Mon", 0])
```

3. The result will should like the following.

```
Converged in 6 iterations.
Expected weekly profit: 2880.0
```

Value iteration gives the optimal policy, but with less computational effort compared to the policy iteration algorithm! It took only total 6 sweeps over the state space with the value iteration while the policy iteration arrived at the same optimal policy after 20 sweeps (17 for policy evaluation and 3 for policy improvement).

Now, remember our discussion around generalized policy improvement. You can in fact combine the policy improvement step with a truncated policy evaluation step, which, in some sophisticated examples where the state values change significantly after the policy improvement, converge faster than both policy iteration and value iteration algorithms.

Great work! We have covered how to solve the prediction problem for MDPs using DP and then two algorithms to find optimal policies. And they worked great for our simple example. On the other hand, DP methods suffer from two important drawbacks in practice. Let's discuss what those are next, and why we need the other approaches that we will introduce later in the chapter.

Drawbacks of dynamic programming

DP methods are great to learn to get a solid grasp of how MDPs can be solved. They are also much more efficient compared to direct search algorithms or linear programming methods. On the other hand, in practice, these algorithms are still either intractable or impossible to use. Let's elaborate on why.

Curse of dimensionality

Both the policy iteration and the value iteration algorithms iterate over the entire state space, multiple times, until they arrive at an optimal policy. We also store the policy, the state values, and the action values for each state in a tabular form. Any realistic problem, on the other hand, would have a gigantic number of possible states, explained by a phenomenon called **curse of dimensionality**. This refers to the fact that the possible number of values of a variable (states) grows exponentially as we add more dimensions.

Consider our food truck example. In addition to keeping track of patties, let's assume we also keep track of burger buns, tomatoes, and onions. Also assume that the capacity for each of these items is 400, and we have a precise count of the inventory. The possible number of states in this case would be 6×401^4, that is greater than 10^{11}. This is a ridiculous number of states to keep track of for such a simple problem.

One mitigation to the curse of dimensionality is **asynchronous dynamic programming**:

- This approach suggests not sweeping over the entire state space in each iteration of policy improvement but focus on the states that are more likely to be encountered.

- For many problems, not all parts of the state space are of equal importance. Therefore, it is wasteful to wait for a complete sweep of the state space before there is an update to the policy.

- With an asynchronous algorithm, we can simulate the environment in parallel to the policy improvement, observe which states are visited and update the policy and the value functions for those states.

- At the same time, we can pass the updated policy to the agent so the simulation would continue with the new policy.

Given that the agent sufficiently explores the state space, the algorithm would converge to an optimal solution eventually.

A more important tool that we use to address this problem, on the other hand, is **function approximators**, such as deep neural networks. Think about it! What is the benefit in storing a separate policy/state-value/action-value for the inventory levels 135, 136, 137? Not much, really. Function approximators represent what we would like to learn in a much more compact manner (although approximately) compared to a tabular representation. In fact, in many cases, deep neural networks are only meaningful choice for function approximation due to their representation power. That is why, starting with the next chapter, we will exclusively focus on deep reinforcement learning algorithms.

Need for a complete model of the environment

So far, we have relied on the transition probabilities of the environment in our policy evaluation, policy iteration, and value iteration algorithms to obtain optimal policies. This is a luxury that we usually don't have in practice. It is either these probabilities are very difficult to calculate for each possible transition (which is often impossible to even enumerate), or we simply don't know them. You know what is much easier to obtain? A sample trajectory of transitions, either from the environment itself or from its **simulation**. In fact, simulation is a particularly important component in reinforcement learning as we will discuss separately towards the end of this chapter.

Then the question becomes how we use sample trajectories to learn (near) optimal policies. Well, this is exactly what we cover next in the rest of this chapter with Monte Carlo and temporal-difference methods. The concepts you will learn here are at the center of many advanced reinforcement learning algorithms.

Training your agent with Monte Carlo methods

Let's say you would like to learn the chance of flipping heads with a particular, possibly biased, coin:

- One way of calculating this is through a careful analysis of the physical properties of the coin. Although this could give you the precise probability distribution of the outcomes, it is far from being a practical approach.

- Alternatively, you can just flip the coin many times and look at the distribution in your sample. Your estimate could be a bit off if you don't have a large sample, but it will do the job for most practical purposes. The math you need to deal with using the latter method will be incomparably simpler.

Just like in the coin example, we can estimate the state values and action values in an MDP from random samples. **Monte Carlo (MC)** estimation is a general concept that refers to making estimations through repeated random sampling. In the context of RL, it refers to *a collection of methods that estimate state and action values using sample trajectories of complete episodes*. Using random samples is incredibly convenient, and in fact essential, for any realistic RL problem. Because the environment dynamics (state transition and reward probability distributions) are often either:

- Too complex to deal with, or

- They are not known in the first place.

Monte Carlo estimation, therefore, is a powerful method that allows an RL agent to learn optimal policies only from the experience it collects through interacting with its environment, without knowing how the environment works.

In this section, we first look into estimating the state and action values for a given policy with MC methods. Then, we cover how to make improvements towards obtaining optimal policies.

Monte Carlo prediction

As in the DP methods, we need to be able to evaluate a given policy π to be able to improve it. In this section, we cover how to evaluate a policy by estimating the corresponding state and action values. In doing so, we briefly revisit the grid world example from the previous chapter and then go into the food truck inventory replenishment problem.

Estimating the state-value function

Remember that the value of a state s under policy π, $v_\pi(s)$, is defined as the expected cumulative reward when started in state s.

$$v_\pi(s) = E_\pi[G_t|S_t = s] = E_\pi[\sum_{k=0}^{\infty} \gamma^k R_{t+k+1} |S_t = s]$$

MC prediction suggests simply observing (many) sample **trajectories**, sequences of state-action-reward tuples, starting in s, to estimate this expectation. This is similar to flipping a coin to estimate its distribution from a sample.

It is best to explain Monte Carlo methods with an example. In particular, it will be quite intuitive to see how it works in the grid world example; so, let's revisit that next.

Using sample trajectories for state value estimation

Recall that the robot in the grid world receives +1 reward for every move as far as it does not crash. When it does crash into a wall, the episode ends. Assume that this robot can be controlled only to a certain extent. When instructed to go in a particular direction, it follows the command with 70% chance. The robot goes in one of the other three directions with 10% chance for each.

Consider a deterministic policy π illustrated in *Figure 5.3 (a)*. If the robot starts in state (1,2) two example trajectories it can follow, τ_1 and τ_2, and the corresponding probabilities of making the each of the transitions are shown in *Figure 5.3 (b)*.

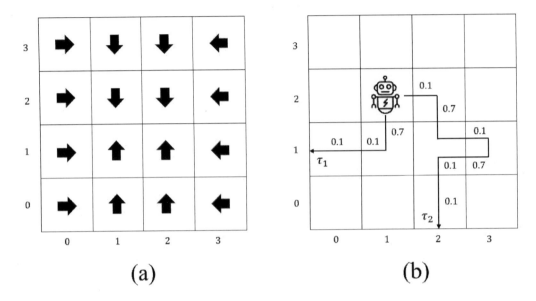

(a)
(b)

Figure 5.3 – a) A deterministic policy π, b) Two sample trajectories under π

> **Tip**
> Notice that the robot follows a random trajectory but the policy itself is deterministic, which means the action taken (command sent to the robot) in a given state is always the same. The randomness comes from the environment due to probabilistic state transitions.

For the trajectory τ_1, the probability of observing it and the corresponding discounted return are as below.

$$\tau_1 : S_0 = (1,2), A_0 = down,$$
$$R_1 = 1, S_1 = (1,1), A_1 = up,$$
$$R_2 = 1, S_2 = (0,1), A_2 = right,$$
$$R_3 = 0, S_3 = crashed$$
$$p_\pi(\tau_1) = 0.7 \cdot 0.1 \cdot 0.1 = 0.007$$
$$G_{\tau_1} = 1 + \gamma 1 + \gamma^2 0$$

And for τ_2

$$\tau_2: S_0 = (1,2), A_0 = down,$$
$$R_1 = 1, S_1 = (2,2), A_1 = down,$$
$$R_2 = 1, S_2 = (2,1), A_2 = up,$$
$$R_3 = 1, S_3 = (3,1), A_3 = left,$$
$$R_4 = 1, S_4 = (2,1), A_4 = up,$$
$$R_5 = 1, S_5 = (2,0), A_5 = up,$$
$$R_6 = 0, S_6 = crashed$$
$$p_\pi(\tau_2) = 0.1 \cdot 0.7 \cdot 0.1 \cdot 0.7 \cdot 0.1 \cdot 0.1 = 0.000049$$
$$G_{\tau_2} = 1 + \gamma 1 + \gamma^2 1 + \gamma^3 1 + \gamma^4 1 + \gamma^5 0$$

For these two example trajectories, we were able to calculate the corresponding probabilities and the returns. To calculate the state-value of $s = (1,2)$, though, we need evaluate the following expression:

$$v_\pi(s) = E_\pi[G_t|S_t = s] = E_\pi[G_\tau|S_t = s] = \sum_i p_\pi(\tau_i) \cdot G_{\tau_i}$$

That means we need to identify:

- Every single possible trajectory τ that can originate from $s = (1,2)$ under policy π,
- The probability of observing τ under π, $p_\pi(\tau)$, and
- The corresponding discounted return, G_τ.

Well, that is an impossible task. Even in this simple problem, there are infinite number of possible trajectories.

This is exactly where Monte Carlo prediction comes to the rescue. It simply tells us to estimate the value of state $(1,2)$ by averaging the sample returns as follows.

$$\hat{v}_\pi(1,2) = \frac{G_{\tau_1} + G_{\tau_2}}{2}$$

That's it! Sample trajectories and returns are all you need to estimate the value of the state.

> **Tip**
>
> Note that v_π denotes the true value of the state, whereas $\hat{v}_\pi$ denotes an estimate.

At this point, you may be asking the following questions:

- *How come is it enough to have two sample returns to estimate a quantity that is the outcome of an infinite number of trajectories?* It is not. The more sample trajectories you have the more accurate your estimate is.

- *How do we know we have enough number of sample trajectories?* That is hard to quantify. But more complex environments, especially when there is a significant degree of randomness, would require more samples for an accurate estimation. It is a good idea, though, check if the estimate is converging as you add more trajectory samples.

- τ_1 *and* τ_2 *have very different likelihoods of occurring. Is it appropriate to assign them equal weights in the estimation?* This is indeed problematic when we have only two trajectories in the sample. However, as we sample more trajectories, we can expect to observe the trajectories in the sample occur proportionally to their true probabilities of occurrence.

- *Can we use the same trajectory in estimating the values of the other states it visits?* Yes! Indeed, that is what we will do in the Monte Carlo prediction.

Let's elaborate on how we can use the same trajectory in estimating the values of different states next.

First-visit vs. every-visit Monte Carlo prediction

If you recall what Markov property is about, it simply tells us all the future depends on the current state, not the past. Therefore, we can think of, for example, τ_1 as three separate trajectories that originate from states $(1,2), (1,1)$ and $(0,1)$. Let's call the latter two trajectories τ_1' and τ_1''. So, we can obtain a value estimate for all the states visited by the trajectories in our sample set. For instance, the value estimate for state $(1,1)$ would be as follows.

$$\hat{v}_\pi(1,1) = G_{\tau_1'}$$
$$G_{\tau_1'} = 1 + \gamma 0$$

Since there is no other trajectory visiting state $(1,1)$, we used a single return to estimate the state-value. Notice the discounts are applied to the rewards according to their time distance to the initial time-step. That is why the exponents of the γ discount reduced by one.

Consider the following set of trajectories in Figure 5.4 and assume we again want to estimate $v(1,2)$. None of the sample trajectories actually originate from state $(1,2)$, but that is totally fine. We can use trajectories τ_1, τ_2 and τ_3 for the estimation. But then there is an interesting case here: τ_3 visits state $(1,2)$ twice. Should we use the return only from its first visit or from each of its visits?

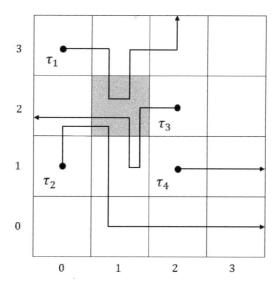

Figure 5.4 – Monte Carlo estimation of $v(\mathbf{1,2})$

Both these approaches are valid. The former method is called **first-visit MC method** and the latter is called **every-visit MC method**. They compare to each other as follows:

- Both converge to true $v_\pi(s)$ as the number of visits goes to infinity.

- First-visit MC methods gives an unbiased estimate of the state-value whereas every-visit MC method is biased.

- The **mean squared error** (**MSE**) of first-visit MC method is higher with fewer samples but lower than every-visit MSE with more samples.

- Every-visit MC method is more natural to use with function approximations.

If it sounds complicated, it is actually not! Just remember these:

- We are trying to estimate a parameter, such as the state-value of s,
  $v_\pi(s) = E_\pi[G_t|S_t = s]$,
- By observing the random variable G_t, the discounted return starting from s, many times.
- It is both valid to consider trajectories from their first visit of s on, or from their every visit on.

Now it is time to implement Monte Carlo prediction!

Implementing first-visit Monte Carlo estimation of the state values

We have used the grid world example to get a visual intuition, and now let's go back to our food truck example for the implementation. Here, we will implement the first-visit MC method, but the implementation can be easily modified to the every-visit MC. This can be done by removing the condition that calculates the return only if the state does not appear in the trajectory up to that point. For the food truck example, since a trajectory will never visit the same state –because day of the week, which is part of the state, changes after every transition– both methods are identical.

Let's follow these steps for the implementation:

1. We start with defining a function that takes a trajectory and calculates the returns from the first visit on for each state that appears in the trajectory.

```python
def first_visit_return(returns, trajectory, gamma):
    G = 0
    T = len(trajectory) - 1
    for t, sar in enumerate(reversed(trajectory)):
        s, a, r = sar
        G = r + gamma * G
        first_visit = True
        for j in range(T - t):
            if s == trajectory[j][0]:
                first_visit = False
        if first_visit:
            if s in returns:
                returns[s].append(G)
            else:
```

```
            returns[s] = [G]
    return returns
```

This function does the following:

a) Takes a dictionary `returns` as input, whose keys are states and values are list of returns calculated in some other trajectories.

b) Takes a list `trajectory` as input, which is a list of state-action-reward tuples.

c) Appends the calculated return for each state to `returns`. If that state is never visited by another trajectory before, it initializes the list.

d) Traverses the trajectory backwards to conveniently calculate the discounted returns. It applies the discount factor in each step.

e) Checks if a state is visited earlier in the trajectory in after each calculation. It saves the calculated return to the `returns` dictionary only for first the visit of a state.

2. Next, we implement a function that simulates the environment for a single episode with a given policy and returns the trajectory.

```
def get_trajectory(env, policy):
    trajectory = []
    state = env.reset()
    done = False
    sar = [state]
    while not done:
        action = choose_action(state, policy)
        state, reward, done, info = env.step(action)
        sar.append(action)
        sar.append(reward)
        trajectory.append(sar)
        sar = [state]
    return trajectory
```

3. Now, implement the first-visit return Monte Carlo function, which simulates the environment for a specified number of episodes/trajectories with given a policy. We keep track of the trajectories and average the returns for each state calculated by the `first_visit_return` function.

```python
def first_visit_mc(env, policy, gamma, n_trajectories):
    np.random.seed(0)
    returns = {}
    v = {}
    for i in range(n_trajectories):
        trajectory = get_trajectory(env, policy)
        returns = first_visit_return(returns,
                                     trajectory,
                                     gamma)
    for s in env.state_space:
        if s in returns:
            v[s] = np.round(np.mean(returns[s]), 1)
    return v
```

4. We make sure that we create an environment instance (or we can simply use the one from the previous sections). Also obtain the base policy, which fills the patty inventory up to 200 or 300 with equal chance.

```python
foodtruck = FoodTruck()
policy = base_policy(foodtruck.state_space)
```

5. Now, let's use the first-visit MC method to estimate the state values from 1000 trajectories.

```python
v_est = first_visit_mc(foodtruck, policy, 1, 1000)
```

6. The result, `v_est`, will look like the following.

```python
{('Mon', 0): 2515.9,
 ('Tue', 0): 1959.1,
 ('Tue', 100): 2362.2,
 ('Tue', 200): 2765.2,
 ...
```

7. Now, remember that we can use DP's policy evaluation method to calculate the true state values for comparison.

```
v_true = policy_evaluation(foodtruck, policy)
```

8. The true state values will look very similar.

```
{('Mon', 0): 2515.0,
 ('Tue', 0): 1960.0,
 ('Tue', 100): 2360.0,
 ('Tue', 200): 2760.0,
 ...
```

9. We can obtain the estimations with different number of trajectories, such as 10, 100 and 1000. Let's do that and compare how the state value estimations get closer to the true values, as shown in *Figure 5.5*.

	M	Tu	W	Th	F
0	2220	1767	1240	550	433
100		1725	1350	1000	633
200			1600	1500	750
300					

$\hat{v}_\pi$ after 10 trajectories

	M	Tu	W	Th	F
0	2532	1918	1538	948	409
100		2354	1763	1203	783
200		3042	2329	3042	1042
300					

$\hat{v}_\pi$ after 100 trajectories

	M	Tu	W	Th	F
0	2518	1967	1441	870	300
100		2374	1824	1264	726
200		2803	2187	1687	1151
300					

$\hat{v}_\pi$ after 1000 trajectories

	M	Tu	W	Th	F
0	2515	1960	1405	850	295
100		2360	1805	1250	695
200		2760	2205	1650	1095
300		3205	2605	2095	1400

v_π, true values

Figure 5.5 – First-visit Monte Carlo estimates vs. true state values

Let's analyze the results a bit more closely:

a) As we collected more trajectories, the estimates got closer to the true state values. You can increase the number of trajectories to even higher numbers to obtain even better estimates.

b) After we collected 10 trajectories, no values were estimated for ("Tue", 200). This is because this state was never visited within those 10 trajectories. This highlights the importance of collecting enough number of trajectories.

c) No values are estimated for states that started the day with 300 units of inventory. This is because, under the base policy, these states are impossible to visit. But then, we have no idea about the value of those states. On the other hand, they might be valuable states that we want our policy to lead us to. This is an **exploration problem** we need to address.

Now we have a way of estimating state values without knowing the environment dynamics and by only using the agent's experience in the environment. Great job so far! However, there remains to be an important problem. With the state value estimates alone, we cannot really improve the policy on hand. To see why this is the case, recall how we improved the policy with the DP methods, such as value iteration:

$$v_\pi^{k+1}(s) := \max_a q_\pi^k(s, a)$$

$$= \max_a E[R_{t+1} + \gamma v_\pi^k(S_{t+1}) \mid S_t = s, A_t = a]$$

$$= \max_a \sum_{s',r} p(s', r \mid s, a)[r + \gamma v_\pi^k(s')]$$

We used the state value estimates *together with the transition probabilities* to obtain action (q) values. We then chose, for each state, the action that maximized the q-value of the state. Right now, since we don't assume the knowledge of the environment, we can't go from the state values to action values.

This leaves us with one option: We need to estimate the action values directly. Fortunately, it will be similar to how we estimated the state values. Let's look into using Monte Carlo methods to estimate the action values next.

Estimating the action-value function

Action values, $q_\pi(s, a)$, represent the expected discounted cumulative return when starting in state s, taking action a, and following the policy π. Consider the following trajectory:

$$S_t, a_t, r_{t+1}, S_{t+1}, a_{t+1}, r_{t+2}, \ldots, r_T, S_T$$

The discounted return observed can be used in estimating $q_\pi(s_t, a_t)$, $q_\pi(s_{t+1}, a_{t+1})$ etc. We can then use them to determine the best action for a given state s, as in the following:

$$a^* = \arg\max_a q(s, a)$$

Here is the challenge: What if we don't have the action-value estimates for all possible a that can be taken in state s? Consider the grid world example. If the policy is always to go right when in state $(0,0)$, we will never have a trajectory that starts with state-action pairs $((0,0), left)$, $((0,0), down)$, or $((0,0), up)$. So, even if one of those actions gives a higher action-value than $((0,0), right)$, we will never discover it. The situation was similar with the base policy in the food truck example. In general, this is the case when we use a deterministic policy, or a stochastic policy that does not take all of the actions with some positive probability.

So, what we have here is essentially an *exploration* problem, which is a fundamental challenge in reinforcement learning.

There are two possible solutions to this:

- Starting the trajectories with a random action selected in a random initial state, and then following a policy π as usual. This is called **exploring starts**. This ensures choosing all state-action pairs at least once, so we can estimate the action-values. The drawback of this approach is that we need to keep starting episodes with random initializations. If we want to learn the action-values from an ongoing interaction with the environment, without frequent restarts, this method will not be too helpful.

- The other and more common solution to the exploration problem is to maintain a policy that selects all actions in any state with positive probability. More formally, we need a policy that satisfies $\pi(a|s) > 0$, for all $a \in A(s)$ and for all $s \in S$; where S is the set of all possible states and $A(s)$ is the set of all possible actions available in state s. Such a policy π is called **soft policy**.

In the next section, we will use soft policies action-value estimation, which will be in turn used for policy improvement.

Monte Carlo control

Monte Carlo control refers to a collection of methods that find (near) optimal policies using the *samples* of discounted return. In other words, this is learning optimal policies from experience. And, since we depend on experience to discover optimal policies, we have to explore, as we explained above. Next, we implement ϵ-**greedy** policies to enable exploration during training, which a particular form of soft policy. After that, we cover two different flavors of Monte Carlo control, namely on-policy and off-policy methods.

Implementing ε-greedy policies

Very similar to what we did in bandit problems, an ε-greedy policy picks an action at random with ε probability; and with $1 - \varepsilon$ probability, it selects the action that maximizes the action-value function. This way, we continue to explore all state-action pairs while selecting the best actions we identify with high likelihood.

Let's now implement a function that converts a deterministic action to an ϵ-greedy one, which we will need later. The function assigns $1 - \varepsilon + \varepsilon/|A(s)|$ probability to the best action, and $\varepsilon/|A(s)|$ probability to all other actions.

```python
def get_eps_greedy(actions, eps, a_best):
    prob_a = {}
    n_a = len(actions)
    for a in actions:
        if a == a_best:
            prob_a[a] = 1 - eps + eps/n_a
        else:
            prob_a[a] = eps/n_a
    return prob_a
```

Exploration is necessary to find optimal policies during training. On the other hand, we would not want to take exploratory actions after the training / during inference, but take the best ones. Therefore, the two policies differ. To make the distinction, the former is called the **behavior policy** and the latter is called the **target policy**. We can make the state and the action values aligned with the former or the latter, leading to two different classes of methods: **on-policy** and **off-policy**. Let's compare the two approaches in detail next.

On-policy vs. off-policy methods

Remember that the state and action values are associated with a particular policy, hence the notation v_π and q_π. On-policy methods estimate the state and the action values for the behavior policy used during training, such as, the one that generates the training data / the experience. Off-policy methods estimate the state and the action values for a policy that is other than the behavior policy, such as the target policy. We ideally want to decouple exploration in training from value estimation. Let's look into why this is the case in detail.

Impact of on-policy methods on value function estimates

Exploratory policies are usually not optimal as they take random actions once in a while for the sake of exploration. Since on-policy methods estimate the state and action values for the behavior policy, that sub-optimality is reflected in the value estimates.

Consider the following modified grid world example to see how involving the effects of the exploratory actions in value estimation could be potentially harmful: The robot needs to choose between going left or right in state 2 of a 3 × 1 grid world, and between up and down in states 1 and 3. The robot follows the actions perfectly, so there is no randomness in the environment. This is illustrated in Figure 5.6:

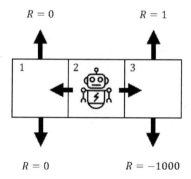

Figure 5.6 – Modified grid world

The robot has an ϵ-greedy policy, which suggests taking the best action with 0.99 chance, and an exploratory action with 0.01 chance. The best policy in state 3 is to go up with a high likelihood. In state 1, the choice does not really matter. The state value estimates obtained in an on-policy manner will then be:

$$v(1) = 0 \cdot p_{up} + 0 \cdot p_{down} = 0$$

$$v(3) = 1 \cdot 0.99 - 1000 \cdot 0.01 = -9.01$$

A policy obtained in an on-policy fashion for state 2 will suggest going left, towards state 1. On the other hand, in this deterministic environment, the robot could perfectly avoid the big penalty when there is no exploration involved. An on-policy method would fail to identify this since the exploration influences the value estimates and yield a sub-optimal policy as a result. On the other hand, in some cases, we may want the agent to take the impact of exploration into account if, for example, the samples are collected using a physical robot and some states are very costly to visit.

Sample efficiency comparison between on-policy and off-policy methods

As mentioned above, off-policy methods estimate the state and the action values for a policy that is different than the behavior policy. On-policy methods, on the other hand, estimate these values only for the behavior policy. When we cover deep RL on-policy methods in the later chapters, we will see that this will require the on-policy methods to discard the past experience once the behavior policy is updated. Off-policy deep RL methods, however, can reuse the past experience again and again. This is a significant advantage in sample efficiency, especially if it is costly to obtain the experience.

Another area where off-policy methods' ability to use the experience generated by a policy other than the behavior policy comes handy is when we want to warm start the training based on the data generated by a non-RL controller, such as classical PID controllers or a human operator. This is especially useful when the environment is hard/expensive to simulate or collect experience from.

Advantages of on-policy methods

The natural question is then why do we even talk about on-policy methods instead of just ignoring them? There are several advantages of on-policy methods:

- As mentioned above, if the cost of sampling from the environment high (actual environment rather than a simulation), we may want to have a policy that reflects the impact of exploration to avoid catastrophic outcomes.

- Off-policy methods, when combined with function approximators, could have issues with converging to a good policy. We will discuss this in the next chapter.

- On-policy methods are easier to work with when the action space is continuous, again, as we will discuss later.

With that, it is finally time to implement first on-policy and then off-policy Monte Carlo methods!

On-policy Monte Carlo control

The GPI framework we described earlier, which suggests going back and forth between some forms of policy evaluation and policy improvement, is also what we use with the Monte Carlo methods to obtain optimal policies. In each cycle, we collect a trajectory from a complete episode, then estimate the action-values and update the policy and so on.

Let's implement an on-policy MC control algorithm and use it to optimize the food truck inventory replenishment:

1. We first create a function that generates a random policy where all actions are equally likely to be taken, to be used to initialize the policy.

```python
def get_random_policy(states, actions):
    policy = {}
    n_a = len(actions)
    for s in states:
        policy[s] = {a: 1/n_a for a in actions}
    return policy
```

2. Next, we build the on-policy first visit MC control algorithm.

```python
import operator
def on_policy_first_visit_mc(env, n_iter, eps, gamma):
    np.random.seed(0)
    states = env.state_space
    actions = env.action_space
    policy = get_random_policy(states, actions)
    Q = {s: {a: 0 for a in actions} for s in states}
    Q_n = {s: {a: 0 for a in actions} for s in states}
    for i in range(n_iter):
        if i % 10000 == 0:
            print("Iteration:", i)
        trajectory = get_trajectory(env, policy)
        G = 0
        T = len(trajectory) - 1
        for t, sar in enumerate(reversed(trajectory)):
            s, a, r = sar
            G = r + gamma * G
            first_visit = True
```

```
            for j in range(T - t):
                s_j = trajectory[j][0]
                a_j = trajectory[j][1]
                if (s, a) == (s_j, a_j):
                    first_visit = False
            if first_visit:
                Q[s][a] = Q_n[s][a] * Q[s][a] + G
                Q_n[s][a] += 1
                Q[s][a] /= Q_n[s][a]
                a_best = max(Q[s].items(),
                             key=operator.itemgetter(1))[0]
                policy[s] = get_eps_greedy(actions,
                                           eps,
                                           a_best)
    return policy, Q, Q_n
```

This is very similar to the first-visit MC prediction method, with the following key differences:

a) Instead of estimating the state values, $v(s)$, we estimate the action values, $q(s, a)$.

b) To explore all state-action pairs, we use ε-greedy policies.

c) This is a first-visit approach, but instead of checking if the state appeared earlier in the trajectory, we check if the state-action pair appeared before in the trajectory before we update the $q(s, a)$ estimate.

d) Whenever we update the $q(s, a)$ estimate of a state-action pair, we also update the policy to assign the highest probability to the action that maximizes the $q(s, a)$, which is $\arg\max_a q(s, a)$.

3. Use the algorithm to optimize the food truck policy.

```
policy, Q, Q_n = on_policy_first_visit_mc(foodtruck,
                                          300000,
                                          0.05,
                                          1)
```

4. Display the `policy` dictionary. You will see that it is the optimal one that we found earlier with DP methods.

```
{('Mon', 0):{0:0.01, 100:0.01, 200:0.01, 300:0.01,
400:0.96},

...
```

That's it! This algorithm does not use any knowledge of the environment dynamics, unlike the DP methods. The agent learns from its interaction with the (simulation of the) environment! And, when we run the algorithm long enough, it converges to the optimal policy.

Great job! Next, let's proceed to off-policy MC control.

Off-policy Monte Carlo control

In an off-policy approach, we have a set of samples (trajectories) collected under some behavior policy b, yet we would like to use that experience to estimate the state and action values under a target policy π. This requires us to use a trick called **importance sampling**. Let's look into what it is next, and then describe the off-policy Monte Carlo control.

Importance sampling

Let's start describing importance sampling in a simple game setting, in which you roll a six-sided die. Depending on what comes up on the die, you receive a random reward. This could be something like this: If it comes 1, you get a reward from a normal distribution with mean 10 and variance 25. There are similar hidden reward distributions for all outcomes, which are unknown to you. Let's denote the reward you receive when the face x comes up by the random variable $H(x), x \in \{1, ... 6\}$.

You want to estimate the expected reward after a single roll, which is

$$E[H] = \sum_{x=1}^{6} E[H(x)]p(x)$$

where $p(x)$ is the probability of observing side x.

Now, assume that you have two dice to choose from, A and B, with different probability distributions. You first pick A, and role the die n times. Your observations are as in the table below:

i	1	2	3	4	5	...	n
x_i	2	6	6	1	3	...	4
$h_i(x_i)$	10	23	0	94	21	...	32

Table 5.1 – Observed rewards after n rolls with die A

Here $h_i(x_i)$ denotes the reward observed after i^{th} roll when the observed side is x_i. The estimated expected reward with die A, $\hat{\mu}_H^A$, is simply given by:

$$\hat{\mu}_H^A = \frac{1}{n} \sum_{i=1}^{n} h_i(x_i)$$

Now, the question is if we can use this data to estimate the expected reward with die B, such as, $\hat{\mu}_H^B$ without any new observations? The answer is yes if we know $p_A(x)$ and $p_B(x)$. Here is how.

In the current estimation, each observation has a weight of 1. Importance sampling suggests scaling these weights according to p_B. Now, consider the observation $(x_1 = 2, h_1(2) = 10)$. If, with die B, we are three times as likely to observe $x = 2$ compared to die A, then we increase the weight of this observation in the sum to 3. More formally, we do the following:

$$\hat{\mu}_H^B = \frac{1}{n} \sum_{i=1}^{n} \frac{p_B(x_i)}{p_A(x_i)} h_i(x_i)$$

Here, the ratio $\rho_x = \frac{p_B(x)}{p_A(x)} = \frac{p_{new}(x)}{p_{old}(x)}$ is called the importance sampling ratio. By the way, the above estimation, $\hat{\mu}_H^B$, is called the **ordinary importance sampling**. We can also normalize the new estimate with respect to the new weights and obtain a **weighted importance sampling** as below:

$$\hat{\mu}_H^B = \frac{\sum_{i=1}^{n} \rho_{x_i} h_i(x_i)}{\sum_{i=1}^{n} \rho_{x_i}}$$

Now, after this detour, let's go back to using this to get off-policy predictions. In the context of Monte Carlo prediction, observing a particular side of the die corresponds to observing a particular trajectory; and the die reward corresponds to the total return.

If you are thinking "well, we don't really know the probability of observing a particular trajectory, that's why we are using Monte Carlo methods, don't we?" You are right, but we don't need to. Here is why. Starting in some s_t, the probability of observing a trajectory $a_t, s_{t+1}, a_{t+1}, ..., s_T$ under a behavior policy b is as follows:

$$\Pr\{a_t, s_{t+1}, a_{t+1}, ..., s_T | s_t; a_{t:T-1} \sim b\} = b(a_t|s_t) \cdot p(s_{t+1}|s_t, a_t)$$
$$\cdot\, b(a_{t+1}|s_{t+1}) \cdot p(s_{t+2}|s_{t+1}, a_{t+1}) \cdot ... \cdot p(s_T|s_{T-1}, a_{T-1})$$
$$= \Pi_{k=t}^{T-1} b(a_k|s_k) p(s_{k+1}|s_k, a_k)$$

The expression is the same for the target policy, except π replaces b. Now, when we calculate the importance sampling ratio, the transition probabilities cancel out and we end up with the following (Sutton & Barto, 2018):

$$\rho_{t:T-1} \triangleq \Pi_{k=t}^{T-1} \frac{\pi(a_k|s_k)}{b(a_k|s_k)}$$

With that, we go from estimating the expectation under the behavior policy

$$E[G_t|s] = v_b(s)$$

to estimating the expectation under the target policy

$$E[\rho_{t:T-1} G_t|s] = v_\pi(s).$$

Let's close this section with a few notes on importance sampling before we implement it:

- In order to be able to use the samples obtained under behavior policy b to estimate the state and action values under π, it is required to have $b(a|s) > 0$ if $\pi(a|s) > 0$. Since we would not want to impose what a could be taken under the target policy, b is usually chosen as a soft policy.

- In the weighted importance sampling, if the denominator is zero, then the estimate is considered zero.

- The formulas above ignored the discount in the return, which is a bit more complicated to deal with.

- The observed trajectories can be chopped with respect to the first-visit or every-visit rule.

- The ordinary importance sampling is unbiased but can have very high variance. The weighted importance sampling, on the other hand, is biased but usually has much lower variance, hence preferred in practice.

This was a quite detour, and we hope you are still there! If you are, let's go back to coding!

Application to the inventory replenishment problem

In our application of the off-policy Monte Carlo method, we use the weighted importance sampling. The behavior policy is chosen as an ϵ-greedy policy, yet the target is a greedy policy maximizing the action-value for each state. Also, we use an incremental method to update the state and action value estimates as below (Sutton & Barto, 2018).

$$W_i = \rho_{t_i:T-1}$$

$$V_n := \frac{\sum_{k=1}^{n-1} W_k G_k}{\sum_{k=1}^{n-1} W_k}, \quad n \geq 2$$

$$V_{n+1} := V_n + \frac{W_n}{C_n}(G_n - V_n), \quad n \geq 1$$

And this:

$$C_{n+1} := C_n + W_{n+1}.$$

Now, the implementation can be done as follows:

1. Let's first define the function for the incremental implementation of the off-policy Monte Carlo.

```python
def off_policy_mc(env, n_iter, eps, gamma):
    np.random.seed(0)
    states = env.state_space
    actions = env.action_space
    Q = {s: {a: 0 for a in actions} for s in states}
    C = {s: {a: 0 for a in actions} for s in states}
    target_policy = {}
    behavior_policy = get_random_policy(states,
                                        actions)
    for i in range(n_iter):
        if i % 10000 == 0:
```

```
                        print("Iteration:", i)
                trajectory = get_trajectory(env,
                                            behavior_policy)
            G = 0
            W = 1
            T = len(trajectory) - 1
            for t, sar in enumerate(reversed(trajectory)):
                s, a, r = sar
                G = r + gamma * G
                C[s][a] += W
                Q[s][a] += (W/C[s][a]) * (G - Q[s][a])
                a_best = max(Q[s].items(),
                            key=operator.itemgetter(1))[0]
                target_policy[s] = a_best
                behavior_policy[s] = get_eps_greedy(actions,
                                                    eps,
                                                    a_best)
                if a != target_policy[s]:
                    break
                W = W / behavior_policy[s][a]
        target_policy = {s: target_policy[s] for s in states}
        return target_policy, Q
```

2. We use the off-policy MC to optimize the food truck inventory replenishment policy.

```
policy, Q = off_policy_mc(foodtruck, 300000, 0.05, 1)
```

3. Finally, display the obtained policy. You will see that it is the optimal one!

```
{('Mon', 0): 400,
 ('Tue', 0): 400,
 ('Tue', 100): 300,
 ('Tue', 200): 200,
 ('Tue', 300): 100,
 ('Wed', 0): 400,
 ...
```

Yay! We are done with the Monte Carlo methods for now. Congratulations, this was not the easiest part! You deserve a break, and next, we will dive into yet another very important topic: Temporal-difference learning.

Temporal-difference learning

The first class of methods to solve MDP we covered in this chapter was DP, which

- Requires to completely know the environment dynamics to be able find the optimal solution.
- Allow us to progress toward the solution with one-step updates of the value functions.

We then covered the MC methods, which

- Only require the ability to sample from the environment, therefore learn from experience, as opposed to knowing the environment dynamics - a huge advantage over DP,
- But need to wait for a complete episode trajectory to update a policy.

Temporal-difference (TD) methods are, in some sense, the best of both worlds: They learn from experience, and they can update the policy after each step by **bootstrapping**. This comparison of TD to DP and MC is illustrated in Table 5.2.

	Dynamic Programming	Monte Carlo Methods	TD Learning
Learns from experience, without knowing environment dynamics	X	✓	✓
Uses bootstrapping	✓	X	✓
Updates policies with partial episode trajectories		X	✓

Table 5.2 – Comparison of DP, MC, and TD learning methods

As a result, TD methods are central in RL, and you will encounter them again and again in various forms. In this section, you will learn how to implement TD methods in tabular form. Modern RL algorithms, which we will cover in the following chapters, implement TD methods with function approximations such as neural networks.

One-step TD learning: TD(0)

TD methods can update a policy after a single state transition or multiple ones. The former version is called one-step TD learning, or TD(0), and it is easier to implement compared to n-step TD learning. We start covering one-step TD learning with the prediction problem. We then introduce an on-policy method, Sarsa, and then an off-policy algorithm, the famous Q-learning.

TD prediction

Remember how we can write the state-value function of a policy π in terms of one-step reward and the value of the next state.

$$v_\pi(s) \triangleq E_\pi[R_{t+1} + \gamma v_\pi(S_{t+1})|S_t = s]$$

When the agent takes an action under policy π while in state S, it observes three random variables realized.

- $A_t = a$
- $R_{t+1} = r$
- $S_{t+1} = s'$

We already know the probability of observing a as part of the policy, but the latter two come from the environment. The observed quantity $r + \gamma v_\pi(s')$ gives us a new estimate for $v_\pi(s)$ based on a single sample. Of course, we don't want to completely discard the existing estimate and replace it with the new one. Because, the transitions are usually random, and we could have as well observed completely different S_{t+1} and R_{t+1} values even with the same action $A_t = a$. *The idea in TD learning is that we use this observation to update the existing estimate $\hat{v}_\pi(s)$ by moving it in the direction of this new estimate.* And the step-size $\alpha \in (0,1]$ controls how aggressively we move towards the new estimate. More formally, we use the following update rule.

$$\hat{v}_\pi(s) := (1 - \alpha)\hat{v}_\pi(s) + \alpha(r + \gamma v_\pi(s'))$$
$$= \hat{v}_\pi(s) + \alpha[r + \gamma v_\pi(s') - \hat{v}_\pi(s)]$$

The term in the square brackets is called the **TD error**. As obvious from the name, it estimates how much the current state-value estimate of $S_t = s$, $\hat{v}_\pi(s)$ is off from the truth based on the latest observation. $\alpha = 0$ would completely ignore the new signal while $\alpha = 1$ would completely ignore the existing estimate. Again, since a single observation is often noisy, and the new estimate itself uses another erroneous estimate $(v_\pi(S_{t+1}))$; the new estimate cannot be solely relied on. Therefore, the α value is chosen between 0 and 1, and often closer to 0.

With that, it is trivial to implement a TD prediction method to evaluate a given policy π and estimate the state values. Follow along to use TD prediction to evaluate the base policy in the food truck example:

1. First, we implement the TD prediction as described above as in the following function.

```python
def one_step_td_prediction(env, policy,
                            gamma, alpha, n_iter):
    np.random.seed(0)
    states = env.state_space
    v = {s: 0 for s in states}
    s = env.reset()
    for i in range(n_iter):
        a = choose_action(s, policy)
        s_next, reward, done, info = env.step(a)
        v[s] += alpha * (reward +
                        gamma * v[s_next] - v[s])
        if done:
            s = env.reset()
        else:
            s = s_next
    return v
```

This function simply simulates a given environment using a specified policy over a specified number of iterations. After each observation, it does a one-step TD update using the given α step size and the discount factor γ.

2. Next, we get the base policy as defined by the `base_policy` function we introduced before.

```python
policy = base_policy(foodtruck.state_space)
```

3. Then, let's estimate the state values using TD prediction for $\gamma = 1$ and $\alpha = 0.01$ over 100K steps.

```
one_step_td_prediction(foodtruck, policy, 1, 0.01,
   100000)
```

4. After rounding, the state-value estimates will look like the following.

```
{('Mon', 0): 2507.0,
 ('Tue', 0): 1956.0
...
```

If you go back to the DP methods section and check what the true state values are under the base policy, which we obtained using the policy evaluation algorithm, you will see that the TD estimates are very much in line with them.

Great! We have successfully evaluated a given policy using the TD prediction and things are working as expected. On the other hand, just like with the MC methods, we know that we have to estimate the action values to be able to improve the policy and find an optimal one in the absence of the environment dynamics. Next, we look into two different methods, Sarsa and Q-learning, which do exactly that.

On-policy control with Sarsa

With slight addition and modifications to the TD(0), we can turn it into an optimal control algorithm. Namely, we will:

- Ensure that we always have a soft policy, such as ϵ-greedy, to try all actions for a given state over time.

- Estimate the action values.

- Improve the policy based on the action-value estimates.

And we will do all of these at each step and using the observations $S_t = s, A_t = a, R_{t+1} = r, S_{t+1} = s', A_{t+1} = a'$, hence the name **Sarsa**. In particular, the action values are updated as follows:

$$\hat{q}_\pi(s,a) := \hat{q}_\pi(s,a) + \alpha[r + \gamma\hat{q}_\pi(s',a') - \hat{q}_\pi(s,a)]$$

Now, let's dive into the implementation!

1. We define the function `sarsa`, which will take as the arguments the environment, the discount factor γ, the exploration parameter ϵ, the learning step size α. Also, implement the usual initializations.

```python
def sarsa(env, gamma, eps, alpha, n_iter):
    np.random.seed(0)
    states = env.state_space
    actions = env.action_space
    Q = {s: {a: 0 for a in actions} for s in states}
    policy = get_random_policy(states, actions)
    s = env.reset()
    a = choose_action(s, policy)
```

2. Next, we implement the algorithm loop, in which we simulate the environment for a single step, observe r and s', choose the next action a' based on s' and the ϵ-greedy policy, and update the action-value estimates.

```python
    for i in range(n_iter):
        if i % 100000 == 0:
            print("Iteration:", i)
        s_next, reward, done, info = env.step(a)
        a_best = max(Q[s_next].items(),
                     key=operator.itemgetter(1))[0]
        policy[s_next] = get_eps_greedy(actions, eps, a_best)
        a_next = choose_action(s_next, policy)
        Q[s][a] += alpha * (reward
                            + gamma * Q[s_next][a_next]
                            - Q[s][a])
        if done:
            s = env.reset()
            a_best = max(Q[s].items(),
                         key=operator.itemgetter(1))[0]
            policy[s] = get_eps_greedy(actions,
                                       eps, a_best)
            a = choose_action(s, policy)
        else:
```

```
        s = s_next
        a = a_next
    return policy, Q
```

3. Then, let's execute the algorithm with a selection of hyper-parameters, such as
    $\gamma = 1, \epsilon = 0.1, \alpha = 0.05$ and over 1M iterations.

```
policy, Q = sarsa(foodtruck, 1, 0.1, 0.05, 1000000)
```

4. The `policy` we obtain is the following:

```
{('Mon', 0): {0: 0.02, 100: 0.02, 200: 0.02, 300: 0.02,
400: 0.92},
 ('Tue', 0): {0: 0.02, 100: 0.02, 200: 0.02, 300: 0.92,
400: 0.02},
 ('Tue', 100): {0: 0.02, 100: 0.02, 200: 0.02, 300: 0.92,
400: 0.02},
...
```

Note that the exploratory actions would be ignored when implementing this
policy after training, and we would simply always pick the action with the highest
probability for each state.

5. The action values, for example, for the state (Monday, 0) (accessed via `Q[('Mon',
0)]`), are as the following.

```
{0: 2049.95351191411,
 100: 2353.5460655683123,
 200: 2556.736260693101,
 300: 2558.210868908282,
 400: 2593.7601273913133}
```

And that's it! We have successfully implemented the TD(0) algorithm for our example.
Notice that, however, the policy we obtain is a near-optimal one, not the optimal one we
obtained with the DP methods. There are also inconsistencies in the policy, such as having
a policy of buying 300 patties both when in states (Tuesday, 0) and (Tuesday, 100). There
are several culprits for not getting the optimal policy:

- Sarsa converges to an optimal solution in the limit, such as, when $n_{iter} \to \infty$. In
  practice, we run the algorithm for a limited number of steps. Try increasing n_{iter}
  and you will see that the policy (usually) will get better.

- The learning rate α is a hyperparameter that needs to be tuned. The speed of the convergence depends on this selection.

- This is an on-policy algorithm. Therefore, the action values reflect the exploration due the ϵ-greedy policy, which is not what we really want in this example. Because, after training, there will be no exploration while following the policy in practice (since we need the exploration just to discover the best actions for each state). The policy we would be using in practice is not the same as the policy we estimated the action values for.

Next, we turn to Q-learning, which is an off-policy TD method.

Off-policy control with Q-Learning

As mentioned above, we would like to isolate the action-value estimates from the exploration effect, which means having an off-policy method. Q-learning is such an approach, which makes it very powerful, and as a result, a very popular one.

Here are how the action values are updated in Q-learning:

$$\hat{q}_\pi(s,a) := \hat{q}_\pi(s,a) + \alpha \left[r + \gamma \max_u \hat{q}_\pi(s',u) - \hat{q}_\pi(s,a) \right]$$

Notice that instead of $\gamma \hat{q}_\pi(s',a')$, we have the term $\gamma \max_u \hat{q}_\pi(s',u)$. The difference may look small, but it is key. *It means that the action the agent uses to update the action-value, u, is not necessarily the one it will take in the next step when in $S_{t+1} = s'$, $A_{t+1} = a'$. Instead, u is an action that maximizes $\hat{q}_\pi(s',\cdot)$, just like what we would use if not in training.* As a result, no exploratory actions are involved in action-value estimates and they are aligned with the policy that would be followed after training.

It means the action the agent takes in the next step, such as, $A_{t+1} = a'$ is not necessarily used in the update. Instead, we use the maximum action-value for the state $S_{t+1} = s'$, i.e., $\max_u \hat{q}_\pi(s',u)$. Such an action u is what we would use after training with those action-values, hence no exploratory actions are involved in action-value estimations.

The implementation of Q-learning is only slightly different than that of Sarsa. Let's go ahead and see Q-learning in action:

1. We start with defining the q_learning function with the usual initializations.

```
def q_learning(env, gamma, eps, alpha, n_iter):
    np.random.seed(0)
    states = env.state_space
```

```
actions = env.action_space
Q = {s: {a: 0 for a in actions} for s in states}
policy = get_random_policy(states, actions)
s = env.reset()
```

2. Then, we implement the main loop, where the action the agent takes in s comes from the ϵ-greedy policy. During the update, the maximum of $q_\pi(s',\cdot)$ is used.

```
for i in range(n_iter):
    if i % 100000 == 0:
        print("Iteration:", i)
    a_best = max(Q[s].items(),
                 key=operator.itemgetter(1))[0]
    policy[s] = get_eps_greedy(actions, eps, a_best)
    a = choose_action(s, policy)
    s_next, reward, done, info = env.step(a)
    Q[s][a] += alpha * (reward
                 + gamma * max(Q[s_next].values())
                 - Q[s][a])
    if done:
        s = env.reset()
    else:
        s = s_next
```

3. We return the policy as stripped of the exploratory actions after the main loop is finished.

```
policy = {s: {max(policy[s].items(),
              key=operator.itemgetter(1))[0]: 1}
          for s in states}
return policy, Q
```

4. Finally, we execute the algorithm with a selection of the hyper-parameters, such as the following.

```
policy, Q = q_learning(foodtruck, 1, 0.1, 0.01, 1000000)
```

5. Observe the returned `policy`.

```
{('Mon', 0): {400: 1},
 ('Tue', 0): {400: 1},
 ('Tue', 100): {300: 1},
 ('Tue', 200): {200: 1},
 ('Tue', 300): {100: 1},
 ...
```

You will see that this hyper-parameter set gives you the optimal policy (or something close to it depending on how randomization plays out in your case).

That concludes our discussion on Q-learning. Next, let's discuss how these approaches can be extended to n-step learning.

n-step TD Learning

In Monte Carlo methods, we collected complete episodes before making a policy update. With TD(0), on the other extreme, we updated the value estimates and the policy after a single transition in the environment. One could possibly find a sweet spot by following a path in between by updating the policy after n-steps of transitions. For $n = 2$, the two-step return looks like the following:

$$G_{t:t+2} \triangleq R_{t+1} + \gamma R_{t+2} + \gamma^2 v_\pi(S_{t+2})$$

And the general form is the following:

$$G_{t:t+n} \triangleq R_{t+1} + \gamma R_{t+2} + \cdots + \gamma^{n-1} R_{t+n} + \gamma^n v_\pi(S_{t+n})$$

This form can be used in the TD update to reduce the weight of the $v_\pi(S_{t+n})$ estimates used in bootstrapping, which could be especially inaccurate at the beginning of the training. We don't include the implementation here as it gets a bit messy, but still wanted to bring this alternative to your attention for you to have it in your toolkit.

With that, we have completed the TD methods! Before finishing the chapter, let's take a closer look into the importance of the simulations in RL.

Understanding the importance of the simulation in reinforcement learning

As we mentioned multiple times so far, and especially in the first chapter when we talked about RL success stories, RL's hunger for data is orders of magnitude greater than that of deep supervised learning. That is why it takes many months to train some complex RL agents, over millions and billions of iterations. Since it is often impractical to collect such data in a physical environment, we heavily rely on simulation models in training RL agents. This brings some challenges along with it:

- Many businesses don't have a simulation model of their processes. This makes it challenging to bring the RL technology to the use of such companies.

- When a simulation model exists, it is often too simplistic to capture the real-world dynamics. As a result, RL models could easily overfit to the simulation environment and may fail in deployment. It takes significant time and resources to calibrate and validate a simulation model to make it sufficiently reflect the reality.

- In general, deploying an RL agent that is trained in simulation in real world is not easy, because, well, they are two different worlds. This is against the core principle in machine learning that says the training and the test should follow the same distribution. This is known as the **simulation-to-real (sim2real)** gap.

- Increased fidelity in simulation comes with slowness and compute resource consumption, which is a real disadvantage for fast experimentation and RL model development.

- Many simulation models are not generic enough to cover scenarios that have not been encountered in the past but likely to be encountered in the future.

- Many commercial simulation software could be hard to integrate (due to the lack of a proper API) with the languages RL packages are naturally available in, such as Python.

- Even when the integration is possible, the simulation software may not be flexible enough to work with the algorithms. For example, it may not reveal the state of the environment, reset it when needed, define terminal states etc.

- Many simulation vendors allow limited number of sessions per license, whereas RL model development is the fastest when you can run thousands of simulation environments in parallel.

In this book, we will cover some techniques to overcome some of these challenges, such as domain randomization for sim2real gap and offline RL for environments without a simulation. However, the key message of this section is that you usually should invest in your simulation model to get the best out of RL. In particular, your simulation model should be fast, accurate, and scalable to many sessions.

With this, we conclude this chapter. Great work! This marks a milestone in our journey with this book. We have come a long way and built a solid foundation of RL solution approaches! Next, let's summarize what we have learned and see what is upcoming in the next chapter.

Summary

In this chapter, we covered three important approaches to solving MDPs: Dynamic programming, Monte Carlo methods, and temporal-difference learning. We have seen that while DP provides exact solutions to MDPs, it requires knowing the precise dynamics of an environment. Monte Carlo and TD learning methods, on the other hand, explore in the environment and learn from experience. TD learning, in particular, can learn from even a single step transitions in the environment. Within the chapter, we also presented on-policy methods, which estimate the value functions for a behavior policy, while off-policy methods for a target policy. Finally, we discussed the importance of the simulator in RL experiments and what to pay attention to when working with one.

Next, we take our journey to a next level and dive into deep reinforcement learning, which will enable us to solve some complex real-world problems. Particularly, in the next chapter, we cover deep Q-learning in detail.

See you there!

References

1. Sutton, R. S., & Barto, A. G. (2018). *Reinforcement Learning: An Introduction.* A Bradford Book. URL: `http://incompleteideas.net/book/the-book.html`

2. Barto, A. (2006). Reinforcement learning. University of Massachusetts - Amherst CMPSCI 687. URL: `https://www.andrew.cmu.edu/course/10-703/textbook/BartoSutton.pdf`

3. Goldstick, J. (2009). Importance sampling. Statistics 406: Introduction to Statistical Computing at University of Michigan. URL: `http://dept.stat.lsa.umich.edu/~jasoneg/Stat406/lab7.pdf`

Section 2: Deep Reinforcement Learning

This part covers state-of-the-art RL algorithms in depth and gives you a solid understanding of the advantages and disadvantages of each algorithm.

This section contains the following chapters:

- *Chapter 6, Deep Q-Learning at Scale*
- *Chapter 7, Policy-Based Methods*
- *Chapter 8, Model-Based Methods*
- *Chapter 9, Multi-Agent Reinforcement Learning*

6

Deep Q-Learning at Scale

In the previous chapter, we covered **dynamic programming (DP)** methods to solve Markov decision processes, and then mentioned that they suffer two important limitations: DP i) assumes complete knowledge of the environment's reward and transition dynamics; ii) uses tabular representations of state and actions, which is not scalable as the number of possible state-action combinations is too big in many realistic applications. We have addressed the former by introducing the **Monte Carlo (MC)** and **temporal-difference (TD)** methods, which learn from their interactions with the environment (often in simulation) without needing to know the environment dynamics. On the other hand, the latter is yet to be addressed, and this is where deep learning comes in. **Deep reinforcement learning (deep RL or DRL)** is about utilizing neural networks' representational power to learn policies for a wide variety of situations.

As great as it sounds, though, it is quite tricky to make function approximators work well in the context of RL since the theoretical convergence guarantees that we had in tabular Q-learning are lost. Therefore, the story of deep Q-learning, to a great extent, is about the tricks that make neural networks work well for RL. This chapter takes you to a tour of what fails with function approximators and how to address them. Once we make neural networks get along with RL, we then face another challenge: the great hunger for data in deep RL that is even more severe than that of deep supervised learning. This requires us developing highly scalable deep RL algorithms, which we also do in this chapter for deep Q-learning using a powerful library, called **Ray**. Finally, we introduce you to RLlib, a production-grade RL library based on Ray. So, the focus throughout the chapter will be to deepen of your understanding of the connections between various deep Q-learning approaches, what works and why; and leveraging Ray and RLlib to build scalable RL implementations.

Without further ado, let's get started! Specifically, here is what this chapter covers:

- From tabular Q-learning to deep Q-learning

- Deep Q-Networks

- Extensions to DQN: Rainbow

- Distributed deep Q-learning

- Implementing scalable deep Q-learning algorithms using Ray

- Using RLlib for production-grade deep reinforcement learning

From tabular Q-learning to deep Q-learning

When we covered the tabular Q-learning method in *Chapter 5, Solving the Reinforcement Learning Problem*, it should have been obvious that we cannot really extend those methods to most real-life scenarios. Think about an RL problem which uses images as input. A 128 × 128 image with three 8-bit color channels would lead to $256^{128 \times 128 \times 3}$ possible images, a number that your calculator won't be able to calculate. For this very reason, we need to use function approximators to represent the value function. Given their success in supervised and unsupervised learning, neural networks / deep learning emerges as the clear choice here. On the other hand, as we mentioned in the introduction, the convergence guarantees of tabular Q-learning fall apart when function approximators come in. This section introduces two deep Q-learning algorithms, the Neural Fitted Q-iteration and online Q-learning, and then discusses what does not go so well with them. With that, we set the stage for the modern deep Q-learning methods that we will discuss in the following sections.

Neural Fitted Q-iteration

The **Neural Fitted Q-iteration algorithm (NFQ)** aims to fit a neural network that represents the action values, the Q-function, to target Q-values, which are:

- Sampled from an environment, and

- Bootstrapped by the previously available Q-values (Riedmiller, 2015).

Let's first go into how NFQ works, and then discuss some practical considerations in NFQ and its limitations.

The algorithm

Recall that in tabular Q-learning, action values are learned from samples collected from the environment, which are (s, a, r, s') tuples, by repeatedly applying the following update rule.

$$Q(s, a) := Q(s, a) + \alpha \left[r + \gamma \max_{a'} Q(s', a') - Q(s, a) \right]$$

where Q represents an estimate of the action values of the optimal policy, q_* (and note that we started using the capital Q which is the convention in the deep RL literature). The goal is to update the existing estimate $Q(s, a)$ towards a "target" value, $y = r + \gamma \max_{a'} Q(s', a')$, by applying the *sampled Bellman optimality operator* to the sample (s, a, r, s'). NFQ has a similar logic with the following differences:

- Q-values are represented by a neural network parameterized by θ, instead of a table, which we denote by Q_θ.

- Instead of updating Q-values with each sample incrementally, NFQ collects a batch of samples from the environment and fit the neural network to the target values at once.

- There are multiple rounds of calculating the target values and fitting the parameters to be able to obtain new target values with the latest Q function.

After this overall description, here is the NFQ algorithm in detail:

1. Initialize θ and a policy π.

2. Collect a set of N samples $\{(s_i, a_i, r_i, s_i') \mid i = 1, ..., N\}$ using the policy π.

3. Apply the sampled Bellman optimality operator to obtain the target values, $y_i = r_i + \gamma \max_{a_i'} Q_\theta(s_i', a_i')$, to all samples $i = 1, ..., N$. Except, if s_i' is a terminal state, set $y_i = r_i$.

4. Obtain θ by minimizing the gap between Q_θ and the target values. More formally, $\theta := \arg\min_\theta \sum_{i=1}^{N} L(Q_\theta(s_i, a_i), y_i)$, where L is a loss function such as squared error, $\frac{1}{2}(Q_\theta(s_i, a_i) - y_i)^2$.

5. Update π with respect to the new Q_θ.

There can be numerous improvements that can be done on fitted Q-iterations, but it is not our focus here. Instead, next, we mention a couple of essential considerations while implementing the algorithm.

Practical considerations in fitted Q-iteration

To make fitted Q-iteration work in practice, there are several important points to pay attention to, which we discuss here:

- Policy π should be a soft policy allowing enough exploration of different state-action pairs during sample collection, such as an ϵ-greedy policy. The rate of exploration, therefore, is a hyperparameter.

- Setting ϵ too large could be problematic as some states could only be reached after sticking with a good policy (once it starts to improve) for a number of steps. An example is that, in a video game, later levels are reached only after finishing the earlier steps successfully, which a highly random policy is unlikely to achieve.

- When the target values are obtained, chances are these values use inaccurate estimates for the action values because we bootstrap with inaccurate $Q_\theta(s_i', a_i')$. Therefore, we need to repeat steps 2 and 3 K times to hopefully obtain more accurate target values in the next round. This gives us another hyperparameter, K.

- The policy that we initially used to collect samples is probably not good enough to lead the agent to some parts of the state space, similar to the case with high ϵ. Therefore, it is usually a good idea to collect more samples after updating the policy, add them to the sample set and repeat the procedure.

- Note that this is an off-policy algorithm, so the samples could come from the chosen policy or somewhere else, such as an existing non-RL controller deployed in the environment.

Even with these improvements, in practice, it may be difficult to solve MDPs using NFQ. Let's look into the why in the next section.

Challenges with the fitted Q-iteration

Although there are some successful applications with the fitted Q-iteration, it suffers from several major drawbacks:

- It requires learning θ from scratch every time we repeat step 3 using the target batch on hand. In other words, step 3 involves an $^{\arg}\min_{\theta}()$ operator, as opposed a gradual update of θ with new data like we have in gradient descent. In some applications, RL models are trained over billions of samples. Training a neural network over billions of samples again and again with updated target values is impractical.

- Sarsa and Q-learning-like methods have convergence guarantees in the tabular case. However, as we mentioned, such theoretical guarantees are lost when function approximations are used.

- Using function approximations with Q-learning, an off-policy method using bootstrapping, is especially unstable, which is called **the deadly triad**.

Before going into how to address these, let's dive into a bit more detail with the latter two points. Now, this will involve a bit theory, understanding which is going to help you gain a deeper intuition about the challenges in deep RL. On the other hand, if you don't feel like it, feel free to skip to the Online Q-learning section.

Convergence issues with function approximators

To explain you why the convergence guarantees with Q-learning are lost when function approximators are used, let's remember why tabular Q-learning converges in the first place:

- The definition of $q_\pi(s, a)$ is the expected discounted return if we deviate from policy π only once at the beginning while in state s by choosing action a, but then following the policy for the rest of the horizon:

$$q_\pi(s, a) = E[R_{t+1} + \gamma v_\pi(S_{t+1}) \mid S_t = s, A_t = a]$$

- The Bellman optimality operator, denoted by $\mathcal{B}$, takes an action-value function q, s and a, and maps to the following quantity:

$$\mathcal{B}q(s, a) = E\left[R_{t+1} + \gamma \max_{a'} q(S_{t+1}, a') \mid S_t = s, A_t = a\right]$$

Note the use of $^{\max}_a q(s', a)$ inside the expectation rather than following some other policy π. $\mathcal{B}$ is an operator, a function, *different than the definition of the action-value function.*

- If and only if the action value function is optimal, $\mathcal{B}$ maps q back to q for all s and a.

$$q_*(s, a) = E\left[R_{t+1} + \gamma \max_{a'} q_*(S_{t+1}, a') \mid S_t\right]$$

$$q_* = \mathcal{B}q_*$$

More formally, the unique fixed-point of the operator $\mathcal{B}$ is the optimal q, denoted by q_*. This is what the Bellman optimality equation is about.

- $\mathcal{B}$ is a **contraction** mapping, which means that every time we apply it to any two different action-value functions, such as q and q' vectors whose entries are some action-value estimates for all s and a, they get close to each other. This is with respect to the L_∞ norm, which is the maximum of the absolute differences between the (s, a) tuples of q and q':

$$\|Bq - Bq'\|_\infty \le k\|q - q'\|_\infty$$

where $0 < k < 1$.

- If we pick one of these action-value vectors to be the optimal one, we obtain the following relation:

$$\|Bq - q_*\|_\infty \le k\|q - q_*\|_\infty$$

This means that we can get closer and closer to the q_* by starting with some arbitrary q, repeatedly applying the Bellman operator and updating the q values.

- With these, $\mathcal{B}$ turns into an update rule to obtain q_* from an arbitrary q, very similar to how the value iteration method works.

Now, notice that fitting a neural network to a batch of sampled targets does not actually guarantee making the action-value estimates closer to the optimal value for *each* (s, a) tuple. Because the fitting operation does not care about the individual errors -nor does it necessarily have the ability to do so, because it assumes a certain structure in the action-value function due to parametrization- but minimizes the average error. As a result, we lose the contraction property of the Bellman operation with respect to the L_∞ norm. Instead, NFQ fits θ to the target values with respect to an L_2 norm, which does not have the same convergence properties.

> **Info**
>
> For a detailed and more visual explanation of why the value function theory
> fails with function approximations, check out Prof. Sergey Levine's lecture at
> `https://youtu.be/doR5bMe-Wic?t=3957`, which also inspired
> this section. The entire course is available online, and it is a great resource for
> you to go deeper into the theory of reinforcement learning.

With that, now let's go into the famous deadly triad that gives another perspective into
why it is problematic to use function approximators with bootstrapping in off-policy
algorithms, such as Q-learning.

The deadly triad

(Sutton & Barto, 2018) coins the term the *deadly triad* that suggests an RL algorithm is
likely to diverge if it involves using all of the following:

- Function approximators,
- Bootstrapping,
- Off-policy sample collection.

They provide this simple example to give an intuition about the problem:

- Consider a part of an MDP that consists of two states, left and right.
- There is only one action on the left, which is to go right with a reward of 0.
- The observation in the left state is 1, and it is 2 in the right state.
- A simple linear function approximator is used to represent the action-values with
  one parameter, w.

This is represented in the following figure:

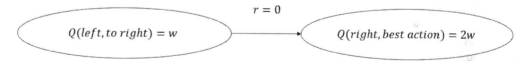

Figure 6.1 – A diverging MDP fragment (source – Sutton & Barto, 2018)

Now, imagine that a behavior policy only samples from the state on the left. Also imagine that the initial value of w is 10 and $\gamma = 0.99$. The TD error is then calculated as

$$\delta = r + \gamma Q(right, best\ action) - Q(left, to\ right)$$
$$= 0 + 0.99 \cdot 2w - w$$
$$= 0.98w$$
$$= 9.8$$

Now, if the linear function approximation is updated with the only data on hand, transition from left to right, say using $\alpha = 0.1$, then the new w becomes $10 + 0.1 \cdot 9.8 = 10.98$. *Note that this updates the action-value estimate of the right state as well.*

In the next round, the behavior policy again only samples from the left and the new TD error becomes:

$$\delta = 0.98w = 10.76$$

It is even greater than the first TD error! You can see how this will diverge eventually. The problem occurs due to:

- This is an off-policy method and the behavior policy happens to visit only one part of the state-action space.

- A function approximator is used, whose parameters are updated based on the limited sample we have, but the value estimates for the unvisited state-actions also get updated with that.

- We bootstrap and use the bad value estimates from the state-actions we never actually visited to calculate the target values.

This simple example illustrates how it can destabilize the RL methods when these three factors come together. For other examples and a more detailed explanation on the topic, we recommend you read the related sections in (Sutton & Barto, 2018).

Now that we have only talked about challenges, we finally start addressing them. Remember that NFQ required us to completely fit the entire neural network to the target values on hand and how we looked for a more gradual update. This is what online Q-learning gives us, which we introduce next. On the other hand, online Q-learning introduces other challenges, that we will address with deep Q-networks in the following section.

Online Q-learning

As we mentioned above, one of the disadvantages of fitted Q-iteration is that it requires finding the $\arg\min_{\theta} \sum_{i=1}^{N} L(Q_\theta(s_i, a_i), y_i)$ with each batch of samples, which is impractical when the problem is complex and requires a lot of data for training. Online Q-learning is the other extreme: it takes a gradient step to update θ after observing every single sample (s_i, a_i, r_i, s_i'). Next, let's go into the details of the online Q-learning algorithm.

The algorithm

The online Q-learning algorithm works as follows:

1. Initialize θ_0 and a policy π_0, initialize the environment and observe s_0.

    For $t = 1$ to T do:

2. Take some action a_{t-1} using a policy π_{t-1} given the state s_{t-1}, observe r_t and s_t, which form the tuple $(s_{t-1}, a_{t-1}, r_t, s_t)$.

3. Obtain the target value $y_t = r_t + \gamma \max_a Q_{\theta_{t-1}}(s_t, a)$, except, if s_t is a terminal state, set $y_t = r_t$.

4. Take a gradient step to update $\theta_t := \theta_{t-1} - \alpha \nabla_\theta L(Q_{\theta_{t-1}}(s_{t-1}, a_{t-1}), y_t)$, where α is the step size.

5. Update the policy to π_t with respect to the new Q_{θ_t}.

    End for

As you can see, the key difference compared to the NFQ is to update the neural network parameters after each (s, a, r, s') tuple sampled from the environment. Here are some additional considerations about online Q-learning:

*   Similar to the NFQ algorithm, we need a policy that continuously explores the state-action space. Again, this can be achieved using an ϵ-greedy policy or another soft policy.

*   Also similar to the fitted Q-iteration, the samples may come from a policy that is not relevant to what the Q network is suggesting, as this is an off-policy method.

Other than these, there can be numerous other improvements to the online Q-learning method. We will momentarily focus on deep Q-networks, a breakthrough improvement over Q-learning, rather than discussing somewhat less important tweaks to the online Q-learning. But before doing so, let's go into why it is difficult to train the online Q-learning in its current form.

Challenges with online Q-learning

The online Q-learning algorithm suffers from the following issues:

- **The gradient estimates are noisy**: Similar to the other gradient descent methods in machine learning, online Q-learning aims to estimate the gradient using samples. On the other hand, it uses a single sample while doing so, which results in noisy estimates that make it hard to optimize the loss function. Ideally, we should use a minibatch with more than one sample to estimate the gradient.

- **The gradient step is not truly gradient descent**: This is because $\nabla_\theta L(Q_{\theta_{t-1}}(s_{t-1}, a_{t-1}), y_t)$ includes y_i, which we treat as a constant while it is not. y_t itself depends on θ, yet we ignore this fact by not taking its derivative with respect to θ.

- **Target values are updated after each gradient step, which becomes a moving target the network is trying to learn from**: This is unlike supervised learning where the labels (of images, let's say) don't change based on what the model predicts; and it makes the learning very difficult.

- **The samples are not independent and identically distributed (i.i.d.)**: In fact, they are usually highly correlated since an MDP is a sequential decision setting and what we observe next highly depends on the actions we have taken earlier. This is another deviation from the classical gradient descent, which breaks its convergence properties.

Because of all these challenges, and what we mentioned in general in the NFQ section regarding the deadly triad, the online Q-learning algorithm is not quite a viable method to solve complex RL problems. This changed with the revolutionary work of **deep Q-networks (DQN)**, which addressed the latter two challenges we mentioned above. In fact, it is with the DQN that we started talking about deep reinforcement learning. So, without further ado, let's dive into discussing DQN.

Deep Q-networks

DQN is a seminal work by (Mnih et al., 2015) that made deep RL a viable approach to complex sequential control problems. The authors demonstrated that a single DQN architecture can achieve super-human level performance in many Atari games without any feature engineering, which created a lot of excitement regarding the progress of AI. Let's look into what makes DQN so effective compared to the algorithms we mentioned earlier.

Key concepts in deep Q-networks

DQN modifies online Q-learning with two important concepts by using experience replay and a target network, which greatly stabilize the learning. We describe these concepts next.

Experience replay

As mentioned earlier, simply using the experience sampled sequentially from the environment leads to highly correlated gradient steps. DQN, on the other hand, stores those experience tuples, (s_i, a_i, r_i, s'_i), in a replay buffer (memory), an idea that was introduced back in 1993 (Lin, 1993). During learning, the samples are drawn from this buffer uniformly at random, which eliminates the correlations between the samples used training the neural network and gives i.i.d.-like samples.

Another benefit of using experience replay over online Q-learning is that experience is reused rather than discarded, which reduces the amount of interaction necessary with the environment - an important benefit given the need for vast amounts of data in RL.

An interesting note about the experience replay is that there is evidence that a similar process is taking place in animal brains. Animals appear to be replaying their past experience in their hippocampus, which contributes to their learning (McClelland, 1995).

Target networks

Another problem with using bootstrapping with function approximations is that it creates a moving target to learn from. This makes an already-challenging undertaking, such as, training a neural network from noisy samples, a task that is destined for failure. The key insight presented by the authors is to create a copy of the neural network that is only used to generate the Q-value estimates used in sampled Bellman updates. Namely, the target value for sample j is obtained as:

$$y_j = r_j + \gamma \max_{a'_j} Q_{\theta'}\left(s'_j, a'_j\right)$$

where θ' is the parameters of a target network, which is updated every C time steps by setting $\theta' := \theta$.

Creating a lag in updating the target network potentially makes its action-value estimations slightly stale compared to the original network. On the other hand, in return, the target values become stable, and the original network can be trained.

Before giving you the full DQN algorithm, let's also discuss the loss function it uses.

The loss function

With the experience replay and the target network introduced, the DQN minimizes the following loss function:

$$L(\theta) = \mathbb{E}_{(s,a,r,s') \sim U(D)} \left[\left(r + \gamma \max_{a'} Q_{\theta'}(s',a') - Q_\theta(s,a) \right)^2 \right]$$

where D is the replay buffer, from which a minibatch of (s, a, r, s') tuples are drawn uniformly at random to update the neural network.

Now it's finally time to give the complete algorithm.

The DQN algorithm

The DQN algorithm consists of the following steps:

1. Initialize θ and a replay buffer D with a fixed capacity M. Set the target network parameters as $\theta' := \theta$.

2. Set the policy π to be an ϵ-greedy with respect to Q_θ.

3. Given the state s and the policy π, take an action a and observe r and s'. Add the transition (s, a, r, s') to the replay buffer D. If $|D| > M$, eject the oldest transition from the buffer.

4. If $|D| \geq N$, uniformly sample a random minibatch of N transitions from D, else return to step 2.

5. Obtain the target values, $y_j = r_j + \gamma \max_{a_j'} Q_{\theta'}(s_j', a_j')$, $j = 1, ..., N$; except, if s_j' is a terminal state, set $y_j = r_j$.

6. Take a gradient step to update θ, which is $\theta := \theta - \alpha \nabla_\theta J(\theta)$.

   Here, $J(\theta) = \frac{1}{N} \sum_{j=1}^{N} L(Q_\theta(s_j, a_j), y_j) = \frac{1}{N} \sum_{j=1}^{N} (Q_\theta(s_j, a_j) - y_j)^2$.

7. Every C steps, update the target network parameters, $\theta' := \theta$.

8. Return to step 1.

The DQN algorithm can be illustrated as in the diagram in *Figure 6.2*.

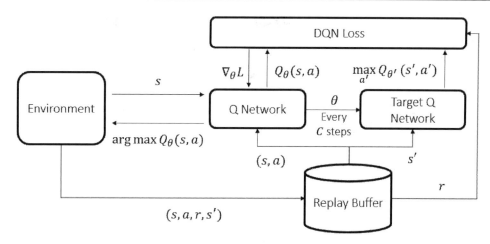

Figure 6.2 – DQN algorithm overview (source Nair et al., 2015)

After the seminal work of DQN, there have been many extensions proposed to improve it in various papers. (Hessel et al., 2018) combined some of the most important of those and called them Rainbow, which we turn to next.

Extensions to DQN: Rainbow

The Rainbow improvements bring in significant performance boost over the vanilla DQN and they have become standard in most Q-learning implementations. In this section, we discuss what those improvements are, how they help, and what their relative importance are. At the end, we talk how DQN and these extensions collectively overcome the deadly triad.

The extensions

There are six extensions to DQN included in the Rainbow algorithm. These are: i) double Q-learning, ii) prioritized replay, iii) dueling networks, iv) multi-step learning, v) distributional RL, and iv) noisy nets. Let's start describing them with double Q-learning.

Double Q-learning

One of the well-known issues in Q-learning is that the Q-value estimates we obtain during learning is higher than the true Q-values because of the maximization operation $\max_a Q_\theta(s, a)$. This phenomenon is called **maximization bias**, and the reason we run into it is that we do a maximization operation over noisy observations of the Q-values. As a result, we end up estimating not the maximum of the true values but the maximum of the possible observations.

For two simple illustrations of how this happens, consider the examples in *Figure 6.3*:

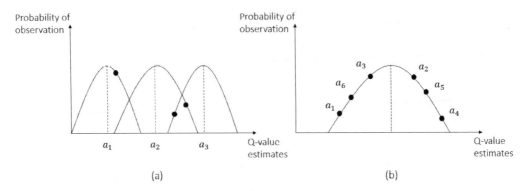

Figure 6.3 – Two examples of maximization bias

Figures 6.3 (a) and 6.3 (b) show the probability distributions of obtaining various Q-value estimates for the available actions for a given state s, where the vertical lines correspond to the true action-values.

- In (a), there are three available actions. After some round of sample collection, just by chance, the estimates we obtain happen to be $Q(s, a_2) > Q(s, a_3) > Q(s, a_1)$. Not only is the best action incorrectly predicted as a_2, but its action-value is overestimated.

- In (b), there six available actions with the same probability distribution of Q-value estimates. Although their true action-values are the same, when we take a random sample, an order will appear between them just by chance. Moreover, since we take the maximum of these noisy observations, chances are it will be above the true value and again the Q-value is overestimated.

Double Q-learning proposes a solution to the maximization bias by decoupling finding the maximizing action and obtaining an action-value estimate for it by using two separate action-value functions, Q_1 and Q_2. More formally, we find the maximizing action using one of the functions:

$$a^* = \arg\max_a Q_1(s, a)$$

Then obtain the action-value using the other function as $Q_2(s, a^*)$.

In tabular Q-learning, this requires the extra effort of maintaining two action-value functions. Q_1 and Q_2 are then swapped randomly in each step. On the other hand, DQN already proposes maintaining a target network with parameters θ' dedicated to providing action-value estimates for bootstrapping. Therefore, we implement double Q-learning on top of DQN to obtain the action-value estimate for the maximizing action as follows:

$$Q_{\theta'}\left(s, \arg\max_a Q_\theta(s, a)\right)$$

Then the corresponding loss function for the state-action pair (s_t, a_t) becomes:

$$\left(r_{t+1} + \gamma Q_{\theta'}\left(s, \arg\max_a Q_\theta(s_t, a)\right) - Q_\theta(s_t, a_t)\right)^2$$

That's it! This is how double Q-learning works in the context of DQN. Now, let's go into the next improvement, prioritized replay.

Prioritized replay

As we mentioned, DQN algorithm suggests sampling the experiences from the replay buffer uniformly at random. On the other hand, it is natural to expect that some of the experience will be more "interesting" than others, in the sense that there will be more to learn from them for the agent. This is especially the case in hard-exploration problems with sparse rewards where there are a lot of uninteresting "failure" cases and only a few "successes" with non-zero rewards. (Schaul et al., 2015) proposes using the TD-error to measure how "interesting" or "surprising" an experience is to the agent is. The probability of sampling a particular experience from the replay buffer is then set to be proportional to the TD-error. Namely, the probability of sampling an experience encountered at time t, p_t, has the following relationship with the TD error:

$$p_t \propto \left|r_{t+1} + \gamma \arg\max_{a'} Q_{\theta'}(s_t, a') - Q_\theta(s_t, a_t)\right|^\omega$$

where ω is a hyperparameter controlling the shape of the distribution. Note that for $\omega = 0$, this gives a uniform distribution over the experiences while larger ω values put more and more weight on experiences with large TD error.

Dueling networks

One of the common situations encountered in RL problems is that in some states, actions taken by the agent have little or no effect on the environment. As an example, consider the following:

- A robot moving in a grid world should avoid a "trap" state, from which the robot cannot escape through its actions.

- Instead, the environment randomly transitions the robot out of this state with some low probability.

- While in this state, the robot loses some reward points.

In this situation, the algorithm needs to estimate the value of the trap state, so that it knows it should avoid it. On the other hand, trying to estimate the individual action-values is meaningless as it would be just chasing the noise. It turns out that this harms the DQN's effectiveness.

Dueling networks propose a solution to this issue through an architecture that simultaneously estimates the state-value and the action **advantages** in parallel streams for a given state. The **advantage value** of an action in a given state, as it could be apparent from the term, is the additional expected cumulative reward that comes with choosing that action instead of what the policy in use, π, suggests. It is formally defined as follows:

$$A^\pi(s, a) = Q^\pi(s, a) - V^\pi(s)$$

So, choosing the action with the highest advantage is equivalent to choosing the action with the highest Q value.

By obtaining the Q values from the explicit representations of the state value and the action advantages, as represented in *Figure 6.4*, we enable the network to have a good representation of the state-value without having to accurately estimate each action-value for a given state.

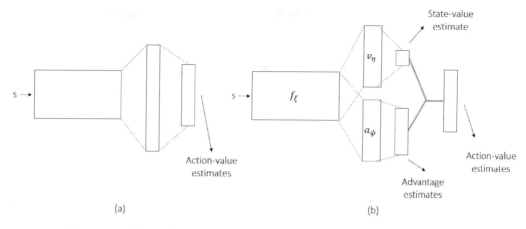

Figure 6.4 – (a) Regular DQN, and (b) dueling DQN (source: Wang et al., 2016)

At this point, you might expect that the action-value estimates are just obtained in this architecture using the formula we gave above. It turns out that this vanilla implementation does not work well. This is because this architecture alone does not enforce the network to learn the state and action values in the corresponding branches, because they are supervised indirectly through their sum. For example, the sum would not change if you were to subtract 100 from the state value estimate and add 100 to all advantage estimates. To overcome this issue of "identifiability," we need to remember this: In Q-learning, the policy is to pick the action with the highest Q value. Let's represent this best action with a^*. Then we have the following:

$$Q(s, a^*) = V(s)$$

which leads to $A(s, a^*) = 0$. To enforce this, one way of obtaining the action-value estimates is to use the following equation:

$$Q_\theta(s, a) = v_\eta\left(f_\xi(s)\right) + a_\psi\left(f_\xi(s), a\right) - \max_{a'} a_\psi\left(f_\xi(s), a'\right)$$

where f_ξ, v_η and a_ψ represents the common encoder, state-value, and advantage streams; and $\theta = \{\xi, \eta, \psi\}$. On the other hand, the authors use the following alternative which leads to a more stable training:

$$Q_\theta(s, a) = v_\eta\left(f_\xi(s)\right) + a_\psi\left(f_\xi(s), a\right) - \frac{\sum_{a'} a_\psi\left(f_\xi(s), a'\right)}{N_{actions}}$$

With this architecture, the authors obtained state-of-the-art results at the time on the Atari benchmarks, proving the value of the approach.

Next, let's look into another important improvement over DQN: multi-step learning.

Multi-step learning

In the previous chapter, we mentioned that a more accurate target value for a state-action pair can be obtained by using multi-step discounted rewards in the estimation obtained from the environment. In such cases, the Q-value estimates used in bootstrapping will be discounted more heavily, diminishing the impact of the inaccuracies of those estimates. Instead, more of the target value will come from the sampled rewards. More formally, the TD error in a multi-step setting becomes the following:

$$R_t^{(n)} \triangleq \sum_{k=0}^{n-1} \gamma^{(k)} r_{t+k+1}$$

$$R_t^{(n)} + \gamma^{(n)} \arg\max_{a'} Q_{\theta'}(s_{t+n}, a') - Q_\theta(s_t, a_t)$$

You can see that with increasing n, the impact of the $\arg\max_{a'} Q_{\theta'}(s_{t+n}, a')$ term diminishes since $0 < \gamma < 1$.

The next extension is distributional RL, one of the most important ideas in value-based learning.

Distributional reinforcement learning

In the traditional Q-learning setting, the action-value function estimates the expected discounted return when action a taken in state s and then the target policy is followed. Distributional RL model proposed by (Bellemare et al., 2017) instead learns a probability mass function over discrete support **z** for state values. This **z** is a vector with $N_{atoms} \in \mathbb{N}^+$ atoms, where $z^i = v_{min} + (i-1)\dfrac{v_{max} - v_{min}}{N_{atoms} - 1}$, $i \in \{1, ..., N_{atoms}\}$. The neural network architecture is then modified to estimate $p_\theta^i(s_t, a_t)$ on each **atom i**. When distributional RL is used, the TD error can be calculated using **Kullbeck-Leibler (KL)** divergence between the current and the target distributions.

To give an example here, let's say the state-value in an environment for any state can range between $v_{min} = 0$ and $v_{max} = 100$. We can discretize this range into 11 atoms, leading to a **z** $= \{0, 10, 20, ..., 100\}$. The value network then estimates, for a given s, what is the probability that its value is 0, 10, 20, and so on. It turns out that this granular representation of the value function leads to a significant performance boost in deep Q-learning. Of course, the additional complexity here is that v_{min}, v_{max}, and N_{atoms} are additional hyperparameters to be tuned.

Finally, we introduce the last extension, noisy nets.

Noisy nets

The exploration in the regular Q-learning is controlled by ϵ that is fixed across the state space. On the other hand, some states may require higher exploration than others. Noisy nets introduce noise to the linear layers of the action-value function, whose degree is learned during training. More formally, noisy nets replace the linear layer:

$$y = wx + b$$

with

$$y \triangleq (\mu^w + \sigma^w \odot \epsilon^w)x + \mu^b + \sigma^b \odot \epsilon^b$$

where μ^w, σ^w, μ^b and σ^b are learned parameters, whereas ϵ^w and ϵ^b are random variables with fixed statistics, and $\odot$ denotes element-wise product. With this setup, the exploration rate becomes part of the learning process, which is helpful especially in hard-exploration problems (Fortunato et al. 2017).

This concludes the discussion on the extensions. Next, we turn to discussing the results from the combination of these extensions.

The performance of the integrated agent

The contribution of the Rainbow paper is that it combines all of the improvements above in a single agent. As the result, they obtain then-state-of-the-art results on the famous Atari 2600 benchmarks, showing the importance of bringing these improvements together. Of course, a natural question is whether each individual improvement contributed significantly to the outcome. The authors demonstrate results from some ablations to answer this, which we discuss next.

How to choose which extensions to use: Ablations to Rainbow

The Rainbow paper arrives at the following findings in terms of the significance of the individual extensions:

- Prioritized replay and multi-step learning turned out to be the most important extensions contributing to the result. Taking these extensions out of the Rainbow architecture led to the highest decrease in performance, indicating their significance.

- Distributional DQN was shown to be the next important extension, which became more apparent especially in the later stages of the trainings.

- Removing noisy nets from the Rainbow agent led to decreases in performance, although, its effect was not as significant as the other extensions mentioned above.

- Removing the dueling architecture and double Q-learning had not notable effect on the performance.

Of course, the effects of each of these extensions depend on the problem at hand, and their inclusion becomes a hyperparameter. However, these results show that prioritized replay, multi-step learning, and distributional DQN are important extensions to try while training an RL agent.

Before we close this section, let's revisit the discussion on the deadly triad and try to understand why it turns out to be less of a problem with all these improvements.

Overcoming the deadly triad

The deadly triad hypothesizes that when off-policy algorithms are combined with function approximators and bootstrapping, training could diverge easily. On the other hand, the aforementioned work in deep Q-learning exhibits great success stories. So, how come can we achieve such results if the rationale behind the deadly triad is accurate?

Hasselt et al. looked into this question and found support for the following hypotheses:

- Unbounded divergence is uncommon when combining Q-learning and conventional deep reinforcement learning function spaces. So, the fact that the divergence could happen does not mean that it will happen. The authors present result that this is not that much of a significant problem to begin with.

- There is less divergence when bootstrapping on separate networks. The target networks introduced in the DQN work help with divergence.

- There is less divergence when correcting for overestimation bias, meaning that double DQN is mitigating divergence issues.

- Longer multi-step returns will diverge less easily as it reduces the influence of bootstrapping.

- Larger, more flexible networks will diverge less easily because their representation power is closer to the tabular representation than function approximators with less capacity.

- Stronger prioritization of updates (high ω) will diverge more easily, which is bad. But then the amount of update can be corrected via importance sampling and that helps preventing divergence.

Those provide great insight into why the situation with deep Q-learning is not as bad as it seemed at the beginning. This is also apparent from the very exciting results that have been reported over the past few years. As a result, deep Q-learning has emerged as a very promising solution approach to RL problems.

This concludes our discussion the theory of deep Q-learning. Next, we turn to a very important dimension in deep RL, which is its scalable implementation.

Distributed deep Q-learning

Deep learning models are notorious for their hunger for data. When it comes to reinforcement learning, the hunger for data is much greater, which mandates parallelization for data collection while training RL models. The original DQN model is a single-threaded process. Despite its great success, it has limited scalability. In this section, we present methods to parallelize deep Q-learning to many (possibly thousands) of processes.

The key insight behind distributed Q-learning is its off-policy nature, which virtually decouples the training from experience generation. In other words, the specific processes/policies that generate the experience do not matter to the training process (although there are caveats to this statement). Combined with the idea of using a replay buffer, this allows us to parallelize the experience generation and store the data in central or distributed replay buffers. In addition, we can parallelize how the data is sampled from these buffers and the action-value function is updated.

Let's dive into the details of distributed deep Q-learning.

Components of a distributed deep Q-learning architecture

In this section, we describe the main components of a distributed deep Q-learning architecture and then go into specific implementations, following the structure introduced in (Nair et al., 2015).

Actors

Actors are processes that interact with a copy of the environment given a policy, take the actions given the state they are in, observe the reward and the next state. If the task is to learn how to play chess, for example, each actor plays its own chess game and collects experience. They are provided by a copy of the Q-network by a **parameter server**, and an exploration parameter, for them to obtain actions.

Experience replay memory (buffer)

When the actors collect experience tuples, they store them in the replay buffer(s). Depending on the implementation, there could be a global replay buffer or multiple local replay buffers, possibly one associated with each actor. When the replay buffer is a global one, the data can still be stored in a distributed fashion.

Learners

A **learner**'s job is to calculate the gradients that will update the Q-network in the parameter server. To do so, a learner carries a copy of the Q-network, samples a minibatch of experiences from the replay memory, calculates the loss and the gradients before communicating them back to the parameter server.

Parameter server

The **parameter server** is where the main copy of the Q-network is stored and updated as the learning progresses. All processes periodically synchronize their version of the Q-network from this parameter server. Depending on the implementation, the parameter server could be comprised of multiple shards to allow storing large amounts of data and reduce communication load per shard.

After introducing this general structure, let's go into the details of the Gorila implementation – one of the early distributed deep Q-learning architectures.

Gorila: General reinforcement learning architecture

The Gorila architecture introduces a general framework to parallelize deep Q-learning using the components we described above. A specific version of this architecture, which is implemented by the authors, bundles an actor, a learner, and a local replay buffer together for learning. Then, one can create many bundles for distributed learning. This architecture is described in the figure below:

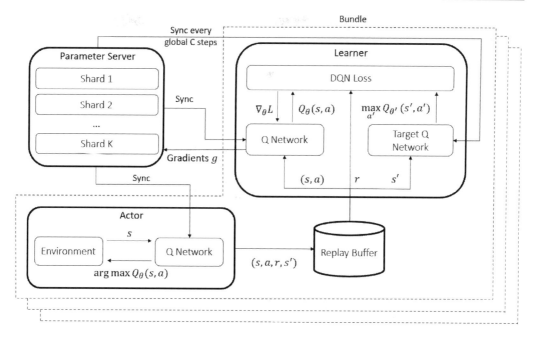

Figure 6.5 – Gorila architecture

Note that the exact flow will slightly change with the Rainbow improvements.

The details of the distributed deep Q-learning algorithm are as follows within a bundle:

1. Initialize a replay buffer D with a fixed capacity M. Initialize the parameter server with some $\boldsymbol{\theta}^+$. Sync the action-value function and the target network with the parameters in the parameter server, $\theta := \theta^+$ and $\theta' := \theta^+$.

    For $episode = 1$ to $M_.$:

2. Reset the environment to an initial state s_1. Sync $\boldsymbol{\theta} := \boldsymbol{\theta}^+$.

    For $t = 1$ to T do:

3. Take an action a_t according to an ϵ-greedy policy given Q_θ and s_t; observe r_t and s_{t+1}. Store the experience in the replay buffer D.

4. Sync $\boldsymbol{\theta} := \boldsymbol{\theta}^+$; sample a random minibatch from D and calculate the target values $\boldsymbol{y}$.

5. Calculate the loss; compute the gradients and send them to the parameter server.

6. Every C gradient updates in the parameter server, sync $\boldsymbol{\theta}' := \boldsymbol{\theta}^+$.

    End for; end for.

Some of the details in the pseudo-code are omitted, such as how to calculate the target values. The original Gorila paper implements vanilla DQN without the Rainbow improvements. However, one could modify it to use, let's say, n-step learning. The details of the algorithm would then need to be filled accordingly.

One of the drawbacks in the Gorila architecture is that it involves a lot of passing of the θ parameters between the parameter server, actors, and learners. Depending on the size of the network, this would mean a significant communication load. Next, we will look into how the Ape-X architecture improves Gorila.

Ape-X: Distributed prioritized experience replay

(Horgan et al., 2018) introduced the Ape-X DQN architecture that achieved some significant improvements over DQN, Rainbow, and Gorila. Actually, the Ape-X architecture is a general framework that could be applied to learning algorithms other than DQN.

Key contributions of Ape-X

Here are the key points in how Ape-X distributes the RL training:

- Similar to Gorila, each actor collects experience from its own instance of the environment.

- Unlike Gorila, there is a single replay buffer in which all the experiences are collected.

- Unlike Gorila, there is a single learner that samples from the replay buffer to update the central Q and target networks.

- Ape-X architecture completely decouples the learner from the actors, and they run at their own pace.

- Unlike the regular prioritized experience replay, actors calculate the initial priorities before adding the experience tuples to the replay buffer, rather than setting them to a maximum value.

- Ape-X DQN adapts the double Q-learning and multi-step learning improvements, in their paper, although other Rainbow improvements can be integrated into the architecture.

- Each actor is assigned different exploration rates, within the spectrum $\epsilon \in [0, 1]$, where actors with low ϵ exploit what has been learned about the environment and actors with high ϵ increases the diversity in the collected experience.

The Ape-X DQN architecture is described in the diagram below.

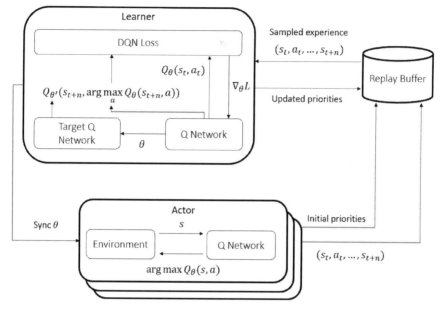

Figure 6.6 – Ape-X architecture for DQN

Now let's go into the details of the algorithms for the actor and the learners

Actor algorithm

Here is the algorithm for the actor:

1. Initialize $\theta_0 := \theta$, ϵ and s_0.

    For $t = 1$ to T do:

2. Take an action a_{t-1} obtained from $\pi_{\theta_{t-1}}(s_{t-1})$ and observe (r_t, s_t).

3. Add the experience (s_{t-1}, a_{t-1}, r_t) to a local buffer

    If the number of tuples in the local buffer exceeds a threshold B do:

4. Obtain τ from the local buffer, a batch of multi-step transitions

5. Calculate P for τ, initial priorities for the experience

6. Send τ and P to the central replay buffer

    End if

7. Sync the local network parameters every C steps from the learner, $\theta_t := \theta$.

    End for

One clarification with the algorithm above: Don't confuse the local buffer with the replay buffer. It is just a temporary storage to accumulate the experience before sending it to the replay buffer, and the learner does not interact with the local buffer. Also, the process that sends data to the replay buffer runs in the background and does not block the process that steps through the environment.

Now, let's look into the algorithm for the learner.

Learner algorithm

Here is how the learner works:

1. Initialize the Q and the target network, $\theta_0, \theta'_0 := \theta_0$.

    For $t = 1$ to T do:

2. Sample a batch of experiences, (id, τ), where the id helps uniquely identify which experience is sampled.

3. Compute the gradients $\nabla_{\theta_t} L$ using τ, θ_t and θ'_t; update network parameters to θ_{t+1} with the gradients.

4. Compute the new priorities p for τ and update the priorities in the replay buffer using the id information.

5. Periodically remove old experience from the replay buffer.

6. Periodically update the target network parameters.

    End for

If you look into the actor and learner algorithms above, they are not that complicated. However, the key intuition of decoupling them brings significant performance gains.

Before we wrap up our discussion in this section, let's discuss some practical details of the Ape-X framework next.

Practical considerations in implementing Ape-X DQN

The Ape-X paper includes additional details about the implementation. Some key ones are:

- The exploration rate for actors $i \in \{0, ..., N-1\}$ as $\epsilon_i = \epsilon^{1+\frac{i}{N-1}\alpha}$ with $\epsilon = 0.4$ and $\alpha = 7$, and these values are held constant during training.

- There is a grace period to collect enough experiences before learning starts, which the authors set to 50K transitions for the Atari environments.

- The rewards and the gradient norms are clipped to stabilize the learning.

So, remember to pay attention to these details in your implementation.

This has been a long journey so far with all the theory and abstract discussions – and thanks for your patience! Now, it is finally time to dive into some practice. In the rest of the chapter, and the book, we will heavily rely on Ray/RLlib libraries. So let's make an introduction into Ray next, and then implement a distributed deep Q-learning agent.

Implementing scalable deep Q-learning algorithms using Ray

In this section, we will implement a parallelized DQN variate using the Ray library. Ray is a powerful, general-purpose, yet simple framework for building and running distributed applications on a single machine as well as on large clusters. Ray has been built for applications that have heterogenous computational needs in mind. This is exactly what modern DRL algorithms require as they involve a mix of long and short running tasks, usage of GPU and CPU resources, and more. In fact, Ray itself has a powerful RL library that is called RLlib. Both Ray and RLlib have been increasingly adopted in academia and industry.

> **Info**
>
> For a comparison of Ray to other distributed backend frameworks such as Spark and Dask, see `https://bit.ly/2T44AzK`. You will see that Ray is a very competitive alternative, even beating Python's own multiprocessing implementation in some benchmarks.

Writing a production-grade distributed application is a complex undertaking, which is not what we aim here. For that, we will cover RLlib in the next section. On the other hand, implementing your own custom DRL -albeit simple- algorithm is highly beneficial, if nothing else, for educational reasons. So, this exercise will help you:

- Introduce you to Ray, which you can also use for tasks other than RL.

- Give you an idea about how to build your custom parallelized DRL algorithm.

- Serve as a steppingstone if you prefer to dive into the RLlib source code.

You can then build your own distributed deep RL ideas on top of this exercise if you prefer to do so.

With that, let's dive in!

A primer on Ray

We start with an introduction to Ray before going into our exercise. This will be rather brief tour to ensure the continuity. For a comprehensive documentation on how Ray works, we refer you to Ray's own website.

> **Info**
>
> Ray and RLlib documentation is available at `https://docs.ray.io/en/latest/index.html`, which includes API references, examples and tutorials. The source code is on GitHub at `https://github.com/ray-project/ray`.

Next, let's discuss the main concepts in Ray.

Main concepts in Ray

Before we go into writing some Ray applications, we first need to discuss the main components they would involve. Ray enables your regular Python functions and classes to run on separate remote processes with a simple Python decorator `@ray.remote`. During execution, Ray takes care of where these functions and classes will live and execute – be it in a process on your local machine or somewhere on the cluster if you have one. In more detail, here is what they are:

- **Remote functions (tasks)** are like regular Python functions except they are executed asynchronously, in a distributed fashion. Once called, a remote function immediately returns an object ID; and a task is created to execute it on a worker process. Note that remote functions do not maintain a state between calls.

- **Object IDs (futures)** are references to remote Python objects, for example, an integer output of a remote function. Remote objects are stored in shared-memory object stores and can be accessed by remote functions and classes. Note that an object ID might refer to an object that will be available in the future, for example, once the execution of a remote function finishes.

- **Remote classes (actors)** are similar to regular Python classes, but they live on a worker process. Unlike remote functions, they are stateful, and their methods behave like remote functions, sharing the state in the remote class. As a side note, the "actor" term here is not to be confused with the distributed RL "actor" – although an RL actor can be implemented using a Ray actor.

Next, let's look into how you can install Ray and use remote functions and classes.

Installing and starting Ray

Ray can be installed through a simple `pip install -U ray` command. To install it together with the RLlib library that we will use later, simply use `pip install -U ray[rllib]`.

> **Info**
>
> Note that Ray is supported on Linux and MacOS. At the time of writing this book, its Windows distribution is still experimental.

So, let's create a virtual environment and install what we need for this chapter:

```
$ virtualenv qenv
$ source qenv/bin/activate
$ pip install ray[rllib]==1.0.1
$ pip install tensorflow==2.3.1
```

Once installed, Ray needs to be initialized before creating any remote functions, objects, or classes:

Chapter06/ray_primer.py

```
import ray
ray.init()
```

Next, let's create a few simple remote functions. In doing so, we are going to use Ray's examples in their documentation.

Using remote functions

As mentioned earlier, Ray converts a regular Python function to a remote one with a simple decorator:

```
@ray.remote
def remote_function():
    return 1
```

Once invoked, this function will be executed on a worker process. Therefore, invoking this function multiple times will create multiple worker processes for parallel execution. To do so, a remote function needs to be called with the `remote()` addition:

```
object_ids = []
for _ in range(4):
    y_id = remote_function.remote()
    object_ids.append(y_id)
```

Note that the function calls will not wait for each other to finish. However, once called, the function immediately returns an object ID. To retrieve the result of a function as a regular Python object via the object ID, we just use `objects = ray.get(object_ids)`. Note that this call waits for the object to be available.

Object IDs can be passed to other remote functions or classes just like regular Python objects.

```
@ray.remote
def remote_chain_function(value):
    return value + 1


y1_id = remote_function.remote()
chained_id = remote_chain_function.remote(y1_id)
```

Several things to note here:

- This creates a dependency between the two tasks. `remote_chain_function` call will wait for the output of the `remote_function` call.

- Within `remote_chain_function`, we did not have to call `ray.get(value)`. Ray handles it whether it is an object ID or object that has been received.

- If the two worker processes for these two tasks were on different machines, the output is copied from one machine to the other.

This was a brief overview of the Ray remote functions. Next, we look into remote objects.

Using remote objects

A regular Python object can be converted to a Ray remote object easily as follows:

```
y = 1
object_id = ray.put(y)
```

This stores the object in the shared-memory object store. Note that remote objects are immutable: Their values cannot be changed after creation.

Finally, let's go over Ray remote classes.

Using remote classes

Using remote classes (actors) in Ray is very similar to remote functions. An example of how to decorate a class with Ray's remote decorator is as follows:

```
@ray.remote
class Counter(object):
    def __init__(self):
        self.value = 0

    def increment(self):
        self.value += 1
        return self.value
```

In order to initiate an object from this class, we use `remote` in addition to calling the class.

```
a = Counter.remote()
```

And again, calling a method on this object requires using `remote`.

```
obj_id = a.increment.remote()
ray.get(obj_id) == 1
```

That's it! This brief overview of Ray sets the foundation for us to go into implementing a scalable DQN algorithm.

Ray implementation of a DQN variate

In this section, we implement a DQN variate using Ray, which will be similar to the Ape-X DQN structure, except we don't implement prioritized replay for simplicity. The code will have the following components:

- `train_apex_dqn.py` is the main script that accepts the training configs and initializes the other components.

- `actor.py` includes the RL actor class that interacts with the environment and collects experience.

- `parameter_server.py` includes a parameter server class that serves the optimized Q model weights to actors.
- `replay.py` includes the replay buffer class.
- `learner.py` includes a learner class that receives samples from the replay buffer, takes gradient steps and pushes the new Q network weights to the parameter server.
- `models.py` includes functions to create a feedforward neural network using TensorFlow/Keras.

We then run this model on Gym's cartpole (v0 version) and see how it performs. Let's get started!

Main script

The initial step in main script is to receive a set of configs to be used during training. This looks like the following:

Chapter06/train_apex_dqn.py

```python
max_samples = 500000
config = {"env": "CartPole-v0",
          "num_workers": 50,
          "eval_num_workers": 10,
          "n_step": 3,
          "max_eps": 0.5,
          "train_batch_size": 512,
          "gamma": 0.99,
          "fcnet_hiddens": [256, 256],
          "fcnet_activation": "tanh",
          "lr": 0.0001,
          "buffer_size": 1000000,
          "learning_starts": 5000,
          "timesteps_per_iteration": 10000,
          "grad_clip": 10}
```

Let's go into some details of some of these configs:

- `env` is the name of the Gym environment.

- `num_workers` is the number of training environments/agents/workers that will be created to collect experience. *Note that each worker consumes a CPU on the computer, so you need to adjust it to your machine.*

- `eval_num_workers` is the number of evaluation environments/agents/workers that will be created to evaluate the policy at that point in training. *Again, each worker consumes a CPU.* Note that these agents have $\epsilon = 0$ since we don't need them to explore the environment.

- `n_step` is the number of steps for multi-step learning.

- `max_eps` will set the maximum exploration rate, ϵ, in training agents, as we will assign each training agent a different exploration rate between $[0, max\_eps]$.

- `timesteps_per_iteration` decides how frequently we run the evaluation. Note that this is not how frequently we take a gradient step as the learner will continuously sample and update the network parameters.

With this config, we create the parameter server, the replay buffer, and the learner. We will go into the details of these classes momentarily. Note that since they are Ray actors, we use `remote` to initiate them.

```
ray.init()
parameter_server = ParameterServer.remote(config)
replay_buffer = ReplayBuffer.remote(config)
learner = Learner.remote(config,
                         replay_buffer,
                         parameter_server)
```

We mentioned that learner is a process on its own that continuously samples from the replay buffer and updates the Q network. We kick the learning off in the main script.

```
learner.start_learning.remote()
```

Of course, this won't do anything alone since the actors are not collecting experiences yet. We next kick off the training actors and immediately let them start sampling from their environments.

```
for i in range(config["num_workers"]):
    eps = config["max_eps"] * i / config["num_workers"]
```

```
actor = Actor.remote("train-" + str(i),
                     replay_buffer,
                     parameter_server,
                     config,
                     eps)
actor.sample.remote()
```

We also start the evaluation actors, but we don't want them to sample yet. That will happen as the learner updates the Q network.

```
for i in range(config["eval_num_workers"]):
    eps = 0
    actor = Actor.remote("eval-" + str(i),
                         replay_buffer,
                         parameter_server,
                         config,
                         eps,
                         True)
```

Finally, the main loop where we alternate between training and evaluation. As the evaluation results improve, we will save the best model that far in the training.

```
total_samples = 0
best_eval_mean_reward = np.NINF
eval_mean_rewards = []
while total_samples < max_samples:
    tsid = replay_buffer.get_total_env_samples.remote()
    new_total_samples = ray.get(tsid)
    if (new_total_samples - total_samples
            >= config["timesteps_per_iteration"]):
        total_samples = new_total_samples
        parameter_server.set_eval_weights.remote()
        eval_sampling_ids = []
        for eval_actor in eval_actor_ids:
            sid = eval_actor.sample.remote()
            eval_sampling_ids.append(sid)
        eval_rewards = ray.get(eval_sampling_ids)
        eval_mean_reward = np.mean(eval_rewards)
```

```
        eval_mean_rewards.append(eval_mean_reward)
        if eval_mean_reward > best_eval_mean_reward:
            best_eval_mean_reward = eval_mean_reward
            parameter_server.save_eval_weights.remote()
```

Note that there is a bit more in the code that is not included here (such as saving the evaluation metrics to TensorBoard). Please see the script on our GitHub repo all the details.

Next, let's look into the details of the actor class.

Reinforcement learning actor class

Here is how the actors will work:

- An RL actor is responsible for collecting experiences from its environment given an exploratory policy.

- The rate of exploration is determined in the main script for each actor and it remains the same throughout the sampling.

- An actor also stores the experiences locally before pushing it to the replay buffer to reduce the communication overhead.

- Also note that we differentiate between a training and evaluation actor since we run the sampling step for the evaluation actors only for a single episode.

- Finally, the actors periodically pull the latest Q network weights to update their policies.

Here is how we construct an actor:

Chapter06/actor.py

```
@ray.remote
class Actor:
    def __init__(self,
                 actor_id,
                 replay_buffer,
                 parameter_server,
                 config,
                 eps,
                 eval=False):
```

```
        self.actor_id = actor_id
        self.replay_buffer = replay_buffer
        self.parameter_server = parameter_server
        self.config = config
        self.eps = eps
        self.eval = eval
        self.Q = get_Q_network(config)
        self.env = gym.make(config["env"])
        self.local_buffer = []
        self.obs_shape = config["obs_shape"]
        self.n_actions = config["n_actions"]
        self.multi_step_n = config.get("n_step", 1)
        self.q_update_freq = config.get("q_update_freq", 100)
        self.send_experience_freq = \
                config.get("send_experience_freq", 100)
        self.continue_sampling = True
        self.cur_episodes = 0
        self.cur_steps = 0
```

The actor uses the following method to sync its policies with the parameter server.

```
    def update_q_network(self):
        if self.eval:
            pid = \
                self.parameter_server.get_eval_weights.remote()
        else:
            pid = \
                self.parameter_server.get_weights.remote()
        new_weights = ray.get(pid)
        if new_weights:
            self.Q.set_weights(new_weights)
```

The reason that the evaluation weights are stored and pulled separately is that since the learner always learns, regardless of what is happening in the main loop, we need to take a snapshot of the Q network for evaluation.

Now, we write the sampling loop for an actor. Let's start with initializing the variables that will be updated in the loop:

```
def sample(self):
    self.update_q_network()
    observation = self.env.reset()
    episode_reward = 0
    episode_length = 0
    n_step_buffer = deque(maxlen=self.multi_step_n + 1)
```

The first thing to do in the loop is to get an action and take a step in the environment:

```
    while self.continue_sampling:
        action = self.get_action(observation)
        next_observation, reward, \
        done, info = self.env.step(action)
```

Our code supports multi-step learning. To implement that, the rolling trajectory is stored in a deque with a maximum length of $n + 1$. When the deque is at its full length, it indicates the trajectory is long enough to make an experience to be stored in the replay buffer:

```
        n_step_buffer.append((observation, action,
                              reward, done))
        if len(n_step_buffer) == self.multi_step_n + 1:
            self.local_buffer.append(
                self.get_n_step_trans(n_step_buffer))
```

We remember the update the counters we have:

```
        self.cur_steps += 1
        episode_reward += reward
        episode_length += 1
```

At the end of the episode, we reset the environment and the episode-specific counters. We also save the experience in the local buffer, regardless of its length. Also note that we break the sampling loop at the end of the episode if this is an evaluation rollout.

```
        if done:
            if self.eval:
                break
```

```
            next_observation = self.env.reset()
            if len(n_step_buffer) > 1:
                self.local_buffer.append(
                    self.get_n_step_trans(n_step_buffer))
            self.cur_episodes += 1
            episode_reward = 0
            episode_length = 0
```

We periodically send the experience to the replay buffer, and also periodically update the network parameters.

```
        observation = next_observation
        if self.cur_steps % \
                self.send_experience_freq == 0 \
                and not self.eval:
            self.send_experience_to_replay()
        if self.cur_steps % \
                self.q_update_freq == 0 and not self.eval:
            self.update_q_network()
    return episode_reward
```

Next, let's go into the details of action sampling. The actions are selected ϵ-greedily, as follows:

```
    def get_action(self, observation):
        observation = observation.reshape((1, -1))
        q_estimates = self.Q.predict(observation)[0]
        if np.random.uniform() <= self.eps:
            action = np.random.randint(self.n_actions)
        else:
            action = np.argmax(q_estimates)
        return action
```

The experience is extracted from the trajectory deque as follows;

```
    def get_n_step_trans(self, n_step_buffer):
        gamma = self.config['gamma']
        discounted_return = 0
        cum_gamma = 1
```

```
        for trans in list(n_step_buffer)[:-1]:
            _, _, reward, _ = trans
            discounted_return += cum_gamma * reward
            cum_gamma *= gamma
        observation, action, _, _ = n_step_buffer[0]
        last_observation, _, _, done = n_step_buffer[-1]
        experience = (observation, action, discounted_return,
                        last_observation, done, cum_gamma)
        return experience
```

And finally, the experience tuples that are stored locally are sent to the replay buffer as follows:

```
def send_experience_to_replay(self):
    rf = self.replay_buffer.add.remote(self.local_buffer)
    ray.wait([rf])
    self.local_buffer = []
```

That's all with the actor! Next, let's look into the parameter server.

Parameter server class

The parameter server is a simple structure that receives the updated parameters (weights) from the learner and serves them to actors. It consists of mostly setters and getters, and a save method. Again, remember that we periodically take a snapshot of the parameters and use them for evaluation. If the results beat the previous best results, the weights are saved.

Chapter06/parameter_server.py

```
@ray.remote
class ParameterServer:
    def __init__(self, config):
        self.weights = None
        self.eval_weights = None
        self.Q = get_Q_network(config)

    def update_weights(self, new_parameters):
        self.weights = new_parameters
```

```
        return True

    def get_weights(self):
        return self.weights

    def get_eval_weights(self):
        return self.eval_weights

    def set_eval_weights(self):
        self.eval_weights = self.weights
        return True

    def save_eval_weights(self,
                          filename=
                          'checkpoints/model_checkpoint'):
        self.Q.set_weights(self.eval_weights)
        self.Q.save_weights(filename)
        print("Saved.")
```

Note that the parameter server stores the actual Q network structure just to be able to use TensorFlow's convenient save functionality. Other than that, only the weights of the neural network, not the full model, are passed between different processes to avoid unnecessary overhead and pickling issues.

Next, we cover the replay buffer implementation.

Replay buffer class

As we mentioned above, for simplicity, we implement a standard replay buffer (without prioritized sampling). As a result, the replay buffer receives experiences from actors and send sampled ones to the learner. It also keeps track of how many total experience tuples it has received that far in the training.

Chapter06/replay.py

```
@ray.remote
class ReplayBuffer:
    def __init__(self, config):
        self.replay_buffer_size = config["buffer_size"]
```

```
        self.buffer = deque(maxlen=self.replay_buffer_size)
        self.total_env_samples = 0

    def add(self, experience_list):
        experience_list = experience_list
        for e in experience_list:
            self.buffer.append(e)
            self.total_env_samples += 1
        return True

    def sample(self, n):
        if len(self.buffer) > n:
            sample_ix = np.random.randint(
                len(self.buffer), size=n)
            return [self.buffer[ix] for ix in sample_ix]

    def get_total_env_samples(self):
        return self.total_env_samples
```

Model generation

Since we are passing only the weights of the Q-network between processes, each relevant actor creates its own copy of the Q-network. The weights of these Q-networks are then set with what is received from the parameter server.

The Q-network is created using Keras as follows:

Chapter06/models.py

```
def get_Q_network(config):
    obs_input = Input(shape=config["obs_shape"],
                      name='Q_input')

    x = Flatten()(obs_input)
    for i, n_units in enumerate(config["fcnet_hiddens"]):
        layer_name = 'Q_' + str(i + 1)
        x = Dense(n_units,
                  activation=config["fcnet_activation"],
```

```
                         name=layer_name) (x)
         q_estimate_output = Dense(config["n_actions"],
                                   activation='linear',
                                   name='Q_output') (x)
    # Q Model
    Q_model = Model(inputs=obs_input,
                    outputs=q_estimate_output)
    Q_model.summary()
    Q_model.compile(optimizer=Adam(), loss='mse')
    return Q_model
```

One important implementation detail here is that this Q-network is not what we want to train. Because, given a state, it predicts Q-values for all possible actions. On the other hand, a given experience tuple includes a target value only for one of these possible actions: the one that got selected in that tuple by the agent. Therefore, when we update the Q-network using that experience tuple, gradients should flow through only the selected action's output. The rest of the actions should be masked. We achieve that by using:

1. A masking input based on the selected action,

2. A custom layer on top of this Q-network that calculates the loss only for the selected action.

That gives us a model that we can train. Here is how we implement the masked loss:

```
def masked_loss(args):
    y_true, y_pred, mask = args
    masked_pred = K.sum(mask * y_pred, axis=1, keepdims=True)
    loss = K.square(y_true - masked_pred)
    return K.mean(loss, axis=-1)
```

And then the trainable model is obtained as follows:

```
def get_trainable_model(config):
    Q_model = get_Q_network(config)
    obs_input = Q_model.get_layer("Q_input").output
    q_estimate_output = Q_model.get_layer("Q_output").output
    mask_input = Input(shape=(config["n_actions"],),
                       name='Q_mask')
    sampled_bellman_input = Input(shape=(1,),
```

```
                                    name='Q_sampled')

    # Trainable model
    loss_output = Lambda(masked_loss,
                         output_shape=(1,),
                         name='Q_masked_out')\
                        ([sampled_bellman_input,
                          q_estimate_output,
                          mask_input])
    trainable_model = Model(inputs=[obs_input,
                                    mask_input,
                                    sampled_bellman_input],
                            outputs=loss_output)
    trainable_model.summary()
    trainable_model.compile(optimizer=
                            Adam(lr=config["lr"],
                            clipvalue=config["grad_clip"]),
                            loss=[lambda y_true,
                                  y_pred: y_pred])
    return Q_model, trainable_model
```

It is this trainable model that the learner will optimize. The compiled Q-network model will never be trained alone, and the optimizer and loss function we specify in it are just placeholders.

Finally, let's look into the learner.

Learner class

The learner's main job is to receive a sample of experiences from the replay buffer, unpack them, and take gradient steps to optimize the Q-network. Here, we only include a part of the class initialization and the optimization step.

The class is initialized as follows:

Chapter06/learner.py

```
@ray.remote
class Learner:
    def __init__(self, config,
```

```
            replay_buffer, parameter_server):
    self.config = config
    self.replay_buffer = replay_buffer
    self.parameter_server = parameter_server
    self.Q, self.trainable = get_trainable_model(config)
    self.target_network = clone_model(self.Q)
```

And now the optimization step. We start with sampling from the replay buffer and updating the counters we keep:

```
def optimize(self):
    samples = ray.get(self.replay_buffer
                .sample.remote(self.train_batch_size))
    if samples:
        N = len(samples)
        self.total_collected_samples += N
        self.samples_since_last_update += N
        ndim_obs = 1
        for s in self.config["obs_shape"]:
            if s:
                ndim_obs *= s
```

Then we unpack the samples and reshape them:

```
        n_actions = self.config["n_actions"]
        obs = np.array([sample[0] for sample \
                    in samples]).reshape((N, ndim_obs))
        actions = np.array([sample[1] for sample \
                    in samples]).reshape((N,))
        rewards = np.array([sample[2] for sample \
                    in samples]).reshape((N,))
        last_obs = np.array([sample[3] for sample \
                    in samples]).reshape((N, ndim_obs))
        done_flags = np.array([sample[4] for sample \
                    in samples]).reshape((N,))
        gammas = np.array([sample[5] for sample \
                    in samples]).reshape((N,))
```

We create the masks to only update the Q value for the action selected in the experience tuple:

```
masks = np.zeros((N, n_actions))
masks[np.arange(N), actions] = 1
dummy_labels = np.zeros((N,))
```

In the main section, we first prepare the inputs to the trainable Q network and then call the fit function on it. In doing so, we use double DQN:

```
# double DQN
maximizer_a = np.argmax(self.Q.predict(last_obs),
                        axis=1)
target_network_estimates = \
    self.target_network.predict(last_obs)
q_value_estimates = \
    np.array([target_network_estimates[i,
                            maximizer_a[i]]
              for i in range(N)]).reshape((N,))
sampled_bellman = rewards + gammas * \
                        q_value_estimates * \
                        (1 - done_flags)
trainable_inputs = [obs, masks,
                    sampled_bellman]
self.trainable.fit(trainable_inputs,
                    dummy_labels, verbose=0)
self.send_weights()
```

Finally, we periodically update the target network.

```
if self.samples_since_last_update > 500:
    self.target_network.set_weights(self.Q.get_weights())
    self.samples_since_last_update = 0
return True
```

For more details, see the full code in `learner.py`.

That's it! Let's look at how this architecture performs in the cartpole environment.

Results

You can kick off training by simply running the main script. Couple things to note before running it:

- Don't forget to activate the Python environment in which Ray is installed.
- Set the total number of workers (for training and evaluation) to be less than the number of CPUs on your machine.

With that, you can kick off the training as follows:

```
python train_apex_dqn.py
```

The full code includes some additions that save the evaluation progress on TensorBoard. You can start TensorBoard within the same folder with scripts as follows:

```
tensorboard --logdir logs/scalars
```

And then go to the default TensorBoard address at `http://localhost:6006/`. The evaluation graph from our experiment looks as follows:

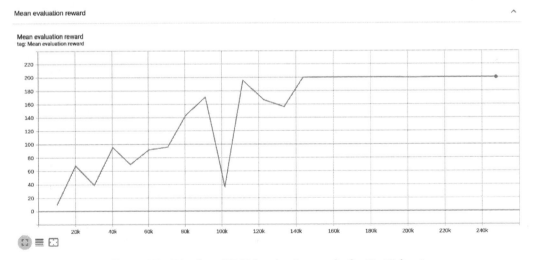

Figure 6.7 – Distributed DQN evaluation results for CartPole-v0

You can see that after 150k iterations or so, the reward reaches the maximum of 200.

Great job! You have implemented a deep Q-learning algorithm that you can scale to many CPUs, even too many nodes on a cluster using Ray! Feel free to improve this implementation, add further tricks, and incorporate your own ideas!

Let's close this chapter with how you can run a similar experiment in RLlib.

RLlib: Production-grade deep reinforcement learning

As we mentioned at the beginning, one of the motivations of Ray's creators is to build an easy-to-use distributed computing framework that can handle complex and heterogenous applications such as deep reinforcement learning. With that, they also created a widely-used deep RL library based on Ray. Training a model similar to ours is very simple using RLlib. The main steps are:

- Import the default training configs for Ape-X DQN as well as the trainer,
- Customize the training configs,
- Train the trainer.

That's it! The code necessary for that is very simple. All you need is the following:

Chapter06/rllib_apex_dqn.py

```python
import pprint
from ray import tune
from ray.rllib.agents.dqn.apex import APEX_DEFAULT_CONFIG
from ray.rllib.agents.dqn.apex import ApexTrainer


if __name__ == '__main__':
    config = APEX_DEFAULT_CONFIG.copy()
    pp = pprint.PrettyPrinter(indent=4)
    pp.pprint(config)
    config['env'] = "CartPole-v0"
    config['num_workers'] = 50
    config['evaluation_num_workers'] = 10
    config['evaluation_interval'] = 1
    config['learning_starts'] = 5000
    tune.run(ApexTrainer, config=config)
```

And your training should start. RLlib has a great TensorBoard logging. Initialize TensorBoard by running:

```
tensorboard --logdir=~/ray_results
```

The results from our training looks like the following:

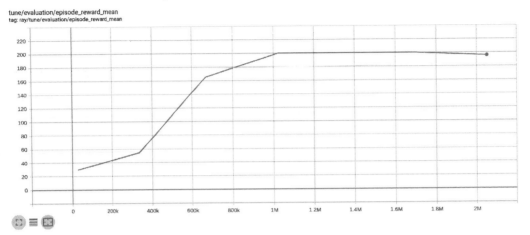

Figure 6.8 – RLlib evaluation results for CartPole-v0

It turns out that our DQN implementation was very competitive! But now, with RLlib, you have access to many improvements from RL literature. You can customize your training by changing the default configs. Please take a moment to go over the very long list of all the available options to you that we print in our code. It looks like the following:

```
{    'adam_epsilon': 1e-08,
     'batch_mode': 'truncate_episodes',
     'beta_annealing_fraction': -1,
     'buffer_size': 2000000,
     'callbacks': <class 'ray.rllib.agents.callbacks.
DefaultCallbacks'>,
     'clip_actions': True,
     'clip_rewards': None,
     'collect_metrics_timeout': 180,
     'compress_observations': False,
     'custom_eval_function': None,
     'custom_resources_per_worker': {},
     'double_q': True,
     'dueling': True,
...
```

Again, the list is long. But this shows the power at your hands with RLlib! We will continue to use RLlib in the following chapters and go into more details.

Congratulations! You have done a great job and accomplished a lot in this chapter. What we have covered here alone gives you an incredible arsenal to solve many sequential decision-making problems. Next chapters will dive into even more advanced material in deep RL, and now you are ready to take on them!

Summary

In this chapter, we have come a long way from using tabular Q-learning to implementing a modern, distributed deep Q-learning algorithm. Along the way, we covered the details of neural fitted Q-iteration, online Q-learning, DQN with rainbow improvements, Gorila, and Ape-X DQN algorithms. We also introduced you to Ray and RLlib, which are powerful distributed computing and deep reinforcement learning frameworks.

In the next chapter, we will go into another class of deep Q-learning algorithms: Policy-based methods. Those methods will allow us to directly learn random policies and use continuous actions.

References

1. Sutton, R. S., Barto, A. G. (2018). Reinforcement Learning: An Introduction. The MIT Press. URL: `http://incompleteideas.net/book/the-book.html`

2. Mnih, V. et al. (2015). Human-level control through deep reinforcement learning. Nature, 518(7540), 529–533.

3. Riedmiller M. (2005) Neural Fitted Q Iteration – First Experiences with a Data Efficient Neural Reinforcement Learning Method. In: Gama J., Camacho R., Brazdil P.B., Jorge A.M., Torgo L. (eds) Machine Learning: ECML 2005. ECML 2005. Lecture Notes in Computer Science, vol 3720. Springer, Berlin, Heidelberg.

4. Lin, L. (1993). Reinforcement learning for robots using neural networks.

5. McClelland, J. L., McNaughton, B. L., & O'Reilly, R. C. (1995). Why there are complementary learning systems in the hippocampus and neocortex: Insights from the successes and failures of connectionist models of learning and memory. Psychological Review, 102(3), 419–457.

6. van Hasselt, H.; Guez, A.; and Silver, D. 2016. Deep reinforcement learning with double Q-learning. In Proc. of AAAI, 2094–2100.

7. Schaul, T.; Quan, J.; Antonoglou, I.; and Silver, D. 2015. Prioritized experience replay. In Proc. of ICLR.

8.   Wang, Z.; Schaul, T.; Hessel, M.; van Hasselt, H.; Lanctot, M.; and de Freitas, N. 2016. Dueling network architectures for deep reinforcement learning. In Proceedings of the 33rd International Conference on Machine Learning, 1995–2003.

9.   Sutton, R. S. 1988. Learning to predict by the methods of temporal differences. Machine learning 3(1):9–44.

10.   Bellemare, M. G.; Dabney, W.; and Munos, R. 2017. A distributional perspective on reinforcement learning. In ICML.

11.   Fortunato, M.; Azar, M. G.; Piot, B.; Menick, J.; Osband, I.; Graves, A.; Mnih, V.; Munos, R.; Hassabis, D.; Pietquin, O.; Blundell, C.; and Legg, S. 2017. Noisy networks for exploration. URL: https://arxiv.org/abs/1706.10295

12.   Hessel, M., Modayil, J., Hasselt, H.V., Schaul, T., Ostrovski, G., Dabney, W., Horgan, D., Piot, B., Azar, M.G., & Silver, D. (2018). Rainbow: Combining Improvements in Deep Reinforcement Learning. URL: https://arxiv.org/abs/1710.02298

13.   Hasselt, H.V., Doron, Y., Strub, F., Hessel, M., Sonnerat, N., & Modayil, J. (2018). Deep Reinforcement Learning and the Deadly Triad. URL: https://arxiv.org/abs/1812.02648

14.   Nair, A., Srinivasan, P., Blackwell, S., Alcicek, C., Fearon, R., Maria, A.D., Panneershelvam, V., Suleyman, M., Beattie, C., Petersen, S., Legg, S., Mnih, V., Kavukcuoglu, K., & Silver, D. (2015). Massively Parallel Methods for Deep Reinforcement Learning. URL: https://arxiv.org/abs/1507.04296

15.   Horgan, D., Quan, J., Budden, D., Barth-Maron, G., Hessel, M., Hasselt, H.V., & Silver, D. (2018). Distributed Prioritized Experience Replay. URL: https://arxiv.org/abs/1803.00933

7
Policy-Based Methods

Value-based methods that we covered in the previous chapter achieve great results in many environments with discrete control spaces. However, a lot of applications, such as robotics, require continuous control. In this chapter, we go into another important class of algorithms, called policy-based methods, which enable us to solve continuous-control problems. In addition, these methods directly optimize a policy network, and hence stand on a stronger theoretical foundation. Finally, policy-based methods are able to learn truly stochastic policies, which are needed in partially observable environments and games, which value-based methods could not learn. All in all, policy-based approaches complement value-based methods in many ways. This chapter goes into the details of policy-based methods to gain you a strong understanding of how they work.

In particular, we discuss the following topics in this chapter.

- Need for policy-based methods
- Vanilla policy gradient
- Actor-critic methods
- Trust-region methods
- Off-policy methods
- Comparison of the policy-based methods in Lunar Lander
- How to pick the right algorithm?
- Open source implementations of policy-based methods

Let's dive right in!

Need for policy-based methods

We start this chapter by first discussing why we need policy-based methods as we have already introduced many value-based methods. Policy-based methods i) are arguably more principled as they directly optimize the policy parameters, ii) allow us to use continuous action spaces, and iii) are able to learn truly random stochastic policies. Let's now go into the details of each of these points.

A more principled approach

In Q-learning, a policy is obtained in an indirect manner by learning action values, which are then used to determine the best action(s). But do we really need to know the value of an action? Most of the time we don't, as they are only proxies to get us to optimal policies. Policy-based methods learn function approximations that directly give policies without such an intermediate step. This is arguably a more principled approach because we can take gradient steps directly to optimize the policy, not the proxy action-value representation. The latter is especially inefficient when there are many actions with similar values, perhaps all uninteresting to us because they are all bad actions.

Ability to use with continuous action spaces

All of the methods we mentioned in the previous section about value-based methods worked with discrete action spaces. On the other hand, there are many use cases for which we need to use continuous action spaces, such as robotics, where discretization of actions results in poor agent behavior. But what is the issue with using continuous action spaces with value-based methods? Neural networks can certainly learn value representations for continuous actions – after all we don't have such a restriction on states. However, remember how we used maximization over actions while calculating the target values:

$$y = r + \gamma \max_{a'} Q(s', a')$$

and while obtaining the best action to act in the environment using $\arg\max_{a} Q(s, a)$. It is not very straightforward to do these maximizations over continuous action spaces, although we can make it work using approaches such as the following:

1. During maximization, sample discrete actions from the continuous action space and use the action with the maximum value. Alternatively, fit a function to the values of the sampled actions and do the maximization over that function, which is called the **cross-entropy method (CEM)**.

2. Instead of using a neural network, use a function approximator, such as a function quadratic in actions, the maximum of which can be analytically calculated. An example of such a work is **Normalized Advantage Functions (NAF)** (Gu et al. 2016).

3. Learn a separate function approximation to obtain the maximum, such as in the **Deep Deterministic Policy Gradient (DDPG)** algorithm.

Now, the downside of CEM and NAF is that they are less powerful compared to a neural network that directly represents a continuous-action policy. DDPG, on the other hand, is still a competitive alternative, which we will cover later in the chapter.

> **Info**
> Most policy-based methods work with both discrete and continuous action spaces.

Ability to learn truly random stochastic policies

Throughout Q-learning, we used soft-policies such as ϵ-greedy to enable the agent to explore in the environment during training. Although this approach works pretty well in practice, and it can be made more sophisticated by annealing the ϵ, it is still not a learned parameter. Policy-based methods can learn random policies that lead to a more-principled exploration during training.

Perhaps a bigger issue is that we may need to learn random policies not just for training but also for inference. There are two reasons why we might want to do this:

- In **partially observable environments** (**POMDPs**), we may have what is called **aliased states**, which emit the same observation although the states themselves are different, for which the optimal actions might be different. Consider the following example:

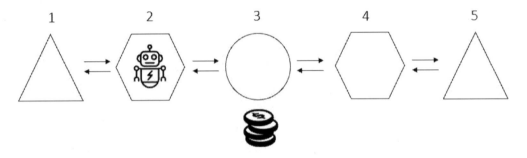

Figure 7.1 – Robot in a partially observable environment

The agent only observes the shapes of the states it is in but cannot tell what the state is. The agent is randomly initialized in a state other than 3, and its goal is to reach the coins in state 3 in a minimum number of steps by going left or right. The optimal action when the agent observes a hexagon is a random one because a deterministic policy (say, to always go left) would make the agent get stuck in either between 1 and 2 (if always left is chosen) or 4 and 5.

- In game settings with adversarial agents, there could be cases where the only optimal policy is a random one. The canonical example for this is the rock-paper-scissors, where the optimal policy is to select an action uniformly at random. Any other policy could be exploited by the opponents in the environment.

The value-based methods don't have the ability to learn such random policies for the inference whereas policy-based methods allow that.

> **Tip**
>
> If the environment is fully observable, and it is not a game setting, there is always a deterministic policy that is optimal (although there could be more than one optimal policy and some of them could be random). In such cases, we don't need a random policy during inference.

With this introduction, let's dive into the most popular policy-based methods. Next, we will give an overview of the vanilla policy gradient to set the stage for more complex algorithms that we will cover later.

Vanilla policy gradient

We start discussing the policy-based methods with the most fundamental algorithm: a vanilla policy gradient approach. Although such an algorithm is rarely useful in realistic problem settings, it is very important to understand it to build a strong intuition and a theoretical background for the more complex algorithms we will cover later.

Objective in the policy gradient methods

In value-based methods, we focused on finding good estimates for action values, with which we then obtained policies. Policy gradient methods, on the other hand, directly focus on optimizing the policy with respect to the reinforcement learning objective - although we will still make use of value estimates. If you don't remember what this objective was, it is the expected discounted return:

$$J(\pi_\theta) = E_{\tau \sim \rho_\theta(\tau)} \left[\sum_{t=0}^{T} \gamma^t R(S_t, A_t) \right]$$

This is a slightly more rigorous way of writing this objective compared to how we wrote it before. Let's unpack what we have here:

- The objective is denoted by J and it is a function of the policy at hand, π_θ.

- The policy itself parametrized by θ, which we are trying to determine.

- The trajectory the agent observes, τ, is a random one, with a probability distribution ρ_θ. It is, as you would expect, a function of the policy, hence a function of θ.

- R is a function (unknown to the agent) that gives a reward based on the environment dynamics given the state S_t and the action A_t.

Now, we have an objective function J that we want to maximize, which depends on parameter θ that we can control. A natural thing to do is to take a gradient step in the ascending direction:

$$\theta_{k+1} = \theta_k + \alpha \nabla_\theta J\left(\pi_{\theta_k}\right)$$

where α is some step size. That's the main idea behind policy gradient methods, which, again, directly optimize the policy.

Now, the million-dollar question (okay, maybe not that much) is how to figure out the gradient term. Let's look into it next.

Figuring out the gradient

Understanding how the gradient of the objective function with respect to the policy parameters θ is obtained is important to get the idea behind different variants of policy gradient methods. Let's derive what we use in the vanilla policy gradient step by step.

A different way of expressing the objective function

First, let's express the objective function slightly differently:

$$J(\pi_\theta) = E_{\tau \sim \rho_\theta(\tau)}[R(\tau)]$$
$$= \int R(\tau)\rho_\theta(\tau)d\tau$$

Here, we just expressed the trajectory and the reward that corresponds to it as a whole rather than individual state-action pairs, $\tau = S_0, A_0, S_1, A_1, \dots$. Then, we used the definition of an expectation to write it as an integral (with a slight abuse of notation since we use the same τ both to denote the random variable and a realization of it, but it should be apparent from the context). Keep in mind that the probability of observing a particular trajectory τ is the following:

$$\rho_\theta(\tau) = \rho_\theta(s_0, a_0, s_1, a_1, \dots)$$

$$= p(s_0) \prod_{t=0}^{\infty} \pi_\theta(a_t|s_t)p(s_{t+1}|s_t, a_t)$$

This is simply a chain of products for probabilities of observing a state, taking a particular action with the policy given the state and observing the next state. Here p denotes the environment transition probabilities.

Next, we use this to find a convenient formula for the gradient.

Coming up with a convenient expression for the gradient

Now let's go back to the objective function. We can write the gradient of it as follows:

$$\nabla_\theta J(\pi_\theta) = \nabla_\theta \int \rho_\theta(\tau) R(\tau) d\tau$$

$$= \int \nabla_\theta \rho_\theta(\tau) R(\tau) d\tau$$

Now we have the term $\nabla_\theta \rho_\theta(\tau)$ we need to deal with. We will do a simple trick to get rid of it:

$$\nabla_\theta \rho_\theta(\tau) = \nabla_\theta \rho_\theta(\tau) \frac{\rho_\theta(\tau)}{\rho_\theta(\tau)} = \rho_\theta(\tau) \nabla_\theta \log \rho_\theta(\tau)$$

which just follows from the definition of $\nabla_\theta \log \rho_\theta(\tau) = \nabla_\theta \rho_\theta(\tau) / \rho_\theta(\tau)$. Putting it back to the integral, we end up with an expectation for the gradient of the objective (be careful, not for the objective itself):

$$\nabla_\theta J(\pi_\theta) = \int \nabla_\theta \rho_\theta(\tau) R(\tau) d\tau$$

$$= \int \rho_\theta(\tau) \nabla_\theta \log \rho_\theta(\tau) R(\tau) d\tau$$

$$= E_{\tau \sim \rho_\theta(\tau)} [\nabla_\theta \log \rho_\theta(\tau) R(\tau)]$$

Now, this will turn out to be a very convenient formula for the gradient. Taking a step back, we now have an expectation for the gradient. Of course, we cannot fully evaluate it because we don't know $\rho_\theta(\tau)$, but we can take samples from the environment.

> **Tip**
> Whenever you see an expectation in RL formulations, you can reasonably expect that we will use samples from the environment to evaluate it.

This formulation forms the essence of the policy gradient methods. Next, let's see how we can conveniently do it.

Obtaining the gradient

Before going into estimating the gradient from samples, we need to get rid of one more term, ρ_θ, because we don't really know what that is. It turns out that we can do so by writing the explicit probability product for the trajectory.

$$\nabla_\theta \log \rho_\theta(\tau) = \nabla_\theta \log \left[p(s_0) \prod_{t=0}^{\infty} \pi_\theta(a_t|s_t) p(s_{t+1}|s_t, a_t) \right]$$

$$= \nabla_\theta \left[\log p(s_0) + \sum_{t=0}^{\infty} \log \pi_\theta(a_t|s_t) + \sum_{t=0}^{\infty} \log p(s_{t+1}|s_t, a_t) \right]$$

When we take the gradient with respect to θ, the first and last terms in the sum drop since they don't depend on θ. With that, we can write this gradient in terms of what we know, namely, $\pi_\theta(a_t|s_t)$, the policy that we possess:

$$\nabla_\theta \log \rho_\theta(\tau) = \sum_{t=0}^{\infty} \nabla_\theta \log \pi_\theta(a_t|s_t)$$

We can then estimate the gradient from a batch of N trajectories as follows:

$$\nabla_\theta J(\pi_\theta) \approx \frac{1}{N} \sum_{i=1}^{N} \nabla_\theta \log \rho_\theta(\tau_i) R(\tau_i)$$

$$= \frac{1}{N} \sum_{i=1}^{N} \left(\sum_{t=0}^{\infty} \nabla_\theta \log \pi_\theta(a_t^i|s_t^i) \right) \left(\sum_{t=0}^{\infty} \gamma^t R(s_t^i, a_t^i) \right)$$

This gradient aims to increase the likelihood of trajectories that have high total rewards, and reduce the ones (or increase less) with low total rewards.

This gives us all the ingredients to put together a policy gradient algorithm, namely REINFORCE, which we turn to next.

REINFORCE

The REINFORCE algorithm, one of the earliest policy gradient methods, uses the ingredients we presented above. We will need a lot of improvements on top of this to come up with methods with which we can attack realistic problems. On the other hand, understanding REINFORCE is useful to formalize these ideas in the context of an algorithm.

REINFORCE works as follows in finite horizon problems with the discount factors ignored.

1.   Initialize a policy π_θ

while some stopping criterion is not met do:

2.   Collect N trajectories $\{\tau^i\}$ from the environment using π_θ

3.   Calculate

$$\nabla_\theta J(\pi_\theta) \approx \frac{1}{N} \sum_{i=1}^{N} \left(\sum_{t=0}^{T} \nabla_\theta \log \pi_\theta \left(a_t^i \mid s_t^i \right) \right) \left(\sum_{t=0}^{T} R(s_t^i, a_t^i) \right)$$

4.   Update $\theta := \theta + \alpha \nabla_\theta J(\pi_\theta)$

end while

The REINFORCE algorithm simply suggests sampling trajectories from the environment using the policy on hand, then estimating the gradient using these samples and taking a gradient step to update the policy parameters.

> **Info**
>
> The fact that the sampled trajectories are used to obtain a gradient estimate for the policy parameters at hand makes policy gradient methods **on-policy**. Therefore, we cannot use samples obtained under a different policy to improve the existing policy, unlike in value-based methods. Having said that, we will have a section at the end of the chapter to discuss several off-policy approaches.
>
> The REINFORCE algorithm requires complete trajectories for network updates, therefore it is a Monte Carlo method.

Next, let's discuss why we need improvements on top of REINFORCE.

The problem with REINFORCE and all policy gradient methods

The most important issue with the policy gradient algorithms in general is the high variance in the $\nabla_\theta J(\pi_\theta)$ estimates. If you think about it, there are many factors contributing to this:

- **Randomness in the environment** could lead to many different trajectories for the agent even with the same policy, whose gradients are likely to vary significantly.

- **Length of sample trajectories** could vary significantly, resulting in very different sums for the log and reward terms,

- **Environments with sparse rewards** could be especially problematic (by the definition of sparse reward),

- **The size of N** is usually kept at few thousands to make the learning practical, but it may not be enough to capture the full distribution of trajectories.

As a result, the gradient estimates we obtain from samples could have a high variance, which is likely to destabilize the learning. Reducing this variance is an important goal to make learning feasible, and we employ various tricks towards this end. Next, we cover the first of those tricks.

Replacing the reward sum with reward-to-go

Let's first rearrange the terms in the gradient estimation as follows:

$$\nabla_\theta J(\pi_\theta) \approx \frac{1}{N} \sum_{i=1}^{N} \left(\sum_{t=0}^{T} \nabla_\theta \log \pi_\theta\left(a_t^i \middle| s_t^i\right) \left(\sum_{t=0}^{T} R(s_t^i, a_t^i) \right) \right)$$

This original form implies that each of the $\nabla_\theta \log \pi_\theta\left(a_t^i \middle| s_t^i\right)$ terms are weighed by the total reward obtained throughout the entire trajectory. Intuition, on the other hand, tells that we should be weighing the log term only by the sum of rewards following that state-action in time pair as they cannot affect what came before it (causality). More formally, we can write the gradient estimate as follows:

$$\nabla_\theta J(\pi_\theta) \approx \frac{1}{N} \sum_{i=1}^{N} \left(\sum_{t=0}^{T} \nabla_\theta \log \pi_\theta\left(a_t^i \middle| s_t^i\right) \left(\sum_{t'=t}^{T} R(s_{t'}^i, a_{t'}^i) \right) \right)$$

It turns out that this still gives us an unbiased estimate of the gradient. The variance also reduces as the sums get smaller as we add less reward terms, and as a result, the weights that multiply the log terms get smaller. The $\sum_{t'=t}^{T} R(s_{t'}^{i}, a_{t'}^{i})$ is called the reward-to-go at time t. Notice that how this is actually an estimate for $Q(s_t^i, a_t^i)$. We will make use of it later in the actor-critic algorithms.

This improvement over the REINFORCE algorithm is a form of a *vanilla policy gradient* method. Next, we show how to use the RLlib vanilla policy gradient implementation.

Vanilla policy gradient using RLlib

RLlib allows us to use the vanilla policy gradient with multiple rollout workers (actors) to parallelize the sample collection. You will notice that, unlike in value-based methods, the sample collection will be synchronized with network weight updates as the vanilla policy gradient algorithm is an on-policy method.

> **Info**
>
> Since policy gradient methods are on-policy, we need to make sure that the samples we use to update the neural network parameters (weights) come from the existing policy suggested by the network. This requires synchronizing the policy in use across the rollout workers.

The overall architecture of the parallelized vanilla policy gradient is therefore as follows:

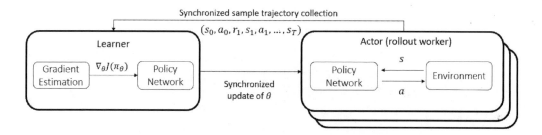

Figure 7.2 – Vanilla policy gradient architecture

At this point it is worth noting that RLlib implementation transmits samples as (s, a, r, s') from actors to the learner and concatenates them in the learner to restore the full trajectories.

Using the vanilla policy gradient in RLlib is pretty simple and very similar to how we used value-based methods in the previous chapter. Let's train a model for the OpenAI Lunar Lander environment with continuous action space. Follow along!

1. First, to avoid running into issues with Gym and Box2D packages, install Gym using the following inside the virtual environment you created in the previous chapter:

```
pip install gym[box2d]==0.15.6
```

2. Then go to implementing the Python code. Import the packages we need for argument parsing, Ray and Tune.

```
import argparse
import pprint
from ray import tune
import ray
```

3. Import the vanilla **policy gradient** (**PG**) trainer class and the corresponding config dictionary.

```
from ray.rllib.agents.pg.pg import (
    DEFAULT_CONFIG,
    PGTrainer as trainer)
```

Note that this part will be different when we want to use different algorithms.

4. Create a main function, which receives the Gym environment name as an argument.

```
if __name__ == "__main__":
    parser = argparse.ArgumentParser()
    parser.add_argument('--env',
                        help='Gym env name.')
    args = parser.parse_args()
```

5. Modify the config dictionary with the number of GPUs we want to use for training, the number of CPUs we want to use for sample collection and evaluation.

```
    config = DEFAULT_CONFIG.copy()
    config_update = {
            "env": args.env,
            "num_gpus": 1,
```

```
        "num_workers": 50,
        "evaluation_num_workers": 10,
        "evaluation_interval": 1
    }
config.update(config_update)
pp = pprint.PrettyPrinter(indent=4)
pp.pprint(config)
```

The `print` statement is for you to see what other configurations are available to you if you want to change it. You can modify things like the learning rate, for example. For now, we are not going into such hyper-parameter optimization details. And for the vanilla policy gradient, the number of hyper-parameters is considerably less than a more sophisticated algorithm will involve. One final note, the reason we set a separate set of evaluation workers is to make the training consistent with the off-policy algorithms we will introduce later. Normally, we don't need to do that since on-policy methods follow the same policy during training and evaluation.

6. Implement the section to initialize Ray and train the agent for a given number of iterations.

```
ray.init()
tune.run(trainer,
        stop={"timesteps_total": 2000000},
        config=config
    )
```

7. Save this code in a Python file, say `pg_agent.py`. You can then train the agent for as follows:

```
python pg_agent.py --env "LunarLanderContinuous-v2"
```

8. Monitor the training on TensorBoard:

```
tensorboard --logdir=~/ray_results
```

The training progress will look like the following:

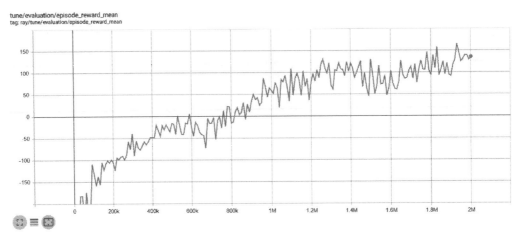

Figure 7.3 – Training progress for a vanilla policy gradient agent in Gym's continuous Lunar Lander

That's it about vanilla policy gradient method! Not a bad performance for an algorithm without much of the improvements that we will introduce in the upcoming sections. Feel free to try this algorithm with the other Gym environments. Hint: The Pendulum environment could give you some headaches.

> **Tip**
>
> To save the best performing models while training the model with Tune, you will need to write a simple wrapper training function, which is described here: `https://github.com/ray-project/ray/issues/7983` You save the model whenever you observe an improvement in the evaluation score.

Next, we cover a more powerful class of algorithms: Actor-critic methods.

Actor-critic methods

Actor-critic methods propose further remedies to the high variance problem in policy gradient algorithm. Just like REINFORCE and other policy gradient methods, actor-critic algorithms have been around for decades now. Combining this approach with deep reinforcement learning, however, has enabled them to solve more realistic RL problems. We start this section my presenting the ideas behind the actor-critic approach, and later we define them in more detail.

Further reducing the variance in policy-based methods

Remember that earlier, to reduce the variance in gradient estimates, we replaced the reward sum obtained in a trajectory with a reward-to-go term. Although a step in the right direction, it is usually not enough. We now introduce two more methods to further reduce this variance.

Estimating the reward-to-go

The reward-to-go term, $\sum_{t'=t}^{T} R(s_{t'}, a_{t'})$, obtained in a trajectory is an estimate of the action-value $Q^{\pi}(s_{t'}^{i}, a_{t}^{i})$ under the existing policy π_{θ}.

> **Info**
>
> Notice the difference between the action-value estimate we use here $Q^{\pi}(s, a)$ and what the Q-learning methods estimate, $Q(s, a)$. The former estimates the action-value under the existing behavior policy π, whereas the latter estimates the action-value under the target policy that is $\arg\max_{a} Q(s, a)$.

Now, every trajectory that visits a particular (s, a) pair is likely to yield a different reward-to-go estimate. This adds to the variance in gradient estimates. What if we could use a single estimate for a given (s, a) in a policy update cycle? That would eliminate the variance caused by those noisy reward-to-go (action-value) estimates. But how do we obtain such an estimate? The answer is to train a neural network that will generate that estimate for us. We then train this network using the sampled reward-to-go values. When we query it to obtain an estimate for a specific state-action pair, it gives us a single number rather than many different estimates, which, in turn reduces the variance.

In essence, what such a network does is that it evaluates the policy, which is why we call it the **critic**, while the policy network tells the agent how to **act** in the environment – hence the name **actor-critic**.

> **Info**
>
> We don't train the critic network from scratch after each policy update. Instead, just like the policy network, we apply gradient updates with new sampled data. As a result, the critic is biased towards the old policies. However, we are willing to make this trade-off to reduce the variance.

Last but not least, we use baselines to reduce the variance, which we turn to next.

Using a baseline

The intuition behind the policy gradient methods is that we would like to adjust the parameters of the policy so that actions that result in high-reward trajectories become more likely, and ones that led to low-reward trajectories become less likely:

$$\nabla_\theta J(\pi_\theta) = \nabla_\theta \int \rho_\theta(\tau) R(\tau) d\tau$$

$$\theta := \theta + \alpha \nabla_\theta J(\pi_\theta)$$

One shortcoming in this formulation is that the direction and the magnitude of the gradient steps heavily determined by the total reward in the trajectory, $R(\tau)$. Consider the following two examples:

- A maze environment which the agent tries to exit in minimum time. The reward is the negative of the time elapsed until the exit.

- The same maze environment but the reward is \$1M, minus a dollar penalty for each second passed until the exit.

Mathematically, these two are the same optimization problems. Now, think about what gradient steps a particular trajectory obtained under some policy π_θ would lead to under these two different reward structures. The first reward structure would lead to a negative gradient step for all trajectories (although some smaller than others) regardless of the quality of the policy, and the second reward structure would (almost certainly) lead to a positive gradient step. Moreover, under the latter, the impact of the elapsed seconds would be negligible since the fixed reward is too big, making the learning for the policy network very difficult.

Ideally, we want to measure the **relative** reward performance observed in a particular trajectory as a result of the sequence of actions taken in it compared to the other trajectories. This way we can take positive gradient steps in the direction of the parameters that result in high-reward trajectories and take negative gradient steps for the others. To measure the relative performance, a simple trick is to subtract a baseline b from the reward sum.

$$\nabla_\theta J(\pi_\theta) = \nabla_\theta \int \rho_\theta(\tau)(R(\tau) - b) d\tau$$

The most obvious choice for the baseline is the average trajectory reward, sampled as:

$$b = \frac{1}{N} \sum_{i=1}^{N} R(\tau^i)$$

It turns out that subtracting such a term still gives an unbiased estimate for the gradient, but with less variance, and the difference could be dramatic in some settings. So, using baselines is almost always good.

When combined with using reward-to-go estimates, a natural choice for baseline is the state value, which results in the following gradient estimate:

$$\nabla_\theta J(\pi_\theta) \approx \frac{1}{N}\sum_{i=1}^{N}\left(\sum_{t=0}^{T}\nabla_\theta \log \pi_\theta\left(a_t^i|s_t^i\right) A^\pi\left(s_t^i, a_t^i\right)\right)$$

$$A^\pi\left(s_t^i, a_t^i\right) = Q^\pi\left(s_t^i, a_t^i\right) - V^\pi\left(s_t^i\right)$$

where $A\left(s_t^i, a_t^i\right)$ is the **advantage** term, which measures how much the agent is better off by taking action a_t in state s_t as opposed to following the existing policy.

Having a critic estimating the advantage, directly or indirectly, gives rise to the **advantage actor-critic** algorithms, which we cover next.

Advantage Actor-Critic: A2C

What we have covered so far is almost there to put together what is known as the A2C algorithm. Let's discuss in a bit more detail how to estimate the advantage term before going into the full algorithm and the RLlib implementation.

How to estimate the advantage

There are different ways of estimating the advantage using a critic. The critic network could:

- Directly estimate $A^\pi(s, a)$,
- Estimate $Q^\pi(s, a)$, from which we can recover $A^\pi(s, a)$.

Note that both of these approaches involve maintaining a network that gives outputs that depend on both the state and the action. However, we can get away with a simpler structure. Remember the definition of action-value:

$$q_\pi(s_t, a_t) = E[R_{t+1} + \gamma v_\pi(S_{t+1}) \mid S_t = s_t, A_t = a_t]$$

When we sample a transition of a single step, we already observe the reward and the next state, and obtain a tuple $(S_t = s_t, A_t = a_t, R_{t+1} = r_{t+1}, S_{t+1} = s_{t+1})$. We can therefore obtain the estimate $Q^\pi(s_t, a_t)$ as follows:

$$Q^\pi(s_t, a_t) = r_{t+1} + \gamma V^\pi(s_{t+1})$$

where V^π is some estimate of the true state value v_π.

> **Info**
>
> Notice the nuances in the notation. q_π and v_π represent the true values where Q^π and V^π are their estimates. S_t, A_t and R_t are random variables, whereas s_t, a_t and r_t are their realizations.

We can finally estimate the advantage as follows:

$$A^\pi(s_t, a_t) = r_{t+1} + \gamma V^\pi(s_{t+1}) - V^\pi(s_t)$$

This allows us to use a neural network that simply estimates the state values to obtain an advantage estimate. To train this network, we can do bootstrapping to obtain the target values for state values. So, using a sampled tuple $(s_t, a_t, r_{t+1}, s_{t+1})$, the target for $V^\pi(s)$ is calculated as $r_{t+1} + \gamma V^\pi(s_{t+1})$ (same as the $Q^\pi(s_t, a_t)$ estimate because we happen to obtain the actions from the existing stochastic policy).

Before presenting the full A2C algorithm, let's take a look at the implementation architecture.

A2C architecture

A2C suggests synchronized sample collection between different agents, that is all of the rollout workers use the same policy network at a given to collect samples. Those samples are then passed to the learner to update the actor (policy network) and the critic (value network). In this sense, the architecture is pretty much the same with the vanilla policy gradient, for which we provided the schema above. Except, this time, we have a critic network. Then the question is how to bring the critic network in.

The design of the actor and critic can range from completely isolated neural networks, as shown in the figure below on the left, to a completely shared design (except the last layers).

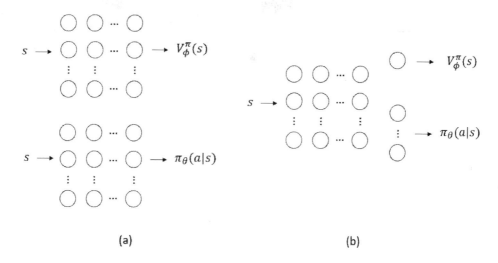

Figure 7.4 – Isolated vs shared neural networks

The advantage of the isolated design is that it is usually more stable. This is because the variance and the magnitude of the target values of the actor and critic targets could be very different. Having them share the neural network requires a careful tuning of the hyperparameters such as learning rate and otherwise the learning would be unstable. On the other hand, using a shared architecture has the advantage of cross-learning and using common feature extraction capabilities. This could come especially handy when feature extraction is a major part of training, such as when observations are images. Of course, any architecture in between is also possible.

Finally, it is time to present the A2C algorithm.

A2C algorithm

Let's put together all these ideas together and form the A2C algorithm:

1. Initialize the actor and critic network(s), θ and ϕ.

    while some stopping criterion is not met **do**:

2. Collect a batch of N samples $\{(s_i, a_i, r_i, s_i')\}_{i=1}^N$ from the (parallel) environment(s) using π_θ.

3. Obtain the state-value targets $\{y_i | y_i = r_i + \gamma V_\phi^\pi(s_i')\}_{i=1}^N$.

4. Use gradient descent to update ϕ with respect to a loss function $L(V_\phi^\pi(s_i), y_i)$, such as squared loss.

5. Obtain the advantage value estimates

$$\left\{A^{\pi}(s_i, a_i) \middle| A(s_i, a_i) = r_i + \gamma V^{\pi}_{\phi}(s'_i) - V^{\pi}_{\phi}(s_i)\right\}^{N}_{i=1}$$

6. Calculate

$$\nabla_{\theta} J(\pi_{\theta}) \approx \frac{1}{N} \sum_{i=1}^{N} \nabla_{\theta} \log \pi_{\theta}(a_i|s_i) A^{\pi}(s_i, a_i)$$

7. Update $\theta := \theta + \alpha \nabla_{\theta} J(\pi_{\theta})$.

8. Broadcast the new θ to the rollout workers.

    end while

Note that we could also use multi-step learning rather than using a single-step estimation for advantage estimates and state value targets. We will present a generalized version of multi-step learning at the end of the actor-critic section. But now, let's see how you can use RLlib's A2C algorithm.

A2C using RLlib

To train an RL agent in RLlib using A2C is very similar to how we did it for the vanilla policy gradient. Therefore, rather than presenting the full flow again, we just describe what the difference is. The main difference is to import the A2C class.

```
from ray.rllib.agents.a3c.a2c import (
    A2C_DEFAULT_CONFIG as DEFAULT_CONFIG,
    A2Ctrainer as trainer)
```

You can then train the agent the same way as the vanilla policy gradient agent. Instead of presenting the results from our training here, we will compare all the algorithms at the end of this chapter.

Next, we present another famous actor-critic algorithm: A2C

Asynchronous Advantage Actor-Critic: A3C

A3C is pretty much the same with A2C in terms of the loss functions and how it uses the critic. In fact, A3C is a predecessor of A2C, although we presented them here in reverse order for pedagogical reasons. The difference between A2C and A3C are architectural and how the gradients are calculated and applied. Next, let's discuss the A3C architecture.

A3C architecture

A3C architecture differs from that of A2C as follows:

- The asynchrony in A3C is due to the fact the rollout workers pull the θ parameters from the main policy network at their own pace, not in sync with other workers.

- As a result, the workers are likely to be using different policies at the same time.

- To avoid calculating gradients at the central learner using samples that are likely to have been obtained under different policies, the gradients are calculated by the rollout workers with respect to the policy parameters in use at that time in the worker.

- What is passed to the learner is therefore not the samples but the gradients.

- Those gradients are applied to the main policy network, again, asynchronously as they arrive.

The following diagram describes the A3C architecture:

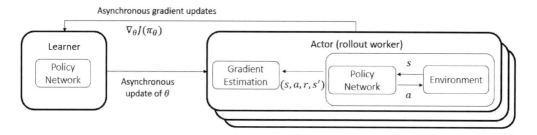

Figure 7.5 – A3C architecture

There are two important downsides to A3C:

- The gradients that update the main policy network are likely to be obsolete and obtained under a different θ than what is in the main policy network. This is theoretically problematic as those are not the true gradients for the policy network parameters.

- Passing around gradients, which could be a large vector of numbers especially when the neural network is big, could create a significant communication overhead compared to passing only samples.

The main motivation behind A3C despite these disadvantages is to obtain decorrelated samples and gradient updates, similar to a role played by experience replay in deep Q-learning. On the other hand, in many experiments people found A2C is as good as A3C and sometimes even better. As a result, A3C is not very commonly used. Still, we have presented it, so you understand how these algorithms have evolved and what are the key differences between them. Let's also look into how you can use RLlib's A3C module.

A3C using RLlib

RLlib's A3C algorithm can simply be accessed by importing the corresponding trainer class:

```
from ray.rllib.agents.a3c.a3c import (
    DEFAULT_CONFIG,
    A3CTrainer as trainer)
```

Then, you can train an agent following the code we provided earlier in the section.

Finally, we close the discussion in this section with a generalization of multi-step RL in the context of policy gradient methods.

Generalized Advantage Estimators

We previously mentioned that one can use multi-step estimates for the advantage function. Namely, instead of using only a single step transition as in:

$$A^\pi(s_t, a_t) = r_{t+1} + \gamma V^\pi(s_{t+1}) - V^\pi(s_t)$$

using n-step transitions could yield a more accurate estimate of the advantage function:

$$A_n^\pi(s_t, a_t) = -V^\pi(s_t) + r_{t+1} + \gamma r_{t+2} + \cdots + \gamma^n V^\pi(s_{t+n})$$

Of course, when $n = \infty$, we are simply back to using sampled reward-to-go, which we had abandoned to reduce the variance in the advantage estimation. On the other hand, $n = 1$ is likely to introduce too much bias towards the existing V^π estimates. Therefore, the hyper-parameter n is a way to control the bias-variance trade-off in while estimating the advantage.

A natural question is then whether we have to use a "single" n in the advantage estimation. For example, we can calculate advantage estimates using A_1^π, A_2^π and A_3^π, and take their average. What about taking a weighted average (convex combination) of all possible A_n^π, up to infinity? That is exactly what the **generalized advantage estimator (GAE)** does. More specifically, it weighs the A_n^π terms in an exponentially decaying fashion:

$$A_{GAE(\lambda)}^\pi(s_t, a_t) = (1 - \lambda)(A_1^\pi + \lambda A_2^\pi + \lambda^2 A_3^\pi + \lambda^3 A_4^\pi + \cdots)$$

$$= \sum_{l=0}^{\infty} (\lambda\gamma)^l \delta_{t+l}$$

where $\delta_{t+l} = r_{t+l+1} + \gamma V^\pi(s_{t+l+1}) - V^\pi(s_{t+l})$ and $0 \le \lambda \le 1$ is a hyperparameter Therefore, GAE gives us another knob to control the bias-variance trade-off. Specifically, $\lambda = 0$ results in A_1^π, which has high bias; and $\lambda = 1$ results in A_n^π, which is equivalent to using the sampled reward-to-to minus the baseline, which has high bias. Any value of $\lambda \in (0,1)$ is a compromise between the two.

Let's close this section by noting that you can turn on or off the GAE in RLlib's actor-critic implementations using the config flag `"use_gae"` along with `"lambda"`.

This concludes our discussion on actor-critic functions. Next, we look into recent approaches called **trust-region methods** that have resulted in significant improvements over A2C and A3C.

Trust-region methods

One of the important developments in the world of policy-based methods has been the evolution of the trust-region methods. In particular, TRPO and PPO algorithms have led to significant improvement over the algorithms like A2C and A3C. For example, the famous Dota 2 AI agent which reached expert-level performance competitions was trained using PPO and GAE. In this section, we go into the details of those algorithms to help you gain a solid understanding of how they work.

> **Info**
>
> Prof. Sergey Levine, who co-authored the TRPO and PPO papers, goes deep into the details of the math behind these methods in his online lecture more than we do in this section. That lecture is available at `https://youtu.be/uR1Ubd2hAlE` and I highly recommend you watch it to improve your theoretical understanding of these algorithms.

Without further ado, let's dive in!

Policy gradient as policy iteration

In the earlier chapters, we described how most of the RL algorithms can be thought as a form of policy iteration, alternating between policy evaluation and improvement. You can think of policy gradient methods in the same context:

- Sample collection and advantage estimation: policy evaluation,

- Gradient step: policy improvement.

Now we will use a policy iteration point of view to set the stage for the upcoming algorithms. First, let's look at how we can quantify the improvement in the RL objective.

Quantifying the improvement

In general, a policy improvement step aims to improve the policy on hand as much as possible. More formally, the objective is the following:

$$\max_{\theta'} \mathcal{L}(\theta')$$

$$\mathcal{L}(\theta') = J(\pi_{\theta'}) - J(\pi_\theta)$$

where θ is the existing policy. Using the definition of J and some algebra, we can show the following:

$$\mathcal{L}(\theta') = E_{\tau \sim \rho_{\theta'}(\tau)} \left[\sum_t \gamma^t A^{\pi_\theta}(S_t, A_t) \right]$$

Let's unpack what this equation tells us:

- The improvement obtained by a new policy θ' over an existing policy θ can be quantified using the advantage function under the existing policy.

- The expectation operation we need for this calculation is under the new policy θ'.

Remember that it is almost never practical to fully calculate such expectations or advantage functions. We always estimate them using the policy on hand, θ in this case, and interacting with the environment. Now, the former is a happy point since we know how to estimate advantages using samples – the previous section was all about this. We also know that we can collect samples to estimate expectations, which is what we have in $\mathcal{L}(\theta')$. The problem here, though, is that the expectation is with respect to a new policy θ'. We don't know what θ' is, in fact, that is what we are trying to find out. So we cannot collect samples from the environment using θ'. Everything from here on will be about how to get around this problem so that we can iteratively improve the policy.

Getting rid of θ'

Let's expand this expectation and write it down in terms of the marginal probabilities that compose $\rho_{\theta'}(\tau)$:

$$\mathcal{L}(\theta') = \sum_t E_{S_t \sim p_{\theta'}(S_t)} \left[E_{A_t \sim \pi_{\theta'}(A_t|S_t)} [\gamma^t A^{\pi_\theta}(S_t, A_t)] \right]$$

which uses the following:

$$\rho_{\theta'}(\tau) = \rho_{\theta'}(s_0, a_0, s_1, a_1, \dots)$$

$$= p(s_0) \prod_{t=0}^{\infty} \pi_{\theta'}(a_t|s_t) p_{\theta'}(s_{t+1}|s_t, a_t)$$

We can get rid of the θ' in the inner expectation using importance sampling:

$$\mathcal{L}(\theta') = \sum_t E_{S_t \sim p_{\theta'}(S_t)} \left[E_{A_t \sim \pi_\theta(A_t|S_t)} \left[\frac{\pi_{\theta'}(A_t|S_t)}{\pi_\theta(A_t|S_t)} \gamma^t A^{\pi_\theta}(S_t, A_t) \right] \right]$$

Now, getting rid of the θ' in the outer expectation is the challenging part. *The key idea is to stay "sufficiently close" to the existing policy during the optimization, that is* $\pi_{\theta'} \approx \pi_\theta$. In that case, it can be shown that $p_{\theta'}(S_t) \approx p_\theta(S_t)$, and we can replace the former with the latter.

One of the key questions here how to measure the "closeness" of the policies so that we can make sure the approximation above is valid. A popular choice for such measurements due to its nice mathematical properties is the **Kullback-Leibler (KL)** divergence.

> **Info**
>
> If you are not too familiar with the KL divergence or if you need to refresh your mind, a nice explanation of it is available here: `https://youtu.be/2PZxw4FzDU?t=226`

Using the approximation due to the closeness of the policies and bounding this closeness results in the following optimization function:

$$\max_{\theta'} \mathcal{L}(\theta') \approx \sum_t E_{S_t \sim p_\theta(S_t)} \left[E_{A_t \sim \pi_\theta(A_t|S_t)} \left[\frac{\pi_{\theta'}(A_t|S_t)}{\pi_\theta(A_t|S_t)} \gamma^t A^{\pi_\theta}(S_t, A_t) \right] \right]$$

$$s.t. \quad D_{KL}\big(\pi_{\theta'}(A_t|S_t) \,\|\, \pi_{\theta'}(A_t|S_t)\big) \leq \epsilon$$

where ϵ is some bound.

Next, let's see how we can use other approximations to further simplify this optimization problem.

Using Taylor series expansion in the optimization

Now that we have a function $\mathcal{L}(\theta')$ and we know that we evaluate it in a close proximity of another point θ, this should ring bells to use a Taylor series expansion.

> **Info**
>
> If you need to refresh your mind on Taylor series, or deepen your intuition, a great resource is this video: `https://youtu.be/3d6DsjIBzJ4`.
> I also recommend subscribing to the channel – 3Blue1Brown is one of the best resources to visually internalize many math concepts.

The first order expansion at θ is:

$$\mathcal{L}(\theta') \approx \mathcal{L}(\theta) + \nabla_\theta \mathcal{L}(\theta)^T (\theta' - \theta)$$

Notice that the first term does not depend on θ', so we can get rid of it in the optimization. Also note that the gradient term is with respect to θ rather than θ', which should come handy.

Our goal then becomes:

$$\max_{\theta'} \nabla_\theta \mathcal{L}(\theta)^T (\theta' - \theta)$$

$$s.t. \quad D_{KL}\big(\pi_{\theta'}(A_t|S_t) \,\|\, \pi_{\theta'}(A_t|S_t)\big) \leq \epsilon$$

Finally, let's look into how we can calculate the gradient term.

Calculating $\nabla_\theta \mathcal{L}(\theta)$

First, let's look at what $\nabla_{\theta'}\mathcal{L}(\theta')$ looks like. Remember that we can write the following:

$$\nabla_{\theta'}\pi_{\theta'}(A_t|S_t) = \pi_{\theta'}(A_t|S_t)\nabla_{\theta'}\log\pi_{\theta'}(A_t|S_t)$$

because, by definition, $\nabla_{\theta'}\log\pi_{\theta'}(A_t|S_t) = \nabla_{\theta'}\pi_{\theta'}(A_t|S_t)/\pi_{\theta'}(A_t|S_t)$. Then we can write:

$$\nabla_{\theta'}\mathcal{L}(\theta') \approx \sum_t E_{S_t \sim p_\theta(S_t)}\left[E_{A_t \sim \pi_\theta(A_t|S_t)}\left[\frac{\pi_{\theta'}(A_t|S_t)}{\pi_\theta(A_t|S_t)}\,\gamma^t\nabla_{\theta'}\log\pi_{\theta'}(A_t|S_t)\,A^{\pi_\theta}(S_t,A_t)\right]\right]$$

Now, remember that we are looking for $\nabla_\theta\mathcal{L}(\theta)$, not $\nabla_{\theta'}\mathcal{L}(\theta')$. Replacing all θ' with θ results in the following:

$$\nabla_\theta\mathcal{L}(\theta) \approx \sum_t E_{S_t \sim p_\theta(S_t)}\left[E_{A_t \sim \pi_\theta(A_t|S_t)}[\gamma^t\nabla_\theta\log\pi_\theta(A_t|S_t)\,A^{\pi_\theta}(S_t,A_t)]\right]$$

$$= \nabla_\theta J(\pi_\theta)$$

We have arrived at a result that should look familiar! The $\nabla_\theta\log\pi_\theta(A_t|S_t)\,A^{\pi_\theta}(S_t,A_t)$ is exactly what goes into the gradient estimate $\nabla_\theta J(\pi_\theta)$ in advantage actor-critic. The objective of maximizing the policy improvement between policy updates has led us to the same objective with a regular gradient ascent approach. Of course, we should not forget the constraint. So, the optimization problem we aim to solve has become the following:

$$\max_{\theta'} \nabla_\theta J(\pi_\theta)^T(\theta' - \theta)$$

$$s.t. \quad D_{KL}\big(\pi_{\theta'}(A_t|S_t) \,\|\, \pi_\theta(A_t|S_t)\big) \le \epsilon$$

This is a key result! Let's unpack what we have obtained so far:

- Regular actor-critic with gradient ascent and trust-region methods have the same objective of moving in the direction of the gradient.

- The trust-region approach aims to stay close to the existing policy through limiting the KL divergence.

- Regular gradient ascent, on the other hand, moves in the direction of the gradient with a particular step size, as in $\theta' := \theta + \alpha\nabla_\theta J(\pi_\theta)$.

- Regular gradient ascent, therefore, aims to keep θ' closer to θ, as opposed to keeping $\pi_{\theta'}$ close to π_θ.

- Using a single step size for all dimensions in θ as the regular gradient ascent does may result in very slow convergence, or not converging at all, since some dimensions in the parameter vector could have much greater impact on the policy (change) than others.

> **Tip**
>
> The key objective in the trust-region methods is to stay sufficiently close to the existing policy π_θ while updating the policy to some $\pi_{\theta'}$. This is different than simply aiming to keep θ' closer to θ, which is what the regular gradient ascent does.

So, we know that π_θ and $\pi_{\theta'}$ should be close, but have not discussed how to achieve this. In fact, two different algorithms, TRPO and PPO will handle this requirement differently. Next, we turn to details of the TRPO algorithm.

TRPO: Trust Region Policy Optimization

TRPO is an important algorithm that precedes PPO. Let's understand in this section how it handles the optimization problem we arrived at above and what the challenges are with the TRPO solution.

Handling the KL divergence

The TRPO algorithm approximates the KL divergence constraint with its second-order Taylor expansion:

$$D_{KL}(\pi_{\theta'} \parallel \pi_\theta) \approx \frac{1}{2}(\theta' - \theta)^T F(\theta' - \theta)$$

where F is called the Fisher information matrix and defined as follows:

$$F = E_{\pi_\theta}[\nabla_\theta \log \pi_\theta(A|S) \nabla_\theta \log \pi_\theta(A|S)^T]$$

where the expectation is to be estimated from the samples. Note that if θ is an m dimensional vector, F becomes an $m \times m$ matrix.

> **Info**
>
> Fisher information matrix is an important concept that you might want to learn more about, and the Wikipedia page is a good start: https://en.wikipedia.org/wiki/Fisher_information

This approximation results in the following gradient update step (we omit the derivation):

$$\theta' := \theta + \alpha^j \sqrt{\frac{2\epsilon}{\nabla_\theta J(\pi_\theta)^T F \nabla_\theta J(\pi_\theta)}} F^{-1} \nabla_\theta J(\pi_\theta)$$

where ϵ and α are hyper-parameters, $\alpha \in (0,1)$ and $j \in \{0,1,...\}$.

If this looks scary to you, you are not alone! TRPO is indeed not the easiest algorithm to implement. Let's next look into what kind of challenges TRPO involves.

Challenges with TRPO

Here are some of the challenges involved in implementing TRPO:

- Since the KL divergence constraint is approximated with its second order Taylor expansion, there could be cases where the constraint is violated.

- This is where the α^j term comes in: It shrinks the magnitude of the gradient update until the constraint is satisfied. To this end, there is a line search followed once $\nabla_\theta J(\pi_\theta)$ and F is estimated: Starting with 0, j increases by one until the magnitude of the update shrinks enough so that the constraint is satisfied.

- Remember that F is an $m \times m$ matrix, which could be huge depending on the size of the policy network and therefore expensive to store.

- Since F is estimated through samples, given its size, there could be a lot of inaccuracies introduced during the estimation.

- Calculating and storing F^{-1} is even a more painful step.

- To avoid the complexity of dealing with F and F^{-1}, the authors use the conjugate gradient algorithm which allows to take gradient steps without building the whole matrix and taking the inverse.

As you can see, implementing TRPO could be complex and we omit the details of its implementation. That is why a simpler algorithm that works along the same lines, PPO, is more popular and more widely used, which we cover next.

PPO: Proximal Policy Optimization

PPO is again motivated by maximizing the policy improvement objective:

$$E_{S_t \sim p, A_t \sim \pi_\theta} \left[\frac{\pi_{\theta'}(A_t|S_t)}{\pi_\theta(A_t|S_t)} A^{\pi_\theta}(S_t, A_t) \right]$$

while keeping $\pi_{\theta'}$ close to π_θ. There are to variants of PPO: PPO-Penalty and PPO-Clip. The latter is simpler, which we focus on here.

PPO-clip surrogate objective

A simpler way of achieving the closeness between the old and new policy compared to TRPO is to clip the objective so that deviating from the existing policy would not bring in additional benefits. More formally, PPO-clip maximizes the surrogate objective below:

$$\max_{\theta'} E_{S_t \sim p, A_t \sim \pi_\theta} \left[\min \left(\frac{\pi_{\theta'}(A_t|S_t)}{\pi_\theta(A_t|S_t)} A^{\pi_\theta}(S_t, A_t), g(\epsilon, A^{\pi_\theta}(S_t, A_t)) \right) \right]$$

Where g is defined as follows:

$$g(\epsilon, A) = \begin{cases} (1 + \epsilon)A^{\pi_\theta}(S_t, A_t), & A^{\pi_\theta}(S_t, A_t) \geq 0 \\ (1 - \epsilon)A^{\pi_\theta}(S_t, A_t), & A^{\pi_\theta}(S_t, A_t) < 0 \end{cases}$$

This simply says, if the advantage A is positive, then the minimization takes the form:

$$\min \left(\frac{\pi_{\theta'}(A_t|S_t)}{\pi_\theta(A_t|S_t)}, 1 + \epsilon \right) A^{\pi_\theta}(S_t, A_t)$$

which therefore clips the maximum value the ratio can take. This means even if the tendency is to increase the likelihood of taking the action A_t in state S_t because it corresponds to a positive advantage, we clip how much this likelihood can deviate from the existing policy. As a result, further deviation does not contribute to the advantage.

Conversely, if the advantage is negative, the expression instead becomes:

$$\max \left(\frac{\pi_{\theta'}(A_t|S_t)}{\pi_\theta(A_t|S_t)}, 1 - \epsilon \right) A^{\pi_\theta}(S_t, A_t)$$

which in similar ways limits how much the likelihood of taking the action A_t in state S_t can decrease. This ratio is bounded by $1 - \epsilon$.

Next, let's layout the full PPO algorithm.

PPO algorithm

The PPO algorithm works as follows:

1. Initialize the actor and critic network(s), θ and ϕ.

    while some stopping criterion is not met **do**:

2. Collect a batch of N samples $\{(s_i, a_i, r_i, s_i')\}_{i=1}^{N}$ from the (parallel) environment(s) using π_θ.

3. Obtain the state-value targets $\{y_i | y_i = r_i + \gamma V_\phi^\pi(s_i')\}_{i=1}^{N}$.

4. Use gradient descent to update ϕ with respect to a loss function $L(V_\phi^\pi(s_i), y_i)$, such as squared loss.

5. Obtain the advantage value estimates

$$\{A^\pi(s_i, a_i) | A(s_i, a_i) = r_i + \gamma V_\phi^\pi(s_i') - V_\phi^\pi(s_i)\}_{i=1}^{N}$$

6. Take a gradient ascent step towards maximizing the surrogate objective function

$$E_{S_t \sim p, A_t \sim \pi_\theta}\left[\min\left(\frac{\pi_{\theta'}(A_t|S_t)}{\pi_\theta(A_t|S_t)} A^{\pi_\theta}(S_t, A_t), g(\epsilon, A^{\pi_\theta}(S_t, A_t))\right)\right]$$

and update θ. Although we don't provide the explicit form of this gradient update, it can be easily achieved through packages like TensorFlow.

7. Broadcast the new θ to the rollout workers.

    end while

Finally, note that the architecture of a PPO implementation would be very similar to that f A2C with synchronous sampling and policy updates in the rollout workers.

PPO using RLlib

Very similar to how we imported the agent trainer classes before for the earlier algorithms, the PPO class can be imported as follows:

```
from ray.rllib.agents.ppo.ppo import (
    DEFAULT_CONFIG,
    PPOTrainer as trainer)
```

Again, we will present the training results later in the chapter.

That concludes our discussion on trust-region methods. The last class of algorithms we present in this chapter is the off-policy approaches for policy-based methods.

Revisiting off-policy Methods

One of the challenges with policy-based methods is that they are on-policy, which requires collecting new samples after every policy update. If it is costly to collect samples from the environment, then training on-policy methods could be really expensive. On the other hand, the value-based methods we covered in the previous chapter are off-policy but they only work with discrete action spaces. Therefore, there is a need for a class of methods that work with continuous action spaces and off-policy. In this section, we cover such algorithms. Let's start with the first one: Deep Deterministic Policy Gradient.

DDPG: Deep Deterministic Policy Gradient

DDPG, in some sense, is an extension of deep Q-learning to continuous action spaces. Remember that deep Q-learning methods learn a representation for action values, $Q(s, a)$. The best action is then given by $\arg\max_a Q(s, a)$ in a given state s. Now, if the action space is continuous, learning the action-value representation is not a problem. However, then, it would be quite cumbersome to execute the max operation to get the best action over a continuous action space. DDPG addresses this issue. Let's see how next.

How DDPG handles continuous action spaces

DDPG simply learns another approximation, $\mu_\phi(s)$, that estimates the best action given the state. If you wonder why this works, consider the following thought process:

- DDPG assumes that the continuous action space is differentiable with respect to a.

- For a moment, also assume that the action values, $Q(s, a)$, is known or has been learned.

- Then the problem simply becomes to learn a function approximation, $\mu_\phi(s)$, whose input is s, output is a and the parameters are ϕ. The "reward" for the optimization procedure is simply provided by $Q(s, a)$.

- We can therefore use a gradient ascent method to optimize ϕ. Over time, the learned action values will hopefully converge and be less of a moving target for the policy function training.

> **Info**
>
> Because DDPG assumes differentiability of the policy function with respect to action, it can only be used with continuous action spaces.

Next, let's look into a bit more detail of the DDPG algorithm.

DDPG algorithm

Since the DDPG is an extension deep Q-learning, plus learning a policy function, we don't need to write the full algorithm here. In addition, many approaches we discussed in the previous chapter, such as prioritized experience replay or multi-step learning, can be used to form a DDPG variate. The original DDPG algorithm, on the other hand, closer to the DQN algorithm and uses:

- **Replay buffer** to store experience tuples, from which the sampling is done uniformly at random.

- **Target network** which is updated using Polyak averaging as in $\theta_{target} := \rho\theta_{target} + (1 - \rho)\theta$, rather than syncing it with the behavior network every C steps.

DDPG then replaces the target calculation in the DQN algorithm:

$$y = r + \gamma \max_{a'} Q_{\theta_{target}}(s', a')$$

with this one:

$$y = r + \gamma Q_{\theta_{target}}\left(s', \mu_{\phi_{target}}(s')\right)$$

Another important difference between DQN and DDPG is that DQN uses ϵ-greedy actions during training. The policy network in DDPG, however, provides a deterministic action for a given state, hence the word "deterministic" in the name. To enable exploration during training, some noise is added to the action. More formally, the action is obtained as follows:

$$a = clip(\mu_{\phi_{target}}(s) + \epsilon, a_{Low}, a_{High})$$

where ϵ can be chosen as a white noise (although the original implementation uses what is called OU noise). In this operation, a_{Low} and a_{High} represent the boundaries of the continuous action space.

That's what DDPG is about. Let's look into how it can be parallelized next.

Ape-X DDPG

Given the similarity between deep Q-learning and DDPG, parallelization for DDPG can easily be achieved using the Ape-X framework. In fact, the original Ape-X paper presents DDPG next to DQN in their implementation. It improves the regular DDPG performance orders of magnitude in some benchmarks. The authors also show that the wall-clock time performance consistently increase with increased number of rollout workers (actors).

DDPG and Ape-X DPG using RLlib

The trainer class and the configs for DDPG can be imported as follows:

```
from ray.rllib.agents.ddpg.ddpg import(
    DEFAULT_CONFIG,
    DDPGTrainer as trainer)
```

Similarly, for Ape-X DDPG:

```
from ray.rllib.agents.ddpg.apex import (
    APEX_DDPG_DEFAULT_CONFIG as DEFAULT_CONFIG,
    ApexDDPGTrainer as trainer)
```

That's it! The rest is pretty much the same with the training flow we described at the beginning of the chapter. Now, before going into algorithms that improve DDPG, let's discuss where DDPG algorithm falls short.

DDPG shortcomings

Despite its initial popularity, there are several issues that the algorithm runs into:

- It can be quite sensitive to the hyper-parameter selections,
- It runs into the issue of maximization bias while learning the action values,
- Spikes in the action-value estimates (which are potentially erroneous) are exploited by the policy network and derails the learning.

Next, we look into the TD3 algorithm, which introduces a set of improvements to address these issues.

TD3: Twin Delayed Deep Deterministic Policy Gradient

The deal with the TD3 algorithm is that it addresses the function approximation errors in DDPG. As a result, it greatly outperforms DDPG, PPO, TRPO and SAC in terms of the maximum reward in OpenAI's continuous control benchmarks. Let's look into what TD3 proposes.

TD3 improvements over DDPG

There are three main improvements in TD3 over DDPG:

- It learns two (twin) Q networks rather than one, which in turn creates two target Q networks. The y targets are then obtained using the following:

$$y = r + \gamma \min_{i=1,2} Q_{\theta_{target,i}}\big(s', a'(s')\big)$$

  where $a'(s')$ is the target action for a given state s'. This is a form of double Q-learning to overcome the maximization bias.

- During training, the policy and the target networks are updated more slowly compared to the Q network updates, where the recommended cycle is to have a policy update for every two Q network update, hence the word "delayed" in the algorithm name.

- The target action, $a'(s')$, is obtained after some noise is added to the policy network outcome:

$$a'(s') = clip(\mu_{\phi_{target}}(s') + clip(\epsilon, -c, c), a_{Low}, a_{High})$$

  where ϵ is some white noise. Note that this is a different noise than what is used to explore in the environment. The role of this noise is to act as a regularizer and prevent the policy network to exploit some action values that are incorrectly estimated by the Q network as very high and non-smooth in its region.

> **Info**
> Just like DDPG, TD3 can only be used with continuous action spaces.

Next, let's see how you can train an RL agent using RLlib's TD3 implementation.

TD3 using RLlib

The TD3 trainer class can be imported as follows:

```
from ray.rllib.agents.ddpg.td3 import (
    TD3_DEFAULT_CONFIG as DEFAULT_CONFIG,
    TD3Trainer as trainer)
```

On the other hand, if you look into the code in the `td3.py` module of RLlib, you will see that it simply modifies the default DDPG configs and uses the DDPG trainer class under the hood. This means that TD3 improvements are optionally available in the DDPG trainer class, and you can modify them to obtain an Ape-X TD3 variant.

That's it with TD3. Next, we discuss SAC.

SAC: Soft actor-critic

SAC is another popular algorithm that outperforms TD3 in different benchmarks. It uses entropy that measures how diverse/random the actions suggested by a policy are as part of the reward to encourage exploration:

$$J(\pi_\theta) = E_{\tau \sim \rho_\theta(\tau)} \left[\sum_{t=0}^{\infty} \gamma^t (R(S_t, A_t) + \alpha H(\pi_\theta)) \right]$$

where H is the entropy term and α is the corresponding weight.

> **Tip**
> SAC can be used both with continuous and discrete action spaces.

To import the SAC trainer, use the following code:

```
from ray.rllib.agents.sac.sac import (
    DEFAULT_CONFIG,
    SACTrainer as trainer)
```

The final algorithm we will discuss is IMPALA.

IMPALA: Importance Weighted Actor-Learner Architecture

IMPALA is an algorithm that is of policy-gradient type, as opposed to DDPG, TD3 and SAC, which are essentially value-based methods. As a result, IMPALA is not completely an off-policy method. Actually, it is similar to A3C but with the following key differences:

- Unlike A3C, it sends sampled experiences (asynchronously) to the learner(s) rather than parameter gradients. This significantly reduces the communication overhead.

- When a sample trajectory arrives, chances are it was obtained under a policy that is several updates behind the policy in the learner. IMPALA uses truncated importance sampling to account for the policy lag while calculating the value function targets.

- IMPALA allows multiple synchronous worker learners to calculate gradients from samples.

The IMPALA trainer class can be imported in RLlib as follows:

```
from ray.rllib.agents.impala.impala import (
    DEFAULT_CONFIG,
    ImpalaTrainer as trainer)
```

This concludes our discussion on algorithms. Now the fun part! Let's compare their performances in OpenAI's continous-control Lunar Lander environment!

Comparison of the policy-based methods in Lunar Lander

Below is a comparison of evaluation reward performance progress for different policy-based algorithms over a single training session in the Lunar Lander environment:

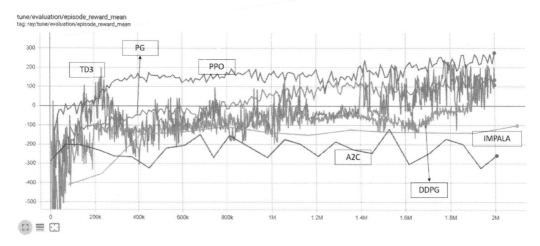

Figure 7.6 – Lunar Lander training performance of various policy-based algorithms

To also give a sense of how long each training session took and what was the performance at the end of the training, below is TensorBoard tooltip for the plot above:

Name	Smoothed	Value	Step	Time	Relative
A2C/A2C_LunarLanderContinuous-v2_0_2020-06-18_08-41-51em03j9y1	-258.6	-258.6	2.008M	Thu Jun 18, 08:46:23	4m 20s
DDPG/DDPG_LunarLanderContinuous-v2_0_2020-06-19_10-26-51qi9ksy28	152.2	152.2	1.92M	Sat Jun 20, 20:36:22	1d 10h 9m 3s
IMPALA/IMPALA_LunarLanderContinuous-v2_0_2020-06-19_07-09-128aho1rgt	-102.5	-102.5	2.101M	Fri Jun 19, 07:11:23	1m 55s
PG/PG_LunarLanderContinuous-v2_0_2020-06-18_08-30-48apnloyfy	135.2	135.2	2M	Thu Jun 18, 08:41:25	10m 26s
PPO/PPO_LunarLanderContinuous-v2_0_2020-06-18_09-20-47x6c75xg2	276.3	276.3	2M	Thu Jun 18, 10:03:57	42m 48s
TD3/TD3_LunarLanderContinuous-v2_0_2020-06-19_07-12-23t8zc4ihc	108.4	108.4	2M	Fri Jun 19, 10:19:40	3h 6m 49s

Figure 7.7 – Wall-clock time and end-of-training performance comparisons

Before going into further discussions, let's make the following disclaimer: The comparisons here should not be taken as a benchmark of different algorithms for multiple reasons:

- We did not perform any hyper-parameter tuning,
- The plots come from a single training trial for each algorithm. Training an RL agent is a highly stochastic process and a fair comparison should include the average of at least 5-10 training trials.
- We use RLlib's implementations of these algorithms, which could be less or more efficient than other open source implementations.

After this disclaimer, let's discuss what we observe in these results:

- PPO attains the highest reward at the end of the training.

- Vanilla policy gradient algorithm is the fastest (in terms of wall-clock time) to reach a "reasonable" reward.

- TD3 and DDPG are really slow in terms of wall-clock time although they achieve higher rewards than A2C and IMPALA.

- The TD3 training graph is significantly more unstable compared to other algorithms.

- At some point, TD3 achieved higher rewards than PPO with the same number of samples.

- IMPALA was super-fast to reach (and go beyond) 2M samples.

You can extend this list, but the idea here is that different algorithms could have different advantages and disadvantages. Next, let's discuss what criteria you should consider in picking an algorithm for your application.

How to pick the right algorithm?

As in all machine learning domains, there is no silver bullet in terms of which algorithm to use for different applications. There are many criteria you should consider, and in some cases some of them will be more important than others.

Here are different dimensions of algorithm performances that you should look into when picking your algorithm.

- **Highest reward**: When you are not bounded by compute and time resources and your goals is simply to train the best possible agent for your application, highest reward is the criterion you should pay attention to. PPO and SAC are promising alternatives here.

- **Sample efficiency**: If your sampling process is costly / time-consuming, then sample efficiency (achieving higher rewards using less samples is important). When this is the case, you should look into off-policy algorithms as they reuse past experiences for training as on-policy methods are often incredibly wasteful in how they consume samples. SAC is a good starting point in this case.

- **Wall-clock time efficiency**: If your simulator fast and/or you have resources to do massive parallelization, PPO, IMPALA and Ape-X SAC are often good choices.

- **Stability**: Your ability to achieve good rewards without running many trials with the same algorithm, and them improving consistently during training is also important. Off-policy algorithms could be hard to stabilize. PPO is often a good choice in this respect.

- **Generalization**: If an algorithm requires extensive tuning for each environment you train it for, this could cost you a lot of time and resources. SAC, due to its use of entropy in its reward, is known to be less sensitive to hyper-parameter choices.

- **Simplicity**: Having an algorithm that is easy to implement is important to avoid bugs and ensure maintainability. That is the reason TRPO has been abandoned in favor of PPO.

That is the end of the discussion on the algorithm picking criteria. Lastly, let's go into some resources where you can find easy-to-understand implementations of these algorithms.

Open source implementations of policy-gradient methods

In this chapter we have covered many algorithms. It is not quite possible to explicitly implement all these algorithms given the space limitations here. We instead relied on RLlib implementations to train agents for our use case. RLlib is open source, so you can go to `https://github.com/ray-project/ray/tree/releases/1.0.1/rllib` and dive into implementations of these algorithms.

Having said that, RLlib implementations is built for production systems and therefore involve many other implementations regarding error-handling, and preprocessing. In addition, there is a lot of code reuse, resulting in implementations of with multiple class inheritances. A much easier set of implementations is provided by OpenAI's Spinning Up repo at `https://github.com/openai/spinningup`. I highly recommend you go into that repo and dive into the implementation details of these algorithms we discussed in this chapter.

> **Info**
> OpenAI Spinning Up is a great resource also to see an overview of RL topics and algorithms, available at `https://spinningup.openai.com`

That's it! We have come a long way and covered policy-based methods in depth. Congratulations in reaching this important milestone!

Summary

In this chapter, we covered an important class of algorithms called policy-based methods. These methods directly optimize a policy network unlike the value-based methods we covered in the previous chapter. As a result, they have stronger theoretical foundation. In addition, they can be used with continuous action spaces. With this, we have covered model-free approaches in detail. In the next chapter, we go into model-based methods, which aim to learn the dynamics of the environment the agent is in.

References

1. OpenAI. (2018). Spinning Up. URL: `https://spinningup.openai.com/en/latest/spinningup/rl_intro2.html`

2. Williams R. (1992). Simple Statistical Gradient-Following Algorithms for Connectionist Reinforcement Learning. Machine Learning, 8, 229-256. URL: `https://link.springer.com/article/10.1007/BF00992696`

3. Sutton, R. et al. (1999). Policy Gradient Methods for Reinforcement Learning with Function Approximation. NIPS. URL: `https://bit.ly/31OMFs7`

4. Silver, D. et al. (2014). Deterministic Policy Gradient Algorithms. Journal of Machine Learning Research. URL: `http://proceedings.mlr.press/v32/silver14.pdf`

5. Mnih, Volodymyr, et al. (2016). Asynchronous Methods for Deep Reinforcement Learning. arXiv.org, `http://arxiv.org/abs/1602.01783`.

6. Gu, Shixiang, et al. (2016). Continuous Deep Q-Learning with Model-Based Acceleration. arXiv.org, `http://arxiv.org/abs/1603.00748`

7. Schulman, John, et al. (2017). Trust Region Policy Optimization. arXiv.org, `http://arxiv.org/abs/1502.05477`

8. Schulman, John, et al. (2017). Proximal Policy Optimization Algorithms. arXiv.org, `http://arxiv.org/abs/1707.06347`.

9. Espeholt, Lasse, et al. (2018). IMPALA: Scalable Distributed Deep-RL with Importance Weighted Actor-Learner Architectures. arXiv.org, `http://arxiv.org/abs/1802.01561`.

10. Fujimoto, Scott, et al. (2018). Addressing Function Approximation Error in Actor-Critic Methods. arXiv.org, `http://arxiv.org/abs/1802.09477`.

11. Haarnoja, Tuomas, et al. (2018). Soft Actor-Critic: Off-Policy Maximum Entropy Deep Reinforcement Learning with a Stochastic Actor. arXiv.org, `http://arxiv.org/abs/1801.01290`.

12. Haarnoja, Tuomas, et al. (2019). Soft Actor-Critic Algorithms and Applications. arXiv.org, `http://arxiv.org/abs/1812.05905`.

13. Christodoulou, Petros. (2019). Soft Actor-Critic for Discrete Action Settings. arXiv.org, `http://arxiv.org/abs/1910.07207`.

14. Lillicrap, Timothy P., et al. (2019). Continuous Control with Deep Reinforcement Learning. arXiv.org, `http://arxiv.org/abs/1509.02971`.

15. OpenAI, et al. (2019). Dota 2 with Large Scale Deep Reinforcement Learning. arXiv.org, `http://arxiv.org/abs/1912.06680`.

8
Model-Based Methods

All of the deep **reinforcement learning** (**RL**) algorithms we have covered so far were **model-free**, which means they did not assume any knowledge about the transition dynamics of the environment but learned from sampled experiences. In fact, this was a quite deliberate departure from the dynamic programming methods to save us from requiring a model of the environment. In this chapter, we swing the pendulum back a little bit and discuss a class of methods that rely on a model, called **model-based methods**. These methods can lead to improved sample efficiency by several orders of magnitude in some problems, making it a very appealing approach, especially when collecting experience is as costly as in robotics. Having said this, we still will not assume that we have such a model readily available, but we will discuss how to learn one. Once we have a model, it can be used for decision-time planning and improving the performance of model-free methods.

This important chapter includes the following topics:

- Introducing model-based methods
- Planning through a model
- Learning a world model
- Unifying model-based and model-free approaches

Let's get started.

Introducing model-based methods

Imagine a scene in which you are traveling in a car on an undivided road and you face the following situation. Suddenly, another car in the opposing direction approaches you fast in your lane as it is passing a truck. Chances are your mind automatically simulates different scenarios about how the next scenes might unfold:

- The other car might go back to its lane right away or drive even faster to pass the truck as soon as possible.
- Another scenario could be the car steering toward your right, but this is an unlikely scenario (in a right-hand traffic flow).

The driver (possibly you) then evaluates the likelihood and risk of each scenario, together with their possible actions too, and makes the decision to safely continue the journey.

In a less sensational example, consider a game of chess. Before making a move, a player "simulates" many scenarios in their head and assesses the possible outcomes of several moves down the road. In fact, being able to accurately evaluate more possible scenarios after a move would increase the chances of winning.

In both of these examples, the decision-making process involves picturing multiple "imaginary" rollouts of the environment, evaluating the alternatives, and taking an appropriate action accordingly. But how do we do that? We are able to do so because we have a mental model of the world that we live in. In the car driving example, drivers have an idea about possible traffic behaviors, how other drivers might move, and how physics works. In the chess example, players know the rules of the game, which moves are good, and possibly what strategies a particular player might use. This "model-based" thinking is almost the natural way to plan our actions, and different than a model-free approach that would not leverage such priors on how the world works.

Model-based methods, since they leverage more information and structure about the environment, could be more sample-efficient than model-free methods. This comes especially handy in applications where sample collection is expensive, such as robotics. So, this is such an important topic that we cover in this chapter. We will focus on two main aspects of model-based approaches:

- How a model of the environment (or *world model*, as we will refer to it) can be used in the optimal planning of actions
- How such a model can be learned when one is not available

In the next section, we start with the former and introduce some of the methods to use for planning when a model is available. Once we are convinced that learning a model of the environment is worth it and we can indeed obtain good actions with the optimal planning methods, we will discuss how such models can be learned.

Planning through a model

In this section, we first define what it means to plan through a model in the sense of optimal control. Then, we will cover several planning methods, including the cross-entropy method and covariance matrix adaptation evolution strategy. You will also see how these methods can be parallelized using the Ray library. Now, let's get started with the problem definition.

Defining the optimal control problem

In RL, or in control problems in general, we care about the actions an agent takes because there is a task that we want to be achieved. We express this task as a mathematical objective so that we can use mathematical tools to figure out the actions toward the task – and in RL, this is the expected sum of cumulative discounted rewards. You of course know all this, as this is what we have been doing all along, but this is a good time to reiterate it: We are essentially solving an optimization problem here.

Now, let's assume that we are trying to figure out the best actions for a problem with a horizon of T time steps. As examples, you can think of the Atari games, Cartpole, a self-driving car, a robot in a grid world, and more. We can define the optimization problem as follows (using the notation in *Levine, 2019*):

$$a_1, ..., a_T = \arg \max_{a_1,...,a_T} J(a_1, ..., a_T)$$

All this says is how to find a sequence of actions, where a_t corresponds to the action at time step t, that maximizes the score over a T steps. Note here that a_t could be multi-dimensional (say d) if there are multiple actions taken in each step (steering and acceleration/brake decisions in a car). Let's also denote a sequence of T actions using $A = [a_1, ..., a_T]$. So, our concern is to find such an A that maximizes J.

At this point, there are different optimization and control styles we may pick. Let's look into those next.

Derivative-based and derivative-free optimization

When we see an optimization problem, a natural reaction for solving it could be "let's take the first derivative, set it equal to zero," and so on. But don't forget that, most of the time, we don't have J as a closed-form mathematical expression that we can take the derivative of. Take playing an Atari game, for example. We can evaluate what $J(A)$ is for a given A by just playing it, but we would not be able to calculate any derivatives. This matters when it comes to the type of optimization approach we can use. In particular, note the following types:

- **Derivative-based methods** require taking the derivative of the objective function to optimize it.

- **Derivative-free methods** rely on systematically and repeatedly evaluating the objective function in search of the best inputs.

Therefore, we will rely on the latter here.

This was about what kind of optimization procedure we will use, which, at the end, gives us some A. Another important design choice is about how to execute it, which we turn to next.

Open-loop, closed-loop, and model predictive control

Let's start explaining different types of control systems with an example: Imagine that we have an agent that is a soccer player in a forward position. For the sake of simplicity, let's assume that the only goal of the agent is to score a goal when it receives the ball. At the first moment of possessing the ball, the agent can do either of the following:

- Come up with a plan to score, close their eyes and ears (that is, any means of perception), and then execute the plan until the end (either scoring or losing the ball).

- Or, the agent can keep their means of perception active and modify the plan with the latest information available from the environment as it happens.

The former would be an example of **open-loop control**, where no feedback from the environment is used while taking the next action, whereas the latter would be an example of **closed-loop control**, which uses environmental feedback. In general, in RL, we have closed-loop control.

> **Tip**
>
> Using closed-loop control has the advantage of taking the latest information into account when planning. This is especially advantageous if the environment and/or controller dynamics are not deterministic, so a perfect prediction is not possible.

Now, the agent can use feedback, the most recent observation from the environment at time t, in different ways. Specifically, the agent can do the following:

- Choose the action from a policy π given o_t, that is, $\pi(a|o_t)$.
- Resolve the optimization problem to find A for the subsequent T time steps.

The latter is called **model predictive control** (**MPC**). To reiterate, in MPC, the agent repeats the following loop:

1. Come up with an optimal control plan for the next T steps.
2. Execute the plan for the first step.
3. Proceed to the next step.

Note that the way we posed the optimization problem so far does not give us a policy π yet. Instead, we will search for a good A using derivative-free optimization methods.

Next, let's discuss a very simple derivative-free method: random shooting.

Random shooting

The random shooting procedure simply involves the following steps:

1. Generating a bunch of candidate action sequences uniformly at random, say N of them.
2. Evaluate each of $J(A_1), ..., J(A_N)$.
3. Take the action A_i that gives the best $J(A_i)$, that is, $\arg\max_i J(A_i)$.

As you can tell, this is not a particularly sophisticated optimization procedure. Yet, it can be used as a baseline to compare more sophisticated methods against.

> **Tip**
> Random search-based methods could be more effective than you might think.
> *Mania et al.* outline such a method to optimize policy parameters in their
> paper *"Simple random search provides a competitive approach to RL,"* which,
> as is apparent from its name, yields some surprisingly good results (*Mania
> et al., 2018*).

To make our discussion more concrete, let's introduce a simple example. But before doing
so, we need to set up the Python virtual environment that we will use in this chapter.

Setting up the Python virtual environment

You can install the packages we will need inside a virtual environment as follows:

```
$ virtualenv mbenv
$ source mbenv/bin/activate
$ pip install ray[rllib]==1.0.1
$ pip install tensorflow==2.3.1
$ pip install cma==3.0.3
$ pip install gym[box2d]
```

Now, we can proceed to our example.

Simple cannon shooting game

Some of us are old enough to have enjoyed the old *Bang! Bang!* game on Windows 3.1 or
95. The game simply involves adjusting the shooting angle and velocity of a cannonball to
hit the opponent. Here, we will play something even simpler: We have a cannon for which
we can adjust the shooting angle (θ). Our goal is to maximize the distance, d, that the ball
covers on a flat surface with a fixed initial velocity v_0. This is illustrated in *Figure 8.1*:

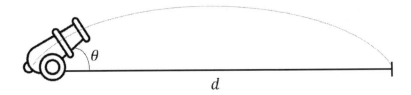

Figure 8.1 – Simple cannon shooting game to maximize **d** by adjusting **θ**

Now, if you remember some high-school math, you will realize that there is really no game here: The maximum distance can be reached by setting $\theta = 45°$. Well, let's pretend that we don't know it and use this example to illustrate the concepts that we have introduced so far:

- The action is θ, the angle of the cannon, which is a scalar.

- This is a single-step problem, that is, we just take one action and the game ends. Therefore $T = 1$, and $A = [a_1]$.

Let's now code this up:

1. We have access to the environment that will *evaluate the actions we consider before we actually take them*. We don't assume to know what the math equations and all the dynamics defined inside the environment are. In other words, we can call the `black_box_projectile` function to get d for a θ we pick and for a fixed initial velocity and gravity:

```python
from math import sin, pi
def black_box_projectile(theta, v0=10, g=9.81):
    assert theta >= 0
    assert theta <= 90
    return (v0 ** 2) * sin(2 * pi * theta / 180) / g
```

2. For the random shooting procedure, we just need to generate N actions uniformly randomly between 0° and 90°, for which we can use something like the following:

```python
import random
def random_shooting(n, min_a=0, max_a=90):
    return [random.uniform(min_a, max_a) for i in
range(n)]
```

3. We also need a function to evaluate all the candidate actions and pick the best one. For this, we will define a more general function that we will need later. It will pick the best M **elites**, that is, the M best actions:

```python
import numpy as np
def pick_elites(actions, M_elites):
    actions = np.array(actions)
    assert M_elites <= len(actions)
    assert M_elites > 0
    results = np.array([black_box_projectile(a)
```

```
                              for a in actions])
         sorted_ix = np.argsort(results)[-M_elites:][::-1]
         return actions[sorted_ix], results[sorted_ix]
```

4.   The loop to find the best action is then simple:

```
n = 20
actions_to_try = random_shooting(n)
best_action, best_result = pick_elites(actions_to_try, 1)
```

That's it. The action to take is then at `best_action[0]`. To reiterate, we have not done anything super interesting so far. This was just to illustrate the concepts, and to prepare you for a more interesting method that is coming up next.

Cross-entropy method

In the cannon shooting example, we evaluated some number of actions we generated in our search for the optimal action, which happens to be $\theta = 45°$. As you can imagine, we can be smarter in our search. For example, if we have a budget to generate and evaluate 100 actions, why blindly use them up with uniformly generated actions? Instead, we can do the following:

1.   Generate some number of actions to begin with (this could be done uniformly at random).

2.   See which region in the action space seems to be giving better results (in the cannon shooting example, the region is around 45°).

3.   Generate more actions in that part of the action space.

We can repeat this procedure to guide our search, which will lead to a more efficient use of our search budget. In fact, this is what the **cross-entropy method** (CEM) suggests!

Our previous description of the CEM was a bit vague. A more formal description is as follows:

1.   Initialize a probability distribution $f(A; v)$ with parameter v.

2.   Generate N samples (solutions, actions) from f, $A_1, ..., A_N$.

3.   Sort the solutions from the highest reward to the lowest, indexed as $i_1, ..., i_N$, $J(A_{i_1}) \geq J(A_{i_2}) \geq, ..., \geq J(A_{i_N})$.

4.   Pick the best M solutions, elites, $A_{i_1}, ..., A_{i_M}$ and fit the distribution f to the elites.

5.   Go back to *step 2* and repeat until a stopping criterion is satisfied.

The algorithm, in particular, identifies the best region of actions by fitting a probability distribution to the best actions in the current iteration, from which the next generation of actions is sampled. Due to this evolutionary nature, it is considered an **evolution strategy** (**ES**).

> **Tip**
> The CEM could prove promising when the dimension of the search, that is the action dimension times T, is relatively small, say less than 50. Also note that CEM does not use the actual rewards in any part of the procedure, saving us from worrying about the scale of the rewards.

Next, let's implement the CEM for the cannon shooting example.

Simple implementation of the cross-entropy method

We can implement the CEM with some slight modifications to the random shooting method. In our simple implementation here, we do the following:

- Start with a uniformly generated set of actions.
- Fit a normal distribution to the elites to generate the next set of samples.
- Use a fixed number of iterations to stop the procedure.

This can be implemented as follows:

```
from scipy.stats import norm
N, M_elites, iterations = 5, 2, 3
actions_to_try = random_shooting(N)
elite_acts, _ = pick_elites(actions_to_try, M_elites)
for r in range(iterations - 1):
    mu, std = norm.fit(elite_acts)
    actions_to_try = np.clip(norm.rvs(mu, std, N), 0, 90)
    elite_acts, elite_results = pick_elites(actions_to_try,
                                            M_elites)
best_action, _ = norm.fit(elite_acts)
```

If you add some `print` statements to see the outcome from the execution of this code, it will look like the following:

```
--iteration: 1
actions_to_try: [29.97 3.56 57.8 5.83 74.15]
```

```
elites: [57.8  29.97]
--iteration: 2
fitted normal mu: 43.89, std: 13.92
actions_to_try: [26.03 52.85 36.69 54.67 25.06]
elites: [52.85 36.69]
--iteration: 3
fitted normal mu: 44.77, std: 8.08
actions_to_try: [46.48 34.31 56.56 45.33 48.31]
elites: [45.33 46.48]
The best action: 45.91
```

You might be wondering why we need to fit the distribution instead of picking the best action we have identified. Well, it does not make much sense for the cannon shooting example where the environment is deterministic. However, when there is noise/stochasticity in the environment, picking the best action that we encountered would mean overfitting to the noise. Instead, we fit the distribution to a set of elite actions to overcome that. You can refer to `Chapter08/rs_cem_comparison.py` in the GitHub repo for the full code.

The evaluation (and action generation) steps of the CEM can be parallelized, which would reduce the wall-clock time to make a decision. Let's implement it next and use the CEM in a more sophisticated example.

Parallelized implementation of the cross-entropy method

In this section, we use the CEM to solve OpenAI Gym's Cartpole-v0 environment. This example will differ from the cannon shooting in the following ways:

- The action space is binary, corresponding to left and right. So, we will use a multivariate Bernoulli distribution as the probability distribution.
- The maximum problem horizon is 200 steps. However, we will use MPC to plan for a 10-step lookahead in each step and execute the first action in the plan.
- We use the Ray library for parallelization.

Now, let's look into some of the key components of the implementation. The full code is available in the GitHub repo.

Chapter08/cem.py

Let's start describing the code with the section that samples a sequence of actions from a multivariate Bernoulli (for which we use NumPy's `binomial` function), A_i, and executes it over the planning horizon to estimate the reward:

```python
@ray.remote
def rollout(env, dist, args):
    if dist == "Bernoulli":
        actions = np.random.binomial(**args)
    else:
        raise ValueError("Unknown distribution")
    sampled_reward = 0
    for a in actions:
        obs, reward, done, info = env.step(a)
        sampled_reward += reward
        if done:
            break
    return actions, sampled_reward
```

The `ray.remote` decorator will allow us to easily kick off a bunch of these workers in parallel.

The CEM runs in the following method of the CEM class we create:

1. We initialize the parameters of the Bernoulli distribution for a horizon of `look_ahead` steps as `0.5`. We also determine the number of elites based on a specified fraction of the total samples:

    ```python
    def cross_ent_optimizer(self):
        n_elites = int(np.ceil(self.num_parallel * \
                               self.elite_frac))
        if self.dist == "Bernoulli":
            p = [0.5] * self.look_ahead
    ```

2. For a fixed number of iterations, we generate and evaluate actions on parallel rollout workers. Note how we copy the existing environment to the rollout workers to sample from that point on. We refit the distribution to the elite set:

    ```python
    for i in range(self.opt_iters):
        futures = []
    ```

```
        for j in range(self.num_parallel):
            args = {"n": 1, "p": p,
                    "size": self.look_ahead}
            fid = \
                rollout.remote(copy.deepcopy(self.
env),
                                            self.dist,
args)
            futures.append(fid)
        results = [tuple(ray.get(id))
                            for id in futures]
        sampled_rewards = [r for _, r in results]
        elite_ix = \
            np.argsort(sampled_rewards)[-n_
elites:]
        elite_actions = np.array([a for a,
                        _ in results])[elite_
ix]
        p = np.mean(elite_actions, axis=0)
```

3. We finalize the plan based on the latest distribution parameters:

```
    actions = np.random.binomial(n=1, p=p,
                    size=self.look_
ahead)
```

Executing this code will solve the environment and you will see the cartpole staying alive for the maximum horizon!

That is how a parallelized CEM can be implemented using Ray. So far, so good! Next, we will go a step further and use an advanced version of the CEM.

Covariance matrix adaptation evolution strategy

The **covariance matrix adaptation evolution strategy** (**CMA-ES**) is one of the state-of-the-art black-box optimization methods. Its working principles are similar to that of the CEM. On the other hand, the CEM uses a constant variance throughout the search. The CMA-ES dynamically adapts the covariance matrix.

We again use Ray to parallelize the search with the CMA-ES. But this time, we defer the inner dynamics of the search to a Python library called `pycma`, which is developed and maintained by Nikolaus Hansen, creator of the algorithm. You already installed this package when you created the virtual environment for this chapter.

> **Info**
>
> The documentation and the details of the `pycma` library are available at
> `https://github.com/CMA-ES/pycma`.

The main difference of the CMA-ES from the CEM implementation is its use of the CMA library to optimize the actions:

```python
def cma_es_optimizer(self):
    es = cma.CMAEvolutionStrategy([0] \
                                * self.n_tot_actions, 1)
    while (not es.stop()) and \
            es.result.iterations <= self.opt_iter:
        X = es.ask()  # get list of new solutions
        futures = [
            rollout.remote(self.env, x,
                        self.n_actions,
                        self.look_ahead)
            for x in X
        ]
        costs = [-ray.get(id) for id in futures]
        es.tell(X, costs)  # feed values
        es.disp()
    actions = [
        es.result.xbest[i * self.n_actions : \
                    (i + 1) * self.n_actions]
        for i in range(self.look_ahead)
    ]
    return actions
```

You can find the full code in `Chapter08/cma_es.py` in our GitHub repo. It solves the Bipedal Walker environment, and the output will look like the following from the CMA library:

```
(7_w,15)-aCMA-ES (mu_w=4.5,w_1=34%) in dimension 40
(seed=836442, Mon Nov 30 05:46:55 2020)
Iterat #Fevals   function value   axis ratio  sigma  min&max std
t[m:s]
      1      15 7.467667956594279e-01 1.0e+00 9.44e-01  9e-01  9e-
01 0:00.0
      2      30 8.050216186274498e-01 1.1e+00 9.22e-01  9e-01  9e-
01 0:00.1
      3      45 7.222612141709712e-01 1.1e+00 9.02e-01  9e-01  9e-
01 0:00.1
     71    1065 9.341667377266198e-01 1.8e+00 9.23e-01  9e-01
1e+00 0:03.1
    100    1500 8.486571756945928e-01 1.8e+00 7.04e-01  7e-01  8e-
01 0:04.3
Episode 0, reward: -121.5869865603307
```

You should see your bipedal walker taking 50 to 100 steps out of the box! Not bad!

Next, let's touch on another important class of search methods, known as **Monte Carlo tree search** (**MCTS**).

Monte Carlo tree search

A natural way of planning future actions is for us to first think about the first step, then condition the second decision on the first one, and so on. This is essentially a search on a decision tree, which is what MCTS does. It is a strikingly powerful method that has seen broad adaptation in the AI community.

> **Info**
>
> MCTS is a powerful method that played a key role in DeepMind's victory against Lee Sedol, a world champion and legend in the game of Go. Therefore, MCTS deserves a broad discussion; and rather than cramming some content into this chapter, we defer its explanation and implementation to the blog post at `https://int8.io/monte-carlo-tree-search-beginners-guide/`.

In this section so far, we have discussed the different methods with which an agent can plan through a model of an environment where we assumed such a model exists. In the next section, we look into how the model of the world (that is, the environment) that the agent is in can be learned.

Learning a world model

In the introduction to this chapter, we reminded you how we departed from dynamic programming methods to avoid assuming that the model of the environment an agent is in is available and accessible. Now, coming back to talking about models, we need to also discuss how a world model can be learned when not available. In particular, in this section, we discuss what we aim to learn as a model, when we may want to learn it, a general procedure for learning a model, how to improve it by incorporating the model uncertainty into the learning procedure, and what to do when we have complex observations. Let's dive in!

Understanding what model means

From what we have done so far, a model of the environment could be equivalent to the simulation of the environment in your mind. On the other hand, model-based methods don't require the full fidelity of a simulation. Instead, what we expect to get from a model is the next state given the current state and action. Namely, when the environment is deterministic, a model is a function f:

$$f(s_{t+1}|s_t, a_t)$$

If the environment is stochastic, we then need a probability distribution over the next state, p, to sample from:

$$p(s_{t+1}|s_t, a_t)$$

Contrast this to a simulation model that often has explicit representations of all the underlying dynamics, such as motion physics, customer behavior, and market dynamics, depending on the type of environment. The model we learn will be a black box and is often represented as a neural network.

> **Info**
>
> A world model that we learn is not a replacement for a full simulation model.
> A simulation model often has a much greater capability of generalization;
> and it is also of a greater fidelity as it is based on explicit representations of
> environment dynamics. On the other hand, a simulation can act as a world
> model, as in the previous section.

Note that, for the rest of the section, we will use f to represent the model. Now, let's
discuss when we may want to learn a world model.

Identifying when to learn a model

There could be various reasons for learning a world model:

- A model may not exist, even as a simulation. This means the agent is being trained
  in the actual environment, which would not allow us to do imaginary rollouts for
  planning.

- A simulation model may exist, but it could be too slow or computationally
  demanding to be used in planning. Training a neural network as a world model can
  allow exploring a much wider range of scenarios during the planning phase.

- A simulation model may exist, but it may not allow rollouts from a particular state
  onward. This could be because the simulation may not reveal the underlying state
  and/or it may not allow the user to reset it to a desired state.

- We may want to explicitly have a representation of the state/observation that has
  a predictive power for the future states, which then removes the need for having
  complex policy representations or even rollout-based planning for the agent. This
  approach has biological inspirations and has proved to be effective, as described
  by *Ha et al., 2018*. You can access an interactive version of the paper at `https://worldmodels.github.io/`, which is a very good read on this topic.

Now that we have identified several cases where learning a model might be necessary,
next, let's discuss how to actually do it.

Introducing a general procedure to learn a model

Learning a model of f (or p for stochastic environments) is essentially a supervised
learning problem: we want to predict the next state from the current state and action.
However, note the following key points:

- We don't start the process with data on hand like in a traditional supervised learning
  problem. Instead, we need to generate the data by interacting with the environment.

- We don't have a (good) policy to start interacting with the environment either. After all, it is our goal to obtain one.

So, what we need to do first is to initialize some policy. A natural choice is to use a random policy so that we can explore the state-action space. On the other hand, a pure random policy may not get us far in some hard exploration problems. Consider training a humanoid robot for walking, for example. Random actions are unlikely to make the robot walk, and we would not be able to obtain data to train a world model for those states. This requires us to do planning and learning simultaneously, so that the agent both explores and exploits. To that end, we can use the following procedure (*Levine, 2019*):

1. Initialize a soft policy $\pi(a|s)$ to collect data tuples $(s, a, s')_i$ into a dataset $\mathcal{D}$.

2. Train f to minimize $\sum_i \|f(s_i, a_i) - s'_i\|^2$.

3. Plan through f to choose actions.

4. Follow an MPC: execute the first planned action and observe the resulting s'.

5. Append the obtained (s, a, s') to $\mathcal{D}$.

6. Every M steps, go to *step 3*; every N steps, go to *step 2*.

This approach will eventually get you a trained f, which you can use with an MPC procedure at inference time. On the other hand, as it turns out, the performance of an agent using this procedure is often worse than what a model-free approach would do. In the next section, we look into why this happens and how the problem can be mitigated.

Understanding and mitigating the impact of model uncertainty

When we train a world model as in the procedure we just described, we should not expect to obtain a perfect one. This should not be surprising, but it turns out that when we plan through such imperfect models using rather good optimizers such as the CMA-ES, those imperfections hurt the agent performance badly. Especially when we use high-capacity models such as neural networks, in the presence of limited data, there will be lots of errors in the model, incorrectly predicting high-reward states. To mitigate the impact of model errors, we need to take the uncertainty in the model predictions into account.

Speaking of uncertainty in model predictions, there are two types, and we need to differentiate between them. Let's do that next.

Statistical (aleatoric) uncertainty

Consider a predictive model that predicts the outcome of the roll of a six-sided fair die. A perfect model will be highly uncertain about the outcome: any side can come up with equal likelihood. This might be disappointing, but it is not the model's "fault." The uncertainty is due to the process itself and not because the model is not correctly explaining the data it observes. This type of uncertainty is called **statistical** or **aleatoric uncertainty**.

Epistemic (model) uncertainty

In another example, imagine training a predictive model to predict the outcome of the roll of a six-sided die. We don't know whether the die is fair or not, and in fact, this is what we are trying to learn from the data. Now, imagine that we train the model just based on a single observation, which happens to be a 6. When we use the model to predict the next outcome, the model may predict a 6, because it is all the model has seen. However, this would be based on very limited data, so we would be highly uncertain about the model's prediction. This type of uncertainty is called **epistemic** or **model uncertainty**. And it is this type of uncertainty that is getting us into trouble in model-based RL.

Let's see some ways of dealing with model uncertainty in the next section.

Mitigating the impact of model uncertainty

Two common ways of incorporating model uncertainty into model-based RL procedures are to use Bayesian neural networks and ensemble models.

Using Bayesian neural networks

A Bayesian neural network assigns a distribution over each of the parameters in θ (the parameters of the network) rather than a single number. This gives us a probability distribution, $p(\theta|\mathcal{D})$, to sample a neural network from. With that, we can quantify the uncertainty over the neural network parameters.

> **Info**
> Note that we used Bayesian neural networks in *Chapter 3, Contextual Bandits*. Revisiting that chapter might refresh your mind on the topic. A full tutorial is available from *Jospin et al., 2020*, if you want to dive deeper.

With this approach, whenever we are at the planning step, we sample from $p(\theta|\mathcal{D})$ multiple times to estimate the reward for an action sequence A.

Using ensemble models with bootstrapping

Another method to estimate uncertainty is to use bootstrapping, which is easier to implement than a Bayesian neural network but also a less principled approach. Bootstrapping simply involves training multiple (say 10) neural networks for f, each using data resampled from the original dataset with replacement.

> **Info**
>
> If you need a quick refresher on bootstrapping in statistics, check out this blog post by Trist'n Joseph: `https://bit.ly/3fQ37r1`.

Similar to the use of Bayesian networks, this time, we average the reward given by these multiple neural networks to evaluate an action sequence A during planning.

With that, we conclude our discussion on incorporating model uncertainty into model-based RL. Before we wrap up this section, let's touch on how to consume complex observations to learn a world model.

Learning a model from complex observations

Everything we have described so far can get a bit complicated to implement when we have one or both of the following:

- Partially observable environments, so the agent sees o_t rather than s_t.

- High-dimensional observations, such as images.

We have an entire chapter coming up on partial observability in *Chapter 11, Achieving Generalization and Overcoming Partial Observability*. In that chapter, we will discuss how keeping a memory of past observations helps us uncover the hidden state in the environment. A common architecture to use is the **long short-term memory (LSTM)** model, which is a particular class of **recurrent neural network (RNN)** architectures. Therefore, representing f using an LSTM would be a common choice in the face of partial observability.

When it comes to dealing with high-dimensional observations, such as images, a common approach is to encode them in compact vectors. **Variational autoencoders (VAEs)** are the choice when it comes to obtaining such representations.

> **Info**
>
> A nice tutorial on VAEs by Jeremy Jordan is available at `https://www.jeremyjordan.me/variational-autoencoders/`.

When the environment is both partially observable and emitting image observations, we would then have to first convert images to encodings, use an RNN for f that predicts the encoding that corresponds to the next observation, and plan through this f. *Ha et al., 2018,* used a similar approach to deal with images and partial observability in their "*World Models*" paper.

This concludes our discussion on learning a world model. In the next and final section of this chapter, let's discuss how we can use the approaches we have described so far to obtain a policy for an RL agent.

Unifying model-based and model-free approaches

When we went from dynamic programming-based approaches to Monte Carlo and temporal-difference methods in *Chapter 5, Solving the Reinforcement Learning Problem,* our motivation was that it is limiting to assume that the environment transition probabilities are known. Now that we know how to learn the environment dynamics, we will leverage that to find a middle ground. It turns out that with a learned model of the environment, the learning with model-free methods can be accelerated. To that end, in this section, we first refresh our minds on Q-learning, then introduce a class of methods called **Dyna**.

Refresher on Q-learning

Let's start with remembering the definition of the action-value function:

$$Q(s, a) = E\left[R_{t+1} + \gamma \max_{a'} Q(S_{t+1}, a') \mid S_t = s, A_t = a\right]$$

The expectation operator here is because the transition into the next state is probabilistic, so S_{t+1} is a random variable along with R_{t+1}. On the other hand, if we know the probability distribution of S_{t+1} and R_{t+1}, we can calculate this expectation analytically, which is what methods such as value iteration do.

In the absence of information on the transition dynamics, methods such as Q-learning estimate the expectation from a single sample of (r, s'):

$$Q(s, a) := Q(s, a) + \alpha \left[r + \gamma \max_{a'} Q(s', a') - Q(s, a)\right]$$

Dyna algorithms are based on the idea that, rather than using a simple (r, s') sampled from the environment, we can come up with a better estimation of the expectation using a learned model of the environment by sampling many (r, s') from it given (s, a).

> **Tip**
>
> So far in our discussions, we have implicitly assumed that reward r can be calculated once (s, a, s') is known. If that is not the case, especially in the presence of partial observability, we may have to learn a separate model for $g(r|s, a, s')$.

Next, let's more formally outline this idea.

Dyna-style acceleration of model-free methods using world models

The Dyna approach is a rather old one (*Sutton, 1990*) that aims to "integrate learning, planning, and reacting." This approach has the following general flow (*Levine, 2019*):

1. While in state s, sample a using $\pi(a|s)$.

2. Observe s' and r, and add the tuple (s, a, r, s') to a replay buffer $\mathcal{B}$.

3. Update the world model $p(s'|s, a)$ and optionally $g(r|s, a, s')$.

   For **1** to K:

4. Sample s from $\mathcal{B}$.

5. Choose some a, either from π, from $\mathcal{B}$, or at random.

6. Sample $s' \sim p(s'|s, a)$ and $r \sim g(r|s, a, s')$.

7. Train on (s, a, r, s') with a model-free RL method (deep Q-learning).

8. Optionally, take further steps after s'.

   End For

9. Go back to *step 1* (and $s := s'$).

That's it! Dyna is an important class of methods in RL, and now you know how it works!

> **Info**
>
> RLlib has an advanced Dyna-style method implementation called **Model-Based RL via Meta-Policy Optimization** or **MBMPO**. You can check it out at `https://docs.ray.io/en/releases-1.0.1/rllib-algorithms.html#mbmpo`. As of Ray 1.0.1, it is implemented in PyTorch, so go ahead and install PyTorch in your virtual environment if you would like to experiment with it.

This concludes our chapter on model-based RL; and congratulations for reaching this far! We only scratched the surface in this broad topic, but now you are equipped with the knowledge to start using model-based methods for your problems! Let's summarize what we have covered next.

Summary

In this chapter, we covered model-based methods. We started the chapter by describing how we humans use the world models we have in our brains to plan our actions. Then, we introduced several methods that can be used to plan an agent's actions in an environment when a model is available. These were derivative-free search methods, and for the CEM and CMA-ES methods, we implemented parallelized versions. As a natural follow-up to this section, we then went into how a world model can be learned to be used for planning or developing policies. This section contained some important discussions about model uncertainty and how learned models can suffer from it. At the end of the chapter, we unified the model-free and model-based approaches in the Dyna framework.

As we conclude our discussion on model-based RL, we proceed to the next chapter for yet another exciting topic: multi-agent RL. Take a break, and we will see you soon!

References

1. Levine, Sergey. (2019). *Optimal Control and Planning*. CS285 Fa19 10/2/19. YouTube. URL: `https://youtu.be/pE0GUFs-EHI`

2. Levine, Sergey. (2019). *Model-Based Reinforcement Learning*. CS285 Fa19 10/7/19. YouTube. URL: `https://youtu.be/6JDfrPRhexQ`

3. Levine, Sergey. (2019). *Model-Based Policy Learning*. CS285 Fa19 10/14/19. YouTube. URL: `https://youtu.be/9AbBfIgTzoo`.

4. Ha, David, and Jürgen Schmidhuber. (2018). *World Models*. arXiv.org, URL: `https://arxiv.org/abs/1803.10122`.

5. Mania, Horia, et al. (2018). *Simple Random Search Provides a Competitive Approach to Reinforcement Learning*. arXiv.org, URL: `http://arxiv.org/abs/1803.07055`

6. Jospin, Laurent Valentin, et al. (2020). *Hands-on Bayesian Neural Networks – a Tutorial for Deep Learning Users*. arXiv.org, `http://arxiv.org/abs/2007.06823`.

7. Joseph, Trist'n. (2020). *Bootstrapping Statistics. What It Is and Why It's Used.* Medium. URL: `https://bit.ly/3fOlvjK`.

8. Richard S. Sutton. (1991). *Dyna, an integrated architecture for learning, planning, and reacting.* SIGART Bull. 2, 4 (Aug. 1991), 160–163. DOI: `https://doi.org/10.1145/122344.122377`

9
Multi-Agent Reinforcement Learning

If there is something more exciting than training a **reinforcement learning** (RL) agent to exhibit intelligent behavior, it is to train multiple of them to collaborate or compete. **Multi-agent RL** (**MARL**) is where you will really feel the potential in artificial intelligence. Many famous RL stories, such as AlphaGo or OpenAI Five, stemmed from MARL, which we introduce you to in this chapter. Of course, there is no free lunch, and MARL comes with lots of challenges along with its opportunities, which we will also explore. At the end of the chapter, we will train a bunch of tic-tac-toe agents through competitive self-play. So, at the end, you will have some companions to play some game against.

This will be a fun chapter, and specifically we will cover the following topics:

- Introducing multi-agent reinforcement learning,
- Exploring the challenges in multi-agent reinforcement learning,
- Training policies in multi-agent settings,
- Training tic-tac-toe agents through self-play.

Let's get started!

Introducing multi-agent reinforcement learning

All of the problems and algorithms we have covered in the book so far involved a single agent being trained in an environment. On the other hand, in many applications from games to autonomous vehicle fleets, there are multiple decision-makers, agents, which train concurrently, but execute local policies (i.e., without a central decision-maker). This leads us to MARL, which involves a much richer set of problems and challenges than single-agent RL does. In this section, we give an overview of MARL landscape.

Collaboration and competition between MARL agents

MARL problems can be classified into three different groups with respect to the structure of collaboration and competition between agents. Let's look into what those groups are and what types of applications fit into each group.

Fully cooperative environments

In this setting, all of the agents in the environment work towards a common long-term goal. The agents are credited equally for the return the environment reveals, so there is no incentive for any of the agents to deviate from the common goal.

Here are some examples to fully cooperative environments:

- **Autonomous vehicle / robot fleets**: There are many applications where a fleet of autonomous vehicles / robots could work towards accomplishing a common mission. One example is disaster recovery / emergency response / rescue missions, where the fleet tries to achieve tasks such as delivering emergency supplies to first responders, shutting of gas valves, removing debris from roads etc. Similarly, transportation problems as in supply chains or in the form of transporting a big object using multiple robots are good examples in this category.

- **Manufacturing**: The whole idea behind Industry 4.0 is to have interconnected equipment and cyber-physical systems to achieve efficient production and service. If you think of a single manufacturing floor, in which there are usually many decision-making equipment, MARL is a natural fit to model such control problems.

- **Smart grid**: In the emerging field of smart grid, many problems can be modeled in this category. An example is the problem of cooling a data center that involves many cooling units. Similarly, control of traffic lights in an intersection is another good example in this area. In fact, in *Chapter 17, Smart City and Cybersecurity*, we will model and solve this problem using MARL.

Before moving into discussing other types of MARL environments, while we are at MARL for autonomous vehicles, let's briefly mention a useful platform, MACAD-Gym, for you to experiment with.

MACAD-Gym for multi-agent connected autonomous driving

MACAD-Gym is a Gym-based library for connected and autonomous driving applications in multi-agent settings, built on top of the famous CARLA simulator.

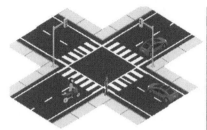  

Figure 9.1 – MACAD-Gym platform (source – MACAD-Gym GitHub repo)

The platform provides a rich set of scenarios involving cars, pedestrians, traffic lights, bikes etc., depicted in Figure 9.1. In more detail, MACAD-Gym environments contain a variety of MARL configurations as in the following example:

```
Environment-ID: Short description
{'HeteNcomIndePOIntrxMATLS1B2C1PTWN3-v0':
'Heterogeneous, Non-communicating, '
'Independent,Partially-Observable '
'Intersection Multi-Agent scenario '
'with Traffic-Light Signal, 1-Bike, '
'2-Car,1-Pedestrian in Town3, '
'version 0'}
```

To see what you can do with MACAD-Gym, check out its Github repo, developed and maintained by Praveen Palanisamy, at https://github.com/praveen-palanisamy/macad-gym.

After this short detour, let's proceed to fully competitive settings in MARL.

Fully competitive environments

In fully competitive environments, the success of one of the agents means failure for the others. Therefore, such settings are modelled as zero-sum games:

$$R^1 + R^2 + \cdots + R^N = 0$$

where R^i is the reward for the ith agent.

Some examples to fully competitive environments are the following:

- **Board games**: This is the classic example for such environments, such as chess, Go, and tic-tac-toe.

- **Adversarial settings**: In situations where we want to minimize the risk of failure for an agent in real-life, we might train it against adversarial agents. This creates a fully competitive environment.

Finally, let's take a look at mixed cooperative-competitive environments.

Mixed cooperative-competitive environments

A third type of environments involves both collaboration and cooperation between agents. These environments are usually modelled as general-sum games:

$$R^1 + R^2 + \cdots + R^N = r$$

Here R^i is the reward for the ith agent and r is some fixed total reward that can be collected by the agents.

Here are some examples to mixed environments:

- **Team competitions**: When there are teams of agents competing against each other, the agents within a team collaborate to defeat the other teams.

- **Economy**: If you think about the economic activities we are involved in, it is a mix of competition and cooperation. A nice example to this is how tech companies such as Microsoft, Google, Facebook, and Amazon compete against each other for certain businesses while collaborating on some open-source projects to advance the software technology.

> **Info**
>
> At this point, it is worth taking a pause to watch OpenAI's demo on agents playing hide-and-seek in teams. The agents develop very cool cooperation and competition strategies after playing against each other for a large number of episodes, inspiring us for the potential in RL towards artificial general intelligence. See Figure 9.2 for a quick snapshot and the link to the video.

Figure 9.2 – OpenAI's agents playing hide-and-seek
(Source: `https://youtu.be/kopoLzvh5jY`)

Now that we have covered the fundamentals, next, let's look into some of the challenges with MARL.

Exploring the challenges in multi-agent reinforcement learning

In the earlier chapters in this book, we discussed many challenges in reinforcement learning. In particular, the dynamic programming methods we initially introduced are not able to scale to problems with complex and large observation and action spaces. Deep reinforcement learning approaches, on the other hand, although capable of handling complex problems, lack theoretical guarantees and therefore required many tricks to stabilize and converge. Now that we talk about problems in which there are more than one agent learning, interacting with each other, and affecting the environment; the challenges and complexities of single-agent RL are multiplied. For this reason, many results in MARL are empirical.

In this section, we discuss what makes MARL specifically complex and challenging.

Non-stationarity

The mathematical framework behind single-agent RL is the Markov decision process (MDP), which establishes that the environment dynamics depend on the state it is in and not the history. This suggests that the environment is stationary, on which many approaches rely for convergence. Now that there are multiple agents in the environment that are learning hence changing their behavior over time, that fundamental assumption falls apart and prevents us analyzing MARL the same way we analyze single-agent RL.

As an example, consider off-policy methods such as Q-learning with replay buffer. In MARL, using such approaches is especially challenging because the experience that was collected a while ago might be wildly different than how the environment (in part, the other agents) responds to the actions of a single agent.

Scalability

One possible solution to non-stationarity is to account for the actions of the other agents, such as using a joint action space. As the number of agents increases, this becomes increasingly intractable, which makes scalability an issue in MARL.

Having said this, it is somewhat easier to analyze how the agent behavior could converge when there are only two agents in the environment. If you are familiar with game theory, a common way to look at such systems is to understand equilibrium points where neither of the agents benefit from changing their policies.

> **Info**
>
> If you need a brief introduction to game theory and Nash equilibrium, check out this video at `https://www.youtube.com/watch?v=0i7p9DNvtjk`

This analysis gets significantly harder when there are more than two agents in the environment, which makes large-scale MARL very difficult to understand.

Unclear reinforcement learning objective

In single-agent RL, the objective is clear: To maximize the expected cumulative return. On the other hand, there is no such a unique objective defined MARL.

Think about a chess game in which we try to train a very good chess agent. To this end, we train many agents competing with each other using **self-play**. How would you set the objective of this problem? First thought could be to maximize the reward of the best agent. But this could result in making all the agents terrible players but one. This would certainly not what we would want.

A popular objective in MARL is to achieve convergence to Nash equilibrium. This often works well, but it also has disadvantages when the agents are not fully rational. Moreover, Nash equilibrium naturally implies overfitting to the policies of the other agents, which is not necessarily desirable.

Information sharing

Another important challenge in MARL is to design the information sharing structure between the agents. There are three alternative information structures we can consider:

- **Fully centralized**: In this structure, all of the information collected by the agents are processed by a central mechanism and the local policies would leverage this centralized knowledge. The advantage of this structure is the full coordination between the agents. On the other hand, this could lead to an optimization problem that won't scale as the number of the agents grow.

- **Fully decentralized**: In this structure, no information is exchanged between the agents and each agent would act based on their local observations. The obvious benefit here is that there is no burden of a centralized coordinator. On the flip side, the actions of the agents would be suboptimal due to their limited information about the environment. In addition, RL algorithms might have a hard time to converge when the training is fully independent due to high partial observability.

- **Decentralized but networked agents**: This structure would allow information exchange between small groups of (neighbor) agents. In turn, this would help the information spread among them. The challenge here would be to create a robust communication structure that would work under different conditions of the environment.

Depending on the objective of the RL problem as well as the availability of computational resources, different approaches could be preferred. Consider a cooperative environment in which a large swarm of robots are trying to achieve a common goal. In this problem, fully centralized or networked control might make sense. In a fully competitive environment, such as a strategy video game, a fully decentralized structure might be preferred since there would be no common goal between the agents.

After this much theory, it is now time to go into practice! Soon, we will train a tic-tac-toe agent that you can play against during your meetings or classes. Let's first describe how we will do the training and then go into implementation.

Training policies in multi-agent settings

There are many algorithms and approaches designed for MARL, which can be classified in the following two broad categories.

- **Independent learning**: This approach suggests training agents individually while treating the other agents in the environment as part of the environment.

- **Centralized training and decentralized execution**: In this approach, there is a centralized controller that uses information from multiple agents during training. At the time of execution (inference), the agents locally execute the policies, without relying on a central mechanism.

Generally speaking, we can take any of the algorithms we covered in one of the previous chapters and use it in a multi-agent setting to train policies via independent learning, which, as it turns out, is a very competitive alternative to specialized MARL algorithms. So rather than dumping more theory and notation on you, in this chapter, we will skip discussing the technical details of any specific MARL algorithm and refer you to literature for that.

> **Info**
>
> An easy and highly recommended read on a comparison of deep MARL algorithms is by (Papoudakis et al. 2020). Just visit the references section to find the link to the paper.

So, we will use independent learning. How does it work, though? Well, it requires us to:

- Have an environment with multiple agents,

- Maintain policies to support the agents,

- Appropriately assign the rewards coming out of the environment to the agents.

It would be tricky for us to come up with a proper framework here to handle the points above. Fortunately, RLlib has a multi-agent environment to come to the rescue. Next, let's see how it works.

RLlib multi-agent environment

RLlib's multi-agent environment flexibly allows us to hook up with one of the algorithms that you already know to use for MARL. In fact, RLlib documentation conveniently shows which algorithms are compatible with this environment type:

Available Algorithms - Overview

Algorithm	Frameworks	Discrete Actions	Continuous Actions	Multi-Agent
A2C, A3C	tf + torch	Yes +parametric	Yes	Yes
ARS	tf + torch	Yes	Yes	No

Figure 9.3 – RLlib's algorithm list shows multi-agent compatibility (Source: `https://docs.ray.io/en/releases-1.0.1/rllib-algorithms.html`)

In that list, you will also see a separate section for MARL-specific algorithms. In this chapter, we will use PPO.

Of course, the next step is to understand how to use an algorithm we selected with a multi-agent environment. At this point, we need to make a key differentiation: *Using RLlib, we will train policies, not the agents (at least directly). An agent will be mapped to one of the policies that are being trained to retrieve actions.*

RLlib documentation illustrates this with the following figure:

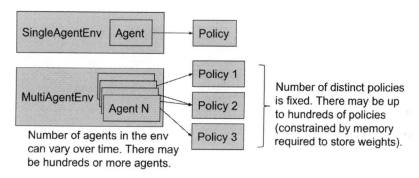

Figure 9.4 – Relationship between agents and policies in RLlib
(source: `https://docs.ray.io/en/releases-1.0.1/rllib-env.html#multi-agent-and-hierarchical`)

In case you have not realized, this gives us a very powerful framework to model a MARL environment. For example, we can flexibly add agents to the environment, remove them, and train multiple policies for the same task. All is fine as far as we specify the mapping between the policies and agents.

With that, let's look into what the training loop in RLlib requires to be used with a multi-agent environment:

1. List of policies with corresponding ids. These are what will be trained.

2. A function that maps a given agent id to a policy id, so that RLlib knows where the actions for a given agent will come from.

Once this is set, the environment will use the Gym convention communicate with RLlib. The difference will be that observations, rewards, and terminal statements will be emitted for multiple agents in the environment. For example, a reset function will return a dictionary of observations like the following:

```
> env.reset()
{"agent_1": [[...]], "agent_2":[[...]], "agent_4":[[...]],...
```

Similarly, the actions by the policies will be passed to the agents from which we received an observation, similar to:

```
... = env.step(actions={"agent_1": ..., "agent_2":...,
"agent_4":..., ...
```

This means that if the environment returns an observation for an agent, it is asking an action back.

So far so good! This should suffice to give you some idea about how it works. Things will be clearer when we go into the implementation!

Soon, we will train tic-tac-toe policies, as we mentioned. The agents that will use these policies will compete against each other to learn how to play the game. This is called **competitive self-play**, which we discuss next.

Competitive self-play

Self-play is a great tool to train RL agents for competitive tasks, which include things like board games, multi-player video games, adversarial scenarios etc. Many of the famous RL agents you have heard about are trained this way, such as AlphaGo, OpenAI Five for Dota 2, and the StarCraft II agent of DeepMind.

> **Info**
>
> The story of OpenAI Five is a very interesting one, showing how the project started and evolved to what it is today. The blog posts on the project gives many beneficial information, from hyperparameters used in the models to how the OpenAI team overcame interesting challenges throughout the work. You can find the project page at `https://openai.com/projects/five/`.

One of the drawbacks of vanilla self-play is that the agents, who only see the other agents trained the same way, tend to overfit to each other's strategies. To overcome this, it makes sense to train multiple policies and pit them against each other, which is also what we will do in this chapter.

> **Info**
>
> Overfitting is such a challenge in self-play that even training multiple policies and simply setting them against each other is not enough. DeepMind created a "League" of agents/policies, like a basketball league, to obtain a really competitive training environment, which led to the success of their StarCraft II agents. They explain their approach in a nice blog at `https://deepmind.com/blog/article/AlphaStar-Grandmaster-level-in-StarCraft-II-using-multi-agent-reinforcement-learning`

Finally, it is time to experiment with multi-agent reinforcement learning!

Training tic-tac-toe agents through self-play

In this section, we will provide you with some key explanations of the code in our Github repo to get a better grasp of MARL with RLlib while training tic-tac-toe agents on a 3x3 board. For the full code, you can refer to `https://github.com/PacktPublishing/Mastering-Reinforcement-Learning-with-Python`.

Figure 9.5 – A 3x3 tic-tac-toe. For the image credit and to learn how it is played, see `https://en.wikipedia.org/wiki/Tic-tac-toe`

Let's started with designing the multi-agent environment.

Designing the multi-agent tic-tac-toe environment

In the game, we have two agents, X and O, playing the game. We will train four policies for the agents to pull their actions from, and each policy can play either an X or O. We construct the environment class as follows:

Chapter09/tic_tac_toe.py

```python
class TicTacToe(MultiAgentEnv):
    def __init__(self, config=None):
        self.s = 9
        self.action_space = Discrete(self.s)
        self.observation_space = MultiDiscrete([3] * self.s)
        self.agents = ["X", "O"]
        self.empty = " "
        self.t, self.state, self.rewards_to_send = \
                            self._reset()
```

Here, 9 refers to the number of squares on the board, each of which can be filled by either X, O, or none.

We reset this environment as follows:

```python
    def _next_agent(self, t):
        return self.agents[int(t % len(self.agents))]


    def _reset(self):
        t = 0
        agent = self._next_agent(t)
        state = {"turn": agent,
                 "board": [self.empty] * self.s}
        rews = {a: 0 for a in self.agents}
        return t, state, rews
```

However, we don't pass this state directly to the policy as it is just full of characters. We process it so that, for the player that is about to play, its own marks are always represented as 1s and the other player's marks are always represented as 2s.

```python
def _agent_observation(self, agent):
    obs = np.array([0] * self.s)
    for i, e in enumerate(self.state["board"]):
        if e == agent:
            obs[i] = 1
        elif e == self.empty:
            pass
        else:
            obs[i] = 2
    return obs
```

This processed observation is what is passed to the policy:

```python
def reset(self):
    self.t, self.state, self.rewards_to_send =\
                        self._reset()
    obs = {self.state["turn"]: \
            self._agent_observation(self.state["turn"])}
    return obs
```

Finally, the `step` method processes the action for the player and proceeds the environment to the next step. For a win, the player gets a 1, and −1 for a loss. Notice that the policies may suggest putting the mark on an already-occupied square, a behavior that is penalized by a −10 points.

Configuring the trainer

We create 4 policies to train, assign them some ids, and specify their observation and action spaces. Here is how we do it:

Chapter09/ttt_train.py

```python
env = TicTacToe()
num_policies = 4
policies = {
    "policy_{}".format(i): (None,
```

```
                              env.observation_space,
                              env.action_space, {})
            for i in range(num_policies)}
```

While creating the config dictionary to pass to the trainer, we map the agents to the policies. To mitigate overfitting, rather than assigning a specific policy to a given agent, we randomly pick the policy to retrieve the action from for the agent that is about to play.

```
    policy_ids = list(policies.keys())
    config = {
        "multiagent": {
            "policies": policies,
            "policy_mapping_fn": (lambda agent_id: \
                        random.choice(policy_ids)),
        },
...
```

During training, we save the models as they improve. Since there are multiple policies involved, as a proxy to measure the progress, we check if the episodes are getting longer with valid moves. Our hope is that as the agents get competitive, more and more games will result in draws, at which point the board is full of marks.

```
    trainer = PPOTrainer(env=TicTacToe, config=config)
    best_eps_len = 0
    mean_reward_thold = -1
    while True:
        results = trainer.train()
        if results["episode_reward_mean"] > mean_reward_thold\
            and results["episode_len_mean"] > best_eps_len:
            trainer.save("ttt_model")
            best_eps_len = results["episode_len_mean"]
        if results.get("timesteps_total") > 10 ** 7:
            break
```

That's it! Now the fun of watching the training!

Observing the results

Initially in the game, there will be lots of invalid moves, resulting in extended episode lengths and excessive penalties for the agents. Therefore, the mean agent reward plot will look like the following:

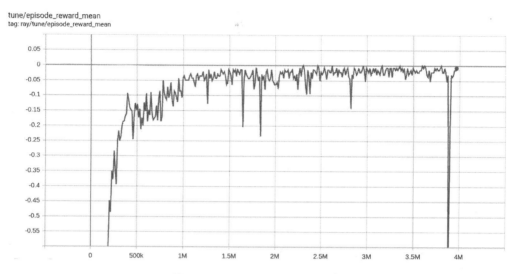

Figure 9.6 – Average agent reward

Notice how this starts in deep negatives to converge to zero, indicating draws as the common result. In the meantime, you should see the episode length converging to 9:

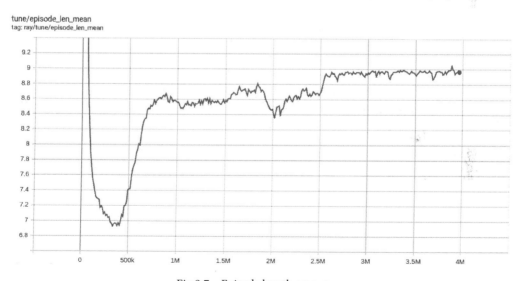

Fig 9.7 – Episode length progress

When you see the competition on fire, you can stop the training! What will be even more interesting is to play against the AI by running the script `ttt_human_vs_ai.py` or watch them compete by running `ttt_ai_vs_ai.py`.

With that, we conclude this chapter. This was a fun one, wasn't it? Let's summarize the learnings from this chapter next.

Summary

In this chapter, we covered multi-agent reinforcement learning. This branch of RL is more challenging than others due to multiple decision-makers influencing the environment and also evolving over time. After introducing some MARL concepts, we explored these challenges in detail. We then proceeded to train tic-tac-toe agents through competitive self-play using RLlib. And they were so competitive that they kept coming to a draw at the end of the training!

In the next chapter, we switch gears to discuss an emerging approach in reinforcement learning, called Machine Teaching, which brings the subject matter expert, you, more actively into the process to guide the training. Hoping to see you there soon!

References

1. Mosterman, P. J. et al. (2014). A heterogeneous fleet of vehicles for automated humanitarian missions. Computing in Science & Engineering, vol. 16, issue 3, pg. 90-95. URL: `http://msdl.cs.mcgill.ca/people/mosterman/papers/ifac14/review.pdf`

2. Papoudakis, Georgios, et al. (2020). Comparative Evaluation of Multi-Agent Deep Reinforcement Learning Algorithms. arXiv.org, `http://arxiv.org/abs/2006.07869`

3. Palanisamy, Praveen. (2019). Multi-Agent Connected Autonomous Driving Using Deep Reinforcement Learning. arxiv.org, `https://arxiv.org/abs/1911.04175v1`

Section 3: Advanced Topics in RL

In this section, you will learn advanced techniques in RL, such as machine learning, which is useful for real-life problems. Also, this section covers various future narratives in RL that will help improve models.

This section contains the following chapters:

- *Chapter 10, Introducing Machine Teaching*
- *Chapter 11, Achieving Generalization and Overcoming Partial Observability*
- *Chapter 12, Meta-Reinforcement Learning*
- *Chapter 13, Exploring Advanced Topics*

10
Introducing Machine Teaching

The great excitement about reinforcement learning is, to a significant extent, due to its similarities to human learning: An RL agent learns from experience. This is also why many consider it as the path to artificial general intelligence. On the other hand, if you think about it, reducing human learning to just trial and error would be a gross underestimation. We don't discover everything we know, in science, art, engineering, from scratch when we are born! Instead, we build on the knowledge and civilization that have evolved over thousands of years! We transfer this knowledge among us through various, structured or unstructured forms of **teaching**. This capability makes it possible for us to gain skills relatively quickly and advance the common knowledge.

When we think from this perspective, what we are doing with machine learning looks quite inefficient: We dump bunch of raw data to algorithms, or expose them to an environment in the case of reinforcement learning, and train them with virtually no guidance. This is partly why machine learning requires so much data and fails at times.

Machine teaching (MT) is an emerging approach that shifts the focus to extracting knowledge from a teacher, rather than raw data, to guide training of machine learning models. In turn, learning new skills and mappings are achieved more efficiently, with less data, time, and compute. In this chapter, we introduce the components of MT for reinforcement learning, some of its most important methods, such as reward function engineering, curriculum learning, demonstration learning, and action masking. At the end, we also discuss the downsides and the future of MT. More concretely, we have the following sections in this chapter:

- Introduction to machine teaching
- Engineering the reward function
- Curriculum learning
- Warm starts and demonstration learning
- Action Masking

Introduction to machine teaching

Machine teaching is the name of a general approach and collection of methods to efficiently transfer knowledge from a teacher, a subject matter expert, to a machine learning model. With that, we aim to make the training much more efficient, and even feasible for tasks that would be impossible to achieve otherwise. Let's talk about what MT is in more detail, why we need it, and what its components are.

Understanding the need for machine teaching

Did you know that the United States is expected to spend about 1.25 trillion dollars, around 5% of its gross domestic product, on education in 2021? This should speak to the existential significance of education for our society and civilization (and many would argue that we should spend more).

We humans have built such a giant system, which we expect people to spend many years in, because we don't expect ourselves to decipher the alphabet or math on our own. And it is not just that, we continuously learn from teachers around us, about how to use some software, how to drive, how to cook, etc. In addition, teaching does not have to be in person: Books, blog posts, manuals, course materials all distill valuable information for us so that we can learn, not just in school, but throughout our lives.

I hope this convinces you the importance of teaching. But if you found this example too populist and perhaps a bit irrelevant to reinforcement learning, let's specifically discuss how machine teaching could help in RL.

Feasibility of learning

Did you ever feel overwhelmed when you were trying to learn something on your own, without a (good) teacher? This is akin to an RL agent not figuring out a path to success and a good policy for the problem on hand. You can think of **hard-exploration problems** with sparse rewards in this context, a serious challenge in RL.

Consider the following example: An RL agent trying to learn chess against a competitive opponent with a reward of +1 for winning, 0 for draw and -1 for losing at the end of the game. The RL agent, while exploring, needs to stumble upon tens of "good moves," one after another, and among many alternative moves at each step, to be able to get its first 0 or +1 reward. Since this is a low likelihood, the training is likely to fail without a huge exploration budget. A teacher, on the other hand, might guide the exploration so that the RL agent discovers at least a few ways to success, from which it can gradually improve upon the winning strategies.

> **Info**
>
> When DeepMind created its AlphaStar agent to play StarCraft II, they used supervised learning to train the agent from past human game logs before going into reinforcement learning-based training. Human players in some sense were the first teachers of the agent, and without them, the training would be impractical or too costly. To support this argument, you can take the example of the OpenAI Five agent trained to play Dota 2. It took almost a year to train the agent.

The following figure shows the agent in action:

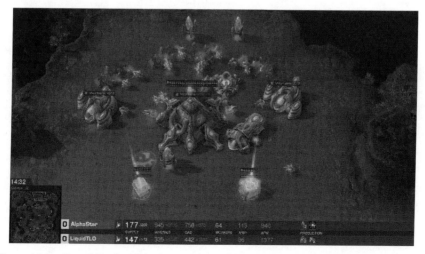

Figure 10.1 – DeepMind's AlphaStar agent in action (source: The AlphaStar Team, 2019)

In summary, having access to a teacher could make the learning feasible in a reasonable amount of time.

Time, data, and compute efficiency

Let's say you have enough compute resources and can afford to try an enormous number of sequences of moves for the RL agent to discover winning strategies in an environment. Just because you can do it doesn't mean that you should do it and waste all these resources. A teacher could help you greatly reduce the training time, data, and compute. You can use the resources you saved to iterate on your ideas and come up with better agents.

> **Tip**
>
> Do you have mentors in your life to help you with your career, education, marriage? Or do you read books about these topics? What is your motivation? You don't want to repeat the mistakes of others, or reinvent what others already know just to waste your time, energy, and opportunities, do you? Machine teaching similarly helps your agent jumpstart in its task.

The benefit of MT goes beyond feasibility of learning or its efficiency. Next, let's talk about another aspect: The safety of your agent.

Ensuring the safety of the agent

A teacher is subject matter expert in a topic. Therefore, a teacher has usually a pretty good idea about what actions under which conditions can get the agent in trouble. The teacher can inform the agent about these conditions by limiting the actions it could take to ensure its safety. For example, while training an RL agent for a self-driving car, it is natural to limit the speed of the car depending on the conditions of the road. This is especially needed if the training happens in real-world, so that the agent does not blindly explore crazy actions to discover how to drive. Even when the training happens in simulation, imposing such limitations will help with the efficient use of the exploration budget, related to the note in the previous section.

Democratizing machine learning

When human teachers train students, they do not worry about the details of the biological mechanisms of learning, such as which chemicals transferred between which brain cells. Those details are abstracted away from the teacher: Neuroscientists and experts who study the brain put out research about effective teaching and learning techniques.

Just like how teachers don't have to be neuroscientists, subject matter experts don't have to be machine learning experts to train machine learning algorithms. Machine teaching paradigm suggests abstracting the low-level details of machine learning away from the machine teacher by developing effective and intuitive teaching methods. With that, it would be much easier for subject matter experts to infuse their knowledge into machines. Eventually, this would lead to democratization of machine learning and its much greater use in many applications.

Data science, in general, requires combining business insights and expertise with mathematical tools and software to create value. When you want to apply RL to business problems, the situation is the same. This often requires either the data scientist to learn about the business, or the subject matter expert to learn data science, or people of both personas working together in a team. This poses a high bar for the adoption of (advanced) machine learning techniques in many settings, because it is rare for these two types of personas to exist at the same time at the same place.

> **Info**
>
> A McKinsey study shows that lack of analytical talent is a major barrier to unlock the value in data and analytics. Machine teaching, its specific tools aside, is a paradigm to overcome these barriers by lowering the bar for entry for non-machine learning experts through creation of intuitive tools to this end. For the study, visit: `https://mck.co/2J3TFEj`.

This vision we have just mentioned is more for the long term as it requires a lot of research and abstractions on the machine learning side. The MT methods we will cover in this chapter, on the other hand, will be pretty technical and for the use of data scientists. For example, we will discuss the **action masking** method to limit the available actions for the agent depending on the state it is in, which will require coding and modifying the neural network outcomes. However, you can envision an advanced machine teaching tool listening to the teacher saying, "don't go over 40 miles-per-hour within the city limits," parsing that command, and implementing action masking under the hood for a self-driving car agent:

Figure 10.2 – Future of machine teaching?

Before closing this section and diving into the details of machine teaching, let me put out a necessary disclaimer.

> **Disclaimer**
>
> One of the most vocal proponents of the machine teaching approach is Microsoft and its Autonomous Systems division. As of the time I am authoring this book, I am an employee in the Autonomous Systems organization of Microsoft, working towards the mission of using machine teaching to create intelligent systems. On the other hand, my goal here is not to promote any Microsoft product or discourse, but to tell you about this emerging topic that I find important. In addition, I do not officially represent Microsoft at any capacity and my view of the topic may not necessarily align with the company's. If you are curious about Microsoft's view of machine teaching, check out the blog post at `https://blogs.microsoft.com/ai/machine-teaching/` and the Autonomous System organization's website at `https://www.microsoft.com/en-us/ai/autonomous-systems`.

Now, it is time to make the discussion more concrete. In the next section, let's overview the elements of machine teaching.

Exploring the elements of machine teaching

As machine teaching is an emerging field, it is hard to formally define its elements. Still, let's look into some of the common components and themes used in it. We have already discussed who the machine teacher is, but let's start with that for the sake of completeness. Then we go into concept, lessons, curriculum, training data, and feedback.

Machine teacher

Machine teacher or simply **teacher** is the subject matter expert of the problem on hand. In the absence of abstractions that decouple machine learning from teaching, this will be the data scientist, you, but this time with the explicit concern of guiding the training using your knowledge of the problem domain.

Concept

Concept is a specific part of the skillset that is needed to solve the problem. Think about training a basketball player in real-life. Training does not consist of only practice games but divided into mastering individual skills as well. Some of those skills are:

- Shooting

- Passing

- Dribbling

- Stopping and landing

Conventional training of a basketball agent would be through playing entire games, with which we would expect the agent to pick up these individual skills. Machine teaching suggests breaking the problem into smaller concepts to learn, such as the skills we listed above. This has several benefits:

- A monolithic task often comes with sparse rewards, which is challenging for an RL agent to learn from. For example, wining the basketball game would be +1 and losing it would be -1. However, the machine teacher would know that winning a game would be possible through mastering the individual skills. To train the agent on individual skills, concepts, there will be rewards assigned to them. This is helpful to get around the sparse reward issue and provide more frequent feedback to the agent in a manner that facilitates learning.

- Credit assignment problem is a serious challenge in RL, which is about the difficulty of attributing the reward in later stages to individual actions in the earlier ones. When the training is broken into concepts, it is easier to see the concepts the agent is not good at. To be specific, this does not solve the credit assignment problem in itself. It is still the teacher that determines whether mastering a particular concept is important. But once these concepts are defined by the teacher, it is easier to isolate what the agent is good at and not.

- As a corollary to the point above, the teacher can allocate more of the training budget to concepts that need more training and/or are difficult to learn. This results in more efficient use of time and compute resources.

> **Info**
> The idea of decomposing monolithic tasks into concepts is central in machine teaching. A successful use of a **concept network** to solve dexterous manipulation tasks with a state-of-the-art performance is by (Gudimella et al. 2017).

For all these reasons, a task that is impractical or costly to solve monolithically can be efficiently solved by breaking it into concepts.

Lessons & curriculum

Another important element in machine teaching is called **curriculum learning**. While training the agent on a concept, exposing it to an expert level difficulty may derail the training. Instead, what makes more sense is to start with some easy settings and increase the difficulty gradually. Each of these difficulty levels makes a separate **lesson**, any they collectively, together with the success thresholds that define the transition criteria from one lesson to the next, to comprise a **curriculum**.

Curriculum learning is one of the important research areas in reinforcement learning and we will elaborate more on that later. A curriculum may be designed by hand by the teacher, or an **auto-curriculum** algorithm can be used.

Training material/data

Related to the previous point, another aspect of machine teaching is to engineer the data that the agent will learn from. For example, the machine teacher could seed the training with data that include successful episodes while using off-policy methods, which can overcome hard exploration tasks. Such data could be obtained from an existing non-RL controller or the teacher's actions. This approach is also called **demonstration learning**.

> **Info**
>
> Demonstration learning is a popular method to train RL agents especially in robotics. An ICRA paper by Nair et al. demonstrates robots how to pick and place objects to seed the training of an RL agent. Check out the video at `https://youtu.be/bb_acElyzDo`.

Conversely, the teacher could steer the agent away from bad actions. An effective way of achieving this is through **action masking**, which limits the available action space given the observation to a desirable set of actions.

Another way of engineering the training data that the agent consumes is to monitor the performance of the agent, identify the parts of the state space that it needs more training in and expose the agent to such states to improve the performance.

Feedback

RL agents learn through feedback in the form of rewards. Engineering the reward function to make the learning easy -and even feasible in some tasks that would have been infeasible otherwise- is one of the most important tasks of a machine teacher. This is usually an iterative process. It is common to revise the reward function many times during the course of a project to get the agent learn the desired behavior. A futuristic machine teaching tool could involve interacting with the agent through natural language to provide this feedback, which would shape the reward function used under the hood.

With this, we have introduced you to machine teaching and its elements. Next, we will go into specific methods. Rather than presenting an entire machine teaching strategy for a sample problem, we will focus on individual techniques. You can use them as building blocks of your machine teaching strategy depending on the needs of your problem. We start with the most common one, reward function engineering, which you might have already used before.

Engineering the reward function

Reward function engineering means crafting the reward dynamics of the environment in an RL problem so that it reflects the objective you have in your mind for your agent and leads the agent to that objective. How you define your reward function might make the training easy, difficult, or even impossible for the agent. Therefore, in most RL projects, a significant effort is dedicated to designing the reward. In this section, we cover some specific cases where you will need to do it and how, then provide a specific example, and finally discuss the challenges that come with engineering the reward function.

When to engineer the reward function

Multiple times in the book, including the previous section when we discussed concepts, we mentioned how sparse rewards pose a problem for learning. One way of dealing with this is to **shape the reward** to make it non-sparse. Sparse reward case, therefore, is a common reason of why we may want to do reward function engineering. Yet, it is not the only one. Not all environments / problems have a predefined reward for you like in an Atari game. In addition, in some cases, there are multiple objectives that you want your agent to achieve. For all these reasons, many real-life tasks require the machine teacher to design the reward function based on their expertise. Let's look into these cases next.

Sparse rewards

When the reward is sparse, meaning that the agent sees a change in the reward (from a constant 0 to positive/negative, from a constant negative to positive, etc.) with unlikely sequences of random actions, the learning gets difficult. That is because the agent needs to stumble upon such a sequence through random trial and error, which makes the problem exploration hard.

Learning chess against a competitive player where the reward is +1 for winning, 0 for draw and -1 for losing at the very end is a good example of an environment with sparse rewards. A classic example used in RL benchmarks is Montezuma's Revenge, an Atari game in which the player needs to collect equipment (keys, torch etc.), open doors etc. to be able to make any progress, which is very unlikely just by taking random actions.

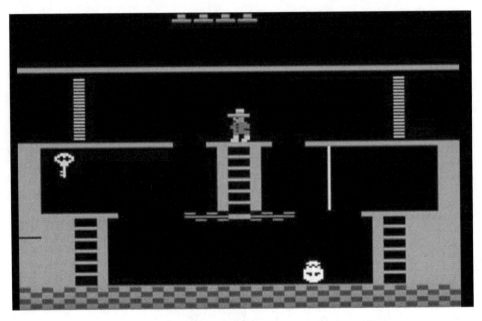

Figure 10.3 – Montezuma's Revenge

In such hard-exploration problems, a common strategy is **reward shaping**, which is to modify the reward to steer the agent towards high rewards. For example, a reward shaping strategy could be to give -0.1 reward to the agent learning chess if it loses the queen, and smaller penalties when other pieces are lost. With that, the machine teacher conveys their knowledge about the queen being an important piece in the game to the agent, although not losing the queen or any other pieces (except the king) in itself is not the game's objective.

We will talk more about reward shaping in detail later.

Qualitative objectives

Let's say you are trying to teach a humanoid robot how to walk. Well, what is walking? How can you define it? How can you define it mathematically? What kind of walking gets a high reward? Is it just about moving forward or are there some elements of aesthetics? As you can see, it is not easy to put what you have in your mind about walking into mathematical expressions.

In their famous work, researchers at DeepMind used the following reward function for the humanoid robot they train to walk:

$$r = \min(v_x, v_{max}) - 0.005\left(v_x^2 + v_y^2\right) - 0.05y^2 - 0.02\|u\|^2 + 0.02$$

where v_x and v_y are velocities along x and y axes, y is the position on the y axis, v_{max} is a cutoff for the velocity reward and u is the control applied on the joints. As you can see, there are many arbitrary coefficients that are likely to differ for other kinds of robots. In fact, the paper uses three separate functions for three separate robot bodies.

> **Info**
>
> If you are curious how the robot walks after being trained with this reward, watch it here: `https://youtu.be/gn4nRCC9TwQ`. The way the robot walks is, how to say, a bit weird...

So, in short, qualitative objectives require crafting a reward function to obtain the behavior intended.

Multi-objective tasks

A common situation in RL is to have multi-objective tasks. On the other hand, conventionally, RL algorithms optimize a scalar reward. As a result, when there are multiple objectives, they need to be reconciled into a single reward. This often results in mixing apples and oranges, and appropriately weighing them in the reward could be quite painful.

When the task objective is qualitative, it is also often multi-objective. For example, the task of driving a car includes elements of speed, safety, fuel efficiency, equipment wear and tear, comfort, etc. You can guess that it is not easy to express what comfort means mathematically. But there are also many tasks in which multiple quantitative objectives need to be optimized concurrently. An example to this is to control an HVAC system to keep the room temperature as close to the specified setpoint as possible while minimizing the cost of energy. In such a problem, it is the machine teacher's duty to balance such trade-offs.

It is very common for an RL task to involve one or more of the situations above. Then, engineering the reward function becomes a major challenge.

After this much discussion, let's focus on reward shaping a little bit more.

Reward shaping

The idea behind reward shaping is to incentivize the agent to move towards success states and discourage it from reaching failure states using positive and negative rewards that are relatively smaller in magnitude with respect to the actual reward (and punishment). If done correctly, this will usually shorten the training time as the agent will not spend as much time while trying to discover how to reach a success state. Here is a simple example to make our discussion more concrete.

Simple robot example

Suppose that a robot is moving on a horizontal axis with 0.01 step sizes. The goal is to reach +1 and avoid -1, which are the terminal states, as shown here:

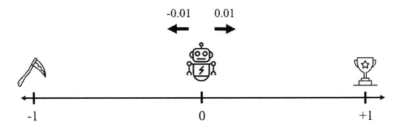

Figure 10.4 – Simple robot example with sparse rewards

As you can imagine, it is very difficult for the robot to discover the trophy when we use sparse rewards, such as, giving +1 for reaching the trophy and -1 for reaching the failure state. If there is a timeout for the task, let's say after 200 steps, the episode is likely to end with that.

In this example, we can guide the robot by giving a reward that increases as it moves towards the trophy. A simple choice could be setting $r = x$, where x is the position on the axis.

There are two potential problems with this reward function:

- As the robot moves right, the incremental relative benefit of moving even farther right gets smaller. For example, going from $x = 0.1$ to $x = 0.11$ increases the step reward by 10% but going from $x = 0.9$ to $x = 0.91$ only 1.1%.

- Since the goal of the agent is to maximize the total cumulative reward, it is not in the best interest of the agent to reach the trophy since that will terminate the episode. Instead, the agent might choose to hang out at 0.99 for forever (or until the time limit is reached.

We can address the first issue by shaping the reward in such a way that the agent gets increasing additional rewards for moving towards the success state. For example, we can set the reward to be $r = x^2 sign(x)$ within the $x \in [-1, 1]$ range:

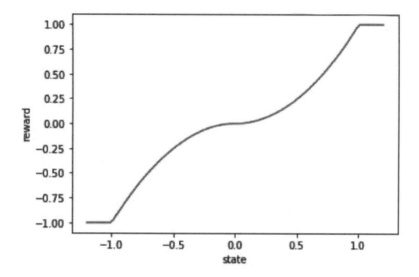

Figure 10.5 – A sample reward shaping where $r = x^2\ sign(x)$

With this, the amount of incentive accelerates as the robot gets closer to the trophy, encouraging the robot even further to go right. The situation is similar for the punishment for going to left.

To address the latter, we should encourage the agent to finish the episode as soon as possible. We need to do that by punishing the agent for every time step it spends in the environment.

This example shows two things: Designing the reward function can get tricky even in such simple problems, and we need to consider the design of the reward function together with the terminal conditions we set.

Before going into specific suggestions for reward shaping, let's also discuss how terminal conditions play a role in agent behavior.

Terminal conditions

Since the goal of the agent is to maximize the expected cumulative reward over an episode, how the episode ends will directly affect the agent behavior. So, we can and should leverage a good set of terminal conditions to guide the agent.

We can talk about several types of terminal conditions:

- **Positive terminal** indicates the agent has accomplished the task (or part of it, depending on how you define success). Such a terminal condition comes with a significant positive reward to encourage the agent to reach there.

- **Negative terminal** indicates a failure state and yields a significant negative reward. The agent will try to avoid such conditions.

- **Neutral terminal** is neither success or failure in itself, but it indicates that the agent has no path to success, and the episode is terminated with a zero reward in the last step. The machine teacher doesn't want the agent to spend any time after that point in the environment but reset back to the initial conditions. Although this does not directly punish the agent, it prevents it from collecting additional rewards (or penalties). So, it is an implicit feedback to the agent.

- **Time limit** bounds the amount of time steps spent in the environment. It encourages the agent to seek high rewards within this budget rather than wandering around for forever. It works as a feedback about what sequences of actions are rewarding in a reasonable amount of time and which ones are not.

In some environments, terminal conditions are preset. But in most cases, the machine teacher has the flexibility to set them.

Now that we have all the components described, let's discuss some practical tips for reward shaping.

Practical tips for reward shaping

Here are some general guidelines you should keep in mind while designing a reward function:

- Keep the step reward between -1 and $+1$ for numerical stability, whenever possible.

- Express your reward (and state) with terms that are generalizable to other versions of your problem. For example, rather than rewarding the agent for reaching a point (x, y), you can incentivize reducing the distance to the target, based on $(\Delta x, \Delta y)$.

- Having a smooth reward function will provide the agent with feedback that is easy to follow.

- The agent should be able to correlate the reward with its observations. In other words, observations must contain some information about what is leading to high or low rewards. Otherwise, there won't be much for the agent base its decisions on.

- The total incentive for getting close to the target states should not outweigh the actual reward of reaching the target state. Otherwise the agent will prefer to focus on accumulating the incentives rather than achieving the actual goal.

- If you would like your agent to complete a task as soon as possible, assign a negative reward to each time step. The agent will try to finish the episode to avoid accumulating negative rewards.

- If the agent can collect more positive rewards by not reaching a terminal state, it will try to collect them before reaching a terminal condition. If the agent is likely to collect only negative rewards by staying inside episode (such as when there is a penalty per time step), it will try to reach a terminal condition. The latter can result in suicidal behavior if the life is too painful for the agent, meaning that the agent can seek any terminal state, including natural ones or failure states, to avoid incurring excessive penalties by staying alive.

Now, we will look at an example of reward shaping using OpenAI.

Example: Reward shaping for mountain car

In OpenAI's mountain car environment, the goal for the car is to reach the goal on top of one of the hills, which is illustrated in Figure 10.6. The action space is to push the car to left, push to right, or apply no force.

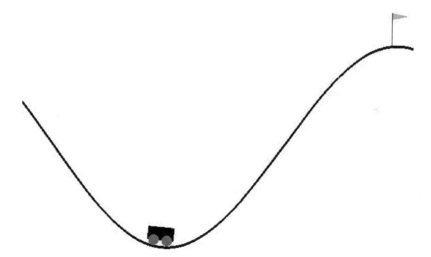

Figure 10.6 – Mountain car environment

Since the force we apply is not enough to climb the hill and reach the goal, the car needs to gradually accumulate potential energy by climbing in opposite directions. Figuring this out is non-trivial, because the car does not know what the goal is until it reaches it, which can be achieved after 100+ steps of correct actions. The only reward in the default environment is -1 per time step to encourage the car to reach the goal as quickly as possible to avoid accumulating negative rewards. The episode terminates after 200 steps.

We will use various machine teaching techniques to train our agent throughout the chapter. To that end, we will have a custom training flow and customized environment with which we can experiment with these methods. Let's get things set up first.

Setting up the environment

Our custom `MountainCar` environment wraps OpenAI's MountainCar-v0, which looks like the following:

Chapter10/custom_mcar.py

```python
class MountainCar(gym.Env):
    def __init__(self, env_config={}):
        self.wrapped = gym.make("MountainCar-v0")
        self.action_space = self.wrapped.action_space
        ...
```

If you visit that file now, it may look complicated since it includes some add-ons we are yet to cover. For now, just know that this is the environment we will use.

We will use Ray/RLlib's Ape-X DQN throughout the chapter to train our agents. Make sure that you have them installed, preferably within a virtual environment.

```
$ virtualenv rlenv
$ source rlenv/bin/activate
$ pip install gym[box2d]
$ pip install tensorflow==2.3.1
$ pip install ray[rllib]==1.0.1
```

With that, next, let's get a baseline performance by training an agent without any machine teaching.

Getting a baseline performance

We will use a single script for all of the trainings. We define a STRATEGY constant at the top of the script, which will control the strategy to be used in the training.

Chapter10/mcar_train.py

```
ALL_STRATEGIES = [
    "default",
    "with_dueling",
    "custom_reward",
    ...
]
STRATEGY = "default"
```

For each strategy, we will kick off 5 different training sessions of 2 million time steps each, so we set NUM_TRIALS = 5 and MAX_STEPS = 2e6. At the end of each training session, we will evaluate the trained agent over NUM_FINAL_EVAL_EPS = 20 episodes. Therefore, the result for each strategy will reflect the average length of 100 test episodes, where lower number indicates better performance.

For most of the strategies, you will see that we have two variants: With and without dueling networks is enabled. When the dueling network is enabled, the agent achieves a near-optimal result (around 100 steps to reach the goal), so it becomes uninteresting for our case. Moreover, when we implement action masking later in the chapter, we won't use dueling networks to avoid complexities in RLlib. Therefore, we focus on the no dueling network case in our example. Finally, note that the results of the experiments will be written to results.csv.

With that, let's train our first agents. When I used no machine teaching, in my case, I obtained the following average episode lengths:

```
STRATEGY = "default"
```

And the outcome is:

```
Average episode length: 192.23
```

Let's see next if reward shaping helps us here.

Solving the problem with a shaped reward

Anyone looking at the mountain car problem could tell that we should encourage the car to go right. At least eventually. In this section, that is what we do: The dip position of the car corresponds to an x position of -0.5. We modify the reward function to give a quadratically increasing reward to the agent for going beyond this position towards right. This happens inside the custom `MountainCar` environment:

```
def step(self, action):
    self.t += 1
    state, reward, done, info = self.wrapped.step(action)
    if self.reward_fun == "custom_reward":
        position, velocity = state
        reward += (abs(position+0.5)**2) * (position>-0.5)
    obs = self._get_obs()
    if self.t >= 200:
        done = True
    return obs, reward, done, info
```

Of course, feel free to try your own reward shaping here to gain a better intuition.

> **Tip**
> Observing a constant step reward for a long time, such as -1, is an example of sparse reward although it is not 0. That is because the agent does not get any feedback on the goodness of its actions from a constant value, until it changes.

We can enable the custom (shaped) reward strategy with the following flag:

```
STRATEGY = "custom_reward"
```

And the outcome we get is something like the following:

```
Average episode length: 131.33
```

This is obviously a significant gain, so, kudos to our shaped reward function! Admittedly, though, it took me several iterations to figure out something that brings in significant improvement. This is because the behavior we encourage is more complex that just going right: We want the agent to go between left and right to speed up. This is a bit hard to capture in a reward function, and it could easily give you headaches.

Reward function engineering in general can get quite tricky and time consuming. So much so that this topic deserves a dedicated section to discuss, which we turn to next.

Challenges with engineering the reward function

The objective in reinforcement learning is to find a policy that maximizes the expected cumulative reward the agent collects. We design and use very sophisticated algorithms to overcome this optimization challenge. In some problems, we use billions of training samples to this end and try to squeeze out a little extra reward. After all this hassle, it is not uncommon to observe that your agent obtains a great reward, but the behavior it exhibits is not exactly what you intended. In other words, the agent learns something different than what you want it to learn. If you run into such a situation, don't get too mad. That is because the agent's sole purpose is to maximize the reward you specified. If that reward does not exactly reflect the objective you had in mind, which is much more challenging that you may think, neither will the behavior of the agent.

Info

A famous example of misbehaving agent due to incorrectly specified reward is OpenAI's CoastRunners agent. In the game, the agent is expected to finish the boat race as quickly as possible while collecting rewards along the course. After training, the agent figured out a way of collecting higher rewards without having to finish the race, defeating the original purpose. You can read more about it on OpenAI's blog: `https://openai.com/blog/faulty-reward-functions/`

As a result, it is of tremendous importance that you specify a good reward function for your task, especially when it includes qualitative and/or complex objectives. Unfortunately, designing a good reward function is more of an art than science, and you will gain intuition through practice and trial and error.

Tip

Alex Irpan, a machine learning researcher at Google, beautifully expresses how important and challenging designing the reward function is: "I've taken to imagining deep RL as a demon that's deliberately misinterpreting your reward and actively searching for the laziest possible local optima. It's a bit ridiculous, but I've found it's actually a productive mindset to have." (Irpan, 2018). François Chollet, author of Keras, says "loss function engineering is probably going to be a job title in the future." (`https://youtu.be/Bo8MY4JpiXE?t=5270`)

Despite these challenges, the tricks we have just covered should give you a running start. The rest will come with experience.

With that, let's conclude our conversation on reward function engineering. This was a long yet necessary one. In the next section, we discuss another topic, curriculum learning, which is not just important in machine teaching, but in reinforcement learning at large.

Curriculum learning

When we learn a new skill, we start with basics. Bouncing and dribbling are the first steps while learning basketball. Doing alley-oops is not something to try to teach in the first lesson. One needs to gradually proceed to advanced lessons, after feeling comfortable with the earlier ones. This idea of following a curriculum, from basics to advanced levels, is the basis of the whole education system. The question is whether machine learning models can benefit from the same approach. It turns out that they can!

In the context of RL, when we create a curriculum, we similarly start with "easy" environment configurations for the agent. This way the agent can get an idea about what success means early on, rather than spending a lot of time by blindly exploring the environment with the hope of stumbling upon success. We then gradually increase the difficulty if we observe the agent is exceeding a certain reward threshold. Each of these difficulty levels are considered a **lesson**. Curriculum learning has been shown to increase training efficiency and making tasks that are infeasible to achieve feasible for the agent.

> Tip
>
> Designing lessons and transition criteria are non-trivial undertakings. It requires significant thought and subject matter expertise. Although we follow manual curriculum design in this chapter, when we revisit the topic in *Chapter 11, Achieving Generalization and Overcoming Partial Observability* and in *Chapter 14, Solving Robot Learning*, we will discuss automatic curriculum generation methods.

In our mountain car example, we create lessons by modifying the initial conditions of the environment. Normally, at the episode beginnings, the environment randomizes the car position around the valley dip ($x = [-0.6, -0.4]$) and sets the velocity (v) to zero. In our curriculum, the car will start in the first lesson close to the goal and with a high velocity towards right. With that, it will easily reach the goal. We will make things gradually closer to the original difficulty as the curriculum progresses.

Namely, here is how we define the lessons:

- Lesson 0: $x = [0.1, \quad 0.4]$, $v = [0, 0.07]$

- Lesson 1: $x = [-0.4, \quad 0.1]$, $v = [0, 0.07]$

- Lesson 2: $x = [-0.6, -0.4]$, $v = [-0.07, 0, 0.07]$

- Lesson 3: $x = [-0.6, -0.1]$, $v = [-0.07, 0, 0.07]$

- Lesson 4 (final / original): $x = [-0.6, -0.4]$, $v = 0$

This is how it is set inside the environment:

```python
def _get_init_conditions(self):
    if self.lesson == 0:
        low = 0.1
        high = 0.4
        velocity = self.wrapped.np_random.uniform(
            low=0, high=self.wrapped.max_speed
        )
    ...
```

We will let the agent to proceed to the next lesson once it is successful enough in the current one. We define this threshold as having an average episode length less than 150 over 10 evaluation episodes. We set the lessons in training and evaluation workers with the following functions:

```python
CURRICULUM_TRANS = 150
...
def set_trainer_lesson(trainer, lesson):
    trainer.evaluation_workers.foreach_worker(
        lambda ev: ev.foreach_env(lambda env: env.set_
lesson(lesson))
    )
    trainer.workers.foreach_worker(
        lambda ev: ev.foreach_env(lambda env: env.set_
lesson(lesson))
    )
    ...
def increase_lesson(lesson):
    if lesson < CURRICULUM_MAX_LESSON:
        lesson += 1
    return lesson    if "evaluation" in results:
        if results["evaluation"]["episode_len_mean"] <
CURRICULUM_TRANS:
```

```
            lesson = increase_lesson(lesson)
            set_trainer_lesson(trainer, lesson)
```

which are then used inside the training flow:

```
            if results["evaluation"]["episode_len_mean"] <
CURRICULUM_TRANS:
                lesson = increase_lesson(lesson)
                set_trainer_lesson(trainer, lesson)
                print(f"Lesson: {lesson}")
```

So, this is how we implement a manual curriculum. If you train the agent with this:

```
STRATEGY = "curriculum"
```

You will see that the performance we get is near optimal!

```
Average episode length: 104.66
```

You just taught a machine something using a curriculum! Pretty cool, isn't it? It should felt like real machine teaching!

Next, we will have another interesting approach: Machine teaching using demonstrations.

Warm starts with demonstrations

A popular technique to demonstrate the agent a way to success is to train it on data that is coming from a reasonably successful controller, such as humans. In RLlib, this can be done via saving the human play data from the mountain car environment:

Chapter10/mcar_demo.py

```
    ...
    new_obs, r, done, info = env.step(a)
    # Build the batch
    batch_builder.add_values(
        t=t,
        eps_id=eps_id,
        agent_index=0,
        obs=prep.transform(obs),
        actions=a,
```

```
        action_prob=1.0,
        action_logp=0,
        action_dist_inputs=None,
        rewards=r,
        prev_actions=prev_action,
        prev_rewards=prev_reward,
        dones=done,
        infos=info,
        new_obs=prep.transform(new_obs),
    )
    obs = new_obs
    prev_action = a
    prev_reward = r
```

This data then can be fed to the training, which is implemented in `Chapter10/mcar_train.py`. We will leave the details of this approach to RLlib's documentation at `https://docs.ray.io/en/releases-1.0.1/rllib-offline.html` and not focus on it here.

Action masking

One final machine teaching approach we will use is action masking. With that, we can prevent the agent to take certain actions in certain steps based on conditions we define. For mountain car, assume that we have this intuition of building momentum before trying to climb the hill. So, we want the agent to apply force to left if the car is already moving left around the valley. So, for these conditions, we will mask all the actions except left.

```
def update_avail_actions(self):
    self.action_mask = np.array([1.0] * \
                        self.action_space.n)
    pos, vel = self.wrapped.unwrapped.state
    # 0: left, 1: no action, 2: right
    if (pos < -0.3) and (pos > -0.8) \
        and (vel < 0) and (vel > -0.05):
        self.action_mask[1] = 0
        self.action_mask[2] = 0
```

In order to be able to use this masking, we need to build a custom model. For the masked actions, we push down all the logits to negative infinity:

```python
class ParametricActionsModel(DistributionalQTFModel):
    def __init__(
        self,
        obs_space,
        action_space,
        num_outputs,
        model_config,
        name,
        true_obs_shape=(2,),
        **kw
    ):
        super(ParametricActionsModel, self).__init__(
            obs_space, action_space,
            num_outputs, model_config, name, **kw
        )
        self.action_value_model = FullyConnectedNetwork(
            Box(-1, 1, shape=true_obs_shape),
            action_space,
            num_outputs,
            model_config,
            name + "_action_values",
        )
        self.register_variables(self.action_value_model.variables())

    def forward(self, input_dict, state, seq_lens):
        action_mask = input_dict["obs"]["action_mask"]
        action_values, _ = self.action_value_model(
            {"obs": input_dict["obs"]["actual_obs"]}
        )
        inf_mask = tf.maximum(tf.math.log(action_mask),
                              tf.float32.min)
        return action_values + inf_mask, state
```

Finally, when using such a model, we turn off dueling to avoid an overly complicated implementation. Also, we register our custom model:

```
if strategy == "action_masking":
    config["hiddens"] = []
    config["dueling"] = False
    ModelCatalog.register_custom_model("pa_model",
                            ParametricActionsModel)
    config["env_config"] = {"use_action_masking": True}
    config["model"] = {
        "custom_model": "pa_model",
    }
```

In order to train your agent with this strategy, set the following:

```
STRATEGY = "action_masking"
```

The performance will be as follows:

```
Average episode length: 147.22
```

This is definitely an improvement over the default case, yet it is behind reward shaping and curriculum learning approaches. Having smarter masking conditions and adding dueling networks can further help with the performance.

With that, we conclude our discussion on machine teaching. Note that this a broad and evolving topic, so what we have done here only scratches the surface. Having said that, you are now equipped with the fundamental approaches and tools of machine teaching. Awesome job! Next, let's summarize what we have covered in the chapter.

Summary

In this chapter, we have covered an emerging paradigm in artificial intelligence, machine teaching, which is about effectively conveying the expertise of a subject matter expert (teacher) to machine learning model training. We discussed how this is similar to how humans are educated: By building on others' knowledge. The advantage of this approach is that it greatly increases data efficiency in machine learning, and, in some cases, makes learning possible that would have been impossible without a teacher. We discussed various methods in this paradigm, including reward function engineering, curriculum learning, demonstration learning, action masking, and concept networks. We observed how some of these methods improved vanilla use of Ape-X DQN significantly.

Besides its benefits, machine teaching also has some challenges and potential downsides: First, it is usually non-trivial to come up with good reward shaping, curriculum, set of action masking conditions etc. This also in some ways defeats the purposes of learning from experience and not having to do feature engineering. Second, when we adapt a machine teaching approach, it is possible to inject the bias of the teacher to the agent, which could prevent it from learning better strategies. The machine teacher needs to avoid such biases whenever possible. Despite these challenges, machine teaching has a potential to become a standard tool in the toolbox of an RL scientist.

In the next section, we will discuss generalization and partial observability, a key topic in RL. In doing so, we will visit curriculum learning again and see how it helps creating robust agents.

See you on the other side!

References

1. Gudimella, Aditya, et al. *Deep Reinforcement Learning for Dexterous Manipulation with Concept Networks*. arXiv.org, `http://arxiv.org/abs/1709.06977`.

2. Bonsai. (2017). *Deep Reinforcement Learning Models: Tips & Tricks for Writing Reward Functions*. Medium. URL: `https://bit.ly/33eTjBv`

3. Bonsai. (2017). *Writing Great Reward Functions – Bonsai*. YouTube. URL: `https://youtu.be/0R3PnJEisqk`

4. Weng, L. (2020). *Curriculum for Reinforcement Learning*. Lil'Log. URL: `https://bit.ly/39foJvE`

5. OpenAI. (2016). *Faulty Reward Functions in the Wild*. OpenAI Blog. URL: `https://openai.com/blog/faulty-reward-functions/`

6. Irpan, A. (2018). *Deep Reinforcement Learning Doesn't Work Yet*. Sorta Insightful. URL: `https://www.alexirpan.com/2018/02/14/rl-hard.html`

7. Heess, Nicolas, et al. (2017). *Emergence of Locomotion Behaviours in Rich Environments*. arXiv.org. URL: `http://arxiv.org/abs/1707.02286`

8. Badnava, Babak, and Nasser Mozayani. (2019). *A New Potential-Based Reward Shaping for Reinforcement Learning Agent*. arXiv.org. URL: `http://arxiv.org/abs/1902.06239`

9. Microsoft Research. (2019). *Reward Machines: Structuring Reward Function Specifications and Reducing Sample Complexity*. YouTube. URL: `https://youtu.be/0wYeJAAnGl8`

10. US Government Finances. (2020). URL: `https://www.usgovernmentspending.com/`

11. The AlphaStar team. (2019). *AlphaStar: Mastering the Real-Time Strategy Game StarCraft II.* DeepMind Blog. URL: `https://bit.ly/39fpDIy`

12. Ng, A., D. Harada, and S. J. Russell (1999). *Policy invariance under reward transformations: Theory and application to reward shaping.* In Proceedings of the Sixteenth International Conference on Machine Learning, pp. 278–287.

11
Achieving Generalization and Overcoming Partial Observability

Deep **reinforcement learning (RL)** has achieved what was impossible with the earlier AI methods, such as beating world champions in games like Go, Dota 2, and StarCraft II. Yet, applying RL to real-world problems is still challenging. Two important obstacles to this end are generalization of trained policies to a broad set of environment conditions and developing policies that can handle partial observability. As we will see in the chapter, these are closely related challenges, for which we will present solution approaches.

Here is what we will cover in this chapter:

- Focusing on generalization in reinforcement learning
- Enriching agent experience via domain randomization
- Using memory to overcome partial observability
- Quantifying generalization via CoinRun

These topics are critical to understand for a successful implementation of RL in real-world settings. So, let's dive right in!

Focusing on generalization in reinforcement learning

The core goal in most machine learning projects is to obtain models that will work beyond training, and under a broad set of conditions during test time. Yet, when you start learning about RL, efforts to prevent overfitting and achieve generalization are not always at the forefront of the discussion, as opposed to how it is with supervised learning. In this section, we discuss what leads to this discrepancy, describe how generalization is closely related to partial observability in RL, and present a general recipe to handle these challenges.

Generalization and overfitting in supervised learning

When we train an image recognition or forecasting model, what we really want to achieve is high accuracy on unseen data. After all, we already know the labels for the data at hand. We use various methods to this end:

- We use separate training, dev, and test sets, for model training, hyperparameter selection, and model performance assessment, respectively. We try to be careful to not modify the model based on the test set, so that it gives a fair assessment of the performance.

- We use various regularization methods, such as penalizing model variance (e.g., L1, L2 regularization) and dropout methods, to prevent overfitting.

- We use as much and diverse data as possible to train the model, which itself has a regularization effect. In the absence of enough data, we leverage data augmentation techniques to generate more.

- We try to curate a training dataset that is of the same distribution with the kind of data we expect to see after model deployment.

Despite all this focus in supervised learning, in RL, we don't seem to have the same mindset when it comes to overfitting and generalization. Let's try to understand what is different in RL, why, and whether generalization is actually of second importance.

Generalization and overfitting in reinforcement learning

Deep supervised learning notoriously requires a lot of data. But the hunger for data in deep reinforcement learning dwarfs the need that of deep supervised learning due to the noise in feedback signals and complex nature of RL tasks. It is not uncommon to train RL models over billions of data points, and over many months. Since it is not quite possible to generate such large data using physical systems, deep RL research has leveraged digital environments, such as simulations and video games for algorithm development and benchmarking. And this has blurred the line between training and test.

Think about it:

- If you train an RL agent to play an Atari game well (which is what most RL algorithms are benchmarked against), such as Space Invaders, and use a lot of data for that, and then if the agent plays Space Invaders very well after training, is there any problem with it? Well, in this case not. As you may have realized, such a training workflow does not involve any effort to prevent overfitting. It may be just that your agent could have memorized a wide variety of scenes in the game. If you care only about Atari games, it may seem like overfitting is not a concern in RL.

- When we depart from Atari settings, and say, train an agent to beat human competitors, such as in Go, Dota 2 and StarCraft II, overfitting starts to appear as a bigger concern. As we saw in the multi-agent RL chapter, such agents are usually trained through self-play. A major danger in that setting for the agents is to overfit to each other's strategies. To prevent that, we usually train multiple agents and make them play against each other in phases, so that a single agent sees a diverse set of opponents (the environment, from a single agent's perspective) and there is less of overfitting.

- Overfitting becomes a huge concern in RL, much more than the two situations we mentioned above, when we train models in simulation and deploy them in a physical environment. This is because, no matter how high-fidelity it is, a simulation is (almost) never the same as the real world. This is called **sim2real gap**. A simulation involves many assumptions, simplifications, and abstractions. It is only a model of the real world, and as we all know, all models are wrong.

We work with models everywhere, so why has this all of a sudden become a major concern in RL? Well, again, training an RL agent requires lots and lots of data (and that's why we needed a simulation in the first place); and training an ML model over similar data for a long time is a recipe for overfitting. So, RL models are extremely likely to overfit to the patterns and quirks of the simulation. There, we really need RL policies to generalize beyond simulation for them to be useful. This is a serious challenge for RL in general, and one of the biggest obstacles in front of bringing RL to real-world applications.

Sim2real gap is a concept that is closely related to partial observability. Let's look into this connection next.

Connection between generalization and partial observability

We mentioned that a simulation is never the same as the real world. Two forms this can manifest itself in are as follows:

- In some problems, you will never get the exact same observations in simulation that you would get in real world. Training a self-driving car is an example of that. The real scenes will always be different.

- In certain problems, you can train the agent on the same observations as you would see in the real world. For example, a factory production planning problem where the observation is the demand outlook, current inventory levels, and machine states. If you know what the ranges for your observations are, you can design your simulation to reflect that. Still, simulation and real-life will be different.

In the former case, it is more intuitive why your trained agent may not generalize well beyond simulation. However, the situation with the latter is a bit more subtle. In that case although observations are the same, the world dynamics may not be between the two environments (and admittedly, this will be also a problem for the former case). Can you recognize what this alludes to? Partial observability. *You can think of the gap between sim and real as a result of partial observability*: There is a state of the environment, hidden from the agent, affecting the transition and reward dynamics. So, even though the agent makes the same observation in simulation and the real world, it does not see this hidden state that we assume to capture the differences between them.

Because of this connection, we cover generalization and partial observability together in this chapter. Having said this,

- Generalization could be still of concern even in fully observable environments; and

- We may have to deal with partial observability even when generalization is not a major concern.

We will look into these dimensions later. Next, let's briefly discuss how we can tackle each of these challenges, before going into details in the later sections.

Achieving generalization with domain randomization

If you are a car driver, think about how you have gained experience over time about driving under different conditions. You may have driven small cars, large vehicles, ones that accelerate fast and slow, ones that are high and low riding etc. In addition, you probably have had driving experience under rain, maybe snow, and on asphalt and gravel. I personally have had these experiences. Then, when I took a test drive with a Tesla Model S for the first time, it felt like a quite different experience at first. But after several minutes I got used to it and started driving pretty comfortably.

Now, as a driver, we often cannot define precisely what differs from one vehicle to another: What the exact differences in weight, torque, traction etc. are, which makes the environment partially observable for us. But our past experience under diverse driving conditions helps us quickly assess the new ones after several minutes of driving. How does this happen? Our brains develop a general physics model for driving (and act accordingly) when the experience is diverse, rather than "overfitting" the driving style to a particular car model and condition.

One of the ways we will deal with overfitting and achieve generalization in RL will be similar to what we described above. We will expose the agent to many different environment conditions, which it cannot necessarily fully observe, during training. This technique is called **domain randomization (DR)**. It will give the agent the necessary experience and understanding to generalize beyond the conditions it is trained under.

A complementary capability for the agent to achieve generalization is to be able to assess the conditions it is in, that is, to overcome partial observability. Let's discuss that next.

Overcoming partial observability with memory

Do you remember what it was like when you first entered your high school classroom? Chances are there were a lot of new faces and you wanted make friends. However, you would not want to approach people just based on your first impression. Although a given scene tells something about people, it reflects only part of who they are. What you really want to do is to make observations over some time before you make a judgement.

The situation is similar in the context of RL. Take this example from the Atari game Breakout:

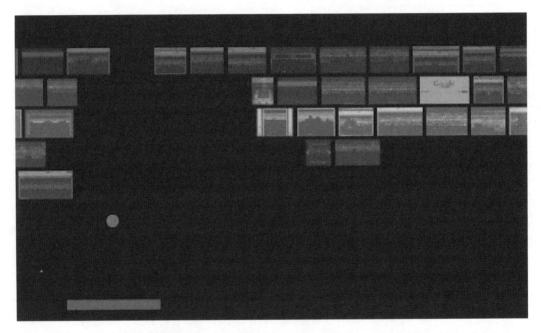

Figure 11.1 – A single frame of an Atari game gives a partial observation of the environment

It is not very clear where the ball is moving towards from a single game frame. If we had another snapshot from a previous timestep, we could estimate the change in position, the velocity of the ball. One more snapshot could help us estimate the change in velocity, acceleration, and so on. So, when an environment is partially observable, taking actions based on not a single observation but a sequence of them results in more informed decisions. In other words, having a **memory** allows an RL agent to uncover what is not observable in a single observation.

There are different ways of maintaining memory in RL models, and we will discuss them in more detail later in the chapter.

Next, let's summarize our discussion related to generalization in RL in the next section.

Recipe for generalization

As it should be clear now after the examples above, three useful ingredients to achieve generalization are:

- Diverse environment conditions to help the agent enrich its experience,
- Model memory to help the agent uncover the underlying conditions in the environment, especially if the environment is partially observable,
- Using regularization methods as in supervised learning.

In the remainder of the chapter, we go into the details of these ingredients. We start with domain randomization next.

Enriching agent experience via domain randomization

DR is simply about randomizing the parameters defining (part of) the environment during training to enrich the training data. It is a useful technique to obtain policies that are robust and generalizable, both in fully and partially observable environments. In this section, we first present a classification of such parameters, in other words, different dimensions of randomization. Then, we discuss two curriculum learning approaches to guide RL training along those dimensions.

Dimensions of randomization

Borrowed from (Rivlin, 2019), a useful categorization of how two environments belonging to the same problem class (e.g., autonomous driving) can differ is as follows.

Different observations for the same/similar states

In this case, two environments emit different observations although the underlying state and transition functions are the same or very similar. An example to this is the same Atari game scene but with different background and texture colors. A more realistic example would be the "cartoonish" look in a visual simulation of an environment versus real images coming from real cameras at the test time for the exact same scene.

Solution: Adding noise to observations

In such cases, what can help with generalization is to add noise to observations, so that the RL model focuses on the patterns that actually matter rather than overfitting to irrelevant details. Later in the chapter, we will discuss a specific approach, called **network randomization**, that will address this problem.

Same/similar observations for different states

Another dimension in which similar environments could differ from each other is related to partial observability, as we mentioned. In such environments, it is common to encounter observations that are the same/similar, with different underlying states/dynamics. When the same observation corresponds to different hidden states, these are called **aliased states**.

A simple example is two separate versions of the mountain car environment with the exact same look but different gravity. Such situations are pretty common in practice with robotics applications. Consider the example of manipulation of objects with a robot hand, as in the famous OpenAI work (which we will discuss in detail later in the chapter). Some of the parameters affecting the environment dynamics, hidden from the agent, are the following:

- Friction coefficient on the object surface
- Gravity
- Object shape and weight
- Power going into actuators

The agent needs to uncover what these hidden states/dynamics are to be able to succeed.

Solution: Training with randomized environment parameters and using memory

As we mentioned, a common approach to take here is to train the agent in many different versions of the environment with different underlying parameters, along with a memory in the RL model to uncover the underlying environment characteristics.

Different levels of complexity for the same problem class

This is the case when we essentially are dealing with the same type of problem but at different levels of complexity. A nice example from (Rivlin, 2019) is the **traveling salesman problem** (**TSP**) with different number of nodes on a graph. The RL agent's job in this environment is to decide which node to visit next at every time step so that all nodes are visited exactly once at minimum cost while going back to the initial node at the end. In fact, many problems we deal in RL naturally face this type of challenge, such as training a chess agent against opponents of different levels of expertise.

Solution: Training at varying levels of complexity with a curriculum

Not so surprisingly, training the agent in environments with varying levels of difficulty is necessary to achieve generalization here. Having said that, using a curriculum that starts with easy environment configurations and gets gradually more difficult, as we described earlier in the book, will potentially make the learning more efficient, and even feasible in some cases which would have been infeasible without a curriculum.

Once we identify the parameters to randomize the environment configurations over, the next step is to systematically expose them to the agent during training. Curriculum learning that we introduced before is a common approach to take here. Let's look into it next in the context of domain randomization.

Curriculum learning for generalization

Let's assume for your robotics application, you have identified two parameters to randomize in your environment with some minimum and maximum values:

- Friction, $k \in [0, 1]$

- Actuator torque: $\tau \in [0.1, 10]$

The goal here is to prepare the agent to act in an environment with unknown friction-torque combination at the test time.

It turns out that, as we mentioned in the previous chapter when we discussed curriculum learning, the training may result in a mediocre agent if you try to train it over the entire range for these parameters right at the beginning. That is because the extreme values of the parameter ranges are likely to be too challenging (assuming they are centered around some reasonable values for the respective parameters) for the agent who has not even figured out the basics of the task. The idea behind curriculum learning is to start with easy scenarios, such as having the first lesson as $k \in [0.4, 0.6]$ and $\tau \in [4.5, 5.5]$ and gradually increase the difficulty in the next lessons by expanding the ranges.

Then the key questions are

- How we should construct the curriculum,
- What the lessons should look like (that is what the next range of parameters after the agent succeeds in the current lesson should be), and
- When to declare success for the existing lesson.

Next, we discuss two methods for curriculum learning that automatically generate and manage the curriculum for an effective domain randomization.

Automatic domain randomization

Automatic domain randomization (ADR) is a method proposed by OpenAI in their research of using a robot hand to manipulate a Rubik's cube. It is one of the most successful robotics applications of RL for several reasons:

- Dexterous robots are notoriously difficult to control due to their high degrees of freedom.
- The policy is trained completely in simulation and then successfully transferred to a physical robot, successfully bridging the sim2real gap.
- During test time, the robot succeeded under conditions that it had never seen during training, such as the fingers being tied, having a rubber glove on, perturbations with various objects etc., which are phenomenal results in terms of generalization capability of the trained policy.

> **Info**
>
> You should check out the blog post for this important research at `https://openai.com/blog/solving-rubiks-cube/`. It contains great visualizations and insights into the results.

ADR was the key method in the success of this application. Next, we discuss how ADR works.

ADR Algorithm

Each environment we create during training is randomized over certain parameters, such as friction and torque as in the example above. To denote this formally,

- We say that an environment e_λ is parametrized by $\lambda \in \mathbb{R}^d$, where the d is the number of parameters (2 in this example).

- When an environment is created, we sample λ from a distribution, $\lambda \sim P_\phi$.

- What ADR adjusts is ϕ of the parameter distribution, therefore changing the likelihood of different parameter samples, making the environment more difficult or easier, depending on whether the agent is successful in the current difficulty.

An example P_ϕ would consist of uniform distributions for each parameter dimension, $\lambda_i \sim U(\phi_i^L, \phi_i^H)$, with $i = 1, \dots, d$. Connecting with our example, $i = 1$ would correspond to the friction coefficient, k. Then, for the initial lesson, we would have $\phi_i^L = 0.4$, $\phi_i^H = 0.6$. This would be similar for the torque parameter, $i = 2$.

Then P_ϕ becomes the following:

$$P_\phi(\lambda) = \prod_{i=1}^{d} U(\phi_i^L, \phi_i^H)$$

ADR suggests the following:

- As the training continues, allocate some of the environments for evaluation to decide whether to update ϕ.

- In each evaluation environment, randomly pick a dimension i, then pick either the upper or the lower bound to focus on, such as $i = 2$ and ϕ_2^L.

- Fix the environment parameter for the dimension picked to the bound chosen. Sample the rest of the parameters from P_ϕ.

- Evaluate the agent performance in the given environment and keep the total reward obtained in that episode in a buffer associated with the dimension and the bound (e.g., $2, L$).

- When there are enough results in the buffer, compare the average reward to the success and failure thresholds you had chosen a priori.

- If the average performance for the given dimension and bound is above your success threshold, expand the parameter range for the dimension, if it is below the failure threshold, decrease the range.

In summary, ADR systematically evaluates the agent performance for each parameter dimension at the boundaries of the parameter range, then expands or shrinks the range depending on the agent performance. You can refer to the paper for a pseudo code of the ADR algorithm, which should be easy to follow with the explanations above.

Next, let's discuss another important method for automatic curriculum generation.

Absolute learning progress with Gaussian mixture models

Absolute Learning Progress with Gaussian Mixture Models (ALP-GMM) is an effective method for automated curriculum learning. The essence of this approach is:

- To identify the parts of the environment parameter space that show the most learning progress (called the ALP value),
- Fit multiple GMM models to the ALP data, with $2, ..., k_{max}$ number of kernels, select the best one,
- Sample the environment parameters from the best GMM model.

This idea has roots in cognitive science and is used to model early vocal developments of infants.

The ALP score for a newly sampled parameter vector p_{new} is calculated as follows:

$$alp_{new} = |r_{new} - r_{old}|$$

where r_{new} is the episode reward obtained with p_{new}; and p_{old} is the closest parameter vector which was obtained in a previous episode, and r_{old} is the episode reward associated with p_{old}. All the (p, r_p) pairs are kept in a database, denoted by $\mathcal{H}$, with which the ALP scores are calculated. The GMM model, however, is obtained using the most recent N (p, ALP_p) pairs.

Note that the parts of the parameter space that have high ALP scores are more likely to be sampled to generate new environments. A high ALP score shows potential for learning for that region, and it can be obtained by observing a large drop or increase in episode reward with the newly sampled p.

> **Info**
>
> The code repo of the ALP-GMM paper is available at `https://github.com/flowersteam/teachDeepRL`, which also contains animations that show how the algorithm works. Also, we use ALP-GMM in *Chapter 14, Solving Robot Learning* to train a robot agent for object grasping.

This concludes our discussion on domain randomization for now. Remember that, when an agent is trained via DR in face of partial observability, there also needs to be a memory mechanism for the agent to uncover the underlying hidden states. Next, we discuss various memory architectures.

Using memory to overcome partial observability

A memory is nothing but a way of processing a sequence of observations as the input to the agent policy. If you worked with other types of sequence data with neural networks, such as in time series prediction or **natural language processing** (**NLP**), you can adopt similar approaches to use observation memory as the input your RL model.

Let's go into more details of how this can be done.

Stacking observations

A simple way of passing an observation sequence to the model is to stitch them together and treat this stack as a single observation. Denoting the observation at time t as o_t, we can form a new observation o'_t to be passed to the model as follows:

$$o'_t = [o_{t-m+1}, o_{t-m+2}, \dots, o_t]$$

where m is the length of the memory. Of course, for $t < m$, we need to somehow initialize the earlier parts of the memory, such as using vectors of zeros that are the same dimension as o_t.

In fact, simply stacking observations is how the original DQN work handled the partial observability in the Atari environments. In more detail, the steps of that preprocessing are as follows:

1. A rescaled $84 \times 84 \times 3$ RGB frame of the screen is obtained.
2. The Y channel (luminance) is extracted to further compress the frame into an $84 \times 84 \times 1$ image. That makes a single observation, o_t.
3. $m = 4$ most recent frames are concatenated to an $84 \times 84 \times 4$ image, forming an observation with memory for the model, o'_t.

Note that only the last step is about the memory and the former steps are not strictly necessary.

The obvious benefit of this method is that it is super simple, and the resulting model is easy to train. The downside is, though, this is not the best way of handling sequence data, which should not be surprising to you if you dealt with time series problems or natural language processing before. Here is an example of why.

Consider the following sentence you speak to your virtual voice assistant, such as Apple's Siri:

"Buy me a plane ticket from San Francisco to Boston"

This is the same as saying:

"Buy me a plane ticket to Boston from San Francisco"

Assuming each word is passed to an input neuron, it is hard for the neural network to readily interpret them as the same sentences:

- Normally each input neuron in a feedforward neural network expects a specific input with a specific meaning. In this example, the same input locations represent different meanings between the two sentences.

- Therefore, if you were to use a feedforward network, you would have to train your network with all different combinations of such sentences.

- A further complexity is that your input size is fixed, but each sentence could be of different length. You can extend this thought to RL problems as well.

Now, stacking observations is good enough in most problems, such as Atari games. But if you are trying to teach your model how to play Dota 2, a strategy video game, then you are out of luck.

Fortunately, we have **recurrent neural networks** (**RNNs**) to come to the rescue.

Using RNNs

RNNs are designed to handle sequence data. A famous RNN variate, **long short-term memory** (**LSTM**) networks, can be effectively trained to handle long sequences. LSTM has been the choice when it comes to handle partial observability in complex environments: It is used in OpenAI's Dota 2 and DeepMind's StarCraft II models, among many others.

> **Info**
> Describing the full details of how RNNs and LSTMs work is the beyond the scope here. If you need a resource to learn (more) about them, Christopher Olah's blog is the place to go: `http://colah.github.io/posts/2015-08-Understanding-LSTMs/`

When using RLlib, LSTM layer can be enabled as below, say while using PPO, followed by some optional hyperparameter changes over the default values:

```
import ray
from ray.tune.logger import pretty_print
from ray.rllib.agents.ppo.ppo import PPOTrainer
from ray.rllib.agents.ppo.ppo import DEFAULT_CONFIG


config = DEFAULT_CONFIG.copy()


config["model"]["use_lstm"] = True
# The length of the input sequence
config["model"]["max_seq_len"] = 8
# Size of the hidden state
config["model"]["lstm_cell_size"] = 64
# Whether to use
config["model"]["lstm_use_prev_action_reward"] = True
```

Note that the input is first fed to the (preprocessing) "model" in RLlib, which is typically a sequence of fully connected layers. The output of the preprocessing is then passed to the LSTM layer.

The fully connected layer hyperparameters can be similarly overwritten:

```
config["model"]["fcnet_hiddens"] = [32]
config["model"]["fcnet_activation"] = "linear"
```

After specifying the environment within the config as a Gym environment name or your custom environment class, the config dictionary is then passed to the trainer class:

```
from ray.tune.registry import register_env
def env_creator(env_config):
    return MyEnv(env_config)    # return an env instance
register_env("my_env", env_creator)
config["env"] = "my_env"
ray.init()
trainer = PPOTrainer(config=config)
while True:
    results = trainer.train()
```

```
    print(pretty_print(results))
    if results["timesteps_total"] >= MAX_STEPS:
        break
print(trainer.save())
```

There are couple things to keep in mind when using and LSTM model as opposed to simple stacking of observations:

- LSTM is often slower to train due to sequential processing of a multi-step input,

- Training LSTM may require more data compared to a feed forward network,

- Your LSTM model could be more sensitive to hyperparameters, so you may have to do some hyperparameter tuning.

Speaking of the hyperparameters, here are some values to try if your training is not progressing well for an algorithm like PPO:

- Learning rate (`config["lr"]`): $10^{-4}, 10^{-5}, 10^{-3}$

- LSTM cell size (`config["model"]["lstm_cell_size"]`): 64, 128, 256

- Layer sharing between the value and policy network(`config["vf_share_layers"]`): Try to make this false if your episode rewards are in hundreds or above to prevent the value function loss from dominating the policy loss. Alternatively, you can also reduce the `config["vf_loss_coeff"]`.

- Entropy coefficient (`config["entropy_coeff"]`): $10^{-6}, 10^{-4}$

- Passing reward and previous action as input (`config["model"]["lstm_use_prev_action_reward"]`): Consider setting this to true to provide more information to the agent in addition to observations, if the past reward and action are also available as inputs at the test time.

- Preprocessing model architecture (`config["model"]["fcnet_hiddens"]` and `config["model"]["fcnet_activation"]`): Try single linear layers.

Hopefully, these will be helpful to come up with a good architecture for your model.

Finally, let's discuss one of the most popular architectures: The Transformer.

Transformer architecture

Over the past several years, the transformer architecture has essentially replaced RNNs in **natural language processing** (**NLP**) applications.

The Transformer architecture has several advantages over LSTM, the most used RNN type:

- LSTM encoder packs all the information obtained from the input sequence into a single embedding layer that is then passed to the decoder. This creates a bottleneck between the encoder and the decoder. The Transformer model, however, allows the decoder to look at each of the elements of the input sequence (at their embeddings, to be precise).

- Since LSTM relies on backpropagation through time, the gradients are likely to explode or vanish throughout the update. The Transformer model, on the other hand, simultaneously look at the each of the input steps and does not run into a similar problem.

- As a result, Transformer models can effectively use much longer input sequences.

For these reasons, Transformer is a competitive alternative to RNNs for RL applications as well.

> **Info**
>
> A great tutorial on the Transformer architecture is, by Jay Alammar, avaliable at `http://jalammar.github.io/illustrated-transformer/` if you would like to catch up on the topic.

Despite their advantages of the original transformer model, it has been shown to be unstable in RL applications. An improvement is proposed (Parisotto et al., 2019), named **Gated Transformer-XL (GTrXL)**.

RLlib has GTrXL implemented as a custom model. It can be used as follows:

```
...
from ray.rllib.models.tf.attention_net import GTrXLNet
...
config["model"] = {
    "custom_model": GTrXLNet,
    "max_seq_len": 50,
    "custom_model_config": {
        "num_transformer_units": 1,
        "attn_dim": 64,
        "num_heads": 2,
        "memory_tau": 50,
```

```
        "head_dim": 32,
        "ff_hidden_dim": 32,
    },
}
```

This gives us another powerful architecture to try in RLlib.

We have come a long way to understand how to achieve generalization in reinforcement learning. Now, it is time to get more practical! In the next section, we introduce an environment, CoinRun, developed to quantify generalization capabilities of RL agents. Also in the next section, we see how regularization techniques used in supervised learning help with RL too.

Take a break, and then we will switch gears.

Quantifying generalization via CoinRun

There are various ways of testing whether certain algorithms/approaches generalize to unseen environment conditions better than others, such as:

- Creating validation and test environments with separate sets of environment parameters,

- Assessing policy performance in real-life deployment.

Real-life deployment may not necessarily be an option, so the latter is not always practical. The challenge with the former is to have consistency and to ensure that validation/test data are indeed not used in training. Also, it is possible to overfit to the validation environment when too many models are tried based on validation performance. One approach to overcome these challenges is to use procedurally generated environments. To this end, OpenAI has created the CoinRun environment to benchmark algorithms on their generalization capabilities. Let's look into it in more detail.

CoinRun environment

In the CoinRun environment, we have a character trying to reach the coin without colliding with the obstacles. The character starts at the far left and the coin is at the far right. The levels are generated procedurally from an underlying probability distribution at various levels of difficulty, as shown here:

Figure 11.2 – Two levels in CoinRun with different levels of difficulty (Source: Cobbe et al., 2018).

Here are more details about the environment's reward function and terminal conditions:

- There are dynamic and static obstacles, causing the character to die when collided, which terminates the episode.

- The only reward is given when the coin is collected, which also terminates the episode.

- There is a time out of 1000-time steps before the episode terminates, unless the character dies or the coin is reached.

Note that the CoinRun environment generates all (training and test) levels from the same distribution, so it does not test out-of-distribution (extrapolation) performance of a policy.

Next, let's install this environment and experiment with it.

Installing the CoinRun environment

You can follow the steps below to install the CoinRun environment:

1. We start with setting up and activating a virtual Python environment since CoinRun needs specific packages. So, in your directory of choice, run:

```
virtualenv coinenv
source coinenv/bin/activate
```

2. Then we install the necessary Linux packages, including a famous parallel computing interface, MPI:

```
sudo apt-get install mpich build-essential qt5-default
pkg-config
```

3. Then, we install the Python dependencies and the CoinRuin package fetched from the GitHub repo:

```
git clone https://github.com/openai/coinrun.git
cd coinrun
pip install tensorflow==1.15.3 # or tensorflow-gpu
pip install -r requirements.txt
pip install -e .
```

Note that we had to install an old TensorFlow version. Officially, TF 1.12.0 is suggested by the creators of CoinRun. However, using a later TF 1.x could help you avoid CUDA conflicts while using GPU.

4. You can try the environment out with your keyboard's arrow keys with the following command:

```
python -m coinrun.interactive
```

Great, and enjoy playing CoinRun! I suggest you familiarize yourself with it to gain a better understanding of the comparisons we will go into later.

> **Info**
>
> You can visit the CoinRun GitHub repo for the full set of commands at
> `https://github.com/openai/coinrun`

The paper that introduced the environment (Cobbe et al., 2018) also mentions how various regularization methods affects generalization in RL, which we discuss next.

The effect of regularization and network architecture on the generalization of RL policies

The authors found that many techniques used in supervised learning to prevent overfitting are also helpful in RL. Since reproducing the results in the paper takes really long time, where each experiment took hundreds of millions of steps, we will not attempt to do it here. Instead, we provide you with a summary of the results and the commands to run various versions of algorithms. But you can observe that, even after 500k time steps, applying the regularization techniques we mention below improves the test performance.

You can see all training options for this environment using the following command:

```
python -m coinrun.train_agent -help
```

Let's start with running a baseline PPO without any regularizations applied.

Vanilla training

You can train an RL agent using PPO with an IMPALA architecture without any improvements for generalization as follows:

```
python -m coinrun.train_agent --run-id BaseAgent --num-levels
500 --num-envs 60
```

Here, `BaseAgent` is an id for your agent that is decided by you, `--num-levels` `500` is to use 500 game levels during training with the default seed used in the paper, `--num-envs 60` kicks off 60 parallel environments for rollouts, which you can adjust according to the number of CPUs available on your machine.

In order to test the trained agent in 3 parallel sessions, with 20 parallel environments in each and 5 levels for each environment, you can run the following command:

```
mpiexec -np 3 python -m coinrun.enjoy --test-eval --restore-id
BaseAgent -num-eval 20 -rep 5
```

The average test reward will be specified in `mpi_out`. In my case, the reward changed from ~5.5 in training after 300K time steps to 0.8 in test.

Also, you can watch your trained agent by running the following:

```
python -m coinrun.enjoy --restore-id BaseAgent -hres
```

which is actually quite fun to do.

Using a larger network

The authors found that, as in supervised learning, using a larger neural network increases generalization by successfully solving more test episodes as it comes with a higher capacity. They also note that, however, there are diminishing returns for generalization with the increase in size, so generalization won't improve linearly with the network size.

To use an architecture with 5 residual blocks instead of 3 with doubled number of channels in each layer, you can add the argument `impalalarge`.

```
python -m coinrun.train_agent --run-id LargeAgent --num-levels
500 --num-envs 60 --architecture impalalarge
```

Again, you can run test evaluations with the run id specified as what you provided for the large agent case.

Diversity in training data

In order to test the importance of diverse training data, the authors compared two types of training, both with a total of 256M time steps, across 100 and then 10,000 game levels (controlled by `--num-levels`). The test performance went from 30% to 90+% success rate (which is also on par with the training performance) with the more diverse data.

> **Tip**
>
> Increasing data diversity acts as a regularizer in supervised and reinforcement learning. This is because the model would have to explain more variation with the same model capacity as diversity increases, forcing it to use its capacity to focus on the most important patterns in the input rather than overfitting to noise.

This emphasizes the importance of randomization of the environment parameters to achieve generalization, which we will separately talk about later in the chapter.

Dropout and L2 regularization

The experiment results show both dropout and L2 regularization improves generalization, bringing in additional around 5% and 8% success on top of ~79% baseline test performance.

> **Tip**
>
> If you need some refresher on dropout and L2 regularization, check out Chitta Ranjan's blog at `https://towardsdatascience.com/simplified-math-behind-dropout-in-deep-learning-6d50f3f47275`.

We explore this in more detail as follows:

- Empirically, the authors find the best L2 weight as 10^{-4} and the best dropout rate as 0.1.

- L2 regularization, empirically, has a higher impact on generalization compared to dropout.

- As expected, training with dropout is slower to converge, to which twice as many time steps (512M) are allocated.

To use a dropout with 0.1 rate on top of the vanilla agent, you can use the following command:

```
python -m coinrun.train_agent --run-id AgentDOut01 --num-levels
500 --num-envs 60 --dropout 0.1
```

Similarly, to use L2 normalization with a weight 0.0001, execute the following:

```
python -m coinrun.train_agent --run-id AgentL2_00001
--num-levels 500 --num-envs 60 --12-weight 0.0001
```

In your TensorFlow RL model, you can add dropout using the Dropout layer, such as in:

```
from tensorflow.keras import layers
...
x = layers.Dense(512, activation="relu")(x)
x = layers.Dropout(0.1)(x)
...
```

And to add L2 regularization, do something like:

```
from tensorflow.keras import regularizers
...
x = layers.Dense(512, activation="relu", kernel_
regularizer=regularizers.12(0.0001))(x)
```

> **Info**
>
> TensorFlow has a very nice tutorial on overfitting and underfitting, which you might want to check out: https://www.tensorflow.org/tutorials/keras/overfit_and_underfit

Next, let's discuss data augmentation.

Using data augmentation

A common method to prevent overfitting is data augmentation, which is modifying / distorting the input, mostly randomly, so that the diversity in the training data increases. When used on images, these techniques include random cropping, changing the brightness, sharpness etc. An example CoinRun scene with data augmentation used looks like the following:

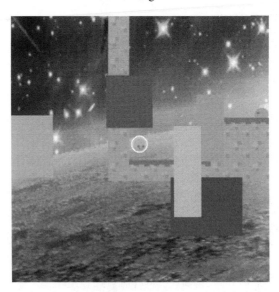

Figure 11.3 – CoinRun with data augmentation (Source: Cobbe et al., 2018).

> **Info**
>
> For TensorFlow tutorial on data augmentation, check out: `https://www.tensorflow.org/tutorials/images/data_augmentation`

Data augmentation, as it turns out, is also helpful in RL, and it gives a lift in the test performance slightly worse than L2 regularization.

Using batch normalization

Batch normalization is one of the key tools in deep learning to stabilize training as well as to prevent overfitting.

> **Info**
>
> If you need a refresher on batch normalization, check out Chris Versloot's blog at `https://bit.ly/3kjzjno`.

In the CoinRun environment, you can enable the batch normalization layers in the training as follows:

```
python -m coinrun.train_agent --run-id AgentL2_00001
--num-levels 500 --num-envs 60 --use-data-augmentation 1
```

This adds a batch normalization layer after every convolutional layer.

When you implement your own TensorFlow model, the syntax for the batch normalization layer is `layers.BatchNormalization()`, with some optional arguments you can pass.

The reported results show that using batch normalization gives the second-best lift to the test performance among all of the other regularization methods (except increasing the diversity in the training data).

Adding stochasticity

Finally, introducing stochasticity/noise into the environment turns out to be the most useful generalization technique, with a ~10% lift to the test performance. Two methods tried in the paper with the PPO algorithm during training:

- Using ϵ-greedy actions (which is usually used with Q-learning approaches),
- Increasing the entropy bonus coefficient (k_H) in PPO, which encourages variance in the actions suggested by the policy.

Some good hyperparameter choices for these methods were $\epsilon = 0.1$ and $k_H = 0.04$, respectively. Something worth noting is that if the environment dynamics are already highly stochastic, introducing more stochasticity may not be as impactful.

Combining all the methods

Using all these regularization methods together during training only slightly improved the boost obtained from the individual methods, suggesting that each of these methods play a similar role to prevent overfitting. Note that it is not quite possible say that these methods will have a similar impact in all RL problems. What we need to keep in mind, though, the traditional regularization methods used in supervised learning can have significant on generalizing RL policies as well.

This concludes our discussion on the fundamental regularization techniques for RL. Next, we look into another method that followed the original CoinRun paper, which is network randomization.

Network Randomization and Feature Matching

Network randomization proposed by (Lee et al., 2020) simply involves using a random transformation of observations, s, as follows:

$$\hat{s} = f(s; \phi)$$

Then, the transformed observation $\hat{s}$ is fed as input to the regular policy network used in the RL algorithm. Here, ϕ is the parameter of this transformation, which is randomly initialized at every training iteration. This can be simply achieved by adding, right after the input layer, a layer that is not trainable and re-initialized periodically. In TensorFlow 2, a randomization layer that transforms the input after each call could be implemented as follows:

```python
class RndDense(tf.keras.layers.Layer):
    def __init__(self, units=32):
        super(RndDense, self).__init__()
        self.units = units

    def build(self, input_shape):
        self.w_init = tf.keras.initializers.GlorotNormal()
        self.w_shape = (input_shape[-1], self.units)
        self.w = tf.Variable(
            initial_value=self.w_init(shape=self.w_shape,
                                      dtype="float32"),
            trainable=True,
        )

    def call(self, inputs):
        self.w.assign(self.w_init(shape=self.w_shape,
                                  dtype="float32"))
        return tf.nn.relu(tf.matmul(inputs, self.w))
```

Note that this custom layer exhibits the following traits:

1. Has weights that are not trainable
2. Assigns random weights to the layer at each call.

A further improvement to this architecture is to do two forward passes, with and without randomized inputs, and enforce the network to give similar outputs. This can be achieved by adding a loss to the RL objective that penalizes the difference:

$$\mathcal{L}_{FM} = \mathbb{E}[\|h(\hat{s}; \theta) - h(s; \theta)\|^2]$$

where θ is the parameters of the policy network, and h is the second from the last layer in the policy network (i.e. the one right before the layer that outputs the actions). This is called **feature matching** and makes the network differentiate noise from the signal in the input.

> **Info**
>
> TensorFlow 1.x implementation of this architecture for the CoinRun environment is available at `https://github.com/pokaxpoka/netrand`. Compare it to the original CoinRun environment by comparing `random_ppo2.py` with `ppo2.py` and `random_impala_cnn` method to `impala_cnn` method under `policies.py`.

Going back to the dimensions of generalization we mentioned earlier, network randomization helps RL policies generalize in all of the three dimensions.

Before we wrap up this chapter, let's also mention another resource & environment that will deepen your understanding on the topic.

Sunblaze environment

We don't have space to cover all methods for generalization in this book, but a useful resource for you to check out is a blog by (Packer & Gao, 2019), which introduces the Sunblaze environments to systematically assess generalization approaches for RL. These environments are modifications to the classic OpenAI Gym environments, which are parametrized to test interpolation and extrapolation performance of algorithms.

> **Info**
>
> You can find the blog post describing the Sunblaze environments and the results at `https://bair.berkeley.edu/blog/2019/03/18/rl-generalization/`.

Congratulations! We have arrived at the end of the chapter! We have covered such important topics that deserve more attention than what our limited space allows here. Go ahead and read the sources in the reference section and experiment with the repos we introduced to deepen your understanding of the topic.

Summary

In this chapter, we have covered an important topic in RL: Generalization and partial observability, which are key for real-world applications. Note that this is an active research area: Keep our discussion here as directional suggestions and the first methods to try for your problem. New approaches come out periodically, so watch out for them. The important thing is you should always keep an eye on the generalization and partial observability for a successful RL implementation outside of video games. In the next section, we will take our expedition to yet a next advanced level with meta-learning. So, stay tuned!

References

1. Cobbe, K., Klimov, O., Hesse, C., Kim, T., & Schulman, J. (2018). *Quantifying Generalization in Reinforcement Learning*. Retrieved from ArXiv: `https://arxiv.org/abs/1812.02341`

2. Lee, K., Lee, K., Shin, J., & Lee, H. (2020). *{Network Randomization: A Simple Technique for Generalization in Deep Reinforcement Learning*. Retrieved from ArXiv: `https://arxiv.org/abs/1910.05396`

3. Rivlin, O. (2019, Nov 21). *Generalization in Deep Reinforcement Learning*. Retrieved from Towards Data Science: `https://towardsdatascience.com/generalization-in-deep-reinforcement-learning-a14a240b155b`

4. Cobbe, K., Klimov, O., Hesse, C., Kim, T., & Schulman, J. (2018). *Quantifying Generalization in Reinforcement Learning*: `https://arxiv.org/abs/1812.0234`

5. Lee, K., Lee, K., Shin, J., & Lee, H. (2020). *"Network Randomization: A Simple Technique for Generalization in Deep Reinforcement Learning."*: `https://arxiv.org/abs/1910.0539`

6. Parisotto, Emilio, et al. (2019) *"Stabilizing Transformers for Reinforcement Learning."*: `http://arxiv.org/abs/1910.06764`

12
Meta-Reinforcement Learning

Humans learn new skills from much fewer data compared to a reinforcement learning agent. Two factors contributing to this are, first, we come with priors in our brains at birth that give us certain capabilities from the get-go; and second, we are able to transfer our knowledge from one skill to another quite efficiently and adapt to new environments fast. Meta-reinforcement learning aims to achieve a similar capability for artificial intelligence agents. In this chapter, we describe what meta-reinforcement learning is, the approaches it uses, and the challenges it faces. Specifically, we cover the following topics:

- Introducing meta-reinforcement learning
- Meta-reinforcement learning with recurrent policies
- Gradient-based meta-reinforcement learning
- Meta-reinforcement learning as partially observed reinforcement learning
- Challenges in meta-reinforcement learning

Introducing meta-reinforcement learning

Meta-reinforcement learning is an intuitive concept, but it could be hard to wrap your mind around it at first. In this section, we make an introduction and discuss the connection between meta-RL and other concepts we covered in the earlier chapters.

Learning to learn

Let's say you are trying to convince a friend of going on a travel together that you really want. There are several arguments coming to your mind. You could talk about:

- The beauty of the nature at your destination,
- How you are so burned out and really need this time away,
- This could be the last chance for a travel together for a while because you will be busy at work.

Well, you know your friend for years and how they love nature, so you recognize that the first argument will be the most enticing one! If it were your mom, perhaps you could use the second one because she cares about you a lot and wants to support you. In either of these situations, you know how to achieve what you want because you have a common past with these individuals.

Now, let's think about another case. Have you ever left a store buying something more expensive than you had originally planned? How were you convinced? Let's think of a car dealership for this example. Hypothetically, the salesperson could figure out how much you care about:

- Your family, and convince you of buying an SUV to make them more comfortable,
- Your look, and convince you of buying a sports car that will attract a lot eyes,
- Your environment, and convince you of buying an electric vehicle with no emissions.

The salesperson does not know you. But through years of experience and training, they learn how to learn about customers very quickly and effectively. They ask you questions, understand your background, discover your interests, figure out your budget. Then, you are presented with some options, and based on what you like and don't like, you end up with an offer package with a make and model, upgrades and options, and a payment plan, all customized for you.

Here, the former of these examples is like reinforcement learning, where an agent has a policy for different tasks to maximize the reward. The latter example corresponds to meta-reinforcement learning, where an agent does not necessarily have a good policy for the task at hand, but has a **procedure** to quickly obtain one to adapt to new tasks to maximize the reward. In these examples, tasks would be different persons to convince. Meta-reinforcement learning is about *learning such a procedure, in other words, learning how to learn* for effective adaptation to new tasks.

After this soft introduction, next, let's formally define meta-RL.

Defining meta-reinforcement learning

In meta-RL, in each episode, the agent faces a task τ_i that comes from a distribution $p(\tau)$, $\tau_i \sim p(\tau)$. A task τ_i is a **Markov decision process** (**MDP**), a variation of the environment, described as $M_i = \langle S, A, P_i, R_i \rangle$, where:

- S is the state space,
- A is the action space,
- P_i is the transition distribution for task τ_i,
- R_i is the reward function for task τ_i.

So, different tasks have the same state and action space, but different transition and reward dynamics. You can think of these as the same environment with different configurations. During the training and test time, we expect the tasks to come from this same distribution, but we don't expect them to the same, which is the setup in a typical machine learning problem. In meta-RL, at the test time, we expect the agent to:

1. Effectively explore to understand the task,
2. Adapt to the task.

You can hopefully start to see why meta-RL is of interest to us. The ability to adapt to new situations could be much more desirable than learning what to do in every single possible situation. The latter would require a lot of learning and training in advance and may not even be completely possible because we may not know all possible situations that we could end up in. So, the latter is an expensive way to ensure "doing well" in relatively unknown environments. And it is not quite how the nature works either. In fact, meta-learning is an essential part of animal learning. Let's explore this connection next.

Relation to animal learning

Artificial neural networks notoriously require a lot of data to be trained. On the other hand, our brains learn much more efficiently from small data. There are two major factors contributing to this:

1. Unlike an untrained artificial neural network, our brains are pretrained and come with **priors** embedded in for vision, audio, and motor skills tasks. Some especially impressive examples are **precocial** animals, such as ducks, whose ducklings are taken to water within two hours of hatching.

2. When we learn new tasks, we learn at two time scales: In a **fast loop**, we learn about the specific task we are dealing with. As we see more examples, in a **slow loop**, we learn **abstractions** that help us generalize our knowledge to new examples very fast. Let's say you learn about a particular cat breed, such as American Curl, and all the examples you have seen are in white and yellow tones. When you see a black cat of this breed, it won't be difficult for you to recognize it. That is because the abstraction you developed will help you recognize this breed from its peculiar ears that curl back towards the back of the skull, not from its color.

One of the big challenges in machine learning is to enable learning from small data similar to above. To mimic (1), we fine-tune trained models for new tasks. For example, a language model that is trained on generic corpora (Wikipedia pages, news articles) can be fine-tuned on a specialized corpus (maritime law) where the amount of data available is limited. And (2) is what meta-learning is about.

> **Tip**
> Empirically, fine-tuning trained models for new tasks doesn't work in reinforcement learning as well as in supervised learning (as in image or language) tasks. It turns out that the neural network representations of RL policies are not as hierarchical as, for example, in image recognition where first layers detect edges and last layers detect complete objects.

To better understand meta-learning capabilities in animals, let's take a look at a canonical example: The Harlow experiment.

The Harlow experiment

The Harlow experiment that explored meta-learning in animals involves a monkey that is shown two objects at a time:

- One of these objects is associated with a food reward, which the monkey had to discover.

- In each step over a six total, the objects are randomly placed in left and right positions.

- The monkey had to learn which object gives them a reward independent of their positions.

- After the six steps are over, the objects were replaced with new ones that are unfamiliar to the monkey and with an unknown reward association.

- The monkey learned a strategy to randomly pick an object in the first step, understand which object gives the reward, and choose that object in the remaining steps regardless of the position of the object.

This experiment nicely expresses the meta-learning capabilities in animals as it involves:

- An unfamiliar environment/task for the agent,

- The agent's effective adaptation to the unfamiliar environment/task through a strategy that involves a necessary exploration, developing a task specific policy on the fly (making a choice based on the object associated with the reward but not its position), and then exploitation.

> **Info**
>
> A famous study that connects the meta-learning in machine learning with the Harlow experiment is by DeepMind, which is nicely outlined in a blog post at `https://deepmind.com/blog/article/prefrontal-cortex-meta-reinforcement-learning-system`

The goal in meta-RL is along the same lines as we will see shortly. For now, let's continue to explore meta-RL's relation to some other concepts we have covered.

Relation to partial observability and domain randomization

One of the main goals in a meta-RL procedure is to uncover the underlying environment/ task at the test time. This could very well be framed as the environment being partially observable; and meta-RL would be a specific approach to deal with it.

In the previous chapter, *Chapter 11, Achieving Generalization and Overcoming Partial Observability*, we discussed that we need (i) memory, and (ii) domain randomization to deal with partial observability. So, how is meta-RL different? Well, memory is still one of the key tools leveraged in meta-RL. We also randomize the environments/tasks while training meta-RL agents, similar to domain randomization. At this point, they may seem indistinguishable to you. However, there is a key difference:

- In domain randomization, the goal of the training for the agent is to develop a robust policy for all variations of an environment over a set of parameter ranges. For example, a robot is trained under a range of friction and torque values with domain randomization. At test time, based on a sequence of observations that carry information about friction and torque in the environment, the agent takes actions using the trained policy. You can also connect domain randomization to the example we provided at the top about convincing someone of your travel plans.

- In meta-RL, the goal of the training for the agent is to develop an adaptation procedure to new environments/tasks, which will potentially lead to different policies at the test time after an exploration period. This is akin to the example of a salesperson.

The difference can be still subtle when it comes to memory-based meta-RL methods, and the training procedure may be identical in some cases. To better understand the difference, remember the Harlow experiment: The idea of domain randomization does not suit to the experiment, since the objects shown to the agent are completely new in every episode. Therefore, the agent does not learn how to act over a range of object in meta-RL. Instead, it learns how to discover the task and act accordingly when it is shown completely new objects.

With that, now it is finally time to discuss several meta-RL approaches.

> **Info**
>
> A pioneer in meta-learning is Prof. Chelsea Finn of Stanford University, who worked with Prof. Sergey Levine of UC Berkeley as her Ph.D. advisor. Prof. Finn has an entire course on meta-learning, available at `https://cs330.stanford.edu/`. In this chapter, we mostly follow the terminology and classification of meta-RL approaches used by Prof. Finn and Prof. Levine.

Let's start with one that uses recurrent policies, called RL2.

Meta-reinforcement learning with recurrent policies

In this section, we cover one of the more intuitive approaches in meta-reinforcement learning that uses recurrent neural networks to keep a memory, also known as the RL2 algorithm. Let's start with an example to motivate this approach.

Grid world example

Consider a grid world where the agent's task is to reach a goal state G from a start state S. These states are randomly placed for different tasks, so the agent has to learn exploring the world to discover where the goals state is, which then is given a big reward. When the same task is repeated, the agent is expected to quickly reach the goal state, which is, adapt to the environment, since there is a penalty incurred for each time step. This is described in Figure 12.1.

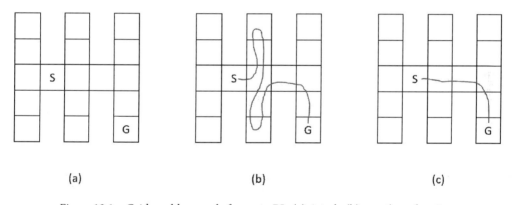

| (a) | (b) | (c) |

Figure 12.1 – Grid world example for meta-RL. (a) A task, (b) agent's exploration of the task, (c) agent's exploitation of what it learned.

In order to excel at the tasked the agent must:

1. Explore the environment (at test time),

2. Remember and exploit what it learned earlier.

Now, since we would like the agent to remember its previous experiences, we need to introduce a memory mechanism, which will be using a **recurrent neural network (RNN)** to represent the policy. There are several points we need to pay attention to:

1. Just remembering the past observations are not enough the goal state changes from task to task. The agent also needs to remember the past actions and rewards, so that it can associate which actions in which states led to which reward to be able to uncover the task.

2. Just remembering the history within the current episode is not enough. Notice once the agent reaches the goal state, the episode ends. If we don't carry the memory over to the next episode, the agent has no way of benefiting from the experience gained in the previous episode.

3. Note that there is no training or updates to the weights of the policy network taking place here. This is all happening at the test time, in an unseen task.

Handling the former is easy: We just need to feed actions and rewards along with the observations to the RNN. To handle the second, we make sure that we *do not reset the recurrent state between episodes*, unless the task changes, so that the memory is not discontinued.

Now, during training, why would the agent learn a policy that explicitly starts a new task with an exploration phase? That is because the exploration phase helps the agent discover the task and collect higher rewards later. If we reward the agent during training based on individual episodes, the agent would not learn this behavior though. That is because exploration has some immediate costs, which are recouped only in future episodes and when that memory is carried across episodes for the same task. To this end, we form **meta-episodes**, or **trials**, which are N episodes of the same task are concatenated together. Again, the recurrent state is not reset within, and the reward is calculated over the meta-episode. This is illustrated in Figure 12.2.

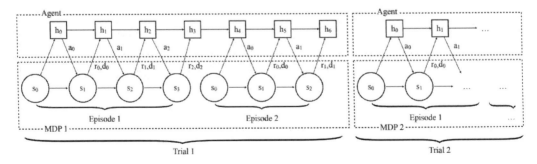

Figure 12.2 – Procedure of agent-environment interaction (source: Duan et al. 2017)

Next, let's see how this can be implemented inside RLlib.

RLlib implementation

About what we mentioned above, meta-episodes can be formed by modifying the environment, so that is not quite related to RLlib. For the rest, we modify the model dictionary inside the agent config:

1. We enable the LSTM model:

    ```
    "use_lstm": True
    ```

2. We pass actions and rewards in addition to observations to the LSTM:

    ```
    "lstm_use_prev_action_reward": True
    ```

3. We make sure that the LSTM input sequence is long enough to cover the multiple episodes within a meta-episode. The default sequence length is 20.

    ```
    max_seq_len": 20
    ```

That is all you need! You can train your meta-RL agents with a few lines of code change!

> **Info**
> This procedure with recurrent policies may not always converge, or when it does, it may converge to bad policies, which is a disadvantage of this approach. Trying training multiple times (with different seeds) and with different hyperparameter settings may help you obtain a good policy, but not guaranteed.

With this, we can proceed to gradient-based approaches.

Gradient-based meta-reinforcement learning

Gradient-based meta-RL methods propose improving the policy by continuing the training at test time so that the policy adapts to the environment it is applied in. The key is that policy parameters right before the adaptation, θ, are set in such a way that the adaptation takes place in just a few shots.

> **Tip**
>
> Gradient-based meta-RL is based on the idea that some initializations of
> policy parameters enable learning from very little data during adaptation.
> The meta-training procedure aims to find such an initialization.

A specific approach in this branch is called **model-agnostic meta-learning (MAML)**,
which is a general meta-learning method that can also be applied in RL. MAML trains the
agent for a variety of tasks to figure out a good θ that facilitates adaptation and learning
from few shots.

Let's see how you can use RLlib for this.

RLlib implementation

MAML is one of the agents implemented in RLlib and can be easily used with Ray's Tune:

```python
tune.run(
    "MAML",
    config=dict(
        DEFAULT_CONFIG,
        ...
    )
)
```

Using MAML requires implementing few additional methods within an environment.
These are namely `sample_tasks`, `set_task`, and `get_task` methods that help
training over various tasks. An example implementation could be on a pendulum
environment, which is implemented in RLlib is as follows (`https://github.
com/ray-project/ray/blob/releases/1.0.0/rllib/examples/env/
pendulum_mass.py`):

```python
class PendulumMassEnv(PendulumEnv, gym.utils.EzPickle,
MetaEnv):
    """PendulumMassEnv varies the weight of the pendulum

    Tasks are defined to be weight uniformly sampled between
    [0.5,2]
    """

    def sample_tasks(self, n_tasks):
        # Mass is a random float between 0.5 and 2
        return np.random.uniform(low=0.5, high=2.0, size=(n_
tasks, ))
```

```
def set_task(self, task):
    """
    Args:
        task: task of the meta-learning environment
    """
    self.m = task

def get_task(self):
    """
    Returns:
        task: task of the meta-learning environment
    """
    return self.m
```

While training MAML, RLlib measures the agent performance before any adaptation to the environment it is in via `episode_reward_mean`. The performance after N gradient steps of adaptation is shown in `episode_reward_mean_adapt_N`. The number of these inner adaptation steps is a config of the agent that can be modified.

```
"inner_adaptation_steps": 1
```

During training, you can see these metrics displayed on TensorBoard:

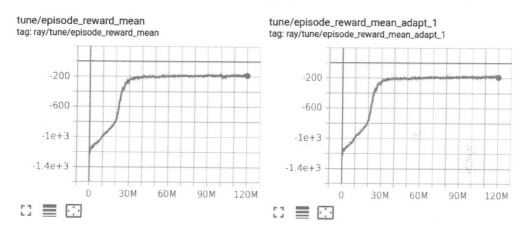

Figure 12.3 – TensorBoard metrics for episode reward before and after one step of adaptation

For the simple pendulum task, you may not see as much of a difference before and after the adaptation. However, these plots will be important to watch when you deal with more complicated tasks.

That's it! Now, let's introduce the last approach in our chapter.

Meta-reinforcement learning as partially observed reinforcement learning

Another approach in meta-RL is to focus on the partially observable nature of the tasks and explicitly estimate the state from the observations until that point in time:

$$p(s_t|o_{1:t})$$

And then form a probability distribution over possible tasks based on their likelihood of being active in that episode, or more precisely, some vector that contains the task information:

$$p(z_t|s_{1:t}, a_{1:t}, r_{1:t})$$

Then, iteratively sample a task vector from this probability distribution and pass that to the policy in addition to state:

1. Sample $z \sim p(z_t|s_{1:t}, a_{1:t}, r_{1:t})$,
2. Take actions from a policy that receives state and task vector as input, $\pi_\theta(a|s, z)$.

With that, we conclude our discussion on three main meta-RL methods. Before we wrap up the chapter, let's discuss some of the challenges in meta-RL.

Challenges in meta-reinforcement learning

The main challenges regarding meta-RL, following (Rakelly, 2019), are as follows:

*   Meta-RL requires a meta-training step over various tasks, which are usually hand-crafted. A challenge here is to create an automated procedure to generate these tasks.

*   The exploration phase that is supposed to be learned during meta-training is in practice is not efficiently learned.

- Meta-training involves sampling from an independent and identical distribution of tasks, which is not a realistic assumption. So, one goal is to make meta-RL more "online" by making it learn from a stream of tasks.

In addition to these challenges, it is important to note meta-RL methods will not work as well as the other methods, such as domain randomization, in complex tasks like robot hand manipulation. As the research in this area progresses, we can expect to see this gap to decrease and meta-RL make its way to mainstream with its unique advantages.

With that, we wrap up this chapter. Congratulations! We have just covered meta-RL, a very important emerging direction in reinforcement learning, which could be also a bit difficult to absorb. Hopefully, this introduction gives you the courage to dive in the literature on this topic and further explore it for yourself.

Conclusion

In this chapter, we covered meta-reinforcement learning, one of the most important research directions in RL as its promise is to train agents that can adapt to new environments very quickly. To this end, we covered three methods: Recurrent policies, gradient-based, and partial observability-based. Currently, meta-RL is at its infancies and not performing as well as the more established approaches, so we covered the challenges in this area as well.

In the next chapter, we will cover several advanced topics in a single chapter. So, stay tuned to further deepen your RL expertise.

References

1. Wang, J.X., Kurth-Nelson, Z., Kumaran, D. et al *Prefrontal cortex as a meta-reinforcement learning system*. Nature Neuroscience 21, 860–868 (2018). https://doi.org/10.1038/s41593-018-0147-8

2. Trazzi, M. (2019). *Meta-Reinforcement Learning*. FloydHub Blog. URL: https://blog.floydhub.com/meta-rl/.

3. Duan, Yan, et al. (2016). *RL^2: Fast Reinforcement Learning via Slow Reinforcement Learning*. arXiv.org, http://arxiv.org/abs/1611.02779

4. Wang, Jane X., et al. (2017). *Learning to Reinforcement Learn*. arXiv.org, http://arxiv.org/abs/1611.05763

5. Gupta A. et al. (2018). *Meta-Reinforcement Learning of Structured Exploration Strategies*. NeurIPS. URL: `https://bit.ly/39XLyUG`

6. Calandra R. et al. (2020). *Workshop on Meta-Learning* (MetaLearn 2020). NeurIPS Workshop. URL: `https://meta-learn.github.io/2020/`

7. Rakelly, K. (2019). *Meta Reinforcement Learning*. UC Berkeley CS285. URL: `https://youtu.be/4qH_h5_V3O4`

13
Exploring Advanced Topics

In this chapter, we cover several advanced topics in reinforcement learning. First of all, we go deeper into distributed reinforcement learning, in addition to our discussion in the previous chapters, which is a key topic to create scalable training architectures. Next, we present curiosity-driven reinforcement learning to handle hard-exploration problems that are not solvable by traditional exploration techniques. Finally, we discuss offline reinforcement learning, which leverages offline datasets rather than environment interactions to obtain good policies. All of these are hot research areas that you will hear more about over the next several years.

So, in this chapter, you will learn about the following:

- Diving deeper into distributed reinforcement learning
- Exploring curiosity-driven reinforcement learning
- Offline reinforcement learning

Let's get started!

Diving deeper into distributed reinforcement learning

As we already mentioned in the earlier chapters, training sophisticated reinforcement learning agents requires massive amounts of data. While one critical area of research is to increase the sample efficiency in RL, the other and complementary direction is about how to best utilize the compute power and parallelization and reduce the wall-clock time and cost of training. We already covered, implemented, and used distributed RL algorithms and libraries in the earlier chapters. So, this section will be an extension of the previous discussions due to the importance of this topic. Here, we present additional material on state-of-the-art distributed RL architectures, algorithms, and libraries. With that, let's get started with SEED RL, an architecture designed for massive and efficient parallelization.

Scalable, efficient deep reinforcement learning: SEED RL

Let's first begin the discussion by revisiting the Ape-X architecture, which was a milestone in scalable RL. The key contribution of the Ape-X is to decouple learning from acting: Actors generate experiences at their own pace, learner learns from the experiences at its own pace, and the actors update their local copies of the neural network policy periodically. An illustration of this flow for Ape-X DQN, which you already saw in *Chapter 6, Deep Q-Learning at Scale* is given in *Figure 13.1*.

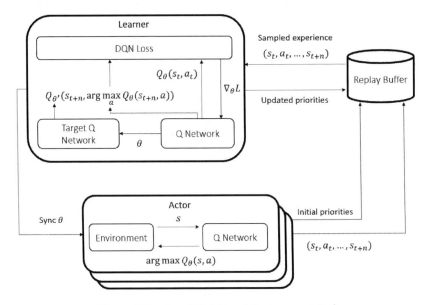

Figure 13.1 – Ape-X DQN architecture, revisited.

Now, let's unpack this architecture from a computation and data communication point of view:

1. Actors, potentially hundreds of them, periodically pull θ parameters, the neural network policy, from a central learner. Depending on the size of the policy network, hundreds of thousands of numbers are pushed from the learner to the remote actors. This creates a big communication load between the learner and the actors, two orders of magnitude larger than what would it take to transfer actions and observations.

2. Once an actor receives the policy parameters, it uses them to infer actions for each step in the environment. In most settings, only the learner uses a GPU and the actors work on CPU nodes. So, in this architecture, a lot of inference have to be done on CPUs, which is much less efficient for this purpose compared to a GPU inference.

3. Actors switch between environment and inference steps, which have different compute requirements. Carrying out both steps on the same node either leads to computational bottlenecks (when it is a CPU node which has to do inference) or underutilization of resources (when it is a GPU node, the GPU capacity is wasted).

To overcome these inefficiencies, the SEED RL architecture makes the following key proposal: *Moving the action inference to the learner.* So, an actor sends its observation to the central learner, where the policy parameters are located, and receives an action back. This way, the inference time is reduced as it is done on a GPU rather than a CPU.

Of course, the story does not end here. What we have described so far leads to a different set of challenges:

*   Since the actor needs to send the observation in each environment step to a remote learner to receive an action, this creates a **latency** issue that did not exist before.

*   While an actor waits for an action, it remains idle, causing *underutilization of the compute resources on the actor node.*

*   Passing individual observations to the learner GPU increases the total *communication overhead with the GPU.*

*   The GPU resources need to be tuned to handle both inference and learning.

To overcome these challenges, SEED RL has the following structure:

- A very fast communication protocol, called **gRPC**, is used to transfer the observations and actions between the actors and the learner.

- Multiple environments are placed on a single actor to maximize the utilization.

- Observations are batched before being passed to the GPU to reduce the overhead.

The fourth challenge of tuning the resource allocation is there, but it is a tuning problem rather than being a fundamental architecture problem. As a result, SEED RL proposes an architecture that can:

- Process millions of observations per second,

- Reduces the cost of experiments, up to 80%,

- Decreases the wall-clock by increasing the training speed up to three times.

The SEED RL architecture is illustrated in *Figure 13.2* taken from the SEED RL paper, which it compares to IMPALA that suffers from similar downsides with Ape-X.

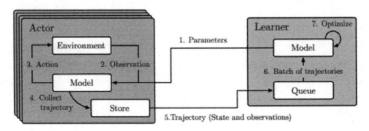

a) IMPALA architecture (distributed version)

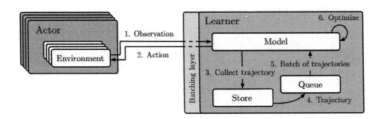

b) SEED architecture

Figure 13.2 – A comparison of IMPALA and SEED architectures (source: Espeholt et al. 2020)

So far so good. For the implementation details, we refer you to (*Espeholt et al. 2020*) and the code repository associated with the paper.

> **Info**
>
> The authors has open sourced SEED RL on `https://github.com/google-research/seed_rl`. The repo has implementations the IMPALA, SAC and the R2D2 agents.

We will cover the R2D2 agent momentarily and then run some experiments. But before we close this section, let's also provide you with one more resource.

> **Info**
>
> If you are interested in diving deeper into the engineering aspects of the architecture, gRPC is a great too to have under your belt. It is a fast communication protocol that is used to connect microservices in many tech companies. Check it out at `https://grpc.io`.

Awesome job! You are now up to date with the state of the art in distributed RL. Next, we cover a state-of-the-art model that is used in distributed RL architectures, R2D2.

Recurrent experience replay in distributed reinforcement learning

One of the most influential contributions to the recent RL literature, which set the state of the art in the classical benchmarks at the time, is the **Recurrent Replay Distributed DQN (R2D2)** agent. The main contribution of the R2D2 work is about effective use of **recurrent neural networks (RNN)** in an RL agent, which is also implemented in a distributed setting. The paper uses **long-short term memory (LSTM)** as the choice of RNN, which we also adopt here in our discussion. So, let's start with what the challenge is with training RNNs when it comes to initializing the recurrent state and then talk about how the R2D2 agent addresses it.

Initial recurrent state mismatch problem in recurrent neural networks

In the previous chapters, we discussed the importance of carrying a memory of observations to uncover partially observable states. For example, rather than using a single frame in an Atari game, which will not convey information such as speeds of the objects, basing the action on a sequence of past frames, from which the speed etc. can be derived, will lead to higher rewards. An effective way of processing a sequence data, as we also mentioned, is using RNNs.

The idea behind a recurrent neural network is to pass the inputs of a sequence to the same neural network one by one, but then also pass information / a memory / a summary of the past steps, h, from one step to the next, which is illustrated in *Figure 13.3*.

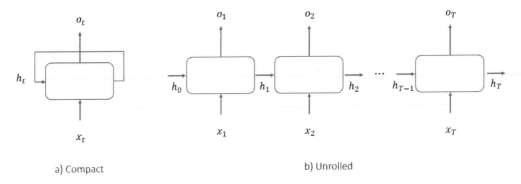

a) Compact   b) Unrolled

Figure 13.3 – A depiction of recurrent neural networks with a) compact,
and b) unrolled representations.

A key question here is to what to use for the initial recurrent state, h_0. Most commonly and conveniently, the recurrent state is initialized as all zeros. This is not a big problem when an actor steps through the environment and this initial recurrent state corresponds to the start of an episode. However, while training from stored samples that correspond to small sections of longer trajectories, such an initialization becomes a problem. Let's see why.

Consider the scenario illustrated in Figure 13.4. We are trying to train the RNN on a stored sample $(o_t = (x_{t-3}, x_{t-2}, x_{t-1}, x_t), a_t, r_t, o_{t+1})$, so the observation is a sequence of four frames that are passed to the policy network. So, x_{t-3} is the first frame and x_t is the last and the most recent frame in the sampled o_t sequence (and the argument is similar for o_{t+1}). As we feed the inputs, the h_t's will be obtained and passed to the subsequent steps and we use zeros for h_0.

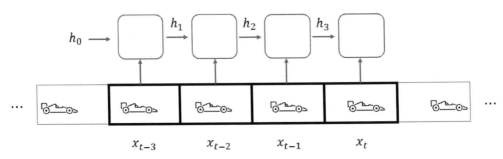

Figure 13.4 – Using a sequence of frames to obtain an action from an RNN

Now, remember that the role of a recurrent state h_i is to summarize what happened up to step i. When we use a vector of zeros for h_0 during training, to generate value function predictions and target values for the Q function for example, it creates several problems, which are related but slightly different from each other:

- It does not any convey meaningful information about what happened before that timestep,

- We use that same vector (of zeros) regardless of what happened before the sampled sequence, which leads to an overloaded representation,

- A vector of zeros, since is not an output of the RNN, is not a meaningful representation to the RNN anyway.

As a result, the RNN gets "confused" about what to make of the hidden states in general and reduces its reliance on memory, which defeats the very purpose of using them.

One solution to this is to record the whole trajectory and process/replay it during training to calculate the recurrent states for each step. This is also problematic because replaying all sample trajectories of arbitrary lengths during training is a lot of overhead.

Next, let's see how the R2D2 agent addresses this issue.

R2D2 solution to the initial recurrent state mismatch

The solution of the R2D2 agent is two folds:

1. Store the recurrent states obtained during the rollouts,

2. Use a burn-in period.

Let's look into these in more detail in the following sections.

Storing the recurrent states from rollouts

While an agent steps through the environment, at the beginning of the episode, it initializes the recurrent state. Then it uses the recurrent policy network to take its actions at each step, and the recurrent states corresponding to each of those observations are also generated. The R2R2 agent sends these recurrent states along with the sampled experience to the replay buffer to later use them to initialize the network at training time instead of vectors of zeroes.

In general, this significantly remedies the negative impact of using zero initialization. However, it is still not a perfect solution: The recurrent states stored in the replay buffer would be stale by the time they are used in training. This is because the network is constantly updated, whereas these states would carry a representation that were generated by an older version of the network, that is, what was used at the rollout time. This is called "**representational drift.**"

To mitigate the representational drift, R2D2 proposes an additional mechanism, which is to use a burn-in period at the beginning of the sequence.

Using a burn-in period

Using a burn-in period works as follows:

- Store a sequence that is longer than what we normally would,

- Use the extra portion at the beginning of the sequence to unroll the RNN with the current parameters,

- With that, produce an initial state that is not stale for after the burn-in portion,

- Don't use the burn-in portion during the backpropagation.

This is depicted in *Figure 13.5*.

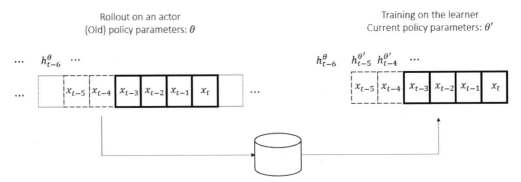

Figure 13.5 – Representation of R2D2's use of stored recurrent states with a 2-step burn-in

So, for the example in the figure, the idea is that rather than using h_{t-4}^{θ} that is generated under some old policy θ:

- Use h_{t-6}^{θ} for to initialize the recurrent state at the training time,

- Unroll the RNN with the current parameters θ' over the burn-in portion to generate an $h_{t-4}^{\theta'}$,

- Which hopefully recovers from the stale representation of h_{t-6}^{θ} and leads to a more accurate initialization than h_{t-4}^{θ} would,

- More accurate in the sense that it is closer to what we would have obtained if we stored and unrolled the entire trajectory from the beginning till $t-4$ using θ'.

So, this was the R2D2 agent. Before we wrap up this section, let's discuss what the R2D2 agent has achieved.

Key results from the R2D2 paper

The R2D2 work has really interesting insights, for which I highly recommend you read the full paper. However, for completeness of our discussion, here is a summary:

- R2D2 quadruples the previous state of the art on the Atari benchmarks that was set by Ape-X DQN, being the first agent achieving super-human level performance on 52 out of 57 games, and with a higher sample efficiency.

- It achieves this using a single set of hyperparameters across all environments, which speaks to the robustness of the agent.

- Interestingly, R2D2 improves the performance even in environments that are considered fully observable, which you would not expect using a memory to help. The authors explain this with the high representation power of LSTM.

- Storing the recurrent states and using a burn-in period are both greatly beneficial, while the former's impact is more. These approaches can be used together, which is the most effective, or individually.

- Using zero start states decrease an agent's capability to rely on the memory.

For your information, in three out of the five environments in which the R2D2 agent could not exceed the human-level performance, it can actually achieve it by modifying the parameters. The remaining two environments, Montezuma's Revenge and Pitfall, are notorious hard-exploration problems, to which we will return in the later sections of the chapter.

With that, let's wrap up our discussion here and go into some hands-on work. In the next section, we are going to use the SEED RL architecture with an R2D2 agent.

Experimenting with SEED RL and R2D2

In this section, we give a short demo of the SEED RL repo and how to use it to train agents. Let's start with setting up the environment.

Setting up the environment

The SEED RL architecture uses multiple libraries such as TensorFlow and gRPC that interact in rather sophisticated ways. To save us from most of the setup, the maintainers of the SEED RL uses Docker containers to train RL agents.

> **Info**
>
> Docker and container technology are among the fundamental tools behind today's Internet services. If you are into machine learning engineering and/or interested in serving your models in a production environment, it is a must to know. A quick bootcamp on Docker by Mumshad Mannambeth is available on `https://youtu.be/fqMOX6JJhGo`.

The setup instructions are available on the SEED RL GitHub page. In a nutshell, they are as follows:

1. Install Docker on your machine.
2. Enable to run Docker as a non-root user.
3. Install `git`.
4. Clone the SEED repository.
5. Start your training for the environments defined in the repo using the run_local.sh script, as in:

```
./run_local.sh [Game] [Agent] [Num. actors]
./run_local.sh atari r2d2 4
```

Just a few additions to this setup are in case your NVIDIA GPU is not recognized by the SEED container, you may have to:

- Install NVIDIA Container Toolkit on `https://docs.nvidia.com/datacenter/cloud-native/container-toolkit/install-guide.html`
- Install NVIDIA Modprobe, for example for Ubuntu, using: `sudo apt-get install nvidia-modprobe`
- Reboot your workstation.

Once your setup is successful, you should see that your agent starts training on a Tmux terminal, as shown on *Figure 13.6*.

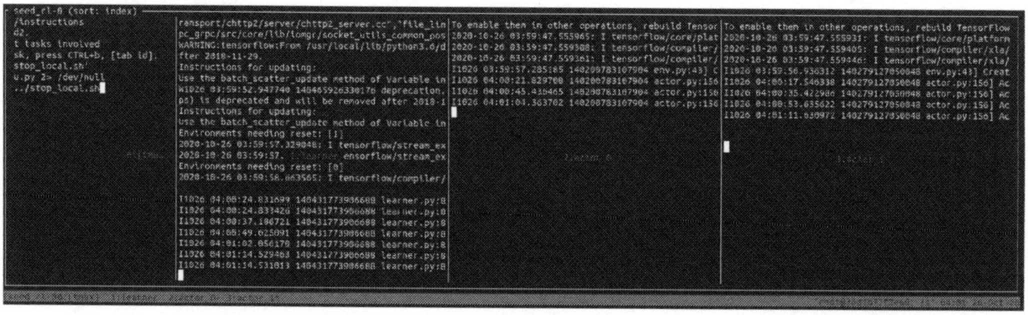

Figure 13.6 – SEED RL training on a Tmux terminal

> **Info**
>
> Tmux is a terminal multiplexer, basically a window manager within the terminal. For a quick demo on how to use Tmux, check out `https://www.hamvocke.com/blog/a-quick-and-easy-guide-to-tmux/`

Now you have SEED, a state-of-the-art RL framework running on your machine! You can plug in your custom environments for training by following the Atari, Football or DMLab example folders.

> **Info**
>
> R2D2 agent is also available at DeepMind's ACME library along with many other agents: `https://github.com/deepmind/acme`

With that, we wrap up our discussion on the state-of-the-art distributed RL architectures and agents, which are behind the most successful RL implementations today. Congratulations to you for elevating your RL skills to this level!

Next, we explore another important topic: Curiosity-driven RL.

Exploring curiosity-driven reinforcement learning

When we discussed the R2D2 agent, we mentioned that there were only few Atari games left in the benchmark set that the agent could not exceed the human performance in. The remaining challenge for the agent was to solve **hard-exploration** problems, which have very sparse and/or misleading rewards. Later work came out of Google DeepMind addressed those challenges as well, with agents called **Never Give Up (NGU)** and **Agent57**, reaching super-human level performance in all of the 57 games used in the benchmarks. In this section, we are going to discuss these agents and the methods they used for effective exploration.

Let's dive in by describing the concepts of hard-exploration and **curiosity-driven learning**.

Curiosity-driven learning for hard-exploration problems

Let's consider a simple grid world illustrated in *Figure 13.7*:

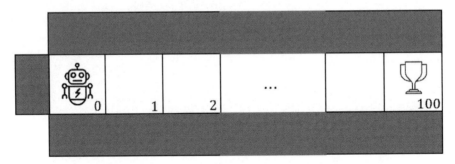

Figure 13.7 – A hard-exploration grid-world problem

Assume the following setting in this grid world:

- There are 102 total states, 101 for the grid world and one for the cliff surrounding it.
- The agent starts in the far left of the world and its goal is to reach the trophy on the far right.
- Reaching the trophy has a reward of 1000, falling off the cliff has a reward of -100, and a -1 reward for each time step passes to encourage quick exploration.

- An episode terminates when the trophy is reached, the agent falls off the cliff, or after 1000 time steps.

- The agent has five actions available to it at every time step, to stay still, to go up, down, left or right.

If you train an agent in the current setting, even with the most powerful algorithms we covered, such as PPO, R2D2 etc., the resulting policy will likely be suicidal:

- It is very difficult to stumble upon the trophy through random actions, so the agent may never discover that there is a trophy with a high reward in this grid world,

- Waiting until the end of the episode results in a total reward of -1000.

- In this dark world, the agent may decide to commit a suicide as early as possible to avoid a prolonged suffering.

Even with the most powerful algorithms, the weak link in this approach is the strategy of exploration through random actions. The probability of stumbling upon the optimal set of moves is $1/5^{100}$.

Tip

To find the expected number of steps it will take for the agent to reach the trophy through random actions, we can use the following equation:

$$m_i = \frac{1}{5}(m_{i-1} + 1) + \frac{1}{5}(m_i + 1) + \frac{1}{5}(m_{i+1} + 1)$$

where m_i is the expected number of steps it will take for the agent to reach the trophy when in state i. We need to generate these equations for all states (it will be slightly different for $i = 0$) and solve the resulting system of equations.

When we discussed the Machine Teaching approach previously, we mentioned that the human teacher can craft the reward function, in this case, to encourage the agent to go right in the world. The downside of this approach is that it may not be feasible to manually craft the reward function in more complex environments. In fact, the winning strategy may not even be known by the teacher to guide the agent.

Then the question becomes how we can encourage the agent to explore the environment efficiently. One good answer is to reward the agent for the states it visited for the first time, for example with a reward of +1 in our grid world. Enjoying discovering the world could make a good motivation for the agent to continue exploring, which will also lead to winning the trophy eventually.

This approach is called **curiosity-driven learning**, which involves giving an **intrinsic reward** to the agent based on the *novelty* of its observations. Then the reward takes the following form:

$$r_t = r_t^e + \beta r_t^i$$

where r_t^e is the extrinsic reward assigned by the environment at time t, r_t^i is the intrinsic reward for the novelty of the observation at time t, and β is a hyperparameter to tune the relative importance of exploration.

Before we discuss the NGU and Agent57 agents, let's look into some practical challenges in curiosity-driven RL.

Challenges in curiosity-driven reinforcement learning

The grid world example we provided above has one of the simplest possible settings. On the other hand, our expectation from RL agents is to solve much sophisticated exploration problems. That, of course, comes with challenges. Let's discuss a few of them here.

Assessing novelty when observations are in continuous space and/ or high dimensional

When we have discrete observations, it could be simple to assess whether an observation is novel or not: We could simply count how many times the agent has seen each observation. When the observation is in continuous space, however, it gets complicated as it is not possible to simply count them. A similar challenge is when the number of dimensions of the observation space /possible number of discrete observations is too big, as it is in an image.

Noisy TV problem

An interesting failure mode for curiosity-driven exploration is to have a source of noise in the environment, such as a noisy TV that displays random frames in a maze.

Figure 13.8 – Noisy TV problem illustrated in OpenAI's experiments (source: OpenAI et al. 2018)

The agent then gets stuck in front of the noisy TV (like a lot of people do) to do meaningless exploration rather than actually discovering the maze.

Life-long novelty

The intrinsic reward as we described it above is given based on the novelty of the observations within an episode. However, we want our agent to avoid making the same discoveries again and again in different episodes as well. In other words, we need a mechanism to assess *life-long novelty* for effective exploration.

There are different ways of addressing these challenges. Next, we will review how the NGU and the Agent57 agents address them, leading to their state-of-the-art performance in the classic RL benchmarks.

Never Give Up

The NGU agent effectively brings together some key exploration strategies. Let's take a look in the following sections.

Obtaining embeddings for observations

The NGU agent obtains embeddings from observations in such a way that it handles the two challenges together regarding a) high dimensional observation space, b) noise in observations. Here is how: Given an (o_t, a_t, o_{t+1}) triplet sampled from the environment, where o_t is the observation and a_t is the action at time t, it trains a neural network to predict action from the two consecutive observations. This is illustrated in *Figure 13.9*.

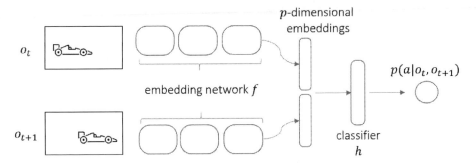

Figure 13.9 – NGU agent embedding network

The embeddings, the p-dimensional representations of the images coming out of the f embedding network, denoted as $f(o_t)$, is what the agent will use to assess the novelty of the observations later.

If you are wondering why there is this fancy setup to obtain some lower dimensional representations of image observations, it is to address the noisy TV problem. Noise in the observations is not useful information while predicting the action that led the environment from emitting observation o_t to o_{t+1} in the next step. In other words, actions taken by the agent would not explain the noise in the observations. Therefore, we don't expect a network that predicts the action from observations to learn representations carrying the noise, at least not dominantly. So, this is a clever way of denoising the observation representations.

Let's next see how these representations are used.

Episodic novelty module

In order to assess how novel an observation o_t is compared to the previous observations in the episode and calculate an episodic intrinsic reward, $r_t^{episodic}$, the NGU agent:

- Stores the embeddings from the observations encountered in an episode in a memory M,

- Compare the $f(o_t)$ to k-nearest embeddings in M,

- Calculate an intrinsic reward that is inversely proportional to the sum of the similarities between $f(o_t)$ and its k neighbors.

This idea is illustrated in *Figure 13.10*:

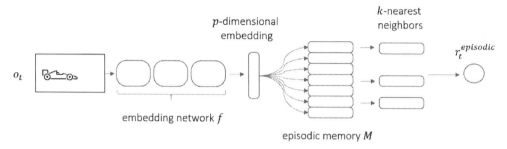

Figure 13.10 – NGU episodic novelty module

To avoid the somewhat crowded notation, we leave the details of the calculation to the paper, but this should give the idea.

Finally, let's discuss how the NGU agent assesses life-long novelty.

Life-long novelty module with random distillation networks

During training, RL agents collect experiences across many parallel processes and over many episodes, leading to billions of observations in some applications. Therefore, it is not quite straightforward to tell whether an observation is a novel one among all.

A clever way to address that is to use **Random Network Distillation (RND)**, which the NGU agent does. RND involves two networks: a random network and a predictor network. Here is how they work:

- The random network is randomly initialized at the beginning of the training. Naturally, it leads to an arbitrary mapping from observations to outputs.

- The predictor network tries to learn this mapping, which is, what the random network does, throughout the training.

- The predictor network's error will be low on previously encountered observations and high on novel ones.

- The higher the prediction error is, the larger the life-long intrinsic reward will be.

The RND architecture is illustrated on *Figure 13.11*.

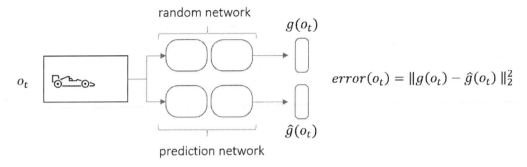

Figure 13.11 – RND architecture in the NGU agent

The NGU agent uses this error to obtain a multiplier, α_t, to scale $r_t^{episodic}$. More specifically,

$$\alpha_t = \max\left(1 + \frac{error(o_t) - \mu_{error}}{\sigma_{error}}, 1\right)$$

where μ_{error} and σ_{error} are the mean and standard deviation of the prediction network errors. So, to obtain a multiplier greater than 1 for an observation, the error, the "surprise," of the predictor network should be greater than the average error it makes.

Now, let's put everything together.

Combining the intrinsic and extrinsic rewards

After obtaining an episodic intrinsic reward and a multiplier based on life-long novelty for an observation, the combined intrinsic reward at time t is calculated as follows:

$$r_t^i = r_t^{episodic} \cdot \min(\alpha_t, L)$$

where L is a hyperparameter to cap the multiplier. Then the episode reward is a weighted sum of the intrinsic and extrinsic rewards:

$$r_t = r_t^e + \beta r_t^i$$

This is it! We have covered some of the key ideas behind the NGU agent. There are more details into it, such as how to set the β values across parallelized actors and then use it to parametrize the value function network, which we leave to the paper.

Before we wrap up our discussion on curiosity-driven learning, let's briefly talk about an extension to the NGU agent, Agent57.

Agent57 improvements

Agent57 extends the NGU agent to set the new state of the art. The main improvements are to:

- Train separate value function network for intrinsic and extrinsic rewards and then combine them,

- Train a population of policies, for which a sliding-window **upper confidence bound (UCB)** method is used to the pick β and discount factor γ during prioritizing one policy over the other.

With that, we conclude our discussion on curiosity-driven reinforcement learning, which has been key to solve hard-exploration problems in RL. Having said that, exploration strategies in reinforcement learning is a broad topic. For a more comprehensive review of the topic, I suggest you read Lilian Weng's blog post (Weng, 2020) on this and then dive into the papers referred in the blog.

Next, we discuss another important area: Offline reinforcement learning.

Offline reinforcement learning

Offline reinforcement learning is about training agents using data recorded during some prior interactions of an agent (likely non-RL, such as a human agent) with the environment, as opposed to directly interacting with it. It is also called **batch reinforcement learning**. In this section, we look into some of the key components of offline RL. Let's get started with an overview of how it works.

An overview of how offline reinforcement learning works

In offline RL, the agent does not directly interact with the environment to explore and learn a policy. *Figure 13.12* contrasts this to on-policy and off-policy settings.

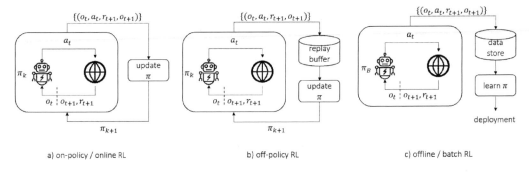

Figure 13.12 – Comparison of on-policy, off-policy, and offline deep RL (adapted from Levine 2020).

Let's unpack what this figure illustrates:

- In on-policy RL, the agent collects a batch of experiences with each policy. Then, it uses this batch to update the policy. This cycle repeats until a satisfactory policy is obtained.

- In off-policy RL, the agent samples experiences from a replay buffer to periodically improve the policy. The updated policy is then used in the rollouts to generate new experience, which gradually replaces the old experience in the replay buffer. This cycle repeats until a satisfactory policy is obtained.

- In offline RL, there is some behavior policy π_B interacting with the environment and collecting experience. This behavior policy does not have to belong to an RL agent. In fact, in most cases, it is either human behavior, a rule-based decision mechanism, a classical controller etc. The experience recorded from these interactions is what the RL agent will use to learn a policy, hopefully improving the behavior policy. So, in offline RL, the RL agent does not interact with the environment.

One of the obvious questions in your mind could be why we cannot just put the offline data into something like a replay buffer and use a DQN agent or alike. This is an important point, so let's discuss that.

Why we need special algorithms for offline learning

Interacting with the environment for an RL agent is necessary to observe the consequences of its actions in different states. Offline RL, on the other hand, does not let the agent to interact and explore, which is a serious limitation. Here are some examples to illustrate this point:

- Let's say we have data from a human driving a car in town. The maximum speed the driver reached as per the logs is 50 mph. The RL agent might infer from the logs that increasing the speed reduces the travel time and may come up with a policy that suggests driving at a 150 mph in town. Since the agent never observed its possible consequences, it does not have a lot of chance to correct its approach.

- While using a value-based method, such as DQN, the Q network is initialized randomly. As a result, some $Q(s, a)$ values will be very high just by chance, suggesting a policy driving the agent to such s and then take the action a. When the agent is able to explore, it can evaluate the policy and correct such bad estimates. In offline RL, it cannot.

So, the core of the problem here is the **distributional shift**, which is the discrepancy between the behavior policy and resulting RL policy.

So, hopefully, you are convinced that offline RL requires some special algorithms. Then the next question is, is it worth it? Why should we bother while we can happily obtain super-human level performances with all the clever approaches and models we discussed so far? Let's see why.

Why offline reinforcement learning is crucial

The very reason that video games are the most common testbed for RL, it is because we can collect the huge amounts of data needed for training. When it comes to training RL policies for real-world applications, such as robotics, autonomous driving, supply chain, finance etc., we need simulations of these processes to be able to collect the necessary amounts of data and wildly explore various policies. *This is arguably the single most important challenge in front of real-world RL.* Here are some reasons why:

- Building a high-fidelity simulation of a real-world process is often very costly and could take years.

- High-fidelity simulations likely require a lot of compute resources to run, making it hard to scale them for RL training.

- Simulations could quickly become stale if the environment dynamics change in a way that is not parametrized in the simulation.

- Even when the fidelity is very high, it may not be high enough for RL. RL is prone to overfitting to errors, quirks, and assumptions of the (simulation) environment it interacts with. So, this creates a sim-to-real gap.

- It could be costly or unsafe to deploy RL agents that might have overfit to simulation.

As a result, a simulation is a rare beast to run into in businesses and organizations. Do you know what we have in abundance? Data. We have processes that generate a lot of data.

- Manufacturing environments have machine logs.

- Retails have data from their past pricing strategies and their results.

- Trading firms have logs of their buy & sell decisions.

- We have, and can obtain, a lot of car driving videos.

Offline reinforcement learning has a potential to drive automation for all those processes and create huge real-world value.

> **Info**
>
> A highly recommended blog post on the importance of offline RL, which also inspired this section, by a top researcher in the area, Prof. Sergey Levine, is at `https://bit.ly/3gjq8Tk`.

After this long but necessary motivation, it is finally time to go into one of the recent offline RL algorithms.

Advantage weighted actor-critic

Offline reinforcement learning is a hot area of research and there are many algorithms that have been proposed. One common theme is to make sure that the learned policy stays close to the behavior policy. A common measure to assess the discrepancy is the KL-divergence:

$$D_{KL}\big(\pi(\cdot\,|s)\|\pi_B(\cdot\,|s)\big) = \sum_{a\in A(s)} \pi(a|s)\log\frac{\pi(a|s)}{\pi_B(a|s)}$$

On the other hand, different from the other approaches, **Advantage weighted actor-critic (AWAC)** exhibits the following traits:

- Does not try fit a model to explicitly learn π_B,

- Implicitly punishes the distributional shift,

- Uses dynamic programming to train to the Q function for data efficiency.

To this end, AWAC optimizes the following objective function:

$$\arg\max_{\pi} \mathbb{E}_{a\sim\pi(\cdot|s)}[A^{\pi_k}(s,a)] \quad s.t. \quad D_{KL}(\pi(\cdot|s)\|\pi_B(\cdot|s)) \leq \epsilon$$

which leads to the following policy update step:

$$\arg\max_{\theta} \mathbb{E}_{s,a\sim Data}\left[\log \pi_\theta(a|s)\frac{1}{Z(s)}\exp\left(\frac{1}{\lambda}A^{\pi_k}(s,a)\right)\right]$$

where λ is a hyperparameter, and $Z(s)$ is a normalization quantity. The key idea here is to encourage actions with higher advantage.

Info

One of the key contributions of AWAC is that the policy that is trained from offline data can then later be fine-tuned effectively by interacting with the environment if that opportunity exits.

We defer the details of the algorithm to the paper (Nair et al. 2020) and the implementation to the RLkit repo at `https://github.com/vitchyr/rlkit`.

Let's wrap up our discussion on offline RL with benchmark datasets and the corresponding repos.

Offline reinforcement learning benchmarks

As offline RL is taking off, researchers from DeepMind and UC Berkeley have created benchmark datasets and repos so that offline RL algorithms can be compared to each other in a standardized way:

- *RL Unplugged* by DeepMind includes datasets from Atari, Locomotion, DeepMind Control Suite environments as well as real-world datasets. It is available at `https://github.com/deepmind/deepmind-research/tree/master/rl_unplugged`

- *D4RL* by UC Berkeley's Robotics and AI Lab (RAIL) includes datasets from various environments such as Maze2D, Adroit, Flow and CARLA. It is available at `https://github.com/rail-berkeley/d4rl`.

Great work! You are now up-to-speed with one of the key emerging fields in RL – offline reinforcement learning.

Summary

In this chapter, we covered several advanced topics that are very hot areas of research. Distributed reinforcement learning is key to be able to scale RL experiments efficiently. Curiosity-driven RL is making solving hard-exploration problems possible through effective exploration strategies. And finally, offline RL has a potential to transform how RL is used for real-world problems by leveraging the data logs already available for many processes.

With this chapter, we conclude the part of our book on algorithmic and theoretical discussions. The remaining chapters will be more applied, starting with robotics applications in the next chapter.

References

1. Espeholt, Lasse, et al. (2020). *SEED RL: Scalable and Efficient Deep-RL with Accelerated Central Inference.* arXiv.org, `http://arxiv.org/abs/1910.06591`.

2. Weng, Lilian. (2020). *Exploration Strategies in Deep Reinforcement Learning.* Lil'Log. URL: `https://bit.ly/3mRohHL`.

3. DeepMind. (2020). *Agent57: Outperforming the Human Atari Benchmark.* DeepMind Blog. URL: `https://bit.ly/3mVaZu4`.

4. OpenAI. (2018). *Reinforcement Learning with Prediction-Based Rewards.* OpenAI Blog. URL: `https://openai.com/blog/reinforcement-learning-with-prediction-based-rewards/`.

5. Pathak, D. (2018). *Large-Scale Study of Curiosity-Driven Learning.* YouTube. URL: `https://youtu.be/C3yKgCzvE_E`.

6. Levine, Sergey. (2020). *Decisions from Data: How Offline Reinforcement Learning Will Change How We Use Machine Learning.* Medium. URL: `https://bit.ly/3gjq8Tk`.

7. Agarwal, R. et al. (2020). *Offline Reinforcement Learning Workshop. Neural Information Processing Systems (NeurIPS)*. URL: `https://offline-rl-neurips.github.io/`.

8. Levine, Sergey, et al. (2020). *Offline Reinforcement Learning: Tutorial, Review, and Perspectives on Open Problems*. arXiv.org, `http://arxiv.org/abs/2005.01643`.

9. Nair, Ashvin, et al. (2020). *Accelerating Online Reinforcement Learning with Offline Datasets*. arXiv.org, `http://arxiv.org/abs/2006.09359`.

10. Agarwal, R. et al. (2020). *An Optimistic Perspective on Offline Reinforcement Learning*. International Conference on Machine Learning (ICML). URL: `https://offline-rl.github.io/`

11. Nair, A. et al. (2020). *AWAC: Accelerating Online Reinforcement Learning with Offline Datasets*. BAIR Blog. URL: `https://bair.berkeley.edu/blog/2020/09/10/awac/`.

Section 4:
Applications of RL

In this section, you will learn about various applications of RL, such as autonomous systems, supply chain management, cybersecurity, and others. We will learn how RL can be used to solve problems in various industries using these techniques. Finally, we will look at some of the challenges in RL and its future.

This section contains the following chapters:

- *Chapter 14, Solving Robot Learning*
- *Chapter 15, Supply Chain Management*
- *Chapter 16, Personalization, Marketing, and Finance*
- *Chapter 17, Smart City and Cybersecurity*
- *Chapter 18, Challenges and Future Directions in Reinforcement Learning*

14

Solving Robot Learning

So far in the book, we have covered many state-of-the-art algorithms and approaches in reinforcement learning. Now, starting with this chapter, we will see them in action to take on real-world problems! We start with robot learning, an important application area for reinforcement learning. To this end, we will train a Kuka robot to grasp objects on a tray using PyBullet physics simulation. We will discuss several ways of solving this hard-exploration problem and solve it both using a manually crafted curriculum as well as using the ALP-GMM algorithm. At the end of the chapter, we will present other simulation libraries for robotics and autonomous driving, which are commonly used to train reinforcement learning agents.

So, this chapter covers:

- Introducing PyBullet
- Getting familiar with the Kuka environment
- Developing strategies to solve the Kuka environment
- Using curriculum learning to train the Kuka robot
- Going beyond PyBullet, into autonomous driving

This is one of the most challenging and fun areas for reinforcement learning. Let's dive right in!

Introducing PyBullet

PyBullet is a popular high-fidelity physics simulation for robotics, machine learning, games, and more. It is one of the most commonly used libraries for robot learning using RL, especially in sim-to-real transfer research and applications.

Figure 14.1 – PyBullet environments and visualizations (source: PyBullet GitHub repo)

PyBullet allows developers to create their own physics simulations. In addition, it has prebuilt environments using the OpenAI Gym interface. Some of those environments are shown in *Figure 14.1*.

In the next section, we will set up a virtual environment for PyBullet.

Setting up PyBullet

It is almost always a good idea to work in virtual environments for Python projects, which is also what we do for our robot learning experiments in this chapter. So, let's go ahead and execute the following commands to install the libraries we will use:

```
$ virtualenv pybenv
$ source pybenv/bin/activate
$ pip install pybullet --upgrade
$ pip install gym
$ pip install tensorflow==2.3.1
$ pip install ray[rllib]==1.0.0
$ pip install scikit-learn==0.23.2
```

You can test whether your installation is working by running:

```
$ python -m pybullet_envs.examples.enjoy_TF_AntBulletEnv_
v0_2017may
```

And if everything is working fine, you will see a cool Ant robot wandering around as in *Figure 14.2*.

Figure 14.2 – Ant robot walking in PyBullet

Great! We are now ready to proceed to the Kuka environment that we will use.

Getting familiar with the Kuka environment

KUKA is a company that offers industrial robotics solutions, which are widely used in manufacturing and assembly environments. PyBullet includes a simulation of a KUKA robot, used for object grasping simulations (*Figure 14.3*).

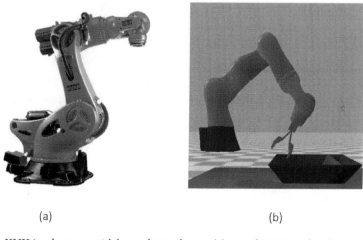

(a)   (b)

Figure 14.3 – KUKA robots are widely used in industry. (a) A real KUKA robot (image source CNC Robotics website), (b) a PyBullet simulation.

There are multiple Kuka environments in PyBullet for:

- Grasping a rectangle block using robot and object position and angles,
- Grasping a rectangle block using camera inputs,
- Grasping random objects using camera/position inputs.

In this chapter, we focus on the first one, which we look into next in more detail.

Grasping a rectangle block using a Kuka robot

In this environment, the goal of the robot is to reach a rectangle object, grasp it, and raise it up to a certain height. An example scene from the environment, along with the robot coordinate system, are shown in *Figure 14.4*.

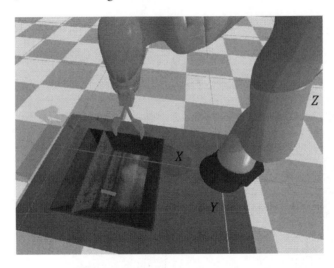

Figure 14.4 – Object grasping scene and the robot coordinate system

The dynamics and initial position of the robot joints are defined in the Kuka class of the pybullet_envs package. We will talk about these details only as much as we need to, but you should feel free to dive into the class definition to better understand the dynamics.

> **Info**
> To better understand the PyBullet environment and how the Kuka class is constructed, you can check out the PyBullet Quickstart Guide at https://bit.ly/323PjmO.

Let's now dive into the Gym environment created to control this robot inside PyBullet.

Kuka Gym environment

The KukaGymEnv wraps the Kuka robot class and turns it into a Gym environment. The action, observation, reward and terminal conditions are defined as below.

Actions

There are three types of actions the agent takes in the environment, which are all about moving the gripper. These actions are:

- Velocity along the x axis,
- Velocity along the y axis,
- Angular velocity to rotate the gripper (yaw).

The environment itself moves the gripper along the z axis towards the tray, where the object is located. When it gets sufficiently close to the tray, it closes the fingers of the gripper to try grasping the object.

The environment can be configured to accept discrete or continuous actions. We will use the latter in our case.

Observations

The agent receives 9 observations from the environment:

- Three observations for the x, y, and z positions of the gripper,
- Three observations for the Euler angles of the gripper with respect to the x, y, and z axes,
- Two observations for the x and y positions of the object **relative** to the gripper,
- One observation for the Euler angle of the object **relative** to the gripper's Euler angle along the z axis.

Reward

The reward for grasping the object successfully and lifting it up to a certain height is 10,000 points. Other than that, there is a slight cost that penalizes the distance between the gripper and the object. Additionally, there is also some energy cost for rotating the gripper.

Terminal conditions

An episode terminates after 1000 steps or when the after the gripper closes, whichever occurs first.

The best way to wrap your mind around how the environment works is actually experiment with it, which you can do next using the following code: `Chapter14/manual_control_kuka.py`

This script allows you to control the robot manually. You can use the "gym-like" control mode, where the vertical speed and the gripper finger angles are controlled by the environment. Alternatively, you can choose the non-gym-like mode to exert more control.

One thing you will notice that even if you keep the speeds along the x and y axes zero, in the gym-like control mode, the robot will change its x and y positions while going down. This is because the default speed of the gripper along the z axis is too high. You can actually verify that in the non-gym-like mode: Values below -0.001 for $posZ$ alter the positions on the other axes too much. We will reduce the speed when we customize the environment to alleviate that.

Now that you are familiar with the Kuka environment, let's discuss some alternative strategies to solve it.

Developing strategies to solve the Kuka environment

The object grasping problem in the environment is a **hard-exploration** problem, meaning that it is unlikely to stumble upon the sparse reward that the agent receives at the end upon grasping the object. Reducing the vertical speed as we will do will make is a bit easier. Still, let's refresh our minds about what strategies we have covered to address these kinds of problems:

- **Reward shaping** is one of the most common **machine teaching** strategies that we discussed earlier. In some problems, incentivizing the agent towards the goal is very straightforward. In many problems, though, it can be quite painful. So, unless there is an obvious way of doing so, crafting the reward function may just take too much time (and expertise about the problem). Also notice that the original reward function has a component to penalize the distance between the gripper and the object, so the reward is already shaped to some extent. We will not go beyond that in our solution.

- **Curiosity-driven learning** incentivizes the agent for discovering new parts of the state space. For this problem, though, we don't need the agent to randomly explore the state space too much as we have already some idea about what it should do. So, we will skip this technique as well.

- **Increasing the entropy of the policy** incentivizes the agent to diversify its actions. The coefficient for this can be set using the `"entropy_coeff"` config inside the PPO trainer of RLlib, which is what we will use. However, our hyperparameter search (we will come to it soon) ended up picking this value as zero.

- **Curriculum learning** is perhaps the most suitable approach here. We can identify what makes the problem challenging for the agent, start training it at easy levels, and gradually increase the difficulty.

So, curriculum learning is what we will leverage to solve this problem. But first, let's identify the dimensions to parametrize the environment to create a curriculum.

Parametrizing the difficulty of the problem

When you experimented with the environment, you may have noticed the factors that make the problem difficult:

- The gripper starts too high to discover the correct sequences of actions to grasp the object. So, the robot joint that adjusts the height will be one dimension we will parameterize. It turns out that this is set in the second element of the `jointPositions` array of the `Kuka` class.

- When the gripper is not at its original height, it may get misaligned with the location of the object along the x axis. We will also parametrize the position of the joint that controls this, which is the fourth element of the `jointPositions` array of the `Kuka` class.

- Randomizing the object position is another source of difficulty for the agent, which takes place for the x and y positions as well as the object angle. We will parametrize the degree of randomization between 0 and 100% for each of these components.

- Even when the object is not randomly positioned, its center is not aligned with the default position of the robot on the y axis. We will add some bias to the y position of the object, again parametrized.

This is great! We know what to do, which is a big first step. Now, we can go into curriculum learning!

Using curriculum learning to train the Kuka robot

The first step before actually kicking off some training is to customize the Kuka class as well as the KukaGymEnv to make them work with the curriculum learning parameters we described above. So, let's do that next.

Customizing the environment for curriculum learning

First, we start with creating a CustomKuka class which inherits the original Kuka class of PyBullet. Here is how we do it:

Chapter14/custom_kuka.py

1. We first need to create the new class, and accept an additional argument, jp_override dictionary, which stands for **joint position override**.

```
class CustomKuka(Kuka):
    def __init__(self, *args,
                    jp_override=None, **kwargs):
        self.jp_override = jp_override
        super(CustomKuka, self).__init__(*args, **kwargs)
```

2. We need this to change the jointPositions array set in the reset method.

```
    def reset(self):
        ...
        if self.jp_override:
            for j, v in self.jp_override.items():
                j_ix = int(j) - 1
                if j_ix >= 0 and j_ix <= 13:
                    self.jointPositions[j_ix] = v
```

Now, it's time to create CustomKukaEnv.

3. Create the custom environment that accepts all these parametrization inputs for curriculum learning.

```
class CustomKukaEnv(KukaGymEnv):
    def __init__(self, env_config={}):
        renders = env_config.get("renders", False)
```

```
        isDiscrete = env_config.get("isDiscrete", False)
        maxSteps = env_config.get("maxSteps", 2000)
        self.rnd_obj_x = env_config.get("rnd_obj_x", 1)
        self.rnd_obj_y = env_config.get("rnd_obj_y", 1)
        self.rnd_obj_ang = env_config.get("rnd_obj_ang",
                                            1)
        self.bias_obj_x = env_config.get("bias_obj_x", 0)
        self.bias_obj_y = env_config.get("bias_obj_y", 0)
        self.bias_obj_ang = \
                    env_config.get("bias_obj_ang", 0)
        self.jp_override = env_config.get("jp_override")
        super(CustomKukaEnv, self).__init__(
                            renders=renders,
                            isDiscrete=isDiscrete,
                            maxSteps=maxSteps)
```

Note that we are also making it RLlib compatible by accepting an `env_config`.

4. We use the randomization parameters in the `reset` method to override the default amount of randomization in the object position.

```
    def reset(self):
        ...
        xpos = 0.55 + self.bias_obj_x + \
                0.12 * random.random() * self.rnd_obj_x
        ypos = 0 + self.bias_obj_y + 0.2 * \
                random.random() * self.rnd_obj_y
        ang = (
            3.14 * 0.5
            + self.bias_obj_ang
            + 3.1415925438 * random.random() * \
            self.rnd_obj_ang)
```

5. Also, we should now replace the old `Kuka` class with `CustomKuka` and pass the joint position override input to it.

```
        ...
        self._kuka = CustomKuka(
            jp_override=self.jp_override,
```

```
urdfRootPath=self._urdfRoot,
timeStep=self._timeStep)
```

6. Finally, we override the step method of the environment to decrease the default speed on the **z** axis.

```
def step(self, action):
    dz = -0.0005
    ...

        ...
        realAction = [dx, dy, dz, da, f]
    obs, reward, done, info = self.step2(realAction)
    return obs, reward / 1000, done, info
```

Also notice that we rescaled the reward (it will end up between -10 and 10) to make the training easy.

Great job! Next, let's discuss what kind of curriculum to use.

Designing the lessons in the curriculum

It is one thing to determine the dimensions to parametrize the difficulty of the problem, and another thing to decide how to expose this parametrization to the agent. We know that the agent should start with easy lessons and move to more difficult ones gradually. This, though, raises some important questions:

- Which parts of the parametrized space are easy?

- What should be the step sizes to change the parameters between lesson transitions? In other words, how should we slice the space into lessons?

- What are the criteria of success for the agent to transition to a next lesson?

- What if the agent fails in a lesson, meaning that its performance is unexpectedly bad? Should it go back to the previous lesson? What is the bar for failure?

- What if the agent cannot transition into the next lesson for a long time? Does it mean that we set the bar for success for the lesson too high? Should we divide that lesson into sub-lessons?

As you can see, these are non-trivial questions to answer when we are designing a curriculum manually. But also remember that in *Chapter 11, Achieving Generalization and Overcoming Partial Observability*, we introduced the **Absolute Learning Progress with Gaussian Mixture Models (ALP-GMM)** method, which handles all these decisions for us. Here, we will implement both, starting with a manual curriculum first.

Training the agent using a manually designed curriculum

We will design a rather simple curriculum for this problem. It will transition the agent to subsequent lessons when it meets the success criteria, without falling back to a previous lesson in case of low performance. The curriculum will be implemented as a method inside the `CustomKukaEnv` class, using the `increase_difficulty` method:

1. We start by defining the delta changes in the parameter values during lesson transitions. For the joint values, we will decrease the joint positions from what is entered by the user (easy) to the original values in the environment (difficult).

```python
def increase_difficulty(self):
    deltas = {"2": 0.1, "4": 0.1}
    original_values = {"2": 0.413184, "4": -1.589317}
    all_at_original_values = True
    for j in deltas:
        if j in self.jp_override:
            d = deltas[j]
            self.jp_override[j] = \
        max(self.jp_override[j] - d, original_values[j])
            if self.jp_override[j] != \
    original_values[j]:
                all_at_original_values = False
```

2. During each lesson transition, we also make sure to increase the randomization of the object position.

```python
self.rnd_obj_x = min(self.rnd_obj_x + 0.05, 1)
self.rnd_obj_y = min(self.rnd_obj_y + 0.05, 1)
self.rnd_obj_ang = min(self.rnd_obj_ang + 0.05,
1)
```

3. Finally, we remember to set the biases to zeros when the object position becomes fully randomized:

```
if self.rnd_obj_x == self.rnd_obj_y == \
                    self.rnd_obj_ang == 1:
    if all_at_original_values:
        self.bias_obj_x = 0
        self.bias_obj_y = 0
        self.bias_obj_ang = 0
```

So far so good, we have almost everything ready to train our agent. One last thing before doing so, let's discuss how to pick the hyperparameters.

Hyperparameter selection

In order to tune the hyperparameters in RLlib, we can use Ray's Tune library. In *Chapter 15, Supply Chain Management*, we will provide you with an example of how it is done. For now, you can just use the hyperparameters we have picked in `Chapter14/configs.py`.

> **Tip**
> In hard-exploration problems, it may make more sense to tune the hyperparameters for a simple version of the problem. This is because without observing some reasonable rewards, the tuning may not pick a good set of hyperparameter values. After we do an initial tuning in an easy environment setting, some of the chosen values can be adjusted later in the process if the learning stalls.

Finally, let's see how we can use the environment we have just created during training with the curriculum we have defined.

Training the agent on the curriculum using RLlib

To proceed with the training, we need the following ingredients:

- Initial parameters for the curriculum,
- Some criteria to define the success (and failure, if needed),
- A callback function that will execute the lesson transitions.

In the code snippet below, we use the PPO algorithm in RLlib, set the initial parameters, and set the reward threshold to 5.5 (empirically determined, feel free to try other values) in the callback function that executes the lesson transitions.

Chapter14/train_ppo_manual_curriculum.py

```
config["env_config"] = {
    "jp_override": {"2": 1.3, "4": -1}, "rnd_obj_x": 0,
    "rnd_obj_y": 0, "rnd_obj_ang": 0, "bias_obj_y": 0.04}


def on_train_result(info):
    result = info["result"]
    if result["episode_reward_mean"] > 5.5:
        trainer = info["trainer"]
        trainer.workers.foreach_worker(
            lambda ev: ev.foreach_env(lambda env:
                        env.increase_difficulty()))


ray.init()
tune.run("PPO", config=dict(config,
                **{"env": CustomKukaEnv,
                    "callbacks": {
                        "on_train_result": on_train_result}}
                    ),
            checkpoint_freq=10)
```

This should kick off the training and you will see the curriculum learning in action! You will notice that as the agent transitions to a next lesson, its performance will drop suddenly once in a while as the environment gets more difficult with lesson transitions.

We will look into the results from this training later. Let's now also implement the ALP-GMM algorithm.

Curriculum learning using absolute learning progress

The ALP-GMM method focuses on where the biggest performance change (absolute learning progress) in the parameter space is and generates parameters around that gap. This idea is illustrated in *Figure 14.5*.

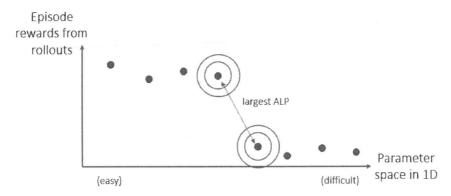

Figure 14.5 – ALP-GMM generates parameters (tasks) around points, between which the biggest episode reward change is observed.

This way, the learning budget is not spent on the parts of the state space that has already been learned, or on the parts that are too difficult to learn for the current agent, but where the agent can take on more difficulties without being overwhelmed.

After this recap, let's go ahead and implement it. We start with creating a custom environment in which the ALP-GMM algorithm will run.

Chapter14/custom_kuka.py

We get the ALP-GMM implementation directly from the source repo accompanying the paper (Portelas et al. 2019) and put it under `Chapter14/alp`. We can then plug that into the new environment we create, `ALPKukaEnv`, the key pieces of which are below:

1. We create the class and define all the minimum and maximum values of the parameter space we are trying to teach the agent.

```
class ALPKukaEnv(CustomKukaEnv):
    def __init__(self, env_config={}):
        ...
        self.mins = [...]
        self.maxs = [...]
        self.alp = ALPGMM(mins=self.mins,
                          maxs=self.maxs,
```

```
                            params={"fit_rate": 20})
    self.task = None
    self.last_episode_reward = None
    self.episode_reward = 0
    super(ALPKukaEnv, self).__init__(env_config)
```

Here, the task is the latest sample from the parameter space generated by the ALP-GMM algorithm to configure the environment.

2. A task is sampled at the beginning of each episode. Once an episode finishes, the task (environment parameters used in the episode) and the episode reward are used to update the GMM model.

```
def reset(self):
    if self.task is not None and \
        self.last_episode_reward is not None:
        self.alp.update(self.task,
                        self.last_episode_reward)
    self.task = self.alp.sample_task()
    self.rnd_obj_x = self.task[0]
    self.rnd_obj_y = self.task[1]
    self.rnd_obj_ang = self.task[2]
    self.jp_override = {"2": self.task[3],
                        "4": self.task[4]}
    self.bias_obj_y = self.task[5]
    return super(ALPKukaEnv, self).reset()
```

3. And finally, we make sure to keep track of the episode reward:

```
def step(self, action):
    obs, reward, done, info = super(ALPKukaEnv,
                                    self).step(action)
    self.episode_reward += reward
    if done:
        self.last_episode_reward = \
                self.episode_reward
        self.episode_reward = 0
    return obs, reward, done, info
```

One thing to note here is that ALP-GMM is normally implemented in a centralized fashion: A central process generates all the tasks for the rollout workers and collects the episode rewards associated with those tasks to process. Here, since we are working in RLlib, it is easier to implemented it inside the environment instances. In order to account for the reduced amount of data collected in a single rollout, we used `"fit_rate": 20`, lower from the original level of 250, so that a rollout worker doesn't wait too long before it fits a GMM to the task-reward data it collects.

After creating the `ALPKukaEnv`, the rest is just a simple call of Ray's `tune.run()` function, which is available in `Chapter14/train_ppo_alp.py`. Note that, unlike in a manual curriculum, we don't specify the initial values of the parameters. Instead, we have passed their bounds the ALP-GMM processes, which guide the curriculum within those bounds.

Now, we are ready to do a curriculum learning bake off!

Comparing the experiment results

We kick off three training sessions using the manual curriculum we described, the ALP-GMM, and one without any curriculum implemented. The TensorBoard view of the training progresses is shown in *Figure 14.6*:

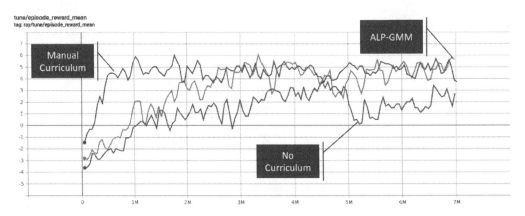

Figure 14.6 – Training progresses on TensorBoard

A first glance might tell you that the manual curriculum and ALP-GMM are close, while not using a curriculum is a distant third. Actually, this is not the case. Let's unpack this plot:

- Manual curriculum goes from easy to difficult, that is why it is at the top, most of the time. In our run, it could not even get to the latest lesson within the time budget. Therefore, the performance shown in the figure is inflated for the manual curriculum.

- The no-curriculum training is always competing at the most difficult level. That is why it is at the bottom most of the time: The other agents are not running against the hardest parameter configurations as they slowly get there.

- ALP-GMM is in the middle for the most part, because it is experimenting with difficult and hard configurations at the same time, while focusing on somewhere in between.

  Since this plot is inconclusive, we evaluate the agents on the original (most difficult) configuration. The results are the following after 100 test episodes for each:

  ```
  Agent ALP-GMM score: 3.71
  Agent Manual score: -2.79
  Agent No Curriculum score: 2.81
  ```

- The manual curriculum performed the worst as it could not get to the latest lesson as of the end of the training.

- The no-curriculum had some success, but starting with the most difficult setting seems to have set it back. Also, the evaluation performance is in line with what is shown on TensorBoard, since the evaluation settings are no different from the training settings in this case.

- ALP-GMM seems to have benefited from gradually increasing the difficulty and performs the best.

- The no-curriculum training's peak point in the TensorBoard graph is similar to the ALP-GMM's latest performance. So, our modification with respect to the vertical speed of the robot diminished the difference between the two. Not using a curriculum, however, causes the agent to not learn at all in many hard-exploration scenarios.

You can find the code for the evaluation in `Chapter14/evaluate_ppo.py`. Also, you can use the script `Chapter14/visualize_policy.py` to watch your trained agents in action, see where they fall short and come up with ideas to improve the performance!

This concludes our discussion on the Kuka example of robot learning. In the next section, we will wrap up this chapter with a list of some popular simulation environments used in training autonomous robots and vehicles.

Going beyond PyBullet into autonomous driving

PyBullet is a great environment to test the capabilities of reinforcement learning algorithms in a high-fidelity physics simulation. Some of the other libraries you will come across at the intersection of robotics and reinforcement learning are:

- Gazebo: `http://gazebosim.org/`,
- MuJoCo (requires license): `http://www.mujoco.org/`,
- Adroit: `https://github.com/vikashplus/Adroit`.

In addition, you will also see Unity and Unreal Engine-based environments used in training reinforcement learning agents.

The next and more popular level of autonomy is of course autonomous vehicles. RL is increasingly experimented in realistic autonomous vehicle simulations as well. The most popular libraries in this area are:

- CARLA: `https://github.com/carla-simulator/carla`,
- AirSim: `https://github.com/microsoft/AirSim`. (Disclaimer: The author is a Microsoft employee at the time of authoring this book and part of the organization developing AirSim.)

With this, we conclude this chapter on robot learning. This is a very hot application area in RL, and there are many environments you can experiment with. I hope you have enjoyed and are inspired by what we have done in this chapter.

Summary

Autonomous robots and vehicles are going to play a huge role in the future of our world; and reinforcement learning is one of the primary approaches to create such autonomous systems. In this chapter, we have taken a peek at what it looks like to train a robot to accomplish an object grasping task, a major challenge in robotics with many applications in manufacturing and warehouse material handling. We used the PyBullet physics simulator to train a Kuka robot in a hard-exploration setting, for which we leveraged both manual and ALP-GMM-based curriculum learning. Now that you have a fairly good grasp of how to utilize these techniques, you can take on other similar problems.

In the next chapter, we will look into another major area for reinforcement learning applications: Supply chain management. Stay tuned for another exciting journey!

References

1. Coumans, E., Bai, Y. (2016-2019). *PyBullet, a Python module for physics simulation for games, robotics and machine learning.* URL: `http://pybullet.org`.

2. Bulletphysics/Bullet3. (2020). *Bullet Physics SDK*, GitHub. URL: `https://github.com/bulletphysics/bullet3`.

3. CNC Robotics. (2018). *KUKA Industrial Robots, Robotic Specialists*. URL: `https://www.cncrobotics.co.uk/news/kuka-robots/`.

4. KUKA AG. (2020). URL: `https://www.kuka.com/en-us`.

5. Portelas, Rémy, et al. (2019). *Teacher Algorithms for Curriculum Learning of Deep RL in Continuously Parameterized Environments.* ArXiv:1910.07224 [Cs, Stat], Oct. 2019. arXiv.org, `http://arxiv.org/abs/1910.07224`.

6. Gonnochenko, Aleksei, et al. (2020). *Coinbot: Intelligent Robotic Coin Bag Manipulation Using Deep Reinforcement Learning and Machine Teaching.* arXiv.org, `http://arxiv.org/abs/2012.01356`.

15
Supply Chain Management

Effective supply chain management is a challenge for many businesses, yet it is key to their profitability and competitiveness. The difficulty in this area comes from a complex set of dynamics affecting supply and demand, business constraints around handling them, and a great uncertainty all along. Reinforcement learning provides us with a key set of capabilities to address such sequential decision-making problems.

In this chapter, we particularly focus on two important problems: Inventory and routing optimization. For the former, we go into the details of creating the environment, understanding the variance in the environment, and hyperparameter tuning to effectively solve it using reinforcement learning. For the latter, we describe a realistic vehicle routing problem of a gig driver working to deliver online meal orders. We then proceed to show why conventional neural networks are limiting while solving problems in varying sizes, and how pointer networks can overcome this. To recap, our topics for the chapter are:

- Optimizing inventory procurement decisions
- Modeling routing problems

Let's jump in!

Optimizing inventory procurement decisions

One of the most important decisions that almost all manufacturers, distributors, and retailers need to make, all the time, is how much inventory to carry to reliably satisfy the customer demand while minimizing the costs. Effective inventory management is key to the profitability and survival of most companies, especially given the razor-thin margins and increased customer expectations in today's competitive landscape. In this section, we use reinforcement learning to address this challenge and optimize inventory procurement decisions.

The need for inventory and the trade off in its management

When you walk into a supermarket, you see items stacked on top of each other. There are probably more of those items in the depot of the supermarket, and more at the warehouse of the distributors, and more at the sites of the manufacturers. If you think about it, there are those huge piles of products just sitting somewhere, waiting to be demanded by customers at some future time. If that sounds like a waste of resources, it largely is. On the other hand, companies have to carry some level of inventory, because:

- The future is uncertain. Customer demand, manufacturing capacity, transportation schedules, raw material availability are all subject to unfold in some unplanned ways.

- It is impossible to operate in a perfect just-in-time manner and manufacture and deliver an item to customers right at the moment they demand it.

Since carrying inventory is mostly unavoidable, the question is then how much. Answering it involves a tricky tradeoff:

- Minimizing the chance of losing customer demand that costs profit, and more importantly, loyalty that will be hard to gain back.

- Minimizing the inventory that costs capital, labor, time, material, maintenance, and warehouse rent and that leads to spoiled or obsolete items and organizational overhead.

So, how would you handle it? Would you make your customer satisfaction an absolute priority or prefer to keep your inventory under control? Well, this balancing act requires careful planning and use of advanced methods, which not all companies have the means for. As a result, most prefer to be "on the safe side" and carry more inventory than they need to, which helps covering up the lack of good planning among other issues. This phenomenon is commonly illustrated as a "sea of inventory" as in *Figure 15.1*:

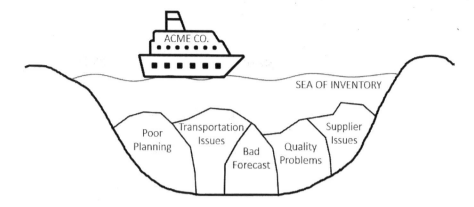

Figure 15.1 – A sea of inventory hides many problems

This is where reinforcement learning could come to the rescue and optimize your inventory decisions in the face of uncertainty. Next, we start building our solution by discussing the components of an inventory optimization problem.

Components of an inventory optimization problem

There are multiple factors that affect the dynamics of an inventory flow and what the best replenishment policy will look like for a given item:

- **Price** of the item at which it is sold is a key factor.

- **Cost of purchase** of the item is another key factor, which, together with the price, determines how much gross profit the business makes per item. This in turn affects how costly it is to lose a unit of customer demand.

- **Inventory holding cost** is the sum of all costs associated with carrying a single unit of inventory over a single time step (day, week, month, and so on). This includes things like, storage rent, cost of capital, and maintenance costs.

- **Loss of customer goodwill** is the monetary cost associated with customer dissatisfaction due to a single unit of lost demand. After all, this reduces customer loyalty and affects future sales. Although dissatisfaction is usually a qualitative measure, businesses need to estimate the monetary equivalent of it to be able to use it in decision making.

- **Customer demand** for the item in a single time step is one of the main factors affecting the decision.

- **Vendor lead time (VLT)** is the lag between the placement of an order with a vendor till its arrival in the inventory. Not surprisingly, VLT is a key factor affecting when to place an order for some anticipated demand.

- **Capacity** limitations, such as how many items can be ordered in a single batch and the storage capacity, will restrict the actions that the agent can take.

These are the main factors that we will consider in our setting here. In addition, we focus on:

- Single item scenario,
- Stochastic customer demand with a Poisson distribution, which will have a deterministic and fixed mean over a given episode,
- Deterministic factors other than demand.

This makes our case tractable while maintaining a sufficient complexity.

> **Tip**
>
> In a real-life setting, most dynamics involve uncertainties. For example, there could be defects in the arrived inventory, the price could change with how obsolete an item becomes, there could be loss in the existing inventory due to weather, there could be return items etc. Estimating the characteristics of all these factors and creating a simulation model of the process is a real challenge, posing a barrier in front of the adoption of reinforcement learning as a tool for such problems.

What we have described is a complex optimization problem, for which there is no tractable optimal solution. However, the single-step version of it, called the **newsvendor problem**, is well studied and widely used. It is a great simplification to develop an intuition about the problem, and it will also help us obtain a near-optimal benchmark for the multi-step case. Let's look into it.

Single-step inventory optimization: The newsvendor problem

When an inventory optimization problem involves:

- Single time step (so no VLT, deterministic arrival of inventory)
- Single item
- Known price, cost of purchase, cost of unsold inventory
- Known (and conveniently Gaussian) demand distribution

The problem is called the newsvendor problem, for which we can obtain a closed-form solution. It was named after a newspaper vendor who aims to plan how many copies to purchase for the day, at a unit cost c, to sell at a unit price p, and return the unsold copies at the end of the day at a unit price r. We then define the following quantities:

- Cost of underage, c_u, is the profit lost due to a single unit of missed demand: $c_u = p - c$.

- Cost of overage, c_o, is the cost of an unsold unit is $c_o = c - r$.

To find the optimal ordering quantity, we then calculate a critical ratio, ρ, as follows:

$$\rho = \frac{c_u}{c_u + c_o}$$

Now, let's unpack how this critical ratio changes with respect to the costs of underage and overage:

- As c_u gets higher, ρ increases. Higher c_u and ρ, means it is costlier to miss customer demand. This suggests being more aggressive in replenishing the inventory to avoid leaving money on the table.

- As c_o gets higher, ρ decreases, and this means it is costlier to have unsold inventory. This suggests that we should be conservative in how much we carry.

It turns out that ρ gives us what percentage of the demand scenarios should be covered to optimize the expected profit at the end of the day. In other words, let's say the demand has a probability distribution function $f(x)$, and a cumulative distribution function (c.d.f.) $F(x)$. The optimal order size is given by $F^{-1}(\rho)$, where F^{-1} is the inverse of the c.d.f.

Let's experiment with this in an example.

Newsvendor example

Assume that the price of an expensive item is p = $2,000, which is sourced at c = $400. The item cannot be returned to the supplier if unsold, and it becomes a waste. So, we have r = $0. In this case the cost of underage is c_u = $1,600, and the cost of overage is c_o = $400, which give us a critical ratio ρ = 0.8. This suggests that the order size should cover the demand with 80% chance. Assuming that the demand has a normal distribution with a mean of 20 and standard deviation of 5 items, the optimal order size is around ~24 items.

You can calculate and plot the optimal order size using the `calc_n_plot_critical_` `ratio` function defined in the file:

Chapter15/Newsvendor plots.ipynb

```
calc_n_plot_critical_ratio(p=2000, c=400, r=0, mean=20, std=5)
```

And you should see the output as follows:

```
Cost of underage is 1600
Cost of overage is 400
Critical ratio is 0.8
Optimal order qty is 24.20810616786457
```

Figure 15.2 illustrates the probability distribution of the demand, the c.d.f., and the value the critical ratio corresponds to for this problem.

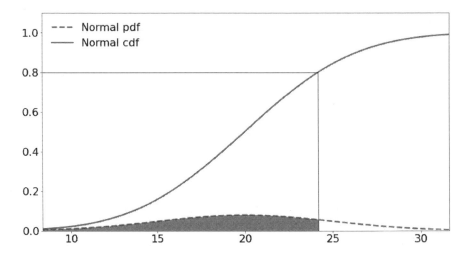

Figure 15.2 – Optimal order size for the example newsvendor problem

This was to give you an intuition into what the solution looks like for a single-step inventory optimization problem. Now, a multi-step problem involves a bunch of other complexities, which we described in the previous section. For example, the inventory arrives with a lag, and the leftover inventory is carried to the next step with a holding cost incurred. Well, this is sequential decision making under uncertainty, which is the forte of reinforcement learning. So, let's use it.

Simulating multi-step inventory dynamics

In this section, we create a simulation environment for the multi-step inventory optimization problem we described.

> **Info**
>
> The rest of this chapter closely follows the problems and environments defined in (Balaji et al., 2019), for which the code is available on `https://github.com/awslabs/or-rl-benchmarks`. We suggest you read the paper for more details on reinforcement learning approaches to classical stochastic optimization problems.

Before we start describing the environment, let's discuss several considerations:

- We would like to create a policy not for a specific product-demand scenario but a broad range of scenarios. Therefore, for each episode, we randomly generate the environment parameters as you will see.

- This randomization increases the variance in gradient estimates, which makes the learning more challenging compared to static scenarios.

With this, let's go into the details of the environment.

Event calendar

In order to correctly apply the step function for the environment, we need to understand when each event takes place. Let's take a look:

1. At the beginning of each day, the inventory replenishment order is placed. Based on the lead time, we record this as the "in-transit" inventory.

2. Next, the items scheduled for the current day arrive. If the lead time is zero, what is ordered at the beginning of the day arrives right away. If the lead time is one day, yesterday's order arrives, and so on.

3. After the shipment is received, the demand materializes throughout the day. If there is not enough inventory to meet the demand, the actual sales will be lower than the demand, and there will be a loss of customer goodwill.

4. At the end of the day, we deduct the sold items (not the total demand) from the inventory and update the state accordingly.

5. Lastly, if the lead time is nonzero, we update in-transit inventory (that is, we shift the inventory set to arrive on t+2 to t+1.)

Now, let's code what we have described.

Coding the environment

You can find the complete code for the environment in our GitHub repo at:

`https://github.com/PacktPublishing/Mastering-Reinforcement-Learning-with-Python/blob/master/Chapter15/inventory_env.py`

Here, we only describe some of the critical parts of the environment.

1. As mentioned earlier, each episode will sample certain environment parameters to be able to obtain a policy that can work across a broad set of price, demand etc. scenarios. We set the maximum values for those parameters, from which we will later generate episode-specific parameters:

```python
class InventoryEnv(gym.Env):
    def __init__(self, config={}):
        self.l = config.get("lead time", 5)
        self.storage_capacity = 4000
        self.order_limit = 1000
        self.step_count = 0
        self.max_steps = 40
        self.max_value = 100.0
        self.max_holding_cost = 5.0
        self.max_loss_goodwill = 10.0
        self.max_mean = 200
```

We use a 5-day lead time, which will be important to determine the observation space (which can be considered equivalent to state space for this problem, so we use the terms interchangeably).

2. Price, cost, holding cost, loss of goodwill, and expected demand are part of the state space, which we assume also visible to the agent. In addition, we need to keep track of the on-hand inventory, and in-transit inventory if the lead-time is nonzero.

```python
        self.inv_dim = max(1, self.l)
        space_low = self.inv_dim * [0]
        space_high = self.inv_dim * \
                     [self.storage_capacity]
        space_low += 5 * [0]
        space_high += [
```

```
                self.max_value,
                self.max_value,
                self.max_holding_cost,
                self.max_loss_goodwill,
                self.max_mean,
            ]
        self.observation_space = spaces.Box(
            low=np.array(space_low),
            high=np.array(space_high),
            dtype=np.float32
        )
```

Note that for a lead time of 5, we have one dimension for the on-hand inventory, and four dimensions (from $t + 1$ to $t + 4$) for the in-transit inventory. As you will see, by adding the in-transit inventory to the state at the end of the step calculation, we can avoid keeping track of the in-transit inventory that will arrive at $t + 5$ (in more general terms, we don't need the $t + l$, l being the lead time).

3. We normalize the action to be between $[0, 1]$, where 1 means ordering at the order limit:

```
        self.action_space = spaces.Box(
            low=np.array([0]),
            high=np.array([1]),
            dtype=np.float32
        )
```

4. One of the very important steps is to normalize the observations. Normally, the agent may not know the bounds of the observations to normalize them. Here we assume that the agent has that information, so, we conveniently do it within the environment class.

```
    def _normalize_obs(self):
        obs = np.array(self.state)
        obs[:self.inv_dim] = obs[:self.inv_dim] / self.
    order_limit
        obs[self.inv_dim] = obs[self.inv_dim] / self.max_
    value
        obs[self.inv_dim + 1] = obs[self.inv_dim + 1] /
    self.max_value
```

```
        obs[self.inv_dim + 2] = obs[self.inv_dim + 2] /
self.max_holding_cost
        obs[self.inv_dim + 3] = obs[self.inv_dim + 3] /
self.max_loss_goodwill
        obs[self.inv_dim + 4] = obs[self.inv_dim + 4] /
self.max_mean
        return obs
```

5. The episode-specific environment parameters are generated within the reset function:

```
def reset(self):
    self.step_count = 0

    price = np.random.rand() * self.max_value
    cost = np.random.rand() * price
    holding_cost = np.random.rand() * min(cost,
                        self.max_holding_cost)
    loss_goodwill = np.random.rand() * \
                        self.max_loss_goodwill
    mean_demand = np.random.rand() * self.max_mean

    self.state = np.zeros(self.inv_dim + 5)
    self.state[self.inv_dim] = price
    self.state[self.inv_dim + 1] = cost
    self.state[self.inv_dim + 2] = holding_cost
    self.state[self.inv_dim + 3] = loss_goodwill
    self.state[self.inv_dim + 4] = mean_demand
    return self._normalize_obs()
```

6. And we implement the step function as we described in the previous section. First, we parse the initial state and received action:

```
def step(self, action):
    beginning_inv_state, p, c, h, k, mu = \
        self.break_state()
    action = np.clip(action[0], 0, 1)
    action = int(action * self.order_limit)
    done = False
```

7. Then, we determine how much we can buy while observing the capacity, add what is bought to the inventory if there is no lead time, and sample the demand.

```
available_capacity = self.storage_capacity \
                   - np.sum(beginning_inv_state)
assert available_capacity >= 0
buys = min(action, available_capacity)
# If lead time is zero, immediately
# increase the inventory
if self.l == 0:
    self.state[0] += buys
on_hand = self.state[0]
demand_realization = np.random.poisson(mu)
```

8. The reward will be the revenue, from which we subtract the purchase cost, the inventory holding cost, and cost of lost customer goodwill.

```
# Compute Reward
sales = min(on_hand,
            demand_realization)
sales_revenue = p * sales
overage = on_hand - sales
underage = max(0, demand_realization
             - on_hand)
purchase_cost = c * buys
holding = overage * h
penalty_lost_sale = k * underage
reward = sales_revenue \
       - purchase_cost \
       - holding \
       - penalty_lost_sale
```

9. Next, we update the inventory levels by shifting the in-transit inventory by a day, adding what is bought at the beginning of the day to the in-transit if the VLT is nonzero.

```
# Day is over. Update the inventory
# levels for the beginning of the next day
# In-transit inventory levels shift to left
```

```
        self.state[0] = 0
        if self.inv_dim > 1:
            self.state[: self.inv_dim - 1] \
                = self.state[1: self.inv_dim]
        self.state[0] += overage
        # Add the recently bought inventory
        # if the lead time is positive
        if self.l > 0:
            self.state[self.l - 1] = buys
        self.step_count += 1
        if self.step_count >= self.max_steps:
            done = True
```

10. At the end, we return the normalized observations and scaled reward to the agent.

```
        # Normalize the reward
        reward = reward / 10000
        info = {
            "demand realization": demand_realization,
            "sales": sales,
            "underage": underage,
            "overage": overage,
        }
        return self._normalize_obs(), reward, done, info
```

Take your time to understand how the inventory dynamics are reflected in the step function. Once you are ready, let's move to developing a benchmark policy.

Developing a near-optimal benchmark policy

An exact solution to this problem is not feasible to derive. Yet, a near-optimal approximation is obtained similar to the newsvendor policy, with two modifications:

- The aggregate demand over $l + 1$ time steps is taken into account instead of single step.

- We also add the loss of goodwill to the cost of underage in addition to the per unit profit.

The reason this is still approximate is that the formula treats multiple steps as a single step and aggregates the demand and supply, meaning that it assumes the demand arrived in a step can be backlogged and satisfied in one of the subsequent steps over the $l + 1$ step horizon. Still, this gives us a near-optimal solution.

Here is how we can code this benchmark policy:

```
def get_action_from_benchmark_policy(env):
    inv_state, p, c, h, k, mu = env.break_state()
    cost_of_overage = h
    cost_of_underage = p - c + k
    critical_ratio = np.clip(
        0, 1, cost_of_underage
            / (cost_of_underage + cost_of_overage)
    )
    horizon_target = int(poisson.ppf(critical_ratio,
                        (len(inv_state) + 1) * mu))
    deficit = max(0, horizon_target - np.sum(inv_state))
    buy_action = min(deficit, env.order_limit)
    return [buy_action / env.order_limit]
```

Notice that after we calculate the critical ratio, we do the following:

- We find the optimal aggregate supply for $l + 1$ steps.

- Then subtract the on-hand inventory and in-transit inventory for the next l time steps.

- Finally, we place the order to cover this deficit, capped by the limit on a single order.

Next, let's look into how we can train an RL agent to solve this problem and how the RL solution compares to this benchmark.

Reinforcement learning solution to the inventory management

There are several factors to take into account while solving this problem:

- Due to the randomizations in the environment, there is a high variance in the reward across episodes.

- This requires us to use higher-than-normal batch and minibatch sizes to better estimate the gradients and have more stable updates to the neural network weights.

- Selecting the winner model is also a problem in the presence of high variance. This is because, if the number of test/evaluation episodes are not large enough, there is a chance to declare a policy as the best just because we happen to evaluate it in a few "lucky" environment configurations.

To handle these challenges, we can adapt the following strategy:

1. Do a limited hyperparameter tuning with limited computation budget to identify a set of good hyperparameters.

2. Train the model with the one or two the best sets of hyperparameters. Save the best models along the way.

3. When you observe the trend of the reward curve is dominated by the noise, increase the batch and minibatch sizes for finer estimation of the gradients and denoising the model performance metrics. Again, save the best model.

4. Depending on your compute budget, repeat this multiple times and pick the winner model.

So, let's implement these steps in Ray/RLlib to obtain our policy.

Initial hyperparameter sweep

We use Ray's Tune library to do the initial hyperparameter tuning. There are two functions we utilize:

- `tune.grid_search()` does a grid search over the specified set of values.
- `tune.choice()` does a random search within the specified set.

For each trial, we also specify the stopping criteria. In our case, we would like to run a trial for a million-time steps.

Chapter15/tune_inv_policy.py

Here is the code for an example search:

```
import ray
from ray import tune
from inventory_env import InventoryEnv
```

```
ray.init()
tune.run(
    "PPO",
    stop={"timesteps_total": 1e6},
    num_samples=5,
    config={
        "env": InventoryEnv,
        "rollout_fragment_length": 40,
        "num_gpus": 1,
        "num_workers": 50,
        "lr": tune.grid_search([0.01, 0.001,
                        0.0001, 0.00001]),
        "use_gae": tune.choice([True, False]),
        "train_batch_size": tune.choice([5000, 10000,
                                20000, 40000]),
        "sgd_minibatch_size": tune.choice([128, 1024,
                                4096, 8192]),
        "num_sgd_iter": tune.choice([5, 10, 30]),
        "vf_loss_coeff": tune.choice([0.1, 1, 10]),
        "vf_share_layers": tune.choice([True, False]),
        "entropy_coeff": tune.choice([0, 0.1, 1]),
        "clip_param": tune.choice([0.05, 0.1, 0.3, 0.5]),
        "vf_clip_param": tune.choice([1, 5, 10]),
        "grad_clip": tune.choice([None, 0.01, 0.1, 1]),
        "kl_target": tune.choice([0.005, 0.01, 0.05]),
        "eager": False,
    },
)
```

To calculate the total tuning budget:

- Take the cross-product of all grid searches since each possible combination has to be tried by definition.

- Multiply that cross-product with the num_samples. That gives the total number of trials that will take place. With the code above, we will have 20 trials.

- During each trial, each `choice` function will select a parameter, uniformly at random, from the corresponding set.

- A given trial stops when the stopping criteria are satisfied.

Whey you execute this, you will see the search progressing. It will look like *Figure 15.3*.

```
== Status ==
Memory usage on this node: 41.3/125.8 GiB
Using FIFO scheduling algorithm.
Resources requested: 51/64 CPUs, 1/1 GPUs, 0.0/65.19 GiB heap, 0.0/22.02 GiB objects
Result logdir: /home/enes/ray_results/PPO
Number of trials: 20 (6 ERROR, 1 PENDING, 1 RUNNING, 12 TERMINATED)
+-----------------------------+------------+------+----------------+
| Trial name                  | status     | loc  |     clip_param |
+-----------------------------+------------+------+----------------+
| PPO_InventoryEnv_90891_00000 | TERMINATED |      |           0.05 |
| PPO_InventoryEnv_90891_00001 | TERMINATED |      |           0.3  |
| PPO_InventoryEnv_90891_00002 | TERMINATED |      |           0.3  |
| PPO_InventoryEnv_90891_00003 | TERMINATED |      |           0.3  |
| PPO_InventoryEnv_90891_00004 | ERROR      |      |           0.1  |
| PPO_InventoryEnv_90891_00005 | TERMINATED |      |           0.3  |
```

Figure 15.3 – Hyperparameter tuning with Ray's Tune

Some trials will error out, unless you are deliberate about the hyperparameter combinations that will form to prevent numerical issues. You can then select the best performing combinations for further training, as illustrated in *Figure 15.4*.

```
-+--------+-------------------+---------+------------+
|  iter  |   total time (s)  |     ts  |    reward  |
-+--------+-------------------+---------+------------|
|   167  |         394.645   | 1002000 |  -25.8308  |
|   167  |         100.572   | 1002000 |  -23.0244  |
|   100  |         392.639   | 1000000 |    4.51787 |
|   100  |          78.4445  | 1000000 |  -20.4601  |
|     7  |           5.30848 |   42000 |  -24.749   |
|    25  |          89.3493  | 1000000 |    3.46016 |
```

Figure 15.4 – A sample performance of a good set of hyperparameters obtained in the search

Nest, let's now do the extensive training.

Extensive training of the model

We now kick off a long training using the selected hyperparameter set (or with multiple sets – in my case the winner set in the previous step did not perform well, but the second set did).

Chapter15/train_inv_policy.py

```
import numpy as np
import ray
from ray.tune.logger import pretty_print
from ray.rllib.agents.ppo.ppo import DEFAULT_CONFIG
from ray.rllib.agents.ppo.ppo import PPOTrainer
from inventory_env import InventoryEnv


config = DEFAULT_CONFIG.copy()
config["env"] = InventoryEnv
config["num_gpus"] = 1
config["num_workers"] = 50
config["clip_param"] = 0.3
config["entropy_coeff"] = 0
config["grad_clip"] = None
config["kl_target"] = 0.005
config["lr"] = 0.001
config["num_sgd_iter"] = 5
config["sgd_minibatch_size"] = 8192
config["train_batch_size"] = 20000
config["use_gae"] = True
config["vf_clip_param"] = 10
config["vf_loss_coeff"] = 1
config["vf_share_layers"] = False
```

Once you set the hyperparameters, you can kick off the training.

```
ray.init()
trainer = PPOTrainer(config=config, env=InventoryEnv)
best_mean_reward = np.NINF
while True:
    result = trainer.train()
```

```
    print(pretty_print(result))
mean_reward = result.get("episode_reward_mean", np.NINF)
 if mean_reward > best_mean_reward:
    checkpoint = trainer.save()
    print("checkpoint saved at", checkpoint)
    best_mean_reward = mean_reward
```

One thing to note here is the size of the batch and minibatch: Normally, the PPO default in RLlib is `"train_batch_size": 4000` and `"sgd_minibatch_size": 128`. However, learning suffers with such small batches given the variance in the environment and rewards. So, the tuning model picked higher batch and minibatch sizes.

Now for the training. At this point, you can develop a logic to adjust various hyperparameters based on the training progress. For simplicity, we will manually observe the progress and then stop when the learning stalls or destabilizes. After that point, we can further train with increased batch sizes to obtain better gradient estimates in the final stages, such as `"train_batch_size": 200000` and `"sgd_minibatch_size": 32768`. This is what such a training process looks like:

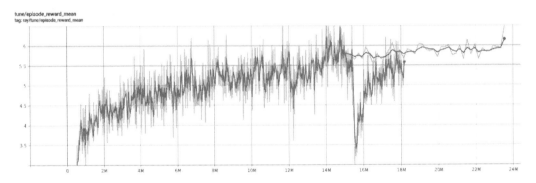

Figure 15.5 – Training started with 20k batch size and continued with
200k batch size to reduce the noise

The fine tuning with a higher batch size helps us denoise the rewards and truly identify high-performing models. We can then compare the benchmark and RL solutions. After 2000 test episodes, the benchmark performance:

```
Average daily reward over 2000 test episodes:
0.15966589703658918.
Average total epsisode reward: 6.386635881463566
```

And the RL model performance:

```
Average daily reward over 2000 test episodes:
0.14262437792900876.
Average total epsisode reward: 5.70497511716035
```

RL performance is within 10% of the near-optimal benchmark solution. We can decrease the gap with further trials and training, but in the presence of such a noise, it is a challenging and time-consuming undertaking. Note that (Balaji et al., 2019) reports metrics that slightly improve the benchmarks, so it is doable.

> **Tip**
> While the RL solution did not outperform the analytical one in this example, note that the RL formulation can take on arbitrarily complex setting, for which the analytical approach will not necessarily be as good of an approximation.

With this, we conclude our discussion on this problem. Great work! We have taken a realistic and noisy supply chain problem from its initial form, modeled it using RL, and solved via PPO on RLlib!

Next, we describe another important supply chain problem, routing optimization. Due to space limitations, we won't be able to solve it here, but refer you to: `https://github.com/awslabs/or-rl-benchmarks/`.

So, let's discuss how you can model and solve a routing optimization problem using RL.

Modeling routing problems

Routing problems are among the most challenging and well-studied in combinatorial optimization. In fact, there are quite a few of researchers who dedicated their entire careers to this area. Recently, RL approaches to routing problems have emerged as an alternative to the traditional operations research methods. We start with a rather sophisticated routing problem, which is about the pick-up and delivery of online meal orders. The RL modeling to this problem, on the other hand, will not be that complex. We will later extend our discussion to more advanced RL models in line of the recent literature in this area.

Pick-up and delivery of online meal orders

Consider a gig driver (our agent) who works for an online platform, similar to Uber Eats or Grubhub, to pick up orders from restaurants and deliver to customers. The goal of the driver is to collect as much tips as possible by delivering many expensive orders. Here are some more details about this environment:

- There are multiple restaurants in the city, which are the pick-up locations for the orders.

- Orders associated to one of these restaurants dynamically arrive on the mobile app.

- The driver has to accept an order to be able to pick it up and deliver.

- If an accepted order is not delivered within a certain time limit since the order creation, a high penalty is incurred.

- If an open order is not accepted by the driver, it disappears after a while, which implies that it is taken by competitive drivers.

- The driver can accept as many orders as they want but can physically carry only a limited number of picked-up orders.

- Different parts of the city generate orders at different tip amounts and different sizes. For example, one region could be generating frequent and expensive orders, making it attractive for the driver.

- Traveling unnecessary distances costs time, fuel, and opportunity to the driver.

Given this environment, at each time step, the driver takes one of the following actions:

- Accept one of the open orders (with known tip).

- Move one step towards a restaurant associated with a particular order (for pick-up).

- Move one step towards a customer location (for delivery).

- Wait and do nothing.

- Move one step towards one of the restaurants (not to pick up an existing order but with the hope that a good, expensive order could be placed soon from that restaurant).

The agent observes the following state to make their decision:

- Coordinates of the driver, the restaurants, and the customers.

- Driver used and available capacity.

- Order statuses (open, accepted, picked up, inactive/delivered/not created).

- Order-restaurant associations.

- Time elapsed since the order creation.

- The tip associated with each order.

For more information, this environment is available at: `https://github.com/ awslabs/or-rl-benchmarks/blob/master/Vehicle%20Routing%20 Problem/src/vrp_environment.py`.

(Balaji et al., 2019) shows that the RL solution to this problem outperforms a **mixed-integer programming** (**MIP**) based approach. This is a rather surprising result since MIP models can find the optimal solution in theory. The reason the MIP solution is outperformed in this case is that:

- It solves a myopic problem for an existing situation while the RL agent learns to anticipate future events and plan accordingly,

- It uses a limited budget as MIP solutions can take really long time. RL inference, on the other hand, happens almost in instantaneously once a policy is trained.

The reported RL performance for such a complex problem is quite encouraging. On the other hand, the way we modeled the problem has limitations since it relies on a fixed state and action space size. In other words, if the state and action space are designed to handle a maximum of N number of orders/restaurants, the trained agent cannot be used for larger problems. On the other hand, MIP models can take any size of input (although large problems can take really long time to solve or become intractable).

Recent research in deep learning has provided us with pointer networks to handle dynamic-size combinatorial optimization problems. Let's look into this next.

Pointer networks for dynamic combinatorial optimization

A pointer network uses a content-based attention mechanism to point to one of its inputs, where the number of inputs can be anything. To explain this better, consider a traveling salesperson problem where the goal is to visit all the nodes located on a 2D plane, exactly once, and come back to the initial node at the end, and do so at the minimum total distance. A sample solution to this problem is illustrated in *Figure 15.6*.

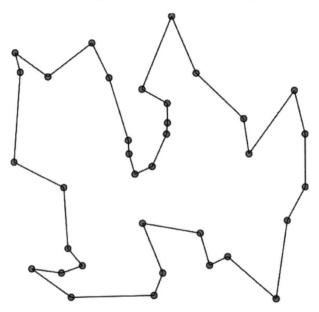

Figure 15.6 – Solution to a traveling salesperson problem (source: https://en.wikipedia.org/wiki/Travelling_salesman_problem)

Each node in this problem is represented by its (x, y) coordinates. A pointer network has the following attributes:

- Uses a recurrent neural network to obtain an embedding e_j from (x_j, y_j) of an input node j in the encoder, and similarly d_i in the decoder at the ith step of the decoding.

- Calculates an attention on the input node j while decoding the ith step as follows:

$$u_j^i = v^T \tanh(W_1 e_j + W_2 d_i)$$

$$a_j^i = softmax(u_j^i)$$

where $v, W_1,$ and W_2 are learnable parameters.

- The input node j with the highest attention a_j^i becomes the ith node to visit on the route.

This attention approach is completely flexible to point to a particular input node without any assumptions on the total number of input nodes. This mechanism is illustrated in *Figure 15.7*.

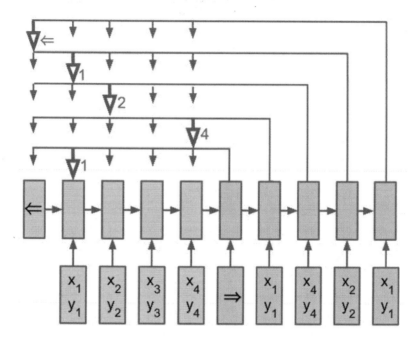

Figure 15.7 – A pointer network (source: Vinyals et al. 2017)

Later work (Nazari et al. 2018) adapted pointer networks to use inside a policy-based reinforcement learning model and obtained very promising results in fairly complex problems compared to open-source routing optimizers. The details of pointer networks and how they are used in the context of RL deserve further space and discussion, which we defer to the papers we cite at the end of the chapter.

With that, we conclude our discussion on reinforcement learning applications for supply chain problems. Let's summarize what we have covered next.

Summary

In this chapter, we covered two important classes of problems in supply chain: Inventory optimization and vehicle routing. These are both very complex problems, and reinforcement learning has recently emerged as a competitive tool to address them. In the chapter, for the former problem, we provided you with a detailed discussion on how the create the environment and solve the corresponding reinforcement learning problem. The challenge in this problem was the high variance across episodes, which we mitigated through a careful hyperparameter tuning procedure. For the latter problem, we described a realistic case of a gig driver who delivers meal orders that dynamically arrive from customers. We discussed how the model can be made more flexible to work with a varying size of nodes via pointer networks.

In the next chapter, we will discuss yet another exciting set of applications around personalization, marketing, and finance. See you there!

References

1. *ORL: Reinforcement Learning Benchmarks for Online Stochastic Optimization Problems*, Balaji, Bharathan, et al. (2019): `http://arxiv.org/abs/1911.10641`

2. *Pointer Networks*, Vinyals, Oriol, et al. (2017): `http://arxiv.org/abs/1506.03134`

3. *Reinforcement Learning for Solving the Vehicle Routing Problem*, Nazari, M, et al. (2018): `http://arxiv.org/abs/1802.04240`

16
Personalization, Marketing, and Finance

In this chapter, we discuss three areas in which reinforcement learning is gaining significant traction. First, we describe how it can be used in personalization and recommendation systems. With that, we go beyond the single-step bandit approaches we covered in the earlier chapters. A related field that can also significantly benefit from reinforcement learning is marketing. In addition to personalized marketing applications, reinforcement learning can help in areas like managing campaign budgets and reducing customer churn. Finally, we discuss the promise of RL in finance and the related challenges. In doing so, we introduce TensorTrade, a Python framework for developing and testing RL-based trading algorithms.

So, in this chapter, we cover:

- Going beyond bandits for personalization,
- Developing effective marketing strategies using reinforcement learning,
- Applying reinforcement learning in finance.

Going beyond bandits for personalization

When we covered multi-armed and contextual bandit problems in the early chapters of the book, we presented a case study that aimed maximizing the click-through rate (CTR) of online ads. This is just one example of how bandit models can be used to provide users with personalized content and experience, a common challenge of almost all online (and offline) content providers, from e-retailers to social media platforms. In this section, we go beyond the bandit models and describe a multi-step reinforcement learning approach to personalization. Let's first start with discussing where the bandit models fall short, and then how multi-step RL can address those issues.

Shortcomings of bandit models

The goal in bandit problems is to maximize the immediate (single step) return. In an online ad CTR maximization problem, this is usually a good way of thinking about the goal: An ad is displayed, the user has clicked, and voila! If not, it's a miss.

The relationship between the user and, let's say, YouTube or Amazon, is much more sophisticated than this. The user experience on such platforms is a journey, rather than an event. The platform recommends some content, and it is not a total miss if the user does not click on it. It could be quite the case that the user finds the presented content interesting and enticing and just continues browsing. Even if that user session does not result in a click or conversion, the user may come back soon knowing that the platform is serving some relevant content to the user interests. Conversely, too many clicks in a session can very well mean that the user is not able to find what they are looking for, leading to a bad experience. This "journey-like" nature of the problem, the fact that the platform (agent) decisions have downstream impact on the customer satisfaction and business value (reward), is what makes multi-step reinforcement learning an appealing approach here.

> **Tip**
>
> Although it is tempting to depart from a bandit model towards multi-step RL, think twice before doing so. Bandit algorithms are much easier to use and have well-understood theoretical properties, whereas it could be quite challenging to successfully train an agent in a multi-step RL setting. Note that many multi-step problems can be cast as a single-step problem by including a memory for the agent in the context and the expected future value of the action in the immediate reward, which then allows us to stay in the bandit framework.

One of the successful implementations of multi-step deep RL for personalization is related to news recommendation, proposed by (Zheng et al. 2018). In the next section, we describe a similar approach to the problem inspired by this work, although our discussion will be at a higher level and broader than what the paper suggests.

Deep reinforcement learning for news recommendation

When we go on our favorite news app, we expect to read some interesting and perhaps important content. Of course, what makes a news interesting or important is different for everyone, so we have a personalization problem. As (Zheng et al. 2018) mention, there are some additional challenges in news recommendation:

- The action space is not fixed. In fact, it is quite the opposite: There are so many news flowing in during a day, each with some unique characteristics, making it hard to think about the problem like a traditional Gym environment.

- User preferences are quite dynamic too: They change and evolve over time. A user group that is more into politics this week can get bored and read about art next week, which is what (Zheng et al. 2018) demonstrate with data.

- As we mentioned, this is a truly multi-step problem. If there are two news that can be displayed, one about a disaster and the other about a sports game, showing the former could have a higher chance of getting clicked due to its sensational nature. It could also lead to the user leave the platform early as their morale decreases, preventing more engagement on the platform.

- What the agent observes about the user is so limited compared to all possible factors playing a role in the user's behavior. Therefore, the environment is partially observable.

So, the problem is to choose which news piece(s) from a dynamic inventory to display to a user, whose interests, one, change over time, and two, are impacted by many factors that the agent does not fully observe.

Let's next describe the components of the RL problem here.

Observation and action space

Borrowed from (Zheng et al. 2018), there are the following pieces of information that make up the observation and action about a particular user and a news piece:

- **User features** related to the features of all the news pieces the user clicked in that session, that day, past week, how many times the user has come to the platform over various time horizons, and so on.

- **Context features** are related to the information about the time of the day, the day of the week, whether it is holiday, election day, and so on.

- **User-news features** about how many times this particular news piece appeared in the feed of this particular user over the past hour, and similar statistics related to the entities, topics, categories in the news.

- **News features** of this particular piece such as topic, category, provider, entity names, click counts over the past hour, past 6 hours, past day, and so on.

Now, this makes up a different observation-action space than what we are used to:

- The first two set of features are more like an observation: The user shows up, requests news content, and the agent observes the user and context-related features.

- Then the agent needs to pick a news piece to display (or a set of news pieces, as in the paper). Therefore, the features related to the news and user-news correspond to an action.

- What is interesting is that the available action set is dynamic, and it carries elements related to the user/observation (in user-news features).

Although this is not a traditional setup, don't let that scare you. We can still estimate, for example, the Q-value of a given observation-action pair: We simply need to feed all these features to a neural network that estimates the Q-value. To be specific, the paper uses two neural networks, one estimating the state-value and the other the advantage, to calculate the Q-value, although a single network can also be used. This is depicted in *Figure 16.1*.

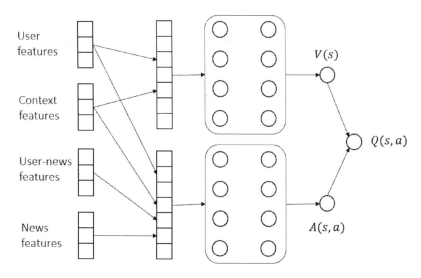

Figure 16.1 – Q-network of a news recommendation agent

Now, compare this to a traditional Q-network:

- A regular Q-network would have multiple heads, one for each action (and plus one for the value estimation if the action heads are estimating advantages rather than Q values). Such a network outputs Q-value estimates for all of the actions in a fixed set for a given observation in a single forward pass.

- In this setup, we need to make a separate forward pass over the network for each available news piece given the user, and then pick the one(s) with highest Q values.

This approach is actually similar to what we used in *Chapter 3, Contextual Bandits.*

Next, let's discuss an alternative modeling approach that we could use in this setup.

Using action embeddings

When the action space is very large and/or it varies each time step, like in this problem, **action embeddings** can be used to select an action given an observation. An action embedding is a representation of the action as a fixed-sized array, usually obtained as an outcome of a neural network.

Here is how it works:

- We use a policy network that outputs, rather than action values, an **intention vector**, a fixed size array of numbers.

- The intention vector carries information about what the ideal action would look like given the observation.

- In the context of the news recommendation problem, such an intention vector would mean something like: "Given these user and context features, this user wants to read about team sports from international leagues that are in finals."

- This intention vector is then compared to the available actions. The action that is "closest" to the "intention" is chosen. For example, a news piece about team sports in a foreign league, but not playing the finals.

- A measure of the closeness is cosine similarity, which is the dot product of an intention and action embedding.

This setup is illustrated in *Figure 16.2*.

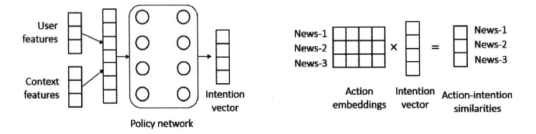

Figure 16.2 – Using action embeddings for news recommendations

> **Info**
> The use of embeddings in this way is something OpenAI introduced to deal with the huge action space in Dota 2. A nice blog explaining their approach is at https://neuro.cs.ut.ee/the-use-of-embeddings-in-openai-five/. This can be also implemented fairly easily in RLlib, which is explained at https://bit.ly/3or8AHz.

Next, let's discuss what the reward function looks like in the news recommendation problem.

Reward function

In the online ad problem that we solved at the beginning of the book, maximizing the CTR was the only objective. In the news recommendation, we would like to maximize the long-term engagement with the user, while also increasing the likelihood of immediate clicks. This requires a measure for user activeness, for which the paper uses a survival model.

Exploration using dueling bandit gradient descent

Exploration is an essential component in reinforcement learning. When we train RL agents in simulation, we don't care about taking bad actions for the sake of learning, except it wastes some of the computation budget. If the RL agent is trained in a real environment, like it usually is in a setting like news recommendation, then exploration will have consequences beyond computational inefficiency and could harm the user satisfaction.

If you think about the common ϵ-greedy approach, during exploration, it takes an action uniformly at random over the entire action space, even we know that some of the actions are really bad. For example, even the agent knows that a reader is mostly interested in politics, it will randomly display news pieces about beauty, sports, celebrities and so on, which the reader might find totally irrelevant.

One way of overcoming this issue is to incrementally deviate from the greedy action to explore, and update the policy if the agent receives a good reward after an exploratory action. Here is how we could do it:

- In addition to the regular Q network, we use an **explore network** $\tilde{Q}$ to generate exploratory actions.

- The weights of $\tilde{Q}$, denoted by $\tilde{W}$, is obtained by perturbing the weights of Q, denoted by W.

- More formally, $\tilde{W} = W \cdot (1 + \alpha \cdot rand(-1,1))$, where α is a some coefficient to control the trade-off between exploration and exploitation, and $rand$ generates a random number between the inputs.

- To obtain a set of news pieces to display to a user, we first generate two sets of recommendations from Q and $\tilde{Q}$, one from each, and then randomly select pieces from both to add to the display set.

- Once the display set is shown to the user, the agent collects the user feedback (reward). If the feedback for the items generated by Q is better, W does not change. Otherwise, the weights are updated $W \coloneqq W + \eta\tilde{W}$, where η is some step size.

Finally, let's discuss how this model can be trained and deployed to get effective outcomes.

Model training and deployment

We already mentioned the dynamic characteristics of user behavior and preferences. (Zheng et al. 2018) overcomes this by training and updating the model frequently in a day, so that the model captures the latest dynamics in the environment.

This concludes our discussion on personalization applications of RL, particularly in a news recommendation setting. Awesome! We have covered some quite useful practical tips and approaches so far! Next, we shift gears towards a related area, marketing, which can also benefit from personalization, and do more using RL.

Developing effective marketing strategies using reinforcement learning

Reinforcement learning can significantly improve marketing strategies in multiple areas. Let's now talk about some of them.

Personalized marketing content

In relation to the previous section, there is always room for more personalization in marketing. Rather than sending the same email or flier to all customers, or having rough customer segmentations, reinforcement learning can help determining the best sequence of personalized marketing content to communicate to individual customers.

Marketing resource allocation for customer acquisition

Marketing departments often make the decisions about where to spend the budget based on subjective judgements and/or simple models. RL can actually come up with pretty dynamic policies to allocate marketing resources, while leveraging the information about the product, responses from different marketing channels, and context information such as time of the year and so on.

Reducing customer churn rate

Retailers have long studied predictive models to identify customers that are about to be lost. After they are identified, usually discount coupons, promotion items and so on are sent to the customer. But the sequence of taking such actions, given the type of the customer and the responses from the earlier actions, is underexplored. RL can effectively evaluate the value of each of these actions and reduce the customer churn.

Winning back lost customers

If you ever subscribed to The Economist magazine, and then made the mistake of quitting your subscription, you probably received many phone calls, mails, emails and notifications. One cannot help but think that whether such spamming is the best approach. It is probably not. An RL-based approach, on the other hand, can help determine which channels to use and when, along with the accompanying perks to maximize the chance of winning the customers back while minimizing the cost of these efforts.

This list can go on. I suggest you take a moment or two to think about what marketing behavior of the companies you are a customer of you find disturbing, ineffective, irrelevant, and how RL can help with that.

Next, our final area for this chapter: Finance.

Applying reinforcement learning in finance

If we need to reiterate RL's promise, it is to obtain policies for sequential decision making to maximize rewards under uncertainty. What is a better match than finance for such a tool? In finance:

- The goal is very much to maximize some monetary reward,
- Decisions made now will definitely have consequences down the road,
- Uncertainty is a defining factor.

As a result, RL is getting increasingly popular in the finance community.

To be clear, this section will not include any examples of a winning trading strategy, well, for obvious reasons: First, the author does not know any; second, even if he did, he would not tell that in a book (and no one would). In addition, there are challenges when it comes to using RL in finance. So, we start this section with a discussion on these challenges. Once we ground ourselves in reality, then we will proceed to defining some application areas and introducing some tools you can use in this area.

Challenges with using reinforcement learning in finance

How much time did it take for you to get a decent score in a video game when you first played it? An hour? Two? In any case, it is a tiny fraction of the experience that an RL agent would need, millions of game frames if not billions, to reach that level. This is because the gradients an RL agent obtains in such environments are too noisy to quickly learn from for the algorithms we are using. And video games are not that difficult after all.

Have you ever wondered what does it take to become a successful trader in the stock market? Years of financial experience, perhaps a Ph.D. in physics or math. Even then, it is difficult for a trader to beat the market performance.

This was perhaps too long of a statement to convince you that it is difficult to make money by trading equities, because:

- Financial markets are highly efficient (although not perfectly), and it is very difficult, if not practically impossible, to predict the market. In other words, the **signal** is very weak in the financial data, and it is almost full of **noise**.

- Financial markets are dynamic. A trading strategy that is profitable today may not last long as others may discover the same and trade on it. For example, if people knew that Bitcoin would trade at $100K at the first solar eclipse, the price would jump to that level now as people would not wait for that day to buy it.

- Unlike video games, financial markets are real-word processes. So, we need to create a simulation of them to be able to collect the huge amounts of data needed to train an RL agent for an environment much noisier than a video game. Remember that all simulations are imperfect, and what the agent learns is likely to be the quirks of the simulation model rather than a real signal, which won't be any useful outside of simulation.

- The real-world data is not that big to easily detect the low signal in it.

So, this was a long, discouraging, yet necessary disclaimer we needed to put out there to let you know that it is far from being a low-hanging-fruit to train a trader agent. Having said that, RL is a tool, a powerful one, and its effective use is up to the capabilities of its user.

Now, it is time to induce some optimism. There are some cool open-source libraries out there for you to work towards creating your trader agent, and TensorTrade is one candidate. It could be helpful for educational purposes and to strategize some trading ideas before going into some more custom tooling.

Introducing TensorTrade

TensorTrade is designed to easily compose Gym-like environments for trading equities. It allows the user to define and glue together various kinds of data streams, feature extractions for observations, action spaces, reward structures, and other convenient utilities you might need to train a trader agent. Since the environment follow the Gym API, it can be easily hooked up with RL libraries, such as RLlib.

In this section, we give a quick introduction to TensorTrade and defer the details of what you can do with it to the documentation.

> **Info**
>
> You can find the TensorTrade documentation at `https://www.tensortrade.org/en/latest/`.

Let's start with installation and then put together some TensorTrade components to create an environment.

Installing TensorTrade

TensorTrade can be installed with a simple pip command as follows:

```
pip install tensortrade
```

If you would like to create a virtual environment to install TensorTrade in, don't forget to also install Ray RLlib.

TensorTrade concepts and components

As we mentioned, TensorTrade environments are modular and composed of multiple components. Let's put together a basic environment here.

Instrument

Instruments in finance are assets that can be traded. We can define U.S. dollar and "TensorTrade Coin" instruments as follows:

```
USD = Instrument("USD", 2, "U.S. Dollar")
TTC = Instrument("TTC", 8, "TensorTrade Coin")
```

The integer arguments above represent the precision of the quantities for those instruments.

Stream

A stream simply refers to an object that streams data, such as price data from a market simulation. For example, we can create a simple sinusoidal USD-TTC price stream as follows:

```
x = np.arange(0, 2*np.pi, 2*np.pi / 1000)
p = Stream.source(50*np.sin(3*x) + 100,
                    dtype="float").rename("USD-TTC")
```

Exchange and data feed

Next, we need to create an exchange to trade these instruments in. We put the price stream we just created in the exchange.

```
coinbase = Exchange("coinbase", service=execute_order)(p)
```

Now that we have price stream defined, we can also define transformations for it and extract some features and indicators. All such features will also be streams and they will be all packed in a data feed.

```
feed = DataFeed([
    p,
    p.rolling(window=10).mean().rename("fast"),
    p.rolling(window=50).mean().rename("medium"),
    p.rolling(window=100).mean().rename("slow"),
    p.log().diff().fillna(0).rename("lr")])
```

If you are wondering what the last line is doing, it is the log ratio of prices in two consecutive time steps to assess the relative change.

Wallet and portfolio

Now, it's time to create some wealth for ourselves and put it in our wallets. Feel free to be generous to yourself.

```
cash = Wallet(coinbase, 100000 * USD)
asset = Wallet(coinbase, 0 * TTC)
portfolio = Portfolio(USD, [cash, asset])
```

Our wallets together make up our portfolio.

Reward scheme

Reward scheme is simply the kind of reward function we want to incentivize our agent with. If you are thinking "there is only one goal, make profit!", well, there is more into it. You can use things like risk-adjusted returns or define your own goal. For now, let's keep things simple and use the profit as the reward.

```
reward_scheme = default.rewards.SimpleProfit()
```

Action scheme

Action scheme defines the type of actions you want your agent to be able to take, such as a simple **buy/sell/hold** all assets (**BSH**), or fractional buys/sells and so on. We also put the cash and assets in it.

```
action_scheme = default.actions.BSH(cash=cash, asset=asset)
```

Putting them all together in an environment

Finally, these can be all put together in to form an environment with some additional parameters.

```
env = default.create(
    feed=feed,
    portfolio=portfolio,
    action_scheme=action_scheme,
    reward_scheme=reward_scheme,
    window_size=25,
    max_allowed_loss=0.6)
```

So, that's the basics of creating an environment in TensorTrade. You can of course go much beyond this, but you get the idea. After this step, it can be easily plugged into RLlib, or virtually any library compatible with the Gym API.

Training RLlib agents in TensorTrade

As you may remember from the earlier chapters, one way of using custom environments in Gym is to put them in a function that returns the environment and register them. So, it looks something like:

```
def create_env(config):
    ...
    return env
register_env("TradingEnv", create_env)
```

The environment name can then be referred to inside the trainer config in RLlib. You can find the full code in Chapter16/tt_example.py on the GitHub repo.

> **Info**
>
> This example mostly follows what is in the TensorTrade documentation. For a more detailed Ray/RLlib tutorial, you can visit https://www.tensortrade.org/en/latest/tutorials/ray.html.

This concludes our discussion on TensorTrade. You can now go ahead and try few trading ideas. When you are back, let's briefly talk about developing machine learning-based trading strategies and wrap up the chapter.

Developing equity trading strategies

What is almost as noisy as the market itself is the information about how to trade them. How to develop effective trading strategies is well beyond the scope of our book. However, here is a blog post that can give you some realistic idea about what to pay attention to when developing ML models for trading. As always, use your judgement and due diligence to decide on what to believe: https://www.tradientblog.com/2019/11/lessons-learned-building-an-ml-trading-system-that-turned-5k-into-200k/.

With that, let's wrap up this chapter.

Summary

In this chapter, we covered three important RL application areas: Personalization, marketing, and finance. For personalization and marketing, this chapter went beyond the bandit applications that are commonly used in these areas and discussed the merits of multi-step RL. We also covered methods such as dueling bandit gradient descent, which is helpful to achieve conservative exploration to avoid excessive reward losses, and action embeddings, which is helpful to deal with large action spaces. We concluded the chapter with a discussion on finance applications of RL, its challenges, and introduced the TensorTrade library.

The next chapter is the last application chapter of the book, in which we will focus on smart city and cybersecurity. Take a break, and join us on the other side!

References

Zheng, G. et al. (2018). DRN: *A Deep Reinforcement Learning Framework for News Recommendation*. WWW '18: Proceedings of the 2018 World Wide Web Conference April 2018, Pages 167–176, `https://doi.org/10.1145/3178876.3185994`.

17
Smart City and Cybersecurity

Smart cities are expected to be one of the defining experiences of the next decades. A smart city collects a lot of data using sensors located in various parts of the city, such as on the roads, utility infrastructures, and water resources. The data are then used to make data-driven and automated decisions, such as how to allocate the city resources, manage the traffic real-time, identify and mitigate infrastructure problems etc. This prospect comes with two challenges: How to program the automation and how to protect the highly-connected city assets from cyberattacks. Fortunately, reinforcement learning can help with both.

In this chapter, we cover three problems related to smart cities and cybersecurity and describe how to model them as RL problems. Along the way, we introduce you to the Flow library, a framework that connects traffic simulation software with RL libraries, and solve an example traffic light control problem.

In particular, here are the problems we address in this chapter:

- Controlling traffic lights to optimize vehicle flow
- Providing ancillary service to power grid
- Detecting cyber-attacks in a smart grid

This will be a fun ride, so let's get started!

Controlling traffic lights to optimize vehicle flow

One of the key challenges for cities is to optimize traffic flows on road networks. There are numerous benefits in reducing traffic congestions, including but not limited to:

- Reducing the time and energy wasted in traffic
- Saving on gas and resulting exhaust emissions
- Increasing vehicle and road lifetime
- Decreasing number of accidents

There has been already a lot of research going in this area; but recently, RL has emerged as a competitive alternative to traditional control approaches. So, in this section, we optimize the traffic flow at a road network by controlling the traffic light behavior using multi-agent reinforcement learning. To this end, we use the Flow framework, which is an open-source library for RL and control experiments on realistic traffic microsimulations.

Introducing Flow

Transportation research significantly relies on simulation software, such as SUMO and Aimsun, for topics such as traffic light control, vehicle route choice, traffic surveillance, and traffic forecast, which involve the optimal control of these agents. On the other side, the rise of deep RL as an alternative to traditional control approaches has led to numerous libraries such RLlib and OpenAI Baselines. Flow is an open source framework that connects these two worlds of traffic simulators and RL libraries.

In this section, as in the previous chapters, we use RLlib as the RL backend. For traffic simulation, we use **SUMO (Simulation of Urban Mobility)**, a powerful open source library that is being developed since the early 2000s.

> **Info**
>
> Here, we will give only a glimpse into applying RL to traffic problems. Detailed
> documentation and tutorials (which we closely follow here) are available on
> the Flow website: `https://flow-project.github.io/` .SUMO
> documentation and libraries are available on `https://www.eclipse.org/sumo/`.

Let's start with installing Flow and SUMO.

Installing Flow and SUMO

In order to install Flow, we create a new virtual environment since it depends on library
versions different than what we used in the earlier chapters.

```
$ sudo apt-get install python3-pip
$ virtualenv flowenv
$ source flowenv/bin/activate
```

To install Flow, we need to download the repo and run the following commands:

```
$ git clone https://github.com/flow-project/flow.git
$ cd flow
$ pip3 install -e .
$ pip3 install ipykernel
$ python -m ipykernel install --user --name=flowenv
```

These commands install the necessary dependencies, including TensorFlow and RLlib.
The last two commands are needed to run Flow on Jupyter Notebook, which is what the
Flow tutorials as well as our example code run on. To install SUMO on Ubuntu 18.04:

```
$ scripts/setup_sumo_ubuntu1804.sh
$ source ~/.bashrc
```

Setup scripts for earlier Ubuntu versions and macOS are also available in the same folder.

You can see Flow and Sumo in action by running (in the flow folder and your virtual
environment activated):

```
$ python examples/simulate.py ring
```

And a window similar to *Figure 17.1* should appear.

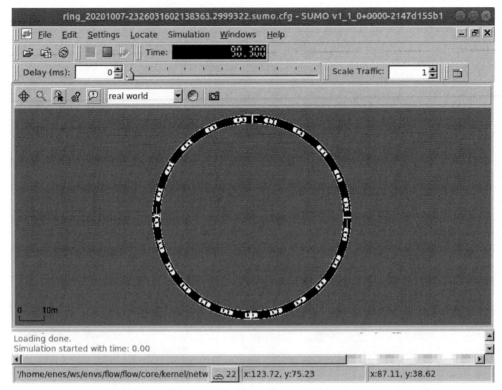

Figure 17.1 – A sample SUMO window simulating the traffic on a ring road

If you run into issues with the setup, Flow documentation can help you with troubleshooting.

Now that we have set things up, let's dive into how to put together a traffic environment using Flow.

Creating an experiment in Flow

Now that we have the setups, we can create environments and experiments in Flow. We will then connect them to RLlib to train RL agents.

There are certain ingredients that go into a Flow experiment:

- **A road network**, such as a ring road (as in Figure 17.1), or a Manhattan-like grid network. Flow comes with a set of predefined networks. For advanced users, it also allows creating custom networks. Traffic lights are defined together with the road network.

- **A simulation backend**, which is not our focus here. We will use the defaults for this.

- **An RL environment** that configures what is controlled, observed, rewarded etc. in the experiment, similar to a Gym environment.

- **Vehicles** are essential to the entire experiment, and their behavior and characteristics are defined separately.

All these components are parametrized, and which are passed to Flow separately. We then pack them all to create a Flow parameters object.

It could be difficult to use a bottom-up approach here and start with individual parameters for each component to compose the big picture. In addition, such details are out of our scope here. Instead, it is much easier to unpack a prebuilt Flow parameters object. Let's do that next.

Analyzing a Flow parameters object

Flow has some benchmark experiments defined for traffic light optimization on a grid network. Let's now take a look at the Flow parameters object for the Grid-0 experiment. Launch Jupyter Notebook and make sure to select the `flowenv` kernel.

Chapter17/Traffic Lights on a Grid Network.ipynb

```
from flow.benchmarks.grid0 import flow_params
flow_params
{'exp_tag': 'grid_0',
 'env_name': flow.envs.traffic_light_grid.
TrafficLightGridBenchmarkEnv,
 'network': flow.networks.traffic_light_grid.
TrafficLightGridNetwork,
 'simulator': 'traci',
 'sim': <flow.core.params.SumoParams at 0x7f25102d1350>,
 'env': <flow.core.params.EnvParams at 0x7f25102d1390>,
 'net': <flow.core.params.NetParams at 0x7f25102d13d0>,
 'veh': <flow.core.params.VehicleParams at 0x7f267c1c9650>,
 'initial': <flow.core.params.InitialConfig at 0x7f25102d6810>}
```

We can, for example, inspect what is inside the network parameters:

```
print(dir(flow_params['net']))
flow_params['net'].additional_params
...
{'speed_limit': 35,
 'grid_array': {'short_length': 300,
   'inner_length': 300,
   'long_length': 100,
   'row_num': 3,
...
```

And of course, a good way to understand what they do is to visually run the experiment:

```
from flow.core.experiment import Experiment
sim_params = flow_params['sim']
sim_params.render = True
exp = Experiment(flow_params)
results = exp.run(1)
```

This will pop up a SUMO screen similar to *Figure 17.2*.

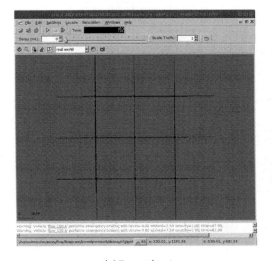

(a) Zoomed out   (b) Zoomed in

Figure 17.2 – SUMO rendering of the grid network

With that, now we have an example up and running. Before we go into RL modeling and training, let's discuss how to get a baseline reward for this experiment.

Getting a baseline reward

The Jupyter notebook in our GitHub repo includes a code snippet taken from the Flow codebase to get a baseline reward on this environment. It has some carefully optimized traffic light phase definitions that lead to a -205 reward on average, which represent the negative of the average delay the vehicles are experiencing. We will use this reward to benchmark the RL result against. Also, feel free to modify the phases (e.g. `minDur` and `maxDur`) to see their impact on the traffic pattern on the network.

With that, we are now ready to define the RL environment.

Modeling the traffic light control problem

As always, we need to define the action, observation and reward for the RL problem. We will do so in the following sections.

Defining the action

We would like to train a single controller for all of the lights at a given intersection that is illustrated in Figure 17.2-b. In the figure, the lights are in a green-red-green-red state. We define a binary action as 0: continue and 1: switch. When instructed to switch, the state of the lights on the figure would become yellow-red-yellow-red, and then red-green-red-green after a few seconds.

The default environment accepts a continuous action for each intersection, $a \in [-1, +1]$, and rounds it up to discretize as we described above.

Single vs. multi-agent modeling

The next design decision we have to make is whether to control all of the traffic lights using a centralized agent or adapt a multi-agent approach. And if we pick the latter, whether to train a single policy for all intersections or train multiple policies.

- The advantage of the centralized approach is that, in theory, we can perfectly coordinate all of the intersections and achieve a better reward. On the other hand, a trained agent may not be easily applied on a different road network. In addition, for larger networks, the centralized approach won't scale easily.

- If we decide to use a multi-agent approach, we don't have a lot of reasons to differentiate between the intersections and the policies they use. So, training a single policy makes more sense.

- Training a single generic policy for all intersections where the agents (the lights at the intersections) collaboratively try to maximize the reward is a scalable and efficient approach. Of course, this lacks the full coordination capabilities of a centralized, single-agent approach. In practice, this would be a tradeoff you would have to evaluate.

So, we will go with the multi-agent setting, in which, the single policy will be trained with the data coming from all of the agents. The agents will retrieve actions from the policy according to their local observations.

With that, let's define the observation.

Defining the observation

The default multi-agent grid environment uses the following as the observations:

- Speeds of the n closest vehicles heading to the intersection,
- Distances of the n closest vehicles heading to the intersection,
- The ids of the road edges that these n vehicles are on,
- The traffic density, average velocity and traffic direction on each of the local edges,
- Whether the lights are currently in a yellow state.

For a more detailed information, you can check the `flow.envs.multiagent.traffic_light_grid` module in the Flow repo.

Finally, let's define the reward.

Defining the reward

The environment has a simple and an intuitive cost definition for a given time step, which measures the average vehicle delay compared to the top speed allowed:

$$cost = \frac{1}{N} \sum_{i=1}^{N} (1 - \frac{v_i}{v_{max}})$$

where v_i is the velocity of the ith of N total vehicles, and v_{max} is the maximum allowed speed. The reward then can be defined as the negative of this cost term.

Now that we have all the formulations in place, it is time to solve problem.

Solving the traffic control problem using RLlib

Since we will use the multi-agent interface of RLlib, we need to:

- Register the environment in RLlib with a name and environment creation function,
- Define the names of the policies we will train, which we have only one, `tlight`,
- Define a function that generates the arguments needed for the RLlib trainer for the policy,
- Define a function that maps agents to the policies, which is again simple do to in our case since all agents map to the same policy.

So, these can be achieved with the following code:

```
create_env, env_name = make_create_env(params=flow_params,
                                       version=0)
register_env(env_name, create_env)
test_env = create_env()
obs_space = test_env.observation_space
act_space = test_env.action_space
def gen_policy():
    return PPOTFPolicy, obs_space, act_space, {}
def policy_mapping_fn(_):
    return 'tlight'
policy_graphs = {'tlight': gen_policy()}
policies_to_train = ['tlight']
```

Once defined, we need to pass these functions and lists to RLlib config:

```
config['multiagent'].update({'policies': policy_graphs})
config['multiagent'].update({'policy_mapping_fn':
                            policy_mapping_fn})
config['multiagent'].update({'policies_to_train':
                            policies_to_train})
```

The rest is the regular RLlib training loop. We use the hyperparameters identified in the Flow benchmarks with PPO. The full code for all of this is available on `Chapter17/ Traffic Lights on a Grid Network.ipynb`.

Obtaining and observing the results

After a couple million training steps, the reward converges around -243, which is a bit lower than the hand-crafted benchmark. The training progress can be observed on TensorBoard:

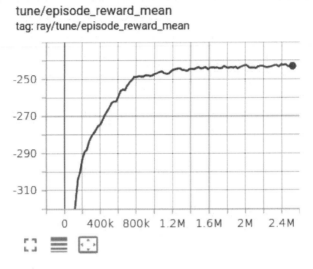

Figure 17.3 – Training progress of the multi-agent traffic light environment in Flow

You can also visualize how the trained agent is doing with a command on Jupyter notebook in the following format:

```
!python /path/to/your/flow/visualize/visualizer_rllib.py /path/
to/your/ray_results/your_exp_tag/your_run_id 100
```

Here the argument at the end refers to the checkpoint number, which is generated regularly during training.

Next, let's also discuss why the RL performance is falling a bit short of the hand-crafted policy.

Further improvements

There are several reasons of why RL may not have reached the baseline performance:

- Lack of more hyperparameter tuning and training: This factor is always there. Usually, there is no way to know whether the performance can be improved with more fiddling with the model architecture and training until you try, which we encourage you to do.

- The baseline policy is exercising a finer control over the yellow light durations, whereas RL did not have a control over that.

- The baseline policy coordinates all the intersections on the network, whereas each RL agent makes local decisions. So, we might be running into the shortcomings of decentralized control here.

- This can be mitigated by adding observations that will help coordinate the agents with their neighbors.

- It is not uncommon for RL algorithms to struggle in crossing the last mile in the optimization and reach the very peak of the reward curve. This may require a fine control over the training procedure with reducing the learning rates, adjusting the batch sizes etc.

So, although there is room for improvement, our agents have successfully learned how to control traffic lights, which is much more scalable than manually crafting policies.

Before we wrap up this topic, let's discuss a few more resource to learn more about the problem and the libraries we used.

Further reading

We have already provided the links to Flow and SUMO documentation. The Flow library and the benchmarks obtained with it are explained in (Wu et al. 2019) and (Vinitsky et al. 2018). In these resources, you will discover additional problems you can model and solve using various RL libraries.

Congratulations! We have done a lot in such a short time and space to leverage reinforcement learning for traffic control problems. Next, we cover another interesting problem, which is to modulate the electricity demand to stabilize a power grid.

Providing ancillary service to power grid

In this section, we describe how reinforcement learning can help with integrating clean energy resources into power grid by managing smart appliances in home and office buildings.

Power grid operations and ancillary services

Transmission and distribution of electricity power from generators to consumers is a massive operation that requires continuous monitoring and control of the system. In particular, the generation and consumption should be nearly equal in a region to keep the electric current at the standard frequency (60 Hz in the United States) to prevent blackouts and damages. This is a challenging undertaking for various reasons:

- Power supply is planned ahead in energy markets with the generators in the region to match the demand.

- Despite the planning, future power supply is uncertain, especially when obtained from renewable resources. The amount of wind and solar may be less or more than expected, causing under or oversupply.

- Future demand is uncertain too, as consumers are mostly free to decide when and how much to consume.

- Failures in the grid, such as at generators or transmission lines, can cause sudden changes in the supply or demand, putting the reliability of the system at risk.

The balance between the supply and demand is maintained by authorities called **Independent System Operators (ISOs)**. Traditionally, ISOs ask generators to ramp up or down their supply based on the changes in the grid, which is an ancillary service provided by generators to ISOs for a price. On the other hand, there are several issues regarding generators providing this service:

- Generators are usually slow to respond to sudden changes in the grid balance. For example, it may take hours to bring in a new generation unit to address a supply deficit in the grid.

- Over the recent years, there has been a significant increase in renewable energy supply, adding to the volatility in the grid.

For these reasons, a line of research has been to enable consumers to provide these ancillary services to the grid. In other words, the goal is to modulate the demand in addition to the supply to better maintain the balance. This requires more sophisticated control mechanisms, which we bring in reinforcement learning to help with.

After this introduction, let's now more concretely define the control problem here.

Describing the environment and the decision-making problem

To reiterate, our goal is to dynamically increase or decrease the total electricity consumption in an area. Let's first describe the parties involved in this setting and their roles.

Independent system operator

The ISO of the region continuously monitors the supply and demand balance, and broadcasts an automated signal to all ancillary service providers in the region to adjust their demand. Let's call this signal y, which is simply a number in $[-1, +1]$. We will come back to what this number precisely means in a moment. For now, let's state that the ISO updates this signal every 4 seconds (which is a particular type of ancillary service called regulation service).

Smart building operator

We assume that there is a **smart building operator (SBO)** that is in charge of modulating the total demand in a (collection of) building(s) to follow the ISO signal. The SBO, which will be our RL agent, operates as follows:

- SBO sells regulation service to the ISO of the region. According to this obligation, the SBO promises to maintain the consumption at a rate of A kW and adjust it up or down, up to R kW at the ISO's request. We assume that A and R predetermined for our problem.

- When $y = -1$, the SBO needs to quickly decrease the consumption in the neighborhood to $A - R$ kW. When $y = +1$, the consumption rate needs to go up to $A + R$ kW.

- In general, the SBO needs to control the consumption to follow $A + Ry$ kW rate.

The SBO controls a population of smart appliances/units, such as **heating**, **ventilation** and **air conditioning (HVAC)** units and **electric vehicles (EVs)**, to abide by the signal. This is where we will leverage RL.

We illustrate this setup in *Figure 17.4*.

Figure 17.4 – Regulation service provision by a smart building operator

Next, let's go a bit more into the details of how smart appliances operate.

Smart appliances

You may feel uncomfortable with the idea that some algorithm is interfering with your appliances and causing them to turn on or off. After all, who would want the TV to shut down to save power while watching the Super Bowl, or turn it on in the middle of the night just because there is excess in electricity generation due to higher-than-anticipated winds outside? This certainly does not make sense. On the other hand, you would be more okay if the AC turned on a minute late or early than normal. Or you would not mind whether your EV reached full battery at 4am or 5am in the morning as far as it is ready for you before you leave the home. So, the point is that some appliances have more room in terms of when to operate, which are of our interest in this case.

We also assume that these appliances are smart and have the following capabilities:

- They can communicate with the SBO to receive the actions.
- They can assess the "utility," which is a measure of how much need there is for the appliance to consume power at a given moment.

Next, let's define appliance utility more specifically.

Defining the utility

Let's give two examples to how the utility changes in different situations. Consider an electric vehicle that needs to be fully charged by 7am in the morning.

- The utility would be high if it is 6am and the battery is still low.
- Conversely, the utility would be low if there is still plenty of time till departure and/or the battery close to full.

Similarly, an air conditioner would have high utility when the room temperature is about to exceed the user comfort zone and low utility when it is close to the bottom.

See *Figure 17.5* for an illustration of these situations.

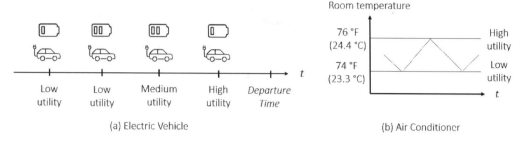

Figure 17.5 – Utility levels under different conditions for an (a) EV and (b) AC

Next, let's discuss why this is a sequential decision-making problem.

Defining the sequential decision-making problem

By now, you may have noticed how SBO actions taken now will have implications later in time. Fully charging the EVs in the system too early may limit how much the consumption may be ramped up later when needed. Conversely, keeping room temperatures too high for too many rooms for too long may cause all ACs to turn on later altogether to bring the room temperatures to normal levels.

In the next section, let's cast this as an RL problem.

Reinforcement learning model

As always, we need to define the action, the observation, and the reward to create a reinforcement learning model.

Defining the action

There are different approaches to how we can define the SBO control:

- First and a more obvious approach would be to directly control each appliance in the system by observing their utilities. On the other hand, this would make the model inflexible and potentially intractable: We would have to modify and retrain the agent when a new appliance is added. In addition, when there are many appliances, the action and observation space would be too big.

- Another approach would be to train a policy for each appliance class (ACs, heating units, EVs etc.) in a multi-agent setting. This would bring in the inherent complexities of multi-agent RL. For example, we would have to design a mechanism for the coordination of individual appliances.

- A middle ground is to apply indirect control. In this approach, the SBO would broadcast its action and let each appliance to decide on what to do for itself.

Let's describe what such an indirect control might look like in more detail.

Indirect control of the appliances

Here is how we define the indirect control/action:

- Assume that there are M appliance types, such as ACs, EVs, refrigerators etc.

- At any given time, an appliance k has a utility U_k that takes a maximum value of 1.

- At every time step, the SBO broadcasts an action $a_i \in [0,1]$ for each appliance type i. Therefore, the action is $a = [a_1, a_2, ..., a_M]$, $a_i \in [0,1]$ and $i = 1, ..., M$.

- Each appliance, when off, checks what the action for its class is once in a while. This won't be at every time step and will depend on its type. For example, AC units might check the broadcast action more frequently than EVs.

- When an appliance k of type i checks the action a_i, it turns on if an only if $U^k \geq a_i$. Therefore, the action acts like a **price** for electricity. The appliance is willing to turn on only when its utility is greater than or equal to the **price**.

- Once turned on, an appliance stays on for a certain time. Then it turns off and starts periodically checking the action again.

With this mechanism, the SBO could influence the demand indirectly. It gives a less precise control over the environment, but at a much reduced complexity compared to a direct or multi-agent control.

Next, let's define the observation space.

Defining the observation

The SBO could use the following observations to make its decisions:

- The ISO signal at time t, y_t , as the SBO is obliged to track it by adjusting its demand.

- Number of appliances that are on at time t for each type, n_t^i. For simplicity, a fixed electricity consumption rate could be assumed for an appliance of type i, e_i.

- Time and date features, such as time of day, day of week, holiday calendar etc.

- Auxiliary information such as weather temperature and forecast.

In addition to making all these observations at each time step, what will be also needed is to keep a memory of the observations. This is a partially observable environment where the energy needs of the appliances, the state of the grid etc. are hidden from the agent. So, keeping a memory will help the agent uncover these hidden states.

Finally, let's describe the reward function.

Defining the reward function

In this model, the reward function consists of two parts: The tracking cost and the utility.

We mentioned that the SBO is obliged to track the ISO signal as it is paid for this service. Therefore, we assign a penalty for deviating from the target implied by the signal at time t:

$$C_t = \left(A + Ry_t - \left(\sum_{i=1}^{M} n_t^i e_i \right) \right)^2$$

where $A + Ry_t$ is the target and $\sum_{i=1}^{M} n_t^i e_i$ is the actual consumption rate at time t.

The second part of the reward function is the total utility realized by the appliances. We want the appliances to turn on and consume energy, but do so when they really need it. An example to why this is beneficial is the following: An AC would consume less energy when the average room temperature is kept closer to the top of the comfort zone (e.g. 76 °F in Figure 17.3), where the utility is the highest than when it is kept closer to the bottom if the outside temperature is above the comfort zone.

We define the total utility realized at time t as:

$$U_t = \sum_{k \in K_t} U_t^k$$

where K_t is the set of appliances that turn on within the discrete time step t. Then the RL objective becomes:

$$\max_{\pi} E \left[\sum_{t} \gamma^t (U_t - \beta C_t) \right]$$

where β is some coefficient to control the tradeoff between utility and tracking cost, and γ is the discount factor.

Terminal conditions

Finally, let's have a word on the terminal conditions for this problem. Normally, this is a continuous task without a natural terminal state. However, we can introduce terminal conditions, for example, to stop the episode if the tracking error is too large. Other than that, we can convert this to an episodic task by taking the episode length as one day.

That's it! We leave the exact implementation of this model out, but you now have a solid idea about how to approach this problem. If you need more details, you can check out the references at the end of this chapter by Bilgin and Caramanis.

Last but not least, let's switch gears to model early detection of cyberattacks in a power grid.

Detecting cyberattacks in a smart grid

Smart cities, by definition, run on intense digital communications between its assets. Besides its benefits, this makes smart cities prone to cyberattacks. As reinforcement learning is finding its way into cybersecurity, in this section, we describe how it can be applied to detecting attacks on a smart power grid infrastructure. Throughout the chapter, we follow the model proposed in (Kurt et al. 2019), while leaving the details to the paper.

Let's start with describing the power grid environment.

The problem of early detection of cyberattacks in a power grid

An electricity power grid consists of nodes, called **buses**, which correspond to generation, demand, or power line intersection points. Grid authorities collect measurements from these buses to make certain decisions such as brining in additional power generation units. To this end, a critical quantity measured is the **phase angle** at each bus (except the reference bus), which makes it a potential target for cyber-attackers, hence our interest in it.

- Not surprisingly, the measurements from the meters are noisy and subject to errors.
- A cyberattack on these meters and their measurements have the potential to mislead the decisions made by grid authorities and cause the system to collapse.
- Therefore, it is important to detect when there is an attack on the system.

- However, it is not easy to differentiate the noise and real system changes from anomalies caused by an attack. Normally, waiting and collecting more measurements are helpful to this end.

- On the other hand, being late in declaring an attack can lead to incorrect decisions in the meantime. Therefore, our goal is to identify such attacks as soon as possible, but without too many false alarms.

So, the set of possible actions that our cybersecurity agent can take is simple: Declare an attack or not. A sample timeline of false and true (but delayed) alarms are illustrated in *Figure 17.6*.

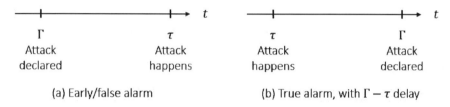

(a) Early/false alarm   (b) True alarm, with $\Gamma - \tau$ delay

Figure 17.6 – A sample timeline of (a) false and (b) true but delayed alarms

Here are the details of the episode lifecycle and rewards:

- Once an attack is declared, the episode terminates.

- If it is a false alarm, a reward of -1 is incurred. If it is a true alarm, the reward is 0.

- If there is an attack but the action is to continue (and don't declare an attack), for each time step, a reward of $-c, c > 0$, is incurred.

- The reward is 0 in all other time steps.

With that, the goal of the agent is to minimize the following cost function (or maximize its negative):

$$P_\tau(\{\Gamma < \tau\}) + cE_\tau[(\Gamma - \tau)^+]$$

where the first term is the probability of a false alarm, the second term is the expected (positive) delay in declaring an attack, and c is the cost coefficient to manage the tradeoff in between.

One missing piece is the observations, which we discuss next.

Partial observability of the grid state

The true state of the system, which is, whether there is an attack or not, is not observable to the agent. Instead, it collects measurements of phase angles, y. A key contribution of (Kurt et al. 2019) is to use the phase angle measurements in the following way:

- Use a Kalman filter to predict the true phase angles from the previous observations.

- Based on this prediction, estimate the expected measurements, μ_y.

- Define η as a measure of the discrepancy between y and μ_y, which then becomes the observation used by the agent.

- Observe η and carry a memory of past observations for the agent's use.

The paper uses a tabular SARSA method to solve this problem by discretizing η, and show the effectiveness of the approach. An interesting extension would be to use deep RL methods without a discretization, and under varying grid topographies and attack characteristics.

With that, we conclude our discussion on the topic and the chapter. Great job, we have done a lot! Let's summarize what we have covered in the chapter.

Summary

Reinforcement learning is posed to play a significant role in automation. Smart city is a great field to leverage the power of RL. In this chapter, we discussed three sample applications: Traffic light control, ancillary service provision by electricity consuming appliances, and detecting cyberattacks in a power grid. The first problem allowed us to showcase a multi-agent setting, we used a price-like indirect control mechanism for the second one, and the last one was a good example of advanced input preprocessing in partially observed environments.

In the next and the last chapter, we will wrap up the book with a discussion on the challenges of real-life reinforcement learning and related future directions.

References

1. Wu, Cathy, et al. (2019). *Flow: A Modular Learning Framework for Autonomy in Traffic*. ArXiv:1710.05465 [Cs]. arXiv.org. URL: `http://arxiv.org/abs/1710.05465`.

2. Vinitsky, E., Kreidieh, A., Flem, L.L., Kheterpal, N., Jang, K., Wu, C., Wu, F., Liaw, R., Liang, E. & Bayen, A.M. (2018). *Benchmarks for reinforcement learning in mixed-autonomy traffic*. Proceedings of The 2nd Conference on Robot Learning, in PMLR 87:399-409. URL: `http://proceedings.mlr.press/v87/vinitsky18a.html`

3. E. Bilgin, M. C. Caramanis, I. C. Paschalidis and C. G. Cassandras. (2016). *Provision of Regulation Service by Smart Buildings*. IEEE Transactions on Smart Grid, vol. 7, no. 3, pp. 1683-1693, May 2016, doi: 10.1109/TSG.2015.2501428.

4. E. Bilgin, M. C. Caramanis and I. C. Paschalidis. (2013). *Smart building real time pricing for offering load-side Regulation Service reserves*. 52nd IEEE Conference on Decision and Control, Florence, 2013, pp. 4341-4348, doi: 10.1109/CDC.2013.6760557.

5. M. Caramanis, I. C. Paschalidis, C. Cassandras, E. Bilgin and E. Ntakou. (2012) *"Provision of regulation service reserves by flexible distributed loads*. IEEE 51st IEEE Conference on Decision and Control (CDC), Maui, HI, 2012, pp. 3694-3700, doi: 10.1109/CDC.2012.6426025.

6. Bilgin, E. (2014). *Participation of distributed loads in power markets that co-optimize energy and reserves*. Dissertation, Boston University.

7. M. N. Kurt, O. Ogundijo, C. Li and X. Wang. (2019). *Online Cyber-Attack Detection in Smart Grid: A Reinforcement Learning Approach*. IEEE Transactions on Smart Grid, vol. 10, no. 5, pp. 5174-5185, Sept. 2019, doi: 10.1109/TSG.2018.2878570.

18

Challenges and Future Directions in Reinforcement Learning

In this last chapter, we summarize our journey that is coming to an end in this book: You have done a lot, so think of this as a celebration and a bird eye view of your achievement! On the other hand, when you take your learnings to use reinforcement learning in real-world problems, you will likely encounter many challenges. Thankfully, deep reinforcement learning is a fast-moving field with a lot of progress to address those challenges. We have already mentioned most of them in the book and implemented solution approaches. In this chapter, we will recap what those challenges and corresponding future directions in RL are. We will wrap up the chapter and the book by going over some resources and strategies for you to deepen your expertise in RL.

So, here is what you will read in this chapter:

- What you have achieved with this book

- Challenges and future directions

- Suggestions for aspiring reinforcement learning experts

- Final words

What you have achieved with this book

First of all, congratulations! You have come a long way to go beyond the fundamentals and to acquire the skills and the mindset to apply reinforcement learning in real-world. Here is what we have done together in this book:

- We have spent a fair amount of time on bandit problems, which have tremendous number of applications in industry and academia.

- We have gone deeper into the theory than a typical applied book to strengthen your foundation in RL.

- We have covered many of the algorithms and architectures behind the most successful applications of RL.

- We have discussed advanced training strategies to get the most out of the advanced RL algorithms.

- We have done hands-on work with realistic case studies.

- Throughout this journey, we have both implemented our versions of some of the algorithms, as well as utilized libraries, such as Ray and RLlib, which power many teams and platforms at the top tech companies for their reinforcement learning applications.

You absolutely deserve to take a moment to celebrate your success!

Now, if you are back, it is time to talk about what is ahead of you. Deep reinforcement learning is at the beginning of its rise. This means multiple things:

- First, it is opportunity. You are now ahead of the game by making this investment and coming this far to the end of this book.

- Second, since this is cutting edge, there are many challenges to be solved until RL becomes a mature, easy-to-use technology.

In the next section we will discuss what those challenges are. That way, you will recognize them when you see them, know that you are not alone, and set your expectations accordingly in terms of what is needed (data, time, compute resource) to solve your problem. But you shall not worry! RL is a highly active and accelerating area of research. So, our arsenal to tackle those challenges is getting stronger by the day. See the number of papers submitted to the NeurIPS conference on RL over the years, compiled and presented by Katja Hofmann, a prominent RL researcher, during the conference in 2019:

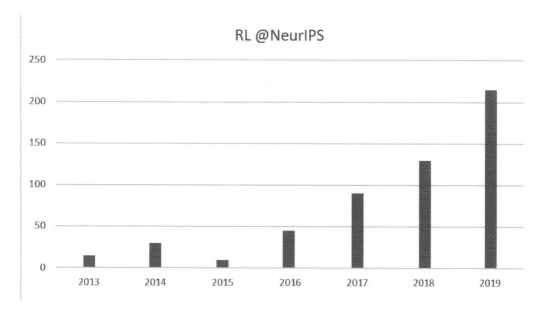

Figure 18.1 – Number of RL contributions to the NeurIPS conference, compiled and presented by Katja Hofmann (source: Hofmann, 2019).

Therefore, while we talk about the challenges, we also talk about the related research directions, so you will know where to look at for the answers.

Challenges and future directions

You could be wondering why we are back to talking about RL challenges after finishing an advanced-level book on this topic. Indeed, throughout the book, we presented many approaches to mitigate them. On the other hand, we cannot claim these challenges are solved. So, it is important to call them out and discuss the future directions for each in a concise list to give you a mental map and a compass to navigate through them.

Let's start our discussion with one of the most important challenges: Sample efficiency.

Sample efficiency

As you are now well aware, it takes a lot of data to train an RL model. OpenAI Five, who became a world-class player in the strategy game Dota 2, took 128,000 CPUs and 256 CPUs to train, over many months, collecting a total of 900 years' worth of game experience **per day** (OpenAI, 2018). RL algorithms are benchmarked on their performances after trained over 10 billion Atari frames (Kapturowski, 2019). This is certainly a lot of compute and resources to just play games. So, sample efficiency is one of the biggest challenges in front of a broader adoption of RL.

Let's look into the directions RL researchers are pursuing to address this challenge.

Sample efficient algorithms

An obvious direction is of course to try to create algorithms that are more sample efficient. Indeed, there is a big push in the research community to this end. We will increasingly compare the algorithms not just based on their best possible performance but how quickly and efficiently they reach those performance levels.

So, the RL community will talk more and more about the following algorithm classes:

- **Off-policy methods,** which don't require data to be collected under the most recent policy, giving them an edge over on-policy methods in terms of sample efficiency.

- **Model-based methods,** which can be orders of magnitude more efficient than their model-free counterparts as they leverage the information they possess on environment dynamics.

- **Models with informed priors,** which limit the hypothesis space of the models to a plausible set. Examples in this direction are to use neural ordinary differential equations and Lagrangian neural networks in RL models (Du, 2020; Shen 2020).

Specialized hardware and software architectures for distributed training

We can expect the progress on the algorithmic frontier to be gradual and slow. For those of us who are excited and impatient enthusiasts, a quicker solution is to dump more compute resources to RL projects, get the most out of the existing resources, and in turn, train bigger and bigger models. So, it is only reasonable to expect what happened in the natural language processing space to happen for RL too: NLP models went from being 8-billion-parameter models to 17-billion, and then to 175-billion in size with OpenAI's GPT-3, in less than a year, thanks to the optimizations in training architectures, and of course, to the supercomputers dedicated to the task.

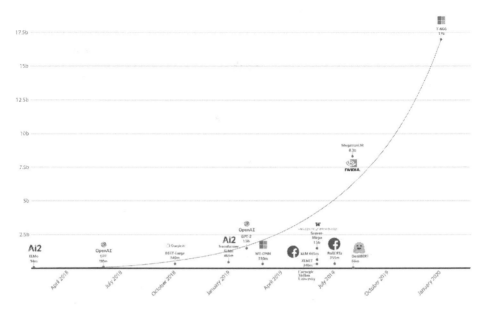

Figure 18.2 – Growth in the biggest NLP model sizes. Vertical axis is the number of parameters. Image modified from (Rosset, 2020).

In the same vein, innovations in RL training architectures, such as in Ape-X and SEED RL (Espeholt, 2019) help the existing algorithms to run more efficiently, a direction we can expect to see more progress in.

Machine teaching

Machine teaching approaches, such as curriculum learning, reward shaping, demonstration learning, aim to infuse context and subject matter expertise into RL training. They often lead to significant sample efficiency during training; and in some cases, they are needed to make learning even feasible. Machine teaching approaches will become increasingly popular in the near future to increase the sample efficiency in RL.

Multi-task, meta, or transfer learning

Since training an RL model from scratch could be very expensive, it only makes sense to reuse the models trained on other relevant tasks. Today, when we want to develop an application that involves image classification, for example, it is rare that we train a model from scratch. Instead, we use one of the pre-trained models and fine-tune it for our application.

> **Info**
>
> As a side note, the ONNX Model Zoo is a collection of pre-trained,
> state-of-the-art models in an open standard format for popular tasks such
> as image classification and machine translation, which I highly recommend
> you take a look: `https://github.com/onnx/models`

Today, transfer learning does not work for RL as well as it works for supervised learning tasks. We can expect to see some progress here to close this gap, which then would lead to RL model repositories. In addition, approaches such as multi-task learning, which is about training models for more than one task, and meta-learning, which is about training models that can efficiently adapt to new tasks, will gain momentum and broader adoption among RL researchers and practitioners.

Reinforcement learning-as-a-service

If you need to translate texts in your app programmatically, one approach is, as we mentioned, to use a pre-trained model. But what if you don't want to invest in the maintenance and continuous development of such models? The answer is often to buy it as a service from companies like Microsoft, Google, and Amazon. Such companies have access to the necessary expertise and huge amounts of data and compute resources to constantly upgrade their models using cutting-edge ML. Doing the same could be a daunting, even an infeasible undertaking for other businesses without the same resources and focus. Hence, we can expect to see RL-as-a-service trend in the industry.

Sample efficiency is a tough nut to crack, but there are developments in multiple frontiers to handle this challenge it as we summarized above.

Next, let's talk about another major challenge: The need for good simulation models.

Need for high-fidelity and fast simulation models

One of the biggest barriers in front of a broader adoption of RL in industry is the absence of simulations of processes that companies are interested in optimizing, either altogether or at a sufficient fidelity. Creating such simulation models often requires a lot of investment. In addition, in some complex tasks, the fidelity of a simulation model won't be high enough for a typical RL approach even after significant development. There are RL innovations in the following frontiers to overcome these challenges:

Offline reinforcement learning to learn directly from data

Most processes in industry don't have simulation models; but they often produce data logs. Offline RL approaches, which aim to learn policies directly from data as opposed to interactions with environment, will be a defining direction for democratization of RL.

Approaches to deal with generalization, partial observability, and non-stationarity

Even in cases where a simulation model of a process exists, it is quite rare for such a model to be of enough fidelity to train an agent that can then be transferred back to the real process without special care. This sim2real gap can be thought of as a form of partial observability, which is often handled through a memory in the RL model. Combined with generalization techniques, such as domain randomization, regularization, and meta-reinforcement learning, we are already seeing very successful examples of sim2real transfer.

Online learning and fine-tuning on the edge

Some of the key capabilities necessary for reliable deployment of RL agents in real-world processes are online learning and fine tuning on the edge. With that, trained agents can continue to learn and adapt to changing conditions in their environments.

In summary, we will witness a shift from RL being a tool to use in video games to being an alternative to traditional control and decision-making methods. Removing the dependencies on high-fidelity simulations will be a facilitating factor to this end.

High-dimensional action spaces

Cartpole, the iconic testbed for RL, has a low-dimensional action space, just like most environments used in RL research. Real-life problems, however, can be quite complex in terms of the number of actions available to the agent, which also often depends on the state the agent is in. Methods such as action embeddings, action masking, and action elimination will come handy to tackle this challenge in realistic scenarios.

Reward function fidelity

Crafting the right reward function that leads an agent to a desired behavior is a notoriously difficult undertaking in RL. Inverse RL approaches, which learn reward from demonstrations, and curiosity-driven learning that relies on intrinsic rewards are promising methods to reduce the dependency on hand-engineering of reward functions.

The challenge with reward function engineering is exacerbated when there are multiple and qualitative objectives. There is a growing literature on multi-objective RL approaches that either deal with each subproblem individually or produce policies for a given mixture of objectives.

Another challenge with respect to reward signals in RL environments is the delay and sparsity of rewards. For example, a marketing strategy controlled by an RL agent might observe rewards days, weeks, or even months after the action is taken. Approaches that deal with causality and credit assignment are critical to be able to leverage RL in such tasks.

These are all important research branches to keep an eye on since real-world RL problems rarely have well-defined, dense, and scalar objectives.

Safety, behavior guarantees, and explainability

While training RL agents in a computer simulation, it is okay, in fact needed, to try random and possibly crazy actions to figure out better policies. For an RL agent competing against the world-class players in a board game, the worst scenario that can happen is to lose, perhaps embarrassingly. The risks are of a different category when an RL agent is in charge of a chemical process or a self-driving car. These are safety-critical systems where the room for error is little-to-none. In fact, this is one of the biggest disadvantages of RL methods compared to traditional control theory approaches, which often come with theoretical guarantees and a solid understanding of the expected behavior. Research on constrained RL and safe exploration is, therefore, crucial to be able to use RL in such systems.

Even when the system is not safety-critical, such as in inventory replenishment problems, a related challenge is explainability of actions suggested by the RL agent in charge. Experts who oversee the decisions in such processes often demand explanations, especially when suggested actions are counterintuitive. Businesses tend to trade accuracy for explanation, which puts black box approaches at a disadvantage. Deep learning has come a long way in explainability, and RL will surely benefit from it. On the other hand, this will be an ongoing challenge for machine learning at large.

Reproducibility and sensitivity to hyper-parameter choices

It is one thing to train an RL model with a close oversight and guidance of many experts for a specific task and after many iterations, yet it is another thing to deploy multiple RL models in production for various environments, which need to be re-trained periodically and hands-of-the-wheel as new data come in. Consistency and resiliency of RL algorithms in terms of producing successful policies under a variety of conditions will be an increasingly important factor for the research community, as well as for practitioners who will get to deal with these models and their maintenance in real life.

Robustness and adversarial agents

Deep learning is known to be brittle with its representations. This lack of robustness allows adversarial agents to manipulate systems that rely on deep learning. This is a major concern and a highly active area of research in the ML community. RL will surely piggyback on the developments in the broader ML research to address robustness issues in this field.

These challenges are important to be aware of, especially for practitioners who want to use RL to solve real-world problems. Hopefully this summary will help with categorizing these challenges and potential solution directions in your mind, some of which we have already implemented in the book. All of these are active areas of research. So, whenever you encounter these challenges, it is a good idea to take a fresh look at the literature.

Before we wrap up, I would like to give my two cents to aspiring reinforcement learning experts.

Suggestions for aspiring reinforcement learning experts

This book is designed for an audience who already know the fundamentals of RL. Now that you have finished this book too, you are well positioned to become an expert in this field. Having said that, RL is big area; and this book is really meant to be a compass and kickstarter for you. At this point, if you decide to go deeper in RL, I will have some suggestions.

Go deeper into the theory

In machine learning, models often fail to produce expected level of performance, at least at the beginning. One big factor that will help you go beyond what comes out of the box is to have a good foundation of the math behind the algorithms you are using. This will help you better understand the limitations and assumptions of those algorithms, identify whether they conflict with the realities of the problem at hand, and give you ideas for addressing them. To this end, here is some advice:

- It is never a bad idea to deepen your understanding of probability and statistics. Don't forget that all these algorithms are essentially statistical models.

- Solid understanding of the basic ideas in RL, such as Q-learning and Bellman equation, is critical to have a good foundation to build the modern RL on. This book serves to the purpose of strengthening your understanding of those topics to some extent. However, I highly recommend you read, multiple times, Rich Sutton and Andrew Barto's "Reinforcement Learning: An Introduction" book, which is essentially the bible of traditional RL.

- Prof. Sergey Levine's UC Berkeley course on Deep RL, which this book has benefited from greatly, is an excellent resource to go deeper into RL theory. This course is available at `http://rail.eecs.berkeley.edu/deeprlcourse/`.

- Another great resource, specific to multi-task and meta learning, is Prof. Chelsea Finn's Stanford course at `https://cs330.stanford.edu/`

- The Deep RL Bootcamp taught by the experts in the field is another excellent resource: `https://sites.google.com/view/deep-rl-bootcamp/home`

As you follow these resources, and refer back to them time to time, you will see your understanding of the topic will become much deeper.

Follow good practitioners and research labs

There are excellent research labs focusing on RL, who also publish their findings in detailed blog posts with a lot of theoretical and practical insights. Here are some examples:

- OpenAI blog: `https://openai.com/blog/`

- DeepMind blog: `https://deepmind.com/blog`

- Berkeley AI Research (BAIR) blog: `https://bair.berkeley.edu/blog`

- Microsoft Research RL group: `https://www.microsoft.com/en-us/research/theme/reinforcement-learning-group/`

- Google AI Blog: `https://ai.googleblog.com/`

Even if you don't read every single post, it is a good idea to monitor them regularly to stay synced with the trends in RL research.

Learn from papers and from their good explanations

One single year in AI research is like one dog year: A lot happens in it. So, the best way to stay up to date is really to follow the research in the area. It will also expose you to the theory and rigorous explanations of the methods. Now, there are two challenges with it:

- There arc a ton of papers published every year, which makes it impossible to read them all,

- It could be daunting to read all the equations and proofs.

To address the former, I suggest you focus on papers accepted to conferences such as NeurIPS, ICLR, ICML, and AAAI. This will be still a lot, so you will still have to develop your own filtering mechanism to pick what to read.

To address the latter, you can check if there are good blog posts explaining the papers you would like to understand better. Some high-quality blogs (not specific to RL) to follow are:

- Lilian Weng's blog: `https://lilianweng.github.io/lil-log/`

- Distill: `https://distill.pub/`

- The Gradient: `https://thegradient.pub/`

- Adrian Colyer's The Morning Paper: `https://blog.acolyer.org/`

- Jay Alammar's blog: `http://jalammar.github.io/`

- Christopher Olah's blog (who is also in the Distill team): `https://colah.github.io/`

- Jian Zhang's blog: `https://medium.com/@jianzhang_23841`

I personally learn a lot from these blogs.

Stay up to date with trends in other fields of deep learning

Most major developments in deep learning, such as the Transformer architecture, take only months to find their way into RL. Therefore, staying up to date with the major trends in the broader ML and deep learning research will help you foresee what is upcoming for RL. The blogs we listed in the previous section will be beneficial to this end.

Read open source repositories

There are just too many algorithms in RL to explain line by line in a book. So, at some point, you need to develop that literacy and directly read good implementations of these algorithms from GitHub repos. Here are my suggestions for you to look into:

- OpenAI Spinning Up website: `https://spinningup.openai.com/` and repo: `https://github.com/openai/spinningup`

- OpenAI Baselines: `https://github.com/openai/baselines`

- Stable Baselines: `https://github.com/hill-a/stable-baselines`

- DeepMind Open Spiel: `https://github.com/deepmind/open_spiel`

- Ray & RLLib: `https://github.com/ray-project/ray`

- Deep Reinforcement Learning Hands On book repo by Maxim Lapan: `https://github.com/PacktPublishing/Deep-Reinforcement-Learning-Hands-On`

In addition to these, many papers now come with open-source implementations, some of which we used in this book. There is a very nice website, `https://paperswithcode.com/`, where you can use to identify such papers.

Practice!

Regardless of how much you read, you will truly learn only by practicing. So, try to get your hands dirty whenever possible. This could be through reproducing RL papers and algorithms, or even better, doing your own RL projects. The benefit you will get by going into the muds of the implementation cannot be replaced by anything else.

I hope this set of resources are helpful for you. To be clear, this is a lot to consume. It will take time to go over these; so, set your targets realistically. Also, be selective about what to read and follow, a skill that you will develop over time.

Final words

Well, it is time to wrap up. I would like to thank you for investing your time and effort in this book. I hope it has been beneficial for you. As a last word, I would like to emphasize that getting good at something takes a long time, and there is no limit to how good you can become. Nobody is expert at everything, even in subdisciplines of ML like reinforcement learning or computer vision. Don't forget that it is a marathon you need to run. Consistency and continuity of your efforts will make the difference, no matter what your goal is. I wish you my best in your journey.

References

1. Hofmann, K. (2019). *Reinforcement Learning: Past, Present, and Future Perspectives.* Conference on Neural Information Processing Systems, Vancouver, Canada. URL: `https://slideslive.com/38922817/reinforcement-learning-past-present-and-future-perspectives`

2. OpenAI (2018). *OpenAI Five.* OpenAI Blog. URL: `https://openai.com/blog/openai-five/`

3. Steven Kapturowski, Georg Ostrovski, Will Dabney, John Quan, & Remi Munos (2019). *Recurrent Experience Replay in Distributed Reinforcement Learning.* In International Conference on Learning Representations.

4. Lasse Espeholt, Raphaël Marinier, Piotr Stanczyk, Ke Wang, & Marcin Michalski. (2019). *SEED RL: Scalable and Efficient Deep-RL with Accelerated Central Inference.* arXiv.org, `http://arxiv.org/abs/1910.06591`.

5. Jianzhun Du, Joseph Futoma, & Finale Doshi-Velez. (2020). *Model-based Reinforcement Learning for Semi-Markov Decision Processes with Neural ODEs.* arXiv.org, `https://arxiv.org/abs/2006.16210`

6. Shen, Paul. (2020). *Neural ODE for Differentiable Reinforcement Learning and Optimal Control: Cartpole Problem Revisited.* The startup. URL: `https://bit.ly/2RROQi3`

7. Rosset, Corby. (2020). *Turing-NLG: A 17-billion-parameter language model by Microsoft.* Microsoft Research Blog. URL: `https://www.microsoft.com/en-us/research/blog/turing-nlg-a-17-billion-parameter-language-model-by-microsoft/`

8. Dulac-Arnold, Gabriel, et al. (2020). *An Empirical Investigation of the Challenges of Real-World Reinforcement Learning.* arXiv.org, URL: `http://arxiv.org/abs/2003.11881`

9. Dulac-Arnold, Gabriel, et al. (2019). *Challenges of Real-World Reinforcement Learning.* arXiv.org, URL: `http://arxiv.org/abs/1904.12901`

10. Irpan, Alex. (2018). *Deep Reinforcement Learning Doesn't Work Yet.* URL: `http://www.alexirpan.com/2018/02/14/rl-hard.html`. Accessed 26 Sept. 2020.

11. Levine, Sergey. (2019). *Deep Reinforcement Learning.* CS285 Fa19 11/18/19. YouTube. URL: `https://youtu.be/tzieElmtAjs?t=3336`. Accessed 26 Sept. 2020.

12. Hoffmann, Katja et al. (2020). *Challenges & Opportunities in Lifelong Reinforcement Learning*. ICML 2020. URL: `https://slideslive.com/38930956/ challenges-opportunities-in-lifelong-reinforcement- learning?ref=speaker-16425-latest`

Other Books You May Enjoy

If you enjoyed this book, you may be interested in these other books by Packt:

Hands-On Reinforcement Learning for Games

Micheal Lanham

ISBN: 978-1-83921-493-6

- Understand how deep learning can be integrated into an RL agent
- Explore basic to advanced algorithms commonly used in game development
- Build agents that can learn and solve problems in all types of environments
- Train a Deep Q-Network (DQN) agent to solve the CartPole balancing problem
- Develop game AI agents by understanding the mechanism behind complex AI
- Integrate all the concepts learned into new projects or gaming agents

PyTorch 1.x Reinforcement Learning Cookbook

Yuxi (Hayden) Liu

ISBN: 978-1-83855-196-4

- Use Q-learning and the state–action–reward–state–action (SARSA) algorithm to solve various Gridworld problems
- Develop a multi-armed bandit algorithm to optimize display advertising
- Scale up learning and control processes using Deep Q-Networks
- Simulate Markov Decision Processes, OpenAI Gym environments, and other common control problems
- Select and build RL models, evaluate their performance, and optimize and deploy them
- Use policy gradient methods to solve continuous RL problems

Leave a review - let other readers know what you think

Please share your thoughts on this book with others by leaving a review on the site that you bought it from. If you purchased the book from Amazon, please leave us an honest review on this book's Amazon page. This is vital so that other potential readers can see and use your unbiased opinion to make purchasing decisions, we can understand what our customers think about our products, and our authors can see your feedback on the title that they have worked with Packt to create. It will only take a few minutes of your time, but is valuable to other potential customers, our authors, and Packt. Thank you!

Index

C

O

Made in the USA
Columbia, SC
26 May 2022

60985524R00298